The Smart Culture

Critical America

General Editors: RICHARD DELGADO and JEAN STEFANCIC

The Smart Culture

Society, Intelligence, and Law

Robert L. Hayman, Jr.

NEW YORK UNIVERSITY PRESS

New York and London

NEW YORK UNIVERSITY PRESS
New York and London

Portions of chapter 7 originally appeared as Robert L. Hayman, Jr., and Nancy Levit, *The Tales of White Folk: Doctrine, Narrative and the Reconstruction of Racial Reality*, 84 CALIFORNIA LAW REVIEW 377 (1996). Reprinted by permission of California Law Review, Inc.

Library of Congress Cataloging-in-Publication Data
Hayman, Robert L.
The smart culture: law, society, and intelligence / Robert L. Hayman, Jr.
p.   cm.
Includes bibliographical references and index.
ISBN 0-8147-3533-9 (alk. paper)
1. Mental health laws—United States.   2. Mentally handicapped—Civil rights—United States. 3. Culture and law.   I. Title.
KF480.H37 1997
323'.0973—dc21   97-29366
                                  CIP

New York University Press books are printed on acid-free paper, and their binding materials are chosen for strength and durability.

Manufactured in the Unites States of America

10 9 8 7 6 5 4 3 2 1

For my family,
who taught me to know better

Do nothing from selfish ambition or conceit, but in humility regard others as better than yourselves. Let each of you look not to your own interests, but to the interests of others.

— PHILIPPIANS 2.3-4

But, after all, nothing is true that forces one to exclude. Isolated beauty ends up simpering; solitary justice ends up oppressing. Whoever aims to serve one exclusive of the other serves no one, not even himself, and eventually serves injustice twice. A day comes when, thanks to rigidity, nothing causes wonder any more, everything is known, and life is spent in beginning over again. These are the days of exile, of desiccated life, of dead souls.

— Albert Camus, RETURN TO TIPASA

Contents

Acknowledgments

I am indebted to many people who, in various ways, made this book possible.

This is, first of all, very much an interdisciplinary effort, and some of the disciplines are not my own. For the science in particular, I have depended on the work of those scholars who have made contemporary understandings accessible to the general public. Ned Block, Stephen Jay Gould, Leon Kamin, and R. C. Lewontin are the most conspicuous examples, but as the notes will indicate, there are others too. Burton Blatt's work exposed the myths of mental retardation, and my own earlier inquiries into that topic benefitted especially from the works (and kind encouragement) of Paul Lombardo and Alexander Tymchuk and the counsel of Fred Rich. My more recent efforts to sift through the primary literature were assisted by a number of doctoral students in psychology at Widener University: at various times, I have benefitted from the research assistance of Ann Christie, Leonard Goldschmidt, and David Nickelsen. Professor Susan Goldberg of Widener University and Professor Martin Levit at the University of Missouri-Kansas City reviewed drafts of selected chapters in an effort to make sure that the science was not obviously wrong; they deserve, of course, no blame for any lingering errors.

For the history too I have benefitted from the efforts of others. The works of Ira Berlin, Carl Degler, Eric Foner, John Hope Franklin, Leon Litwack, James McPherson, Edmund Morgan, and Winton Solberg figure prominently in the text, though again, as the notes reveal, there are many others. Peter Parish's historiography of slavery, Alden Vaughn's historiography of the roots of racism, and Eric Foner's historiographical essay on Reconstruction were particularly valuable to this novice effort. On a more personal note, I must thank William Garfield for teaching me how to learn and appreciate history; I am grateful as well to the History Department at Davidson College for requiring all history majors to take a course in historiography (I am grateful too that they allowed me to graduate, despite an abysmally low History GRE score).

I was more at home with the legal analysis, but here too I must acknowledge certain debts. A. Leon Higginbotham and Thomas Morris have produced wonderful surveys of the law of slavery, and a loose coalition of contemporary legal scholars—the Critical Race Theorists—has generated invaluable critiques of the American law of "race." The works of Derrick Bell, Richard Delgado, Charles Lawrence, and Patricia Williams figure prominently in the text; so too does the work of Martha Minow, on the construction of the many forms of "difference." Alfred Avins's partial collection of the debates over the Reconstruction Amendments provided a useful starting point for research, though I am certain that he would not approve of the way this text builds on his effort. Charles DiMaria, Hamel Vyas, Pamela Krauss, and Aaron Goldstein provided terrific research assistance; the last deserves special thanks for his help in sifting through the microfiche records of the congressional Reconstruction debates. Thanks too to Barbara Carcanague and Noreen McGlinchey of Widener University, and Despina Gimbel and Elyse Strongin at New York University Press, who provided outstanding administrative and technical support to the project. The Widener University School of Law provided a research stipend to fund part of this effort; special thanks to Dean Arthur N. Frakt for his generosity and support.

My more personal debts run the gamut, I suppose, from the ridiculous to the sublime. Close to the former, I feel obliged to acknowledge the constant companionship of Louis Armstrong, Ella Fitzgerald, Louis Jordan, and Bruce Springsteen, who were not, in truth, actually with me, but whose music was a steady inspiration as I pored through the notes and typed up the words. I would also like to thank the folks who populate the personal stories in this text. Some of them would recognize the events but not their names: I changed the names whenever I thought privacy was at issue and accuracy was not. The events, I think, mostly happened as I described them, though I have already discovered that recollections differ on some of the details. But the stories, in any event, are offered as "stories," and their truths are decidedly personal.

Very much at the sublime end of the spectrum, I would like to thank the following family members, not only for giving me most of the stories, but also for their assistance, their support, their tolerance, and their affection: Patricia Eakin, Albert Griffiths, Alma Griffiths, Cynthia Hayman, Tom Hayman, Stephen Heim, Faye Kaufman, Galen Kaufman, Bob Maxwell, Harriet Maxwell, June Pesikey, William Sheridan, Katherine Thomas, Morris Thomas, Ron Whitehorne, and especially my mother, Norine Sheridan. The book is dedicated to them—but really, it is their book anyhow.

Special thanks as well to Niko Pfund at New York University Press for his remarkable patience, steady encouragement, and valuable insights. The same to Richard Delgado and Jean Stefancic, who helped inspire this effort and keep it on track; it would not have happened without them. And the most special of these special thanks to my frequent coauthor and always friend Nancy Levit; I suspected that it might be a real strain to write something without her, and am glad that I didn't have to find out.

Finally, thanks to Alice Eakin, my editor, best friend, and wife. She provided the words when I needed them, and the ideas, and the muse—and a whole world of kindness.

1

Introduction
Smart People

I'm not sure when I found out that some kids had high IQs. When I did find out, I'm not sure I much cared. When we were kids, we had our own ideas about "smart," and they had very little to do with IQs. The third-grade boys, for example, had developed their own distinct intellectual hierarchy: it consisted in small part of baseball trivia, in small part of the aptitude for petty crime, and in very substantial part of the skills—cognitive and otherwise—needed for insulting our peers (and, of course, their families). The girls, meanwhile, probably had their own hierarchy, but in the third grade, that was a mystery we boys had no interest in solving.

In the three-part hierarchy in which the boys subsisted, the ability to insult was undeniably the most important branch of intellect. It was also the most elaborate, itself consisting of three developmental stages: the first came with the recognition that curse words could be used as insults; the second was marked by the ability to use some curse words (one in particular) as participles to modify other curse words; and the third arrived with the realization that almost any curse word could be made doubly insulting by adding -face, -head, or -breath as a suffix. Progress through these stages, it seems to me now, was as much art as science. I remember one poor lad whose social fate was sealed the day he called me a "f—ing ass-head."

There was one insult we used quite a bit, and it was about the only time we showed any interest in the IQ concept. For no specific reason, or at least not for reasons having anything to do with perceptions of intelligence, we found it immensely gratifying to call one another "retards." We had, of course, no idea who or what a "retard" was, and we were fairly liberal in constructing synonyms: "reject" was thought to convey the same message, as were the more elaborate "mental retard," "mental reject," or, less elaborately, "mental." All we knew about any of these terms was that they had all the ingredients for a good insult: they were apparently somehow demeaning; they had quite a funny sound to them; and no one, as far as we knew, would ever confront us with the embarrassing revelation that what we intended as an insult was in fact an accurate description.

All of this changed sometime in the third grade, when we discovered Mrs. Sweeney's "special" class. We had wondered for some time why the window in Mrs. Sweeney's door was covered with cardboard, wondered specifically why we kids weren't supposed to look in. I suppose it never occurred to us that the cardboard also kept the kids inside from looking out, but then, lots of that kind of stuff never occurred to us. What did occur to us was that Mrs. Sweeney's kids had to be "special" in some very strange way, strange enough that we had to be prevented from seeing them. Our imaginations ran wild with the possibilities, and we were not at all disappointed the day Dicky Hollins told us that he knew the secret to those kids, that his mom knew the mother of some kid in Mrs. Sweeney's class, and the kid was, honest-to-god, a retard.

Just what that meant remained a mystery. For all we knew, "retards" were circus freaks or juvenile delinquents or some barely imaginable combination of the two. We deduced that they must be somehow pathetic and perhaps somehow frightening; we knew for sure that they were different from other kids, and that the difference was wildly fascinating.

For months, our school days were preoccupied with the effort to catch a glimpse of the retards. We'd linger outside Mrs. Sweeney's door at lunch time, knock on her door and hide just around the corner, we'd come to school early in the hopes of seeing the retards arrive and stay late to catch them leaving, and through it all, we never saw more than Mrs. Sweeney's disapproving frown. And then Mrs. Sweeney failed to show up for school one morning, and we were sure it was because the retards had killed her, and we anxiously awaited the showdown, the cops versus the retards. But she only had a cold, and she was back early the next day, with the cardboard over her window, preserving the great mystery inside.

The spell was broken on a spring morning. We had a substitute teacher that day, and he was either more gullible or more lazy than most, so when we told him that it was physical fitness week, and that instead of geography we were having extended recess in the morning, he dutifully took us outside to play kickball at 10:30 in the morning, a full ninety minutes before our scheduled break. It did not occur to him, nor did it occur to us, that 10:30 might have been the time set aside for some other kids' recess, and that some other kids might have been on the playground, playing kickball, when we arrived.

But 10:30 was Mrs. Sweeney's time, and she was there when we got to the playground. So too was her class.

"It's them." Dicky Hollins, now our resident authority, made the matter-of-fact pronouncement, and all the boys knew exactly what he meant. We all stood there, transfixed, and watched them play. I recall thinking that some of them looked a little different, but I'm not quite sure how. And that some of them moved a little differently, though again, I could not explain how.

On they played, oblivious, it seemed, to our presence.

We stood silently and watched.

They kicked the ball. They ran. They laughed. They celebrated.

One kid dropped a ball kicked right at him.

We all heard him when he cussed.

And it occurs to me now, as I think about it for the first time, that no other kid called him a name.

Our substitute said something to Mrs. Sweeney, and then, with a very serious look on his face, he said something to our class. The kids in our class started to file back into school, but some of us boys lagged behind, and somebody grabbed me by the arm, and dragged me up the walk to the school, and I kept turning around, just looking. When we all got back to our classroom, the substitute handed out maps of the United States, and he told us to color in the Middle Atlantic states, and when we complained that we didn't have crayons, he told us to use our pencils. He gave us an hour and a half to finish the exercise, and I spent the last eighty-five minutes drawing pictures of Frankenstein, and football players, and World War II fighter planes. And all the time I was thinking about Mrs. Sweeney's kids, and I looked around the room at the other boys in the class, and I knew they were thinking about the same thing too.

I don't remember ever seeing any of Mrs. Sweeney's kids again. Nor do I remember ever saying a word about them to any of my friends, or hearing a word about them from anybody. It was as if the whole day never happened. Except for one thing: after that day, for some reason, none of us ever called any kid a "retard" again.

Carrie Buck was a retard. That, at least, was the prevailing opinion of her in 1924, when the director of the Virginia Colony for the Feeble-minded concluded that the eighteen-year-old resident of the Colony was "feebleminded of the . . . moron class." Carrie's mother was also of limited intellect, a moron as well, according to the director. Carrie was born out of wedlock and, it was assumed, had inherited both her mother's intellectual disabilities and her moral defects: Carrie too, after all, had conceived an illegitimate daughter. For her mental and moral failings, Carrie's foster family arranged to have the young mother institutionalized in the Virginia Colony in January 1924. That September, the Colony, acting under the authority of a Virginia state law, sought to sterilize Carrie Buck.

The director of the Colony, Albert Priddy, had been the chief architect and sponsor of Virginia's sterilization law. The law found its scientific support in eugenics theory, still in vogue in 1920s America, but compulsory sterilization depended upon more than the mere belief in the genetic perfectibility of humanity. For that drastic measure, some odd combination of moral and political values was necessary: a bit of social Darwinism, a bit of political Progressivism, some economic conservatism, a little thinly disguised racism, and, for men like Priddy, a certain priggish disdain for the sexual habits of the poor. Armed with this intellectual grab bag, Priddy had won the near unanimous approval of the Virginia legislature for his sterilization law in March 1924.

But his advocacy was not ended. Similar laws had been struck down by courts in other states, some because they did not afford sufficient procedural protection for their subjects, others because they unfairly targeted only the residents of state institutions. But with his counsel and friend, Aubrey Strode, Priddy had carefully drafted the Virginia law to meet these objections; now, they were determined to find the test case that would secure judicial approval. The case they settled on was Carrie Buck's.

The Virginia law provided for the sterilization of inmates of state institutions where four conditions were met. First, it had to appear that the "inmate is insane, idiotic, imbecile, feeble-minded or epileptic" and, second, that the inmate "by the laws of heredity is the probable potential parent of socially inadequate offspring likewise afflicted." Third, sterilization must not harm "the general health" of the inmate, but rather, as the fourth and final requirement, must promote "the welfare of the inmate and of society." Carrie Buck, the young unwed mother, provided an easy case under the terms of this statute, particularly the way the deck was stacked.

Priddy's petition for the sterilization of Carrie Buck was approved by the Special Board of Directors of the Colony; under the Virginia law, Carrie was entitled to appeal that decision to the Virginia state courts. Her trial was held on November 18, 1924. Aubrey Strode called eight lay witnesses to testify that Carrie was feebleminded and immoral and that her mother and daughter were "below the normal mentally"; he called two physicians to testify to the medical advantages of sterilizing the feebleminded; he called a eugenicist to testify by deposition as to the value of eugenic sterilization as "a force for the mitigation of race degeneracy"; and he called Priddy himself to testify that, for Carrie and society at large, compulsory sterilization "would be a blessing."

Irving Whitehead, Carrie's appointed attorney, called no rebuttal witnesses.

The court approved the sterilization order, and the highest court in Virginia affirmed this decision. Carrie's attorney dutifully appealed to the United States Supreme Court. On May 2, 1927, the Supreme Court, by a vote of eight justices to one, approved the involuntary sterilization of Carrie Buck.

Justice Oliver Wendell Holmes wrote the opinion for the Court. Holmes had already served on the Supreme Court for a quarter century; for twenty years before that, he had been a justice of the Massachusetts Supreme Judicial Court, the last three years as chief justice. He had been educated in private schools, at Harvard College, and at Harvard Law School. He was, by common consensus, a very smart man.

He was able to dispose of Carrie Buck's claim in a few pithy sentences.

We have seen more than once that the public welfare may call upon the best citizens for their lives. It would be strange if it could not call upon those who already sap the strength of the State for these lesser sacrifices, often not felt to be such by those concerned, in order to prevent our being swamped with incompetence. It is better for all the world, if instead of waiting to execute degenerate offspring for crime, or to let them starve for their imbecility, society can prevent those who are manifestly unfit from continuing their kind. The principle that sustains compulsory vaccination is broad enough to cover cutting the Fallopian tubes. Three generations of imbeciles are enough.

Carrie Buck was sterilized on October 19, 1927. Not long after, she was "paroled" from the Colony into the care of a family in Bland, Virginia, for whom she worked as a domestic servant. She married; she and her husband had, of course, no children. Her husband died after twenty-four years of marriage. Carrie eventually remarried and in 1970 moved back to her hometown of Charlottesville, Virginia. For ten years, she and her husband lived there in a one-room, cinder block shed. In 1980 Carrie was hospitalized for exposure and malnutrition; later, she and her husband were taken to a nursing home where, on January 28, 1983, Carrie Buck died at the age of seventy-six.

Not long before her death, Carrie Buck was interviewed by Professor Paul Lombardo of the University of Virginia. He writes:

> Throughout Carrie's adult life she regularly displayed intelligence and kindness that belied the "feeblemindedness" and "immorality" that were used as an excuse to sterilize her. She was an avid reader, and even in her last weeks was able to converse lucidly, recalling events from her childhood. Branded by Holmes as a second generation imbecile, Carrie provided no support for his glib epithet throughout her life.

Carrie Buck, it appears, was no "imbecile" at all. She was poor, she was uneducated, and these no doubt contributed to her "diagnosis." But even under the crude categories of the day, under which "imbeciles" ranked below the various grades of "morons" in the grand hierarchy of "feeblemindedness," Carrie was no "imbecile" and probably was not "feebleminded" at all.

Carrie Buck's attorney might have known better, might have known that Carrie was no imbecile, was no moron, and was perhaps not feebleminded at all. He might have explained all this to the reviewing courts. But Carrie Buck's attorney apparently had other plans. Irving Whitehead, it evolves, was a former member of the Board of Directors of the Virginia Colony for the Feeble-minded and a long time associate of Strode and Priddy's. Indeed, a building at the Colony named in Irving Whitehead's honor was opened just two months before the arrival of a young mother named Carrie Buck.

Irving Whitehead might also have known the truth behind Carrie's moral failings. Carrie's illegitimate daughter was conceived in neither a moral lapse nor an imbecile's folly; she was conceived when Carrie was raped by the nephew of her foster parents. Carrie Buck was institutionalized not to protect her welfare, but to preserve her foster family's good name.

In the end, Carrie Buck was a victim not of nature, but of the people around her. The eventual debunking of the sham that was eugenics merely confirmed what should have been obvious all along: the "science" that dictated Carrie's unwelcome trip to the Colony infirmary was in reality only politics, the cruel politics of inequality.

There is, finally, the matter of Carrie's daughter, the third of the three generations of imbeciles. Relatively little is known of her life, save this: Vivian Buck attended regular public schools for all of her life, before dying of an infectious disease at the age of eight. And in the next to last year of her short life, Carrie Buck's daughter earned a spot on the Honor Roll.[1]

There are no more imbeciles in America, no more morons, no more feebleminded of any type or degree. We eliminated them all, installing in their place people with varying degrees of mental retardation: at first, some were educable or trainable; now their retardation is mild or moderate or severe or profound. And when we determined that we had too many people with mental retardation, we tightened the general definition of the class, eliminating half the mentally retarded population in a single bold stroke that would have made the eugenicists proud.

But some things have not changed. In contemporary America, we still sterilize people with low IQs. When they escape sterilization, we routinely deny them the right to raise their own children. Systematically, too, we deny them the right to marry, to vote, to choose their residence, to live on their own. We have made a history for people with mental retardation that is replete with the normal horrors of discrimination—stigmatization, segregation, disenfranchisement—but we have added to their lot the unique horrors of involuntary sterilizations and psychosurgery. In our words and in our deeds we have been relentless in our efforts to diminish them, to make them lesser people. All of this, because they are not sufficiently smart.[2]

The remarkable furor that followed the publication of Richard Herrnstein and Charles Murray's book *The Bell Curve* tended to obscure the altogether unremarkable thesis of that text. Simply put, its thesis was this: in American society today, smart folks get ahead, and not-so-smart folks don't. As their critics pointed out, Herrnstein and Murray relied on a whole lot of questionable material to make this point, and stretched the bounds of science to posit a slew of weak correlations among various "biological" traits, "intelligence," and assorted indicia of "success." Still, the basic empirical proposition of the text has survived most critical scrutiny: if you are smart, then indeed, you get ahead; if you are not, chances are, you won't.

This, of course, came as good news to smart people throughout the country, and they were not reluctant to express their satisfaction. For them, it was not merely that the inevitable equation of smartness and success ensured their fortunes; what was more important, rather, was that they could feel downright good about their prospects.

There was, after all, a subtext to *The Bell Curve*'s simple story that is almost of moral dimensions. The people who have made it have done so because they are smart; they, in a very clear sense, deserve their success. Conversely, the people who have not made it have failed because they are not-so-smart; they, in an equally clear sense, deserve their failure.

Understandably, then, *The Bell Curve* was not perceived as bringing very good news for the not-so-smart people, who to the extent that they could understand the text's rather simple message, had to be forgiven for finding it just a bit depressing. For these people, after all, there were to be no smiling fortunes; destiny promised them less wealth, less status, less comfort. *The Bell Curve* offered to the not-so-smart people little more than a single lesson in civics: hereafter, they should no longer labor under the illusion that smart people were to blame for their misfortunes.

Indeed, the worst news for the not-so-smart people came in the political subtext of the book, and it was this reading that generated some of the most heated debate. For Herrnstein and Murray, there were clear policy implications to their findings. If smart people get ahead, almost no matter what, and if not-so-smart people fall behind, almost no matter what, then it does not seem to make a great deal of sense to devote massive amounts of energy and resources to the pursuit of social and economic equality. From a pragmatic viewpoint, those efforts were simply futile; moreover, if the moral lesson of their work was correct, then such rampant egalitarianism was simply unjust. New Deals, Great Societies, New Covenants and the like would never alter the basic social hierarchy; they would only flatten the pyramid by unfairly limiting the potential of the gifted and unnaturally rewarding the foibles of the inept.

Thus with one brutally simple idea, *The Bell Curve*, following centuries of "scientific" tradition, undermined the very foundations of the struggle for equality. The preoccupations of welfare state social engineers were no longer justifiable; their emphasis on, in *The Bell Curve*'s words, "changes in economics, changes in demographics, changes in the culture" and solutions founded on "better education, more and better jobs, and specific social interventions" seemed untenable in the face of this natural order. What mattered instead was "the underlying element that has shaped the changes: human intelligence."

Not surprisingly, then, *The Bell Curve* set its sights on what should be easy targets: the practical tools of egalitarians—lawyers and the law. It is law, they suggested, that most clearly embodies our unnatural preoccupation with equality, law that redistributes our resources, levels our opportunities, and reduces our culture to the least common denominator. *The Bell Curve* challenged the fairness and practical wisdom of the full range of legislative enactments and judicial decisions designed to make America a more equal nation. While acknowledging the central place of equality in America's political mythology, *The Bell Curve* called into serious question the realizability of this goal. Antidiscrimination laws are inefficient, desegregation counter-productive, affirmative action unwise, unfair, and perhaps immoral. In the worldview of *The Bell Curve*, the legal devotion to equality must sit in an uneasy tension with the combined effects of liberalism's commitment to individual freedom and the immutable differences in human aptitude. The idea is as old as the Federalists, but now it comes with "new" scientific support: all men, it seems, were not created equal after all; it is only the law that pursues this quixotic vision.

Smart people succeed. From this simple empirical proposition emerged a counterrevolutionary policy prescription: law's egalitarian ideal must invariably accommodate, or yield to, those inexorable commands of nature that distinguish the smart from the not-so-smart. Only smart people *should* succeed.

But *The Bell Curve* eluded a vital dilemma that inheres in its marvelously elegant empirical proposition: it is either tautological or wrong. It evolves that this central proposition holds true only because the terms of the equation, "smartness" and "success," are not just empirical correlates, but definitionally synonymous: the culture rewards smartness with success because "smartness" is, definitionally, the ability to succeed in the culture. And, if any effort is made to imbue the terms with some independent meaning—to define "smartness" without reference to success, or "success" without reference to evidence of smartness—then the whole proposition falls apart: the equation becomes hopelessly confounded by the variables of class and culture, and whatever causal relationship remains between "smartness" and "success" begins to look, at the very least, bidirectional.

As the empirical proposition collapses, so too does the moral and political framework of *The Bell Curve*'s "natural" order, as well as its regressive critique of the law. It is simply not true that, throughout the history of this nation, law has been the great social equalizer, bucking the tides of natural justice. On the contrary, law has been and remains the great defender of the natural order, protecting the bounty of the "smart" from the intrusions of the "not-so-smart" while eluding all insight into the actual construction of those terms.

The Bell Curve got it backwards: law does not impose an artificial equality on a people ordered by nature; on the contrary, law preserves the artificial order imposed on a people who could be, and should be, of equal worth. Because it is culture, not biology, that makes people different. It is culture, not nature, that generates the intellectual hierarchy. And law maintains rather than challenges the smart culture.

I did pretty well in my early years of school. From the first through fifth grades, I got almost all As, and never anything less than a B+, except for in penmanship, where I tended to get mostly Ds. This last wasn't for lack of effort, but for the life of me, I just could not master the cursive style. The disorder persists to this day.

When I was eleven my mom remarried, and we moved from our brick rowhouse into a completely detached split-level home with a driveway, a patio, and a backyard that seemed at the time large enough to get lost in. I changed schools at the same time, and got my first experience with what I now know is called academic tracking.

At my new school, the sixth grade was divided into four sections, A through D, with section A being for the really "smart" kids, B for the less smart kids, and so on down the line. Though I had a section A type record, I got assigned to section B; this, I figure, reflected either a skepticism about the academic standards at my old school or an emphasis on penmanship at the new one.

I did not fare well in section B. In section B, we were expected to talk about stuff, and most of the kids—feeling, I guess, at ease among friends—found this activity not the least bit challenging. I was another story. Most of the talk focused on current events, and while I sort of knew what was going on, and think I understood when I was told, the simple fact was that I could not bring myself to say much about the matter. And so I got mostly As on my homework, and even As on the tests, but when called on in class I was completely unresponsive. Day after day the sixth-grade teacher would call on me, sometimes for opinions, sometimes just to repeat the received wisdom of a prior lesson, and day after day I would sit in silence, staring at my desk, waiting for the teacher to move on.

I had lots of conferences with the teacher, and at least two that I can recall with the principal. They were not terribly productive. Yes, I could hear the teacher's questions; yes, I knew the answers; yes, I knew the importance of sharing the answers with the teacher and the rest of the class. No, I was not trying to embarrass the teacher; no, I was not afraid of being wrong; no, I certainly did not cheat on my homework or on the tests. And no, I was sorry, but I did not know what the problem was, or what anyone should do to fix it.

I guess the principal came up with his own solution, because I spent a couple of days with the kids of section C. The move may have been punitive or it may have been remedial, but, in either event, I loved it. The kids of section C did not bother with current events; our focus was on drawing—and I loved to draw. In science, we drew pictures of solar systems and molecules; in social studies, we drew pictures of historical figures; in math, we drew pictures of numbers, then added anatomical features to convert them into animals or people. Precisely how the kids of section C were expected to contribute to the war against communism I do not know, but I do know our training for service was a heckuva lot more fun than section B's.

At the same time, it worries me some in retrospect that section C's drawing lessons were so thoroughly unencumbered by any actual knowledge of the things to be drawn. I don't remember ever learning anything at all about the physical appearance of molecules or solar systems, let alone anything about what they did or why they were important. And about the only math I remember from my time in Section C is that a 6 is versatile enough to be any animal from a giraffe to a turtle, and a 9 can be the same animal in extreme distress, but a 2 isn't worth a damn for anything but a snake.

We learned just as much about the historical figures. I remember a Thanksgiving lesson that required each of us to draw a picture of Pocahontas, an easy task for me, I having studied at my old school from a textbook that featured a very nice picture of the Thanksgiving heroine. The image stuck with me—she looked like a movie star, and I think I had a crush on her—and so I finished the assignment with ease, producing a credible rendition of Sophia Loren in buckskins with a feather sticking up out of her head. Some of the other kids at my drawing table—in section C we did not use individual desks—did not know Pocahontas as well as I did, and a couple of the boys drew Pocahontas as a very fierce, and very male, Indian warrior, which certainly would have made Captain John Smith's story a more interesting one, but was, as far as I know, largely inconsistent with the historical record. But we all got the same grade on the assignment, except for the one kid who drew Pocahontas holding a bloody scalp, an image, I guess, that ran counter to the sentiments of the holiday.

I did not get to stay in section C all that long. I spent half a day with some other principal-type person taking a slew of tests; a week later, I was in section A. In section A, we seldom talked about current events, and we hardly ever drew. Instead, we diagrammed sentences (kind of like turning numbers into animals, but with correct answers), learned the periodic table (there really is a krypton), bisected triangles (with compasses and protractors), argued about who started the War of 1812 (it was the British, of course), and even wrote and performed a play (based on *Romeo and Juliet*, to every boy's dismay). We had lots of tests in section A, and some were like the ones I took in the principal's office, multiple-choice tests with separate answer sheets where you had to be careful not to mark outside the little circles with your number 2 pencil. Sometimes kids would leave section A, and sometimes new kids would arrive, and always we kept taking the tests.

I did not do all that great my first few weeks in section A, but I eventually got the hang of things and, with help from my teacher, once again started getting As. I made friends in section A, and some of them would be friends clear through high school. I sometimes missed the kids in section B, and also the kids in section C, but I lost touch with all of them. From time to time I wonder what happened to them, and to the kids in section D, whom I never even knew.

I learned a lot in section A, acquired a lot of new skills, gained a lot of new knowledge. We didn't get to draw much or talk about current events, but we learned to think and to write, and we learned lots of new concepts and new words and new phrases. Maybe it was in section A that I learned the meaning of "self-fulfilling prophecy."

George Harley and John Sellers wanted to be police officers. In the District of Columbia, applicants for positions in the Metropolitan Police Department were required to pass a physical exam, satisfy character requirements, have a high school diploma or its equivalent, and pass a written examination. Successful applicants were then admitted into Recruit School, a seventeen-week training course. Upon the completion of their training, recruits were required to pass a written final examination; those who failed the final examination were given assistance until they eventually passed.

The initial examination given to all Department applicants was known as Test 21, an eighty-question multiple-choice test prepared by the U.S. Civil Service Commission. The test purported to measure "verbal ability"; a few sample items follow:

Laws restricting hunting to certain regions and to a specific time of the year were passed *chiefly* to
   a. prevent people from endangering their lives by hunting
   b. keep our forests more beautiful
   c. raise funds from the sale of hunting licenses
   d. prevent complete destruction of certain kinds of animals
   e. preserve certain game for eating purposes

BECAUSE is related to REASON as THEREFORE is related to
   a. result
   b. heretofore
   c. instinct
   d. logic
   e. antecedent

BOUNTY means most nearly
   a. generosity
   b. limit
   c. service
   d. fine
   e. duty

(Reading) "Adhering to old traditions, old methods, and old policies at a time when circumstances demand a new course of action may be praiseworthy from a sentimental point of view, but success is won most frequently by facing the facts and acting in accordance with the logic of the facts." *The quotation best supports the statement that* success is best attained through
   a. recognizing necessity and adjusting to it
   b. using methods that have proved successful
   c. exercising will power
   d. remaining on a job until it is completed
   e. considering each new problem separately

PROMONTORY means most nearly
   a. marsh
   b. monument
   c. headland
   d. boundary
   e. plateau

The police department had determined that a raw score of forty on Test 21 was required for entrance into Recruit School; applicants who failed to attain that score were summarily rejected.

George Harley and John Sellers failed to score at least a forty on Test 21 when they took the test in the early 1970s; as a consequence, they were denied admission into Recruit School. Both Harley and Sellers are black, and it turned out that they were not the only black applicants to "fail" Test 21. From 1968 to 1971, the failure rate for black applicants was 57 percent; in the same time frame, by contrast, 13 percent of the white applicants failed Test 21.

In 1972 Harley and Sellers joined a lawsuit challenging the hiring and promotion practices of the Metropolitan Police Department. They contended, among other things, that reliance on Test 21 amounted to discrimination against black applicants in violation of the Constitution and federal civil rights laws. Test 21, they noted, had never been validated as a predictor of job performance: it was true that high scores on Test 21 were positively correlated with high scores on the Recruit School final examination, but neither Test 21 nor the final examination had been validated with reference to the Recruit School curriculum or the requirements of the job. Neither test, in short, bore any necessary relationship to police training or police work.

But the trial judge, Gerhard Gesell, of the U.S. District Court in the District of Columbia, rejected Harley and Sellers's claim. Judge Gesell ruled, first, that "reasoning and verbal and literacy skills" were significant aspects of work in law enforcement: " [t]he ability to swing a nightstick no longer measures a policeman's competency for his exacting role in this city." Gesell then rejected the argument that Test 21 was an inappropriate measure of those skills. "There is no proof," he wrote, that Test 21 is "culturally slanted to favor whites. . . . The Court is satisfied that the undisputable facts prove the test to be reasonably and directly related to the requirements of the police recruit training program and that it is neither so designed nor operates to discriminate against otherwise qualified blacks."

It was true, Gesell granted, that "blacks and whites with low test scores may often turn in a high job performance." But "[t]he lack of job performance validation does not defeat the Test, given its direct relationship to recruiting and the valid part it plays in this process." The police department, he concluded, "should not be required on this showing to lower standards or to abandon efforts to achieve excellence."

The U.S. Court of Appeals reversed Gesell's decision. It was clear, the court first held, that the use of Test 21 did amount to racial discrimination. The statistical disparity was itself enough to establish that claim; moreover, it arose amid a growing body of evidence suggesting that, as a general rule, "blacks are test-rejected more frequently than whites." "This phenomenon," the court noted, "is the result of the long history of educational deprivation, primarily due to segregated schools, for blacks. Until arrival of the day when the effects of that deprivation have been completely dissipated, comparable performance on such tests can hardly be expected."

The court also rejected the suggestion that the use of the test—and its racially discriminatory effects—could be justified by some objective job-related requirements, that, in legal terms, the discrimination was necessary to advance a "compelling governmental interest." "The assertion of predictive value of Test 21 for achievement in Recruit School is based upon a correlation between Test 21 scores and scores on written examinations given during a 17-week training course," the court noted. "We think this evidence tends to prove nothing more than that a written aptitude test will accurately predict performance on a second round of written examinations, and nothing to counter this hypothesis has been presented to us." "As long as no one with a score below 40 enters Recruit School," the court concluded,

> as long as all recruits pass Recruit School, as long as the Department's actions concede that Recruit School average has little value in predicting job performance, and as long as there is no evidence of any correlation between the Recruit School average and job performance, we entertain grave doubts whether any of this type of evidence could be strengthened to the point of satisfying the heavy burden imposed by [the law].

In 1976, the U.S. Supreme Court reversed yet again, reinstating Judge Gesell's decision. In an opinion that altered the basic fabric of constitutional law—and impossibly hindered, in some views, the legal struggle for equality—the Court held that racially discriminatory effects were not enough to establish a constitutional violation. Rather, the guarantee of "equal protection of the laws" was abridged only by intentional discrimination. Only "purposeful discrimination" could create the type of inequality that required some compelling justification; discriminatory effects required no justification at all. There was, then, no constitutional inequality when black applicants failed Test 21 at four times the rate of their white counterparts; in the absence of proof that the Metropolitan Police Department intended this result, the Constitution was not implicated at all.

Justice Byron White wrote the opinion for the Court. Justice White was the valedictorian of the class of 1938 at the University of Colorado, a Rhodes scholar, and a graduate with high honors from

Yale Law School. He was—and is—a very smart man. But Harley and Sellers's claim, he wrote, left him befuddled: "[W]e have difficulty understanding how a law establishing a racially neutral qualification for employment is nevertheless racially discriminatory and denies 'any person . . . equal protection of the laws' simply because a greater proportion of Negroes fail to qualify than members of other racial or ethnic groups."

Nowhere in his opinion did White explain how he knew that Test 21 was "racially neutral."

Near the close of his opinion for the Court, White did explain why evidence of a racially disparate impact could not suffice to establish a constitutional claim:

> A rule that a statute designed to serve neutral ends is nevertheless invalid, absent compelling justification, if in practice it benefits or burdens one race more than another would be far reaching and would raise serious questions about, and perhaps invalidate, a whole range of tax, welfare, public service, regulatory, and licensing statutes that may be more burdensome to the poor and to the average black than to the more affluent white.

There are, in short, too many racial disparities for the Constitution to redress without proof of an unlawful intent. The unhappy coincidence that black applicants failed Test 21 at four times the rate of their white counterparts could not alone offend the Constitution: validated or not, Test 21 was "race-neutral" because the Court could not afford to believe otherwise.[3]

Before the Civil War, every southern state except Tennessee prohibited the instruction of slaves. After a brief period of promise during Reconstruction, black education was effectively suppressed by the violent reactions of Redemption and the gradual entrenchment of the Jim Crow system. Some of the tools of racial hierarchy were legal, some extralegal. As to the former, racial segregation, combined with grotesque disparities in the allocation of educational resources and radical differences in the focus and depth of the curricula, was both pervasive and effective. As to the latter, a relentless scheme of orchestrated violence, directed principally at educated black Americans, achieved for white supremacy what laws alone could not.

Today, America's white citizens are more likely than its black citizens to receive undergraduate and graduate education, more likely to attend primary and secondary schools in districts with superior resources, and more likely to be enrolled in "advanced" or "college preparatory" courses; its black citizens are more likely to be suspended, expelled, or failed from high school, are more likely to attend overcrowded and underfunded primary and secondary schools, and are more likely to be assigned to remedial education classes, or labeled "mentally retarded." America's black citizens are offered fewer math and science courses as primary and secondary school students, are forced to learn with smaller supplies of texts and equipment, materials that are, in any event, more apt to be hopelessly outdated, and are more likely to be led in their educational efforts by underpaid and underqualified "substitute" teachers.[4]

And white people, for some reason, keep doing better on "race-neutral" tests.

The stories of Carrie Buck and of George Harley and John Sellers are the stories the law usually tells about "smart." They are not stories of unbridled egalitarianism: no wealth is redistributed, no incompetence rewarded, no unqualified applicant gets the prize, no loser suddenly wins. The stories told by the law are the stories told by the culture at large: the smart people get ahead, the not-so-smart people don't. The law, truth be told, ensures this result.

This book is about being "smart"—about its meaning and its consequences. It is about attempts to expand its meaning and make it more inclusive, and it is about attempts to preserve its conventional meaning, to maintain its exclusivity. It is a book about the relationship between "intelligence" and "race," and the way the two phenomena have been created together. It is about the relentless interplay between science and politics in shaping the conventional meaning of both constructs, and the vital role played by law in shielding those conventional meanings from critical scrutiny.

This book, then, is about the deeply rooted cultural myths that surround the concept of smartness: the myths of biology, the myths of merit, and the myths of equality under law. It is about the myths that persuade us, over our better moral judgment, that not all people—and maybe only very few—are smart. It is about, then, the "smart" culture.

The mythology of "smartness" is old: it is an original part of our national fabric. It found full expression during the very founding of the Republic, as a vital part of the effort to reconcile the lofty rhetoric of universal liberty and equality with the undeniable realities of social caste, political exclusion, and chattel slavery. Not all people were in fact created equal, endowed with inalienable rights, and meant to share in the blessings of liberty. What distinguished the included from the excluded were the natural differences in "the faculties of men": Indians, Africans, women, and the poor all were differentiated by "nature," and relegated to the lower rungs of the "natural" order.

That was in the beginning. Four score and a few years later, a reconstructed nation abolished slavery and promised all persons the "equal protection of the law." But the architects of Reconstruction—as a collective whole—were intensely ambivalent, and the promise they offered—of legal equality—was maddeningly ambiguous. Even that promise withered in the face of assertions of natural superiority: separate but equal was in truth only separate, and the inequality was entirely in keeping with the natural order. By the end of the nineteenth century, a new evolutionary science seemed to confirm the inevitability of the American hierarchy: even in a land of unrestrained liberty—and perhaps especially in such a land—only the fittest will thrive. Over a century into the American experiment, social caste and political exclusion remained the general rule, and while chattel slavery yielded to sharecropping and debt peonage and wage labor, the economic order was essentially the same. And whenever it was called upon, the Supreme Court would be there to confirm that it was all perfectly natural.

Another century later, and much finally has changed. Suffrage is now genuinely universal. Public or private discrimination based on race, gender, or disability now violates federal law. The promise of legal equality, at least, is now a reality.

Yet by every social, political, and economic measure, the hierarchies of race, gender, and disability endure. And to explain the reality of inequality in the face of professed equality, we make recourse still to the same old myths:

- The myth of identity: that the salient differences among groups of people—race, gender, disability—are biological.
- The myth of merit: that our social, political, and economic markets are free and neutral, and only occasionally corrupted by the bias of individual discrimination.
- The myth of intelligence: that the unequal outcomes of social, political, and economic competition reflect the inborn inequities of nature.
- The myth of equality under law: that equality can never transcend the empty realm of form, for the law is limited by tradition and powerless in the face of the natural order.

Thus the mythology of smartness endures. And it is all untrue. And the real tragedy is this: by now, we should know better.

We should know that the biological differences among groups of people are trivial, and that the salient differences are generated through the processes of social interaction.

We should know that our markets reflect the preferences of the people who have structured and maintained them, and that these biases—structural and unconscious—constitute the real discrimination.

We should know that unequal outcomes—in education, in employment, and yes, on tests of smartness—reflect the cumulative advantages and disadvantages of centuries of discrimination, and the same biases that pervade all of our culture.

We should know that our laws and traditions are only what we choose to make them, and that equality can be as real as we dare.

All of this we should now know, yet somehow refuse to believe. And in rejecting the liberation offered by contemporary understanding, we have rejected as well the very best of our national heritage. We abandon the egalitarian vision of the people who founded and reconstructed our nation; we embrace instead their tragically flawed mythology.

Smart people do get ahead. They stay ahead. But it is *not* only natural.

One question haunts this book: for all the talk about "socially constructed this" and "culturally determined that," for all the critiques of the "natural order" and all the appeals to equality, isn't it undeniably true that some people—and perhaps some groups of people—are just plain smarter than others?

The answer is simple and obvious: yes, some people—and perhaps some groups of people—are smarter than others.

It's the explanation that's complicated. Because the fact is that both the question and the answer are meaningless unless we are clear about what we mean by "smart." The problem is that we often are not very clear, and we often are not in agreement, and so our assertions about the relative smartness of some people as compared to others are too easily misunderstood, and it becomes far too easy to assume that their profound smartness—and other people's lack of it—is more natural, more inevitable, and more inherently meaningful than it really is.

So let me try to be clear about what I mean when I say that some people—and perhaps some groups of people—are smarter than others.

Some people are less "smart" than others for identifiable physiological reasons. Neurological disorders often have direct effects on cognitive ability; sometimes these disorders may so affect a cognitive ability that we will say that the person is cognitively impaired. If the impairment is spread among a wide enough range of cognitive abilities, it may be possible to say that—in most cultural contexts—the person will be less smart than the norm. Here, however, a certain note of caution is in order: in some discrete contexts, our cognitively impaired person may be quite smart after all—smart, that is, at some things, if not at most.

Some people don't do as well as other people on standardized measurements of "intelligence." Ideally, "intelligence" means the ability to succeed in the culture; standardized measurements of intelligence should thus measure the relative ability to achieve cultural success. Someone with less measured intelligence should then have—if everything goes according to plan—less ability to succeed in the culture. Again, it may be possible to say that in most cultural contexts, the person will be less smart than the norm.

Here, many notes of caution are in order. It is easy to assume that these intelligence differences that we have measured represent natural variations among people, variations that are fixed in the biological makeup of the individual. But that is not necessarily—and probably not often—the case.

Nature, after all, does not dictate which qualities will correlate with cultural achievement. It is for us to decide which aptitudes—which skills and knowledge, talents and abilities, cognitive and affective traits—are valuable and which ones are not. We could exalt formal deduction, or creative analogic reasoning, or practical problem-solving skills, or moral reasoning, or empathic judgment and interpersonal skills. We decide, in other words, what will count as "intelligence."

Nature does not dictate which people will be afforded the optimal chances to acquire the aptitudes for cultural success. It is for us to decide who will receive the optimal chances—the cultural environment, the formal education, the social opportunity—to acquire intelligence. Research now consistently documents the profound effects of environmental stimulation on cognitive development and the equally profound effects of environmental deprivation. It is a social fact that the probabilities of growing up in comparatively stimulating and deprived environments are not equally distributed among race and class: successful people—smart people—are uniquely situated to perpetuate their advantages. And we keep them there. We decide, in other words, who will be afforded the best chance to get "smart" and stay smart.

Nature does not dictate our response to measured differences in intelligence. We decide whether those differences should be simply ignored, actively countered, or preserved as justifications for the prevailing inequities. In the United States, we long ago stopped talking about regional differences in "IQ," as well as most ethnic disparities. The gender disparities, meanwhile, we eliminated by modifying the tests. The disparities of race, however, retain a singular legitimacy. We give them that. We decide, in other words, whether we actually like our hierarchies of "smartness."

All of which is to say that "superior" and "inferior" intelligences are not entirely natural. On the contrary, it is substantially our decisions that make people either more or less "smart."

There is something concededly counterintuitive about all this. We have come to believe in smartness as an inherent quality, as something people are either born with or not. We have come to believe that it is fairly immutable, that individual limitations are pretty much fixed. And we can hardly be faulted for conceiving of it as something universal; it is hard to imagine choosing other things to count as "smart" beyond the things "we" have chosen. So the suggestion that smartness is "made" strikes us as, well, a not-very-smart suggestion.

But then again, we know that people disagree about smartness, about whether a student or a teacher or a politician or a neighbor is "smart." Maybe, then, smartness is not entirely inherent; maybe it does require our subjective assessment.

And we know that people can get smart. They learn knowledge, and skills, and even learn how to learn: even the vaunted "IQ" is not stable. Maybe, then, smartness is not immutable; maybe it depends on our efforts, as both teachers and learners.

And we know that some pretty smart people are not universally smart. The most gifted Japanese haiku poet may be unable to write an instruction manual for English-speaking purchasers of Japanese-made VCRs. And no matter how good the manual, the most brilliant American brain surgeon may never master the art of programmed recording. Law students are trained to "think like lawyers"; medical and nursing students, thank goodness, are not. Maybe smartness is not an abstract, universal entity; maybe it depends on the contexts we construct.

So the idea that smartness is partly "made" is not entirely counterintuitive; on the contrary, it actually confirms our practical experience with the concept. Still, something about the notion of a constructed intelligence seems slightly incredible: too fantastic, perhaps too optimistic. We can't quite shake our skepticism. "Okay," we might say, "you socially constructed wiseguy, answer me this: If people are really as smart as we make them, then do you mean to tell me that a person with mental retardation can be made smart enough to be, say, a nuclear physicist?"

Well, here's one honest answer: probably not. I don't know what it takes to be a nuclear physicist; I don't know whether it takes the kind of aptitudes that are measured by IQ tests. But if it does, then the person with mental retardation—who, by definition, did badly on an IQ test—has farther to go to be a nuclear physicist than the person who is not mentally retarded. She may, in fact, have farther to go than our patience, our resources, and our skill are capable of taking her. If that's the case, then she cannot be a nuclear physicist—or, at least, not a very good one.

But here's the key: not much of this—and maybe not any of it—is natural. We—society, culture, who- or whatever is in charge here—figure pretty heavily in the determination whether a person with mental retardation, or anyone else for that matter, can be a nuclear physicist. Consider:

Being a nuclear physicist is not a natural state: it's a job that we made, requiring attributes that we define.

Competence in that job is not a naturally defined condition: there are questions of degree and subjective judgments that inhere in the determination whether someone is a "qualified" nuclear physicist (or a lawyer, or a judge, or a vice president of a company, or a vice president of the United States).

Training for that competence is not a natural process: our cultural talents and commitments determine who we will train, and how well.

Even the mental retardation that necessitates special training is not a natural condition: we make "mental retardation"—as we make the intelligence of all people—in the complex interactions between the individual and the society in which she lives, interactions that shape her opportunities, the perceptions of her, and even, we now know, the very physiology of her brain, all in a relentless gestalt of intellectual advantage, or disadvantage.

So maybe she can't be a nuclear physicist. We just need to acknowledge, even in this most extreme of examples, that it's at least partly our doing, that with some will or ingenuity, an intervention here, a cultural change there, things might, just might, turn out differently. And as the scenario gets more commonplace—as either the job or her measured intelligence grow closer to the norm—the gaps between what might be and what could be and ultimately what *should* be grow more narrow, and it becomes increasingly likely that if anything stands in the way of our mentally retarded subject—our neighbor, our friend, our sister—it's something that we put there, and something that we can remove.

If it all sounds too altruistic, or too utopian, then it is perhaps important to remember this: not so long ago, we were fairly certain that a woman's aptitudes did not embrace skills from the political realm. "Race" was a disqualifying characteristic throughout social and economic life, due to the perceived cognitive incapacities of some racial groups. We restricted the immigration of certain ethnic groups—most, in fact, except those from Britain and northern Europe—because of the genetic inferiority of the immigrant stock. Feebleminded people were so inferior that we institutionalized them, and sterilized them, to prevent our being swamped with incompetence. In each case, arguments against the conventional wisdom seemed too altruistic, too utopian.

It seems the conceit of each generation that it has reached the state of ultimate enlightenment: each age is a progressive one, each society the most perfectly egalitarian. I know a husband and wife who had a baby boy; the state took their baby away before they could even leave the hospital. They had done nothing wrong except not be smart enough: they both were mentally retarded. A generation or so ago, they would have been simply sterilized; in their day—in our day—they lost their newborn baby to the state. It's an odd kind of progress.

But they got their baby back; they became a family after all. They will need help to succeed; their boy will need help. It is hard to know what will happen to him, hard to know how smart he will be. Maybe, in the next generation, sterilization will be back in vogue. Or maybe his daughter will be a nuclear physicist.

There's one last thing that I think we need to acknowledge, and it's maybe the most important of all. Even if somebody can't be a good nuclear physicist, and even if it is somehow due entirely to her own "natural" limitations, it absolutely does not mean that she is not smart. Here, I think, is the greatest danger in the concept, the most insidious aspect of "smartness" and "intelligence" and "IQ" and "mental retardation." From one perceived inability we induce a general inferiority: someone who doesn't do well on standardized tests becomes "dumb" or even "mentally retarded," and that means that not only will they not become very good nuclear physicists, they also won't become very good citizens, or parents, or people. Being not smart at that one thing means that they are just plain not smart—at anything. And that means that they deserve—in terms of cultural success—nothing.

But it means nothing of the sort, or rather, it *should* mean nothing of the sort. Because there are many kinds of smartness, and people can be smart in many different ways, and the fact that they are not smart—or are not made smart—in one way does not mean that they cannot be smart in many other ways. Really bad nuclear physicists can be really good nurses; really bad nurses can be really good lawyers; really bad lawyers can be really good auto mechanics; really bad auto mechanics can be really good teachers; and any of them—but not necessarily all of them—can be really good mothers and fathers.

Here too we have made the decisions: to ignore the different kinds of smartness; to collapse it all into one general, abstract concept; and to order all the differences, as matters of degree, as more smart or less, as superior and inferior. Here too, in this final crucial way, we make some people smarter than others, by rewarding the smartness of some people and ignoring the smartness of others. We make some people smart, in short, just by choosing to call them that.

So some people are smarter than others. It would be wrong not to admit it. But wrong too not to admit that in most cases, and in most respects, we made them that way.

The remainder of this book examines in detail the mythology of smartness: as it was initially conceived by the founders of 1787 and the reconstructors of 1868; as it persists today in American science and politics; and as it has been maintained by American law. In the process, it confronts one of the most vicious myths of smartness: the myth of "races" of people that are, by nature, intellectually superior and inferior. That myth, it evolves, is an old myth, but not an ancient one; an outmoded myth, but a durable one. And it has been made durable by American law.

This book also examines a competing vision—one also promised by the founders, adopted by the reconstructors, confirmed by science, and realized, in fleeting moments, in American politics and American law. It is a vision of a nature that blesses all people—and all groups of people—and of a community in which equality is not merely a legal concept but a lived condition. It is a vision of a truly smart culture, one in which "smart" means all of us.

2

The First Object of Government
Creation Myths

It is the central contradiction of American life: the absurd divorce between egalitarian ideals and the reality of relentless inequality. It has been with us from the outset, and revolution, civil war, and two national efforts at reconstruction have succeeded more in re-stating the contradiction than in resolving it. We began by declaring all men equal, and a century later guaranteed all persons the equal protection of the law, and after yet another century ensured the civil rights of all Americans—and still our social, economic, and political life is dominated by inequity. There are no castes in America, and yet—maddeningly, undeniably—there are.

The rationalizations have been with us from the outset as well. All men were equal, but, by nature, that principle did not extend to women, or men without property, or American Indians, or, of course, slaves. All persons were guaranteed equality under law but, in the nature of things, that pledge did not eradicate distinctions rooted in biology, and could not redress inequalities that were social, as opposed to legal. Civil rights are guaranteed all Americans, but, naturally, that secures only an equal opportunity to succeed, and cannot ensure equal outcomes. We are, formally, all equal, but we are, really, not equal at all: platitudes aside, there is no denying the natural order.

We do not deny it; on the contrary, we have made it the law. At the founding, Rousseau's communitarian vision yielded to an individualism that exalted, above all, the right to amass very unequal shares of property; protecting the "unequal faculties of acquiring property" became "the first object of government." Over two hundred years later, it still is. Economic liberty leads inexorably to social inequality, and that is natural, that is just. The laws of nature have thus become our rules of law: both represent the same order.

27

Some are, by nature, smarter; they should get, it is only natural, more. These are the myths of our creation, the essence of the smart culture.

Prologue

As a kid, I spent most of my summers living with my grandparents, which is even less of a big deal than it sounds, seeing as how my grandparents lived just across the highway. On the other hand, just across the highway sometimes seemed like another world: the houses there had yards on all four sides—"detached" is what we call them now; as kids, we just called them "huge"—and the backyards were big enough for any game any kid could ever want to play. I had a whole different bunch of friends over at my grandparents', and we played a whole different bunch of games. For a kid, I guess, it really was a different world.

I loved staying with my grandparents. It was a little bit because of the yard and the games but it was mostly because of them. My grandfather was a truck tire salesman and he made his living on the road, and he was great at it and he loved it, until somebody in some regional office somewhere decided that truck tires could not be sold efficiently by traveling salesmen, and they were not confused by the fact that my grandfather was already doing precisely what could not be done. So they moved my grandfather inside a store, and he became an automobile tire salesman, and he was great at this too, but he loved it a lot less. My grandfather was also a repairman—of all things mechanical and of many things familial—and he was like a father to me, and he was, I guess, one of my first real teachers. He taught me how to throw and hit a baseball, and later how to fix a car, and in between he tried to teach me how to ride a bicycle, but at this he failed, as he could not overcome my bike's supernatural attraction to large inanimate objects like parked cars and brick walls and even, with an odds-defying accuracy, the goalposts on a football field. He also taught me my first complete sentence—"Pop-pop can fix any damned thing"—as well as my first lesson in manners, a lesson I proudly displayed to my mother on a city bus one Saturday morning, after a well-dressed man stumbled up the steps and fell to the floor: "Fall down," I shouted helpfully, to my mom and all concerned riders, "and bust the ass!" For this, I had to wash my mouth out with soap, and my grandfather had to wash our new used car.

My grandmother was my teacher too, and in a sense had to do double duty, as she had to help me unlearn a great many of my grandfather's lessons. My grandmother was an executive secretary, and she could type and take shorthand and take minutes and balance books and edit correspondence and I hardly know what else, except that it seems to me a safe guess that she was as much responsible for her company's success as was the company president she worked for, even if he got paid fifteen or twenty times as much. And if my grandfather could fix anything that was broke, my grandmother could heal anything that was hurt: there is no word big enough to describe the love she had for her grandchildren, and none good enough to describe the comfort we felt in her arms. She taught me a lot of things—little things like not to say "ain't" (I still don't), and big things like taking care of the people who need you (I try), but above all, she taught me what it's like to feel safe, and that's just about the best feeling in the world.

I seemed to know all the people in my grandparents' neighborhood, and they all seemed to know me. The Burkhardts lived on one side, and they were sometimes my baby-sitters when my grandparents were at work, and their house always smelled wonderfully like tomato sauce, which was, my grandfather explained, because Mrs. Burkhardt was an Italian. The Sanderses lived on the other side, and they also were sometimes my baby-sitters, and Mrs. Sanders always wore white clothes, and that was because, as my grandmother explained, Mrs. Sanders was a nurse. This simple order could have become mighty complicated on the day that Mrs. Sanders made spaghetti for dinner, but it was soon overwhelmed by a more fundamental truth. Mrs. Sanders, according to my grandmother, worked at St. Francis Hospital because she was a Catholic, and it turned out that Mrs. Burkhardt was also a Catholic, and Tommy Sidowski, who was a kid about my age who lived behind my grandparents, and whom I knew pretty well, and who was, according to my grandfather, a "Polack"—well, he was a Catholic too. Suddenly, the bewildering fragments of identity had yielded their common denominator, and that is why, at the age of six, I became a Catholic, a development that, unfortunately, went completely over the heads of my grandparents, who could not understand why I kept saying that I was a Catholic when, they insisted, I was hardly even a Methodist. My grandparents and I eventually reached an understanding on the matter, and it was agreed that I could become a Catholic later on if I still wanted to, and that arrangement was basically satisfactory to me, though it did not keep me from dipping into the ashtray for the next few Ash Wednesdays. My grandparents even let me be Italian—though only partly, and on my mother's side, whatever that meant—but on my subsequent desire to become a Polack they remained uncompromising. Which was fine, because Tommy Sidowski wasn't even my best friend.

The Sanderses had two boys, Huey and Michael, and Huey was just a year younger than me, and it was Huey who would become my best friend in the world. We started playing together in my grandparents' backyard when I was barely five, and for as long as I can remember, we were playing baseball and baseball-related games. Most of these games we made up, partly because, with just the two of us, it would have been difficult to field two standard teams, but also because it was our unspoken desire that in the games we played, neither one of us should really win or lose. We played some games that we copied from other kids—Wall-Ball was not one of our originals—but also some games that we made up from scratch over the years, games like Up Against the Wall, Off the Roof, Perfect Game, Double Play, and Rundown.

For each of our games we made up rules. The object of Up Against The Wall was for the fielder—we always imagined we were some Phillie outfielder, usually either Johnny Callison or Tony Gonzalez—to make a great leaping catch by hurling his body against the brick wall of my grandparents' house; the "batter" would accommodate by throwing the ball just over the fielder's head. We had a scoring system for the catches: one point for a catch, two points if you juggled the ball and caught it, three points if you caught it above an imaginary line on the wall, and four points if you caught the ball and hit the wall with sufficient force or friction to draw blood. We scored each catch, but did not keep a running tally; the game ended when we had drawn too much blood, or when we broke one of my grandparents' windows.

Off the Roof was our variation on Wall-Ball. The "batter" threw the ball onto my grandparents' roof, and the fielder tried to catch it when it rolled off. This was tougher than it sounds, thanks to my grandparents' rain gutter, which, we discovered one day, caused the ball to hop at impossible heights and angles. You got a hit if the fielder missed the ball, were "out" if the fielder caught it, and lost your turn at bat if you threw the ball over the roof. We scored it like a regular game, but never completed an official one, each effort being called sometime in the middle innings, when my grandfather got tired of getting the ball out of the gutter.

Perfect Game was an effort by a pitcher—usually Huey, as either Jim Bunning or Chris Short—to throw one, that is, to record twenty-seven straight outs. The catcher called the pitches as well as the balls and strikes—and, for that matter, also the play-by-play—which meant that every game ended with the nearly intolerable suspense of a full count on the twenty-seventh batter. Almost every effort was successful, thanks mostly to the propensity of the imaginary batters to chase and foul-off even the wildest pitches. The only exceptions occurred when the pitcher would refuse the benevolent products of the catcher's imagination; the pitcher would then show remarkable fortitude in overcoming the adversity of one walk or sometimes even two.

Double Play was really not much more than our practice of that baseball play. Whichever one of us was the first baseman would throw a groundball to the other fielder, who could be either a shortstop or a second baseman, depending on his identity on that particular day: when Huey was Bobby Wine he played shortstop, when he was Tony Taylor he played second base, I was always Cookie Rojas, who could play any position. The middle infielder, whoever he was, would tag second base, and relay the ball to the first baseman, who would decide, based on a very complex mathematical calculation involving various laws of physics and also little kid's moods, whether the throw was in time to complete the double play. The middle infielder did not always agree with the call, and that prompted occasional rhubarbs, as the infielder went nose to nose with the first base umpire, who, of course, used to be the first baseman, but who had now assumed a distinctly antagonistic persona. Things would get particularly heated—and complicated—when the first baseman would rematerialize and join the fray, and sometimes the combined force of their arguments would persuade the umpire to change his mind. This rarely happened, however, and the rhubarbs were mostly just an excuse to practice cussing. Double Play usually went the full nine innings, the exceptions occurring only when games were suspended on account of the adults overhearing the rhubarbs.

All but one of our games were designed to be played by just two people; the exception was Rundown. Rundown required two fielders and a baserunner: the fielders, stationed at first and second bases, threw the ball back and forth, and the baserunner would at some point attempt to leave first base and get to second or, once caught in a rundown, at least make it safely back to first. There were no points and no scoring; the runner either made it safely or not.

Huey and I could be the fielders in Rundown, but we needed a baserunner, and neither my grandparents nor Huey's mom were generally up to the task. Fortunately, however, Huey's folks had planned ahead, and they provided Huey with a kid brother named Michael, and while Michael was generally no more useful than any other kid brother or sister—his primary function seemed to revolve around whining, which was either the cause or effect of our general indifference to his existence—still Michael made a perfectly adequate, and eventually an absolutely perfect, steady runner in our game.

What was so perfect about Michael was that he was always "out": in all the games of Rundown we played, he never once stole second, nor even made it safely back to first. This required, admittedly, some ingenuity on our part: he seemed, sometimes, like he was going to be safe, as when one of us made a wild throw, and he seemed, on other occasions, like he might actually *be* safe, as when he appeared to be standing on second base before the ball's arrival, but invariably fortune intervened, and Mike would accidentally trip in the base path over our outstretched arms, or overrun the base, propelled by some mysterious natural force that looked strangely like Huey or me. When these physical phenomena were not denying Michael his due, fate nonetheless conspired against him; either Huey or I had invariably called "time-out" (whether or not Michael actually heard us), and "time-out" meant, by rule of course, that the game had to start over. It is a wonder, given his steady misfortune, that Michael continued to play with us, but he did, and he always seemed to have fun.

For Huey and me there was something a bit too crude and obvious about our schemes against Michael, and I suspect we would have soured on them over time. But it never became an issue, thanks to Richie Ashburn, who was a radio announcer for the Phillies, and who explained, as Huey and I listened intently to what was probably another Phillies loss, that some hapless Phillie player had been tagged out at first even though he had apparently singled because, after crossing the bag, he had turned the wrong way. Huey and I looked at each other the instant we heard the call, and we smiled.

A little knowledge can be dangerous, and the knowledge we gained that day was certainly hazardous to Michael's hopes for Rundown success. We had Michael caught in a rundown early in our next game, when Huey's throw bounced off my glove and rolled to my grandparents' fence. I retrieved the ball and threw it to Huey, but Michael had arrived at second base well ahead of the throw. Mike stood on the base and waited. He must have been surprised that Huey did not try to drag him off, and then downright stunned that I did not start yelling, "time out." And as the seconds passed, his bewilderment must have yielded to a sense of triumph, as he stood there on second base, and turned to revel in his victory over his former oppressors. And all of that must have merely compounded his sense of frustration, when Huey slapped him in the chest with his glove, and said, matter-of-factly, "You're out; you turned the wrong way."

Mike, relentlessly gullible, buried his head in his hands. "Good try, Mike," we said, probably less to console him than to maintain his interest in the game. But it was hardly necessary: we could not have deterred Mike if we had tried. With grim determination, Mike dug in for another try.

But, of course, there was no hope. All day long, try as he might, he simply could not avoid turning the wrong way. To his left, to his right, clockwise, or counterclockwise, every way was the wrong way. First base or second base, off the base or on it, he was "out." And what stands out most about that day is how Huey and I ended up laughing about it, soon hysterically, and then so hard that we could barely sputter out what had become Mike's motto. Eventually we didn't even need to say it, we just started laughing and walking toward Mike with the ball, except for the times that we were laughing too hard to walk, and had to crawl. And Mike was laughing so hard that he ended up on the ground with us, and I thought that it was just because Huey and I were laughing so hard, but now I realize that he always knew exactly what we were up to, and that the joke all along wasn't really on him, or even on Huey and me: it was really *our* joke—it belonged to all three of us.

For a brief while, Huey and I tried our rules outside my grandparents' backyard. We played baseball one day with a bunch of other kids, and Huey was playing first base and I was at second, and a kid on the opposing team got a hit, and I, with uncharacteristic bravado, yelled that the kid turned the wrong way. Huey marched up to the kid and tagged him and said, "you're out," and eventually all the kids on our team caught on, and they started yelling, "that's right," and "he's out," and "he turned the wrong way." And the kid complained a little, but it hardly mattered: he was out—he had turned the wrong way.

We kept this up for about a week. Once a game, no matter which way some kid would turn, Huey or I would yell that the kid turned the wrong way, and Huey would tag the kid out. The kid would look puzzled, and somebody on our team would say something about how you have to know the rules, and the kid's teammates would shrug like "hey, what can we do," and sometimes they'd even get mad at the kid for not knowing which way to turn. Then one day I yelled that a kid had turned the wrong way, and Huey went up to tag him, and the kid yelled back, "I only took one step, you idiot!" He was very sure of himself, and he was also very big, and Huey and I both knew, without needing to consult on the matter, that the kid was safe, and that we had a new rule. We decided instead to drop the old one: "you turned the wrong way" was fun with Michael, but it was just a hassle outside my grandparents' backyard.

When I was eleven my mom remarried and we moved away, and I pretty much lost touch with Huey and Mike and the whole gang of kids in my grandparents' neighborhood. I didn't get to spend summers with my grandparents anymore, and Huey made other friends, and I really got to see him only at Christmas. For a few years I still got him Christmas presents, like some baseball cards or comic books, but then he seemed too old for those, and I didn't know what to get him, and then I didn't go see him at all.

It was 1976, and I was a sophomore in college in North Carolina, when my grandparents called me with the news about Huey. He had become the first kid in his family to go to college, and he was nearing the end of his freshman year at the University of Delaware. He was on his way to Florida for his spring break, and he and his friend stopped for gas in North Carolina. They filled the tank and looked for somebody to give their money to, but as the witnesses later explained, there appeared to be no one there. So Huey and his friend got tired of looking and waiting, and they got back in their car, and drove away. At that moment the gas station owner showed up, and he had a rifle, and he shot my friend Huey in the head. Huey died. He was eighteen years old.

The gas station owner was at first not charged, but the attorney general of Delaware intervened, and the man eventually pled guilty to manslaughter and served a year or so in prison, and was reportedly much aggrieved even at that. He was, after all, merely defending what was rightfully his.

Huey and I had played a lot of games when we were kids, and we made up a lot of rules. Some of them were good, and some of them were bad, and, looking back, some of them could have been both, depending on how you used them. But there is in my mind nothing doubtful or contingent or equivocal about this: it's a bad rule—a terrible, vicious, hateful rule—that says it's basically okay to shoot a kid who doesn't pay for a tank of gas. And I cannot help thinking when I remember Huey that somebody, somehow, has us playing a really stupid game, and that somewhere along the line, we—all of us—turned the wrong way.

I didn't go to Huey's funeral, but my grandparents did, and they said it was a pretty rough thing, especially for Huey's mom. But probably nobody took it harder than Michael. Mike was always kind of shy, but after Huey's death, he seemed to close off completely from the rest of the world. It wasn't until his mom died, some twenty years later, that Mike really went outside again. He was thirty-four when he got a job and learned how to drive. It was my grandfather who taught him.

The Original Construction

The United States celebrated the bicentennial of its Constitution in 1987, but the celebrations were momentarily interrupted by a dissenting opinion. It was Supreme Court Justice Thurgood Marshall who sounded a more critical note: the Constitution—as originally constructed in 1787—was not, he said, necessarily worth celebrating. Justice Marshall objected to the "complacent belief" that the founding fathers presented us with a finished product two centuries ago, a completed text with a meaning permanently fixed. For Marshall, the Constitution was and remained a living document; it had to be, because the initial effort was so fundamentally flawed:

> Nor do I find the wisdom, foresight, and sense of justice exhibited by the framers particularly profound. To the contrary, the government they devised was defective from the start, requiring several amendments, a civil war, and momentous social transformation to attain the system of constitutional governments, and its respect for the individual freedoms and human rights, that we hold as fundamental today.

What Marshall saw in the Constitution of 1787 was principally contradiction: a text that purports to represent the voice of "We the people," that asserts at the outset a dedication to justice and to liberty, and that is designed to be the governing charter of a nation premised on the self-evident truths of human equality and inalienable rights, in fact excluded from its protections all but a privileged few, and acquiesced in the complete subordination—through chattel slavery—of a substantial part of its citizenry. As Marshall explained, "Moral principles against slavery, for those who had them, were compromised, with no explanation of the conflicting principles for which the American Revolutionary War had ostensibly been fought."[1]

Marshall's statements evoked the predictable howls of protest: his comments were unpatriotic, unseemly, and ill-tempered. But what Marshall's critics did not say, and what they could not say, was that he was wrong.

The Constitution was written by some very smart people; on this score, Marshall and his critics would agree. But Marshall was revealing an additional, less comfortable truth: that the Constitution was written *for* "smart" people—it protected, above all, the interests of a natural elite. Rights in property were ascendant; individual interest the priority; liberty the governing principle. It was inevitable in such a scheme that the "diversity in the faculties of men" would lead to social and economic inequality, and there was no communitarian ethic, no egalitarian commitment to mitigate the trend. Quite the contrary: the "first object" of the new government was the preservation of the natural order. The rules it established were those dictated by nature, and they were—naturally—the rules of a rigged game: for those born to lose, it would be very difficult to win.

The Spirit of the Nation

The framers of the Constitution of 1787 had choices to make, some theoretical, some practical. Not infrequently, they chose the less egalitarian path, even when that path entangled them in contradiction, They spoke of themselves as "we the people," but they embraced an ethos of liberal individualism that was explicitly at odds with communitarian norms. Those communities, principally in the agrarian South, that continued to champion republican virtues, did so without abandoning their commitment to the traditional hierarchies of social and political life. Lost between these competing ethos—the liberal individualism of northern Federalists on the one hand, the conservative communitarianism of southern Republicans on the other—was any sense of the egalitarian commitments of a Rousseau; indeed, there is no record that the great French philosopher was even mentioned at the 1787 convention. As a result, the founding fathers all could agree with Jefferson's ringing declaration that "all men are created equal" precisely because they shared common ground in *rejecting* that notion, except at an impossible level of political abstraction.

The framers spoke in universal terms about "liberty," "justice," and "equality," but these principles seemed merely instrumental to rights in property, rights that were of real importance only to a privileged few. Thus, partly echoing Locke, they construed "liberty" to mean, above all, the natural right to own private property, to maintain, through the protection of the state, the fruits of one's labor. "Justice" in turn became the protection of property from the democratic impulses of the laboring masses; "equality" then became the equal right to own property, and enjoy the attendant public benefits of propertied status.

And on this score, the framers were more or less explicit about what they were doing. According to Madison's notes on the Philadelphia convention, Charles Pinckney of South Carolina was moved to remark on the singular equality of the American people:

> Among them there are fewer distinctions of fortune & less of rank, than among inhabitants of any other nation. Every freeman has a right to the same protection & security; and a very moderate share of property entitles them to all the honors and privileges the public can bestow: hence arises a greater equality, than is to be found among the people of

any other country, and an equality which is more likely to continue
. . . because in a new country . . . where industry must be rewarded
with competency, there will be few poor, and few dependent.

Madison concurred, but felt compelled to point out that "equality," as
Pinckney would have it, did not include an identity of material
interests. As Shay's Rebellion had made clear, already there were
"different interests"—between creditors and debtors, farmers and
manufacturers, and "particularly the distinction of rich & poor"—and
these would likely intensify over time:

> An increase of population will of necessity increase the proportion of
> those who will labour under all the hardships of life, & secretly sigh for
> a more equal distribution of its blessings. These may in time outnum-
> ber those who are placed above the feelings of indigence. According to
> the equal laws of suffrage, the power will slide into the hands of the
> former. No agrarian attempts have yet been made in this Country, but
> symptoms, of a leveling spirit, as we have understood, have sufficiently
> appeared in a certain quarter to give notice of the future danger.

Hamilton agreed with Madison: "It was certainly true: that nothing
like an equality of property existed: that an inequality would exist as
long as liberty existed, and that it would unavoidably result from that
very liberty itself. This inequality of property constituted the great &
fundamental distinction in Society."[2]

Rousseau had recognized this phenomenon: "It is precisely because
the force of things always tends to destroy equality," he had written,
"that the force of legislation must tend to maintain it." But, writing
in *The Federalist Papers*, Madison made clear, that if Rousseau's
observation was correct, his prescription was wrong: the duty of
government was to preserve inequality.

> The diversity in the faculties of men, from which the rights of property
> originate, is not less an insuperable obstacle to a uniformity of interests.
> The protection of these faculties is the first object of government.
> From the protection of different and unequal faculties of acquiring
> property, the possession of different degrees and kinds of property
> immediately results; and from the influence of these on the sentiments
> and views of the respective proprietors, ensues a division of the society
> into different interests and parties.

"The latent causes of faction," Madison concluded, "are thus sown in the nature of man." Hamilton agreed; inequality was natural, inevitable, and an altogether proper foundation for government:

> All communities divide themselves into the few and the many. The first are the rich and well **born**, the other the mass of the people. The voice of the people has been said to be the voice of God; and however generally this maxim has been quoted and believed, it is not true in fact. The people are turbulent and changing; they seldom judge or determine right. Give therefore to the first class a distinct permanent share in the government. . . . Nothing but a permanent body can check the imprudence of democracy.

The notion was perhaps most fully developed in John Adams's *Discourses on Davila*. There, Adams posited the existence of a "natural aristocracy": "every society," he wrote, "naturally produces an order of men, which it is impossible to confine to an equality of rights." The rhetoric was too strong for some of his countrymen, but the central premise was widely shared: there is a social order, and it is altogether natural.

Perhaps no word dominated the rhetoric of the convention like this one: everything—rights, laws, orders, the government itself—all had to be "natural." Montesquieu—part naturalist, part empiricist—had suggested that the natural law of each nation would vary with its natural conditions: the proper government was the one that consisted with the "spirit of the nation." No authority was cited at the convention more than Montesquieu, and no idea seemed to capture the framers' imagination like this one. The new government had to suit the country's nature: it had to accommodate, not shape, the natural order of things.[3]

America's natural order in turn seemed to depend on three interrelated phenomena. There was, first, human nature. There was near unanimous agreement with Madison's sentiment that self-interest was "sown in the nature of man"; rejected was the Republican vision of an enlightened citizenry, trained in civic virtue, finding its fullest political expression in the idea of the public good. "It is the nature of man," proclaimed James Wilson during the ratification debates, "to pursue his own interest, in preference to the public good." Noah Webster, writing as "A Citizen of America," insisted that "[t]he first and almost only principle that governs men, is *interest*" (emphasis in original). There was no altruism in this conception of humanity; "men are," as Hamilton summarized it, "ambitious, vindictive, and rapacious."

There was, second, natural inequality. The more egalitarian-minded Republicans, following Rousseau, had posited a community of genuine equals: they advocated what for the next two centuries would be cryptically and often pejoratively described as "social equality." But for most of the framers, such a state was inconceivable. Some men, they reasoned, would naturally achieve greater success than others, if they were simply left to pursue their interests; it was the inevitable result of the "diversity in the faculties of men." Thus arose the distinctions between classes—between rich and poor, between creditors and debtors—distinctions that are, as Madison explained in a 1787 letter to Jefferson, "various and unavoidable," due to the "unequal faculties of acquiring" property. These are, Madison explained, "natural distinctions," unlike the "artificial distinctions" created by politics and religion. It was not a great leap to Adams's natural aristocracy, even if, for political reasons, few Federalists—and still fewer Republicans—were openly willing to make it.

There were, finally, natural rights. The notion is generally attributed to Locke, but the American conception is probably somewhat original: Locke's *Treatises on Government* likely relied too heavily on biblical authority for the deists who founded the new nation, and there is no real evidence that the more significant exposition of rights in the *Second Treatise* was even read by the framers. What the Americans fashioned was a conception of natural rights that lacked Locke's rigorous conceptual framework, and perhaps also his conditions. For Locke, the social compact limited the exercise of rights, and even "inalienable rights" of "life" and "property" required the protection of positive law. For the framers, natural rights referred more loosely to freedoms which the government was bound to respect: rights to life, liberty, and property. These were more likely to be genuinely inalienable—they could not be ceded to the state—and genuinely natural—they preceded the state, and gave rise to, but did not depend upon, its positive laws.[4]

The distinction may be more than semantic: it may explain the framers' otherwise remarkable capacity for inequality. The American conception of natural rights clearly underlies Madison's "first object of government"; the social compact cannot embrace limitations on the pursuits of men because liberty is, a priori, essential to political life. Distinctions of property, then, are rooted in an inviolable liberty: inequality becomes a political mandate. This is not Rousseau, of course, and it is not even Locke. It explains, perhaps, why "equality" almost never appears as a first order principle: it is only a condition, as in, for example, John Dickinson's devotion to "equal liberty" or "equal freedom." When the framers do advocate "equality"—as when Noah Webster argues for an "equality of property"—it is almost always "liberty" that is on their minds: Webster's argument is, above all, for the free alienability of property rights, for the accumulation of property not through divine rights of inheritance, but through merit.[5]

America's natural order may not have been rooted in Locke or Rousseau, but it was clearly a product of its times. The modernist shift from the supernatural to the natural simply found full expression in the new nation. The process was manifest in a host of material ways—in the gradual transition, for example, from religious to property qualifications for suffrage—but its most significant impact was on political theory: it was not God, but nature, that defined and limited the realm of the politically possible. All men may have been created equal, and may have been endowed by their creator with inalienable rights, but they did not all evolve in equal ways, and the terms of their rights varied with the nature of things. Thus, in America, did the creator yield to creation.

"Justice," "liberty," and "equality" all assumed meanings constrained by nature; all were shaped by the "spirit" of the American nation. An undeniable part of that spirit was its natural order: generations of Americans would state both an empirical and a political truth when they claimed that theirs was a "white man's government." It was only natural, then, that justice, liberty, and equality should be reduced to fluctuating combinations of obfuscation, oxymoron, and empty formalism; they could then accommodate the harshest forms of economic, social, and political oppression. They could even accommodate slavery.

The Central Paradox

Slavery was not originally a distinct problem, in part because it did not begin as a distinctive condition. The line between servant and slave was hazy in the early colonies; in fact, the defining features of slavery would be contested clear through Reconstruction. In addition, many of the legal disabilities imposed on colonial bondsmen in their various forms—on slaves and servants of African, European, or Native American descent—were suffered by many "free" peoples: Native Americans, propertyless men regardless of their origins, and women. For early colonial thinkers, then, the problem of slavery was really a problem of degree.

But by the time of the Constitutional Convention, slavery was sufficiently distinct in form and fact to pose a peculiar challenge to the new nation's political principles. The gradual separation of slave from servant happened principally as a matter of historical accident, and so too did the gradual correlation of color and condition. But, accident or not, these happened all the same, and by 1787 there was no longer mistaking slavery with any other form of servitude. To be sure, oppression, subordination, and exclusion persisted to varying degrees for many groups. But if these hardships constituted a continuum for eighteenth-century Americans, chattel slavery marked its logical extreme. For the slave, as for no other group, the disabilities were both complete and perpetual: the slave had, by nature, no cognizable rights, and was, also by nature, in every sense the inferior of the citizen. Slavery had become the dichotomous referent for American liberty and equality; thus most historians agree with Edmund Morgan's appraisal that the concurrent rise of liberty and equality, on the one hand, and the institution of African slavery, on the other, would become "the central paradox of American history."[6]

But as Morgan and others have noted, the paradox is not mere coincidence: liberty and equality, as America's founders came to conceive them, were in fact deeply dependent on slavery. Consider:

Slavery provided a frame of reference for the American conception of liberty and an omnipresent reminder of the horrors of lost freedom. The rhetoric of the American Revolution never really did match the reality: the revolt itself had not been a popular one (at most a third of Americans had sought independence, and most of those for economic reasons) and, with perhaps one significant exception, independence had generally failed to produce social change. But the promise of its principles—of liberty and equality—offered a unifying theme for a new people, and slavery offered the rhetorical counterpoint. At the convention, then, Luther Martin could protest the proposed congressional electoral schemes by insisting that the smaller states would be "enslaved," while in a radically different context, Benjamin Franklin could caution against the perpetual "servitude" of legislators. It was a pattern that would persist for generations: each compromise of freedom was liable to be condemned as slavery. Interestingly, no class was more ready to level the charge than the slaveholders: they were ever vigilant against "enslavement" by the Federalists, abolitionists, or the North. Perhaps, as Morgan suggests, "Virginians may have had a special appreciation of the freedom dear to republicans, because they saw every day what life without it could be like." In a certain sense, their commitment to liberty and freedom was there at the beginning, even if it once served different goals: the first Virginia colony—at Roanoake—was founded to liberate African and Indian slaves from the Spanish.[7]

Slavery became the litmus test of American liberty, which embraced, above all other rights, the right to own property, including slaves. The almost incomprehensible notion of "human property" filled the law of slavery with contradictions: the ascendant liberal conception of property held that it must be freely alienable, and it abhorred perpetuities, but the law of human property fully consigned labor—it was freely alienable only for those who sold themselves into bondage—and maintained those laborers in perpetual bondage. The contradictions, of course, were a matter of perspective: for the slaveholder, the law was merely vindicating the rights in this species of property, on terms roughly commensurate with others. Thus Locke, who denounced hereditary slavery, was cited to support the natural rights of slaveholders; and Montesquieu's condemnation of slavery as "absolute power" was used to define the slaveholder's rights. Ultimately, respect for these peculiar property rights became the test of liberty, as well as the precondition to union. Speaking at the Philadelphia convention, Pierce Butler of South Carolina insisted that "[t]he security the South^n States want is that their negroes may not be taken from them, which some gentlemen within or without doors, have a very good mind to do." And, according to Madison's notes on the convention, General Charles Cotesworth Pinckney "reminded the Convention that if the Committee should fail to insert some security to the Southern States agst an emancipation of slaves, and taxes on exports, he sh^d be bound by duty to his State to vote agst their Report." Pinckney, of course, did not have to make good on his threat.[8]

Slavery made possible the universal grant of liberty to freemen by removing from the body politic those groups—labor and the poor—that otherwise posed the chief threat to the political order. Federalists and Republicans shared a fear of the mob: the "faction" that most worried both groups was the democratic majority. But they fashioned quite different solutions. For the Federalists, the passions of the democratic masses needed to be filtered through a more-or-less representative elite—more representative for Madison even before his republican conversion, less representative for the likes of Adams and Hamilton. For the Republicans, the problem had been solved by slavery. The mostly white freedmen in the colonial South always seemed to be on the brink of rebellion: they were largely disempowered because they owned no property, and they were largely without property because of a very artificial land scarcity. Slavery eased the threat posed by the freedmen: with slavery, the number of indentured servants decreased and so too, then, the number of men turning free. Those who were free simply needed to be persuaded that they shared the interests of the master class, a cause advanced principally by the drawing of the color line. Of course, slaves posed their own threat of rebellion, but the conditions of bondage and the harshness of the reprisal (slaves who participated in insurrections faced grisly "exemplary deaths" by slow burning, dismemberment, or by being hanged in chains) tended to mitigate the threat. As a result, slaves proved less dangerous to the privileged class than did free or semifree labor, and the latter groups reaped some of the benefit. As Morgan concludes, "Aristocrats could more safely ensure personal equality in a slave society than in a free one. Slaves did not become leveling mobs."[9]

Slavery provided the economic security needed to permit liberty. It is easier to afford liberty in times of social peace and economic stability, and slavery helped ensure both conditions. In fact, slavery helped ensure American independence: the Revolution itself would not have been possible without the funding secured by tobacco exports, and production of that crop, of course, was in turn made possible by slavery. Fitting, then, that the Virginia Assembly voted in 1780 to reward Revolutionary soldiers with three hundred acres and a slave.[10]

Slavery provided the measure of relative liberty and equality among the white population. By the mid-eighteenth century, the plantation owner, the yeoman farmer, and even the white indentured servant had this in common: they were not slaves. They were, relatively, equal, and they were, as opposed to black Americans, all free; it was true in fact and theory. By the nineteenth century, John Calhoun could brag of slavery that it "was the best guarantee to equality among the whites," and he was probably right. Congressman Henry Wise could insist, without any sense of irony, that "[t]he principle of slavery is a leveling principle; it is friendly to equality. Break down slavery and you would with the same blow break down the great democratic principle of equality among men." As late as 1864, Congressman Aaron Harding would complain that radical Republicans "are making some progress in giving nominal freedom to the slaves, but equally as much in destroying the liberty of the white race."

These various ironies did not go unnoticed. "It always seemed a most iniquitous scheme to me," Abigail Adams wrote to her husband John, during the war for independence, "to fight ourselves for what we are daily robbing and plundering from those who have as good a right to freedom as we have." And Lieutenant Enos Reeves left a slave auction in 1782 wondering, "Is this liberty?—Is this the land of liberty I've been fighting for these six years?"

Similar sentiments were also expressed at the Philadelphia convention. The slave trade provision of the Constitution, which precluded congressional action to abolish the slave trade until 1808, drew the harshest indictments. William Patterson of New Jersey protested against the "indirect encouragem^t of the slave trade; observing that Cong^s in their act relating to the change of the 8 art: of Confed^n had been ashamed to use the term 'slaves' & had substituted a description." Luther Martin of Maryland concurred: "it was inconsistent with the principles of the revolution and dishonorable to the American character to have such a feature in the Constitution." George Mason of Virginia maintained that "Every master of slaves is born a petty tyrant. They bring the judgment of heaven on a Country." John Dickinson of Delaware "considered it as inadmissible on every principle of honor & safety that the importation of slaves should be authorised to the States by the Constitution." And Madison insisted that "Twenty years will produce all the mischief that can be apprehended from the liberty to import slaves. So long a term will be more dishonorable to the National character than to say nothing about it in the Constitution."

In the end, they followed Madison's lead, at least in form. The slave trade provision remained, and so too did the fugitive slave clause, and so too the much-debated three-fifths clause, which enabled the southern states to count each slave as three-fifths of a person for purposes of the census. But the "National character" was not dishonored by the appearance of the terms "slave" or "slavery" anywhere in the federal charter.

The framers, it appears, did indeed take care that the Constitution should not appear to sanction the idea of "property in men." There is good reason to believe that the framers anticipated that the institution was in decline, and that if the Constitution was merely silent on the matter, slavery would fade into the past. Thus, according to Madison's notes, Elbridge Gerry of Massachusetts "thought we had nothing to do with the conduct of the States as to Slaves, but ought to be careful not to give any sanction to it." Roger Sherman of Connecticut "thought it best to leave the matter as we find it. He observed that the abolition of Slavery seemed to be going on in the United States & that the good sense of the several States would probably by degrees compleat it." Sherman's Connecticut colleague, Oliver Ellsworth, offered that "slavery in time will not be a speck in our Country. Provision is already made in Connecticut for abolishing it. And the abolition has already taken place in Massachusetts." Ellsworth did, however, venture that "if it was to be considered in a moral light we ought to go farther and free those already in the Country." But such appeals were growing wearisome for John Rutledge of South Carolina: "Religion & humanity had nothing to do with this question," Rutledge insisted. "Interest alone is the governing principle with nations."[11]

Whether it was due to morality or self-interest, God or humanity, the effort to free the slaves had already begun. This, perhaps, was the one significant social change to follow the American Revolution. In 1777 Vermont declared slavery inconsistent with natural rights; within a generation, the rest of the North would follow. In 1780 abolitionists in Massachusetts failed in their efforts to ban slavery in that state's constitution, but the following year, an African slave named Quock Walker argued that any construction of that constitution that authorized slavery was contrary to the law of God. In a fashion, Chief Justice William Cushing of the Massachusetts Supreme Court agreed: the institution of slavery was inconsistent with the constitutional proclamation that "all men are born free and equal." The rest of New

England abolished slavery, and Pennsylvania, long a home to the antislavery Quakers, did as well. New York adopted a plan of gradual manumission, and in 1804 New Jersey became the last state in the North to announce the institution's demise.

There was also a change in the South. Before the Revolution, slaves were very much at the mercy of their masters: only pecuniary interest ensured their welfare. A 1723 Virginia law, for example, provided that slaves could be punished to the point of death, and any provocation would justify their killing; similarly, a North Carolina law adopted in 1774 punished the willful murder of a slave with just one year in prison. But after the Revolution, southern laws provided greater protection to slaves: by law, at least, they enjoyed the same protection from homicide as that extended to white southerners, with the exception—not insignificant—of those deaths that were incident to "moderate correction." As always, the reality did not necessarily match the ideal: "almost all homicides of slaves," Thomas Morris reports, "from the colonial period to the end of slavery, ended in acquittals, or at most in verdicts of manslaughter, which meant that there had been some legal provocation from the slave." Still, the implications were both obvious and widely accepted: slaves, like all people, had rights.[12] This, of course, only emphasized the contradictions.

The Resolution

In Europe, there was little serious intellectual defense of slavery by the last quarter of the eighteenth century. America's founding generation, meanwhile, could muster little more than ambivalence. Most of the founders professed—genuinely or not—both moral and intellectual disapproval of slavery; many claimed to feel as enslaved by the institution as those held in actual bondage. Jefferson's repugnance is well known, and so too Madison's; even when they advocated the spread of slavery, it was, they claimed, because "diffusion" of the institution would expedite its demise. Adams, meanwhile, favored abolition, and his eldest son, John Quincy, would lead the abolitionist cause in Congress. John Jay was the first president of the New York Society for Promoting the Manumission of Slaves; Hamilton was the second. Hamilton advocated abolition on utilitarian grounds; he believed slavery was unproductive. Franklin urged the same result for reasons that were both scientific—the master-slave hierarchy had no empirical basis—and moral. Washington, meanwhile, found it difficult even to acknowledge the matter. In a 1794 letter to Alexander Spotswood, Washington wrote:

> With respect to the other species of property, concerning which you ask my opinion, I shall frankly declare to you that I do not like to even think, much less talk of it. However, as you have put the question I shall, in a few words, give you *my ideas* of it. Were it not then, that I am principled agt. selling negroes, as you would do cattle in the market, I would not, in twelve months from this date, be possessed of one, as a slave. I shall be happily mistaken, if they are not found to be a very troublesome species of property 'ere many years pass over our heads; (but this by the bye).

Three years later, Washington would write from Mount Vernon that "I wish from my soul that the Legislature of this State could see the policy of a gradual Abolition of Slavery; It would prevt. much future mischief."

It now seems clear that the founding generation responded to slavery's paradox largely by postponing the day of reckoning. Most believed, with Washington, that slavery would bring only "mischief"; most hoped, as he did, that the institution would be abolished. They lacked, for the most part, the courage to realize their convictions; but they believed, probably genuinely, that it was only a matter of time. The contradictions would then be resolved by the simple passing of years; their inaction was justified, in their minds, by the obvious inevitability of slavery's demise.

But the years of the new century passed, and slavery did not die. Paradox, instead, begat paradox: new orders, and new contradictions, emerged. American women of the early nineteenth century had access to only a few low-paying jobs; if they were married, they generally could not contract, and could not control their wages. Most women were forced to labor at home, freeing their male counterparts both to pursue wage labor and to assume civic responsibilities. Thus, as Eric Foner writes, the "vaunted independence of the yeoman depended in considerable measure on the labor of women"; "free labor," he continues, "embodied a contradiction akin in some ways to slavery's . . . free labor for some rested on dependent labor for others."

...ical issue of the nineteenth century wa...
...uliar institution was not simply fading away;
...ntrary, even more firmly entrenched. The
...the invention of the cotton gin, and the develop-
...national markets for cotton all combined to make
...ot just peculiar, but vital.[13]

...grew stronger, so too did the passions aroused by it. On
...e, the abolitionist effort intensified: its supporters grew in
..., their condemnations of slavery grew harsher, and their
...ies to secure its abolition grew bolder. Rifts developed within
...ranks, at first between those who continued to advocate a gradual
...anumission and those who had grown tired of waiting and demanded
instead slavery's immediate demise. Later, the schism shifted terrain,
and it called into question—sharply and directly—the "spirit of the
nation," the character of the United States Constitution.

William Lloyd Garrison pronounced the Constitution "a covenant
with death and an agreement with hell." For him, the document was
beyond redemption; only a radical reconstitution could eliminate the
taint of slavery bequeathed by the founders. Other abolitionists were
less harsh; they thought the founders guilty only of a resolute
neutrality. Salmon Chase, later appointed chief justice of the Supreme
Court by Abraham Lincoln, wrote to Joshua Giddings that "The
Constitution must be vindicated from the reproach of sanctioning the
doctrine of property in men." Chase compiled a comprehensive
collection of the antislavery statements of the framers; "The Constitution," he concluded, "found slavery and left it a state institution." Still
others were outright hopeful. Frederick Douglass had been a dedicated
Garrisonian, but he found Garrison's views on the Constitution
increasingly self-defeating. Douglass chose—as he insisted all open-
minded people could—to see more good in the document than evil:
"interpreted as it *ought* to be interpreted," he proclaimed, "the
Constitution is a GLORIOUS LIBERTY DOCUMENT."[14]

Yet another schism lingered beneath the surface, one that in some
ways went to the very heart of the abolitionist effort. It required
clarification of the moral and political objections to slavery, and forced
a choice among conceptual priorities, between, in simplest terms,
liberty and equality.

The early crusade against slavery was substantially rooted in
religious evangelicalism, and it was a remarkably egalitarian one. The

evangelical message was derived from the Puritan and A
traditions, but, significantly, it departed from those tradit
rejecting their conventional orders—of faith, of knowledge, a
humanity. In the evangelical worldview, faith and truth were
realized, and they were to be realized universally and wit
qualification. "The offer of salvation to all," Donald Matthews wr
"meant the essential humanity of all." The message, then,
essentially egalitarian; abolitionism was simply the secular outgrow
of the evangelical commitment to the equality, under God, of a
human beings. It is not clear that evangelical practice ever completely
transcended the racial order of its day; but it offered real hope. As
Mathews puts it, "When black people spoke in evangelical meetings
they were in practice rather than principle expressing an essential
democracy of experience among people who believed that in worship
God revealed His presence." The full promise of equality, and its
genuine meaning, were thus to be realized through the "theoretically
merciless scrutiny" of evangelical thought.

But as the nineteenth century progressed, this egalitarian evangelicalism gradually yielded to a different temperament. In the South, the
antislavery effort became "futile within the churches and dangerous in
the world," and the effort consequently shifted from abolition to
religious witness through the "Christianizing" of slaves and of slavery.
The positive effects were not insignificant—the peculiar institution did
apparently become a less harsh one in the antebellum era—but the new
paternalism left very much in place the old order. In the North,
meanwhile, the Second Great Awakening gave a distinctively Calvinist
tone to evangelical abolition: individualist in its orientation and
essentially liberal in its commitments, this Yankee evangelicalism easily
merged with the utilitarian challenges to slavery. The result, according
to historian Louis S. Gerteis, was that by the 1830s, "the moral
sentiments of antislavery reform advanced the utilitarian ethic of
liberal capitalism."[15]

The change was apparent in the dispute among abolitionists over the
growing labor movement. The workingmen's movements of the
nineteenth century broadly targeted social and economic inequality;
they sought, not unlike the early evangelicals, a revival of genuine
republican values. Most labor reformers were unhesitatingly opposed
to slavery, but abolitionists did not necessarily return their support.
Some abolitionists—Wendell Phillips, for example, and Nathaniel P.

Rogers—did join labor reformers in urging cooperation as an antidote to unfair competition. But most did not see abolition as an egalitarian or communitarian struggle. They instead followed economist Theodore Sedgwick in opposing slavery on utilitarian grounds: slavery was wrong because it frustrated human progress by denying individual liberty. Most agreed with Sedgwick that society could not be equal because nature was not equal: government was obliged only to leave men equally free—"there shall be no institutions *by law* that shall make men unequal."

Abolitionism became essentially individualistic, meritocratic, and remarkably tolerant of social inequality. Thus in 1831, Garrison's *Liberator* would chide labor reformers: "Poverty," the title of his article proclaimed, "Is Not Slavery." Poverty, Garrison explained to his readers, simply resulted from the natural differences among men; echoing Madison, he insisted that a free society "must, in the nature of things, be full of inequalities." Most black abolitionists were in accord; like their white compatriots, notes George M. Fredrickson, "they accorded legitimacy to what they viewed as just and normal social hierarchies."

Of course, to the slave South, these factional divides and philosophical evolutions could hardly obscure the central abolitionist message: the southern way of business, the southern way of life, was under assault. While the southern statesmen of the founding generation may have evidenced a certain embarrassment and regret over the institution of slavery, the succeeding generations could not afford this luxury: for them, slavery was too pervasive, too vital, to be left exposed by their ambivalence. Increasingly, the passions of abolitionists were matched by those of slavery's defenders: "Intellectual, social, and economic forces," write Oscar Handlin and Lilian Handlin, "fortified one another to create a system permanently grounded in slavery—no longer a necessary evil but justified as a positive good, with the planter replacing the yeoman as a model." The peculiar institution, now vital, became a righteous one.[16]

In the process, slavery's contradictions were at long last resolved. By now, the bondsmen of the South were exclusively of African descent; the coincidence became too obvious to ignore. With help of a nascent science, a physical anthropology of "race," slavery's defenders finally found the resolution to slavery's paradox, and they found it in the color of their bondsmen's skin. Africans—the black "race"—were lawfully subordinated because they were naturally subordinates. All men, it was well settled, were not created equal, and, it now became clear, neither were all races. The answer had been there all along: it was to be found—where else?—in nature.

Slavery found its intellectual defense, and it found it in a pseudo-scientific racism. The natural order thus became a natural racial order. Africans and African Americans became—as a "race"—naturally inferior; more, they were—as a "race"—naturally slaves. Slavery fulfilled nature's plan for the master and slave alike; for both the cultured white master and the uncivilized black slave, it was truly the best arrangement possible. The peculiar institution, in the final analysis, was thus a benevolent one.

The Confirmation: The Dred Scott Case

In 1856 the racial resolution received the official imprimatur of the United States Supreme Court. Dred Scott was an African American; he and his family had been assaulted by a white man who claimed to be Scott's master. Scott filed suit against the white man, but the success of his suit would depend on whether he was free: as a free man, Scott could not be assaulted; as a slave, he remained subject to discipline. Scott argued that he *was* free, in part by virtue of his stay in the Upper Louisiana Territory, an expanse of federal land made free by the Missouri Compromise of 1820. But Scott's very ability to file the suit depended on an interpretation of Article III of the United States Constitution: to sue, he had to be a "citizen."

Chief Justice Roger B. Taney delivered the opinion of the Supreme Court in *Scott v. Sandford*, the "Dred Scott case." Scott, the Court ruled, was not a "citizen," and neither, incredibly, was anyone "whose ancestors were negroes of the African race, and imported into this country, and sold and held as slaves." The entire "African race" was thus excluded from the life of the nation.

Taney purported to be bound by the "true intent and meaning" of the Constitution:

> No one, we presume, supposes that any change in public opinion or feeling, in relation to this unfortunate race, in the civilized nations of Europe or in this country, should induce the court to give to the words

of the Constitution a more liberal construction in their favor than they were intended to bear when the instrument was framed and adopted.

The founders' views on this "unfortunate race" precluded, according to Taney, the conclusion that they were citizens:

> On the contrary, they were at that time considered as a subordinate and inferior class of beings, who had been subjugated by the dominant race, and, whether emancipated or not, yet remained subject to their authority, and had no rights or privileges but such as those who held the power and the Government might choose to grant them.

This Taney knew by examining "the legislation and histories of the times, and the language used in the Declaration of Independence." The former included the laws establishing and maintaining slavery; the latter included the stirring proclamation that "all men are created equal":

> The general words above quoted would seem to embrace the whole human family, and if they were used in a similar instrument at this day would be so understood. But it is too clear for dispute, that the enslaved African race were not intended to be included, and formed no part of the people who framed and adopted this declaration; for if the language, as understood in that day, would embrace them, the conduct of the distinguished men who framed the Declaration of Independence would have been utterly and flagrantly inconsistent with the principles they asserted.

Such a result was inconceivable: "the men who framed this declaration were great men—high in literary acquirements—high in their sense of honor, and incapable of asserting principles inconsistent with those on which they were acting." Thus in the minds of the framers, "[t]he unhappy black race were separated from the white by indelible marks"; they could not be "citizens," and they could not sue.

That should have ended the case. But Taney went on to hold that the Missouri Compromise, on which Scott substantially based his claim of freedom, was unconstitutional. In outlawing slavery in the federal territory, the law exceeded the scope of the powers granted to Congress by the Constitution; moreover, it violated the Fifth Amendment to the Constitution by depriving slaveholders of their liberty and property without "due process of law." The Garrisonian view of the Constitution had received its unholy vindication: the document indeed protected slavery; and abolition—at least by Congress—was impossible without constitutional change.

For slaveholders, the decision in the *Dred Scott* case was a welcome sign that there was yet room for the South in the Union; for abolitionists, it was a sure sign that the "slave power" still reigned supreme. For politicians of every persuasion it became a defining issue: were you for the decision or against it, and if the latter, what would you do? Thus in 1860 the Lincoln candidacy was forced to deal directly with the question whether the decision deserved to be respected as authoritative. Lincoln's repudiation of *Scott v. Sandford* meant that his subsequent election could be seen as something of a constitutional referendum: Lincoln's election, said Illinois governor Richard Yates, "has decided that a construction which is favorable to the idea of freedom shall be given to the Constitution, and not a construction favorable to human bondage." It also meant, of course, secession and civil war.[17]

The years have not been kind to Taney's decision; indeed there is much to criticize. His determination to invalidate the Missouri Compromise is, as a legal matter, only *dicta*—making it ironic, at least, that a jurist so avowedly committed to separating law from politics should undertake such an overtly political project, one wholly unnecessary to the resolution of the legal case. Worse, as a calculated effort to preserve the Union, Taney's opinion was obviously a miserable failure: not even the Supreme Court could remove slavery from the national political conscience. More broadly, Taney's insistence that the meaning of the Constitution cannot evolve to incorporate new understandings seems too rigid and cramped a rule for an organic document; his specific determination—that the "African race" was, and thus still must be, regarded as an inferior race—seems morally obtuse.

Too rarely included among the criticisms of *Scott v. Sandford* is the indictment offered by Justices John McLean and Benjamin R. Curtis in their dissenting opinions. It is the most telling rebuke of all: Taney was, quite simply, wrong.

Slaves may have been, as Taney claimed, "subordinate," but not all slaves were African, and not all subordinated peoples were slaves:

women were subordinate, and minors, and men without property, and no one would suggest that they were not "citizens."

Africans, Taney insisted, had "no rights or privileges" beyond those recognized by their government, but this is either wrong or tautological, depending on one's views of rights: free men, black and white, participated in civil life on equal terms in parts of the now nation, and indeed the descendants of African slaves participated in the ratification decisions

Legislative history, Taney maintained, supports the view that Africans were not citizens, but in fact the leading documents of the day make a strong case against Taney's claim. The Articles of Confederation confer citizenship on all freemen: the qualifier "white" was explicitly rejected. The signatories to the Declaration, it is true, did not literally believe that "all men are created equal," but the inequalities they implicitly excepted were not defined by "race": the author of those words, Thomas Jefferson, never admitted to more than the "possibility" of racial inferiority, and this possibility he happily rejected when the evidence came due. As for the Constitution, it says not a word about "slavery," and no more about "race," and its framers certainly had no unifying "intent." Benjamin Franklin had expressed his view that all races were intellectual equals as early as 1763; and, as McLean puts it, "we know as a historical fact, that James Madison, that great and good man, a leading member in the Federal Convention, was solicitous to guard the language of that instrument so as not to convey the idea that there could be property in man."[18]

For all his protests to the contrary, it is not the "true intent and meaning" of the Constitution that Taney announces; it is instead the meaning that he chooses, informed by the "public opinion" of his day. It was Taney's generation, not Jefferson's and Madison's, that finally resolved slavery's paradox in racial terms; it was his generation, not the founders', that condemned an "unfortunate race" to perpetual servitude. It was one of many ironies that, in this sense, Frederick Douglass was correct after all: the Constitution was what its interpreters make of it.

And some, following Curtis and McLean, continued to insist even after *Scott v. Sandford* that the Constitution could yet be made into something more. Its principles had been betrayed by the Supreme Court's decisions, but at some level they endured, and in some fashion they would be redeemed. Congressman John A. Bingham of Ohio addressed the House of Representatives in January 1857: "It must be apparent that the absolute equality of all, and the equal protection of each, are principles of our Constitution ... The Constitution provides . . . that *no person* shall be deprived of life, liberty, or property without due process of law. It makes no distinction on account of complexion or birth ... This is equality." The Constitution, Bingham went on to observe, permits no title of nobility; this was more than a matter of form:

> Why this restriction? Was it not because all are equal under the Constitution; and that no distinctions should be tolerated, except those which merit originates, and no nobility except that which springs from the practice of virtue, or the honest, well-directed effort of brain, or heart, or hand? There is a profound significance in this restriction of the Constitution. It is an announcement of the equality and brother-hood of the human race.

A decade later, Bingham would write the Fourteenth Amendment.

The First Reconstruction

In April 1860, the United States Senate took up the question whether public education should be afforded to the District of Columbia's children, black and white alike. No large sum of money was implicated, nor was the number of prospective students very large; but the principle, such as it was, certainly seemed worth fighting for.

For some, the attempt to educate black children was a waste of time and money; for others, like James A. Bayard of Delaware, the inherent limitations of "the black race" simply meant that "the extent of education ought to be limited, and precise in its character." Still others had grown tired of these and similar claims: "I have heard long enough," said Daniel Clark of New Hampshire, "in the Senate and elsewhere that the colored people cannot be elevated. They cannot be elevated because you will not try to elevate them."

Yet another view was offered by Albert G. Brown, Democrat from Mississippi. "I will not," Brown insisted, "in this slaveholding community, vote for any proposition which proposes to mingle the negro and the white child in the same school." Brown was willing, however, to allow the black and white communities to be separately taxed to fund separate schools; "but I will vote for no proposition which looks to put white children on an equal footing with negro children, here or elsewhere." Brown preferred that his colleagues concentrate their attention on the needs of white children:

> these children are dearer to us than the little darkies . . . children of your own blood; of your own complexion; of your own race . . . as the white boy is better than the black boy in the judgment of some of us, as the white girl is more entitled to our kindness than the black girl, let us take the whites first; let us provide for our own people, precisely as any man would do for his own children in preference to the children of his neighbor; precisely as a man would take care of his own kith and kin in preference to strangers. These white children are of our own race.

James Harlan of Iowa was moved to inquire: "If it is cheaper to educate the white child at the public expense than to support him as a pauper, or to punish him after years as a criminal, is it not equally true of colored children?"

One answer came from Mississippi Democrat Jefferson Davis:

> In this District of Columbia you have but to go to the jail and find there, by those who fill it, the result of relieving the negro from that control which keeps him in his own healthy and useful condition. It is idle to assume that it is the want of education; it is the natural inferiority of the race; and the same proof exists wherever that race has been left the master of itself—sinking into barbarism or into the commission of crime. . . . In the law, sometimes, it has been attempted to declare their equality; but in fact, socially, and as a practical question, I say it is done nowhere.

"Do gentlemen need more," Davis asked,

> to convince them of the distinction between the races? Do they hope, offending against all the teachings of history; against the marks of God; in violation of the Constitution; and by trampling upon the feelings of the southern representatives here, to found in the District of Columbia an experimental establishment to disprove the inequality of the races?

Bayard concurred, and thus prompted another inquiry from Harlan: "If the negro population were all as well educated as the white people, would they then be our equals?"

Bayard did not hesitate:

> Without entering into the question, which I leave to philologists and ethnologists, as to the unity or diversity of the races, I have no shadow of a doubt, from my own observation of the negro race, of its inferiority. . . . My answer to the honorable Senator is, that, from my reading of the history of the past, from my own personal observation of the character of the race, I believe it would be impossible to carry the civilization of the negro race as a race—I do not speak of individual cases—to equality with the white man with any benefit either to them or the white race.

It was the response Harlan had anticipated. Harlan's defense of black education was, after all, a pragmatic one: it was better to afford education than to absorb the social costs of ignorance. It was not a defense rooted in equality, at least, not the kind of equality Davis and Bayard seemed to fear:

> What do Senators mean by the term equality? Do they mean physical equality? Who has proposed to make the Negro, by law, as beautiful as the Anglo-Saxon; as symmetrical in his proportions; as capable of enduring fatigue, or enduring toil? Who has proposed to make him his equal in intellectual development, or in moral sensibilities? Who has proposed to make him his equal in a social point of view? Nobody. Social equality, I suppose, depends on entirely different laws, and on that subject everybody must be a judge for himself. Will either of those Senators tell me that he will meet on terms of perfect equality every man of his own race, admit every man to his own table, or as a suitable suitor for the hand of his own daughter in matrimony? I apprehend not. Then what kind of equality is referred to? . . . Well, is it political equality that is referred to? Who has proposed to make them the equal of the white race in a political point of view? Nobody.

Henry Wilson of Massachusetts shared Harlan's views: "This negro equality seems to run through the heads of southern gentlemen. There is great alarm about negro equality. Sir, let us educate, if we can, these poor colored children, and enable them, as far as possible, to improve their condition in life."

What followed is an early version of a colloquy that would be replayed countless times over the next two decades—and many times more, right up to the present day. It is at once enlightening and bewildering, as befits, perhaps, its subject. At issue was the meaning, theoretically and practically, of that elusive term "equality."

Davis: The Senator objects to the argument which treats of the proposition of himself and his friends, as the assertion of equality between the negro and white races. Do I understand him as denying the equality, or does he admit the equality?

Wilson: The natural equality of all men I believe in, as far as the rights are concerned. So far as mental or physical equality is concerned, I believe the African race inferior to the white race.

Davis: "Natural equality" would imply that God had created them equal, and had left them equal, down to the present time. Is that what the Senator means?

Wilson: I believe in the equality of rights of all mankind. I do not believe in the equality of the African race with the white race, mentally or physically, and I do not think morally.

Davis: When the Senator says "equality of rights of all men," does he mean political and social rights—political and social equality?

Wilson: I believe that every human being has the right to his life and to his liberty, and to act in this world so as to secure his own happiness. I believe, in a word, in the Declaration of Independence; but I do not, as I have said, believe in the mental or moral or physical equality of some of the races, as against this white race of ours.

Davis: Then the Senator believes and he does not believe, and he changes his position so rapidly in giving his answers that it is impossible to tell what he does believe.

Harlan: Will the Senator allow me to ask him a question?

Davis: Oh, yes.

Harlan: Do you believe in the political and social equality of all individuals of the white race?

Davis: I will answer you, yes; the exact political equality of all white men who are citizens of the United States. That equality may be lost by the commission of crime; but white men, the descendants of the Adamic race, under our institutions, are born equal; and that is the effect of the Declaration of Independence.

Harlan: If the Senator will allow me, being "born equal" is a phrase that involves the proposition that the Senator from Massachusetts has stated. I inquired as to their social and their political equality.

> *Davis*: Their political equality, I stated, exists, unless it is lost by the commission of crime, or some disqualification which attaches to the individual, not to the race. Their social equality will depend upon a great variety of circumstances, being the result of education and many other contingencies. Those are conventional, not political, rights. They do not belong to the institutions of the country. They may be matters of taste. Every man has a right to select his own associates; and he may assert his superiority, and the person he excludes may regard him as an inferior. All that has nothing to do with anything which we have a right to consider. This is not a debating society. We are not here to deal in general theories and mere speculative philosophy, but to treat subjects as political questions.

Seven months later, the "political question" would start to be answered with the election of Abraham Lincoln as president. The slave South seceded from the Union; Jefferson Davis became president of the Confederate States of America. Their rebellion, Davis insisted, was in the name of liberty. In 1863 Union General David Hunter defied military protocol by writing Davis directly to protest the brutal treatment of captured black soldiers; in the process, he shared his thoughts on the slaveholders' conception of liberty:

> You say you are fighting for liberty. Yes you are fighting for liberty: liberty to keep four millions of your fellow-beings in ignorance and degradation;—liberty to separate parents and children, husband and wife, brother and sister;—liberty to steal the products of their labor, exacted with many a cruel lash and bitter tear;—liberty to seduce their wives and daughters, and to sell your own children into bondage;—liberty to kill these children with impunity, when the murder cannot be proven by one of pure white blood. This is the kind of liberty—the liberty to do wrong—which Satan, Chief of the fallen Angels, was contending for when he was cast into Hell.[19]

In the end, a different principle prevailed. After four years of war, in which over six hundred thousand soldiers lost their lives, the United States of America was in need of Reconstruction. By 1868, its amended Constitution would contain an explicit guarantee of equality. But precisely what that meant, and how it was to be realized, remained far from certain.

The Contradictions Reconstructed: The Conundrum of Formal Equality

A review of the Reconstruction debates in Congress leaves the reader with two overwhelming impressions. First, it is clear that constitutional Reconstruction did not proceed through a logical, scripted progression: the Reconstruction amendments to the Constitution—the Thirteenth, Fourteenth, and Fifteenth Amendments—and the civil rights legislation designed to effectuate them, were not simultaneously conceived as parts of a coherent, comprehensive plan. Rather, the Reconstruction effort was, on the whole, quite pragmatic, responding to the evidence and the exigencies of the day. It was undoubtedly held together by a unifying purpose—the protection of the freedmen—but the means of achieving this broad goal were decidedly ad hoc.

Consider the cornerstone of constitutional Reconstruction, section 1 of the Fourteenth Amendment, with its guarantee of the "equal protection of the law." "[T]he principle of the first [section]," noted Congressman Henry J. Raymond during the congressional debates in 1866, "which secures an equality of rights among all the citizens of the United States, has had a somewhat curious history." Indeed it had. It was, recall, John Bingham who wrote this section. In 1857 Bingham had insisted that the Constitution guaranteed "the equality of all, the equal protection of each." It was, at the time, a distinctly minority view; the constitutionalization of slavery in the Dred Scott decision was the clearest testament to that. But in 1865 Congress endeavored to reverse the situation with the Thirteenth Amendment to the Constitution: it abolished slavery, and made all Americans free and equal.

But it made them equal only implicitly. The Thirteenth Amendment contained no expressed guarantee of equality, which is why Republican senator Charles Sumner of Massachusetts, a former lecturer at Harvard Law School, had proposed as a substitute amendment a provision declaring that, "All persons are equal before the law." "[E]quality before the law," Sumner explained, "gives precision to that idea of human rights which is enunciated in our Declaration of Independence. The sophistries of Calhoun, founded on the obvious inequalities of body and mind, are all overthrown by this simple statement." But Lyman Trumbull of Illinois, chair of the Senate

Judiciary Committee, favored the principal amendment; abolish slavery, he reasoned, and equality invariably follows. In deference to his colleague, Sumner withdrew his substitute.

But simply declaring an end to slavery did not in fact ensure equality. The congressional debates of the subsequent years are replete with testimony on the relentless oppression of the freedmen: widespread discrimination by public and private actors, often in collaboration, and not infrequently culminating in the institution of virtual slavery through sharecropping schemes, apprenticeship laws, and the brutal enforcement of "vagrancy" restrictions. The freedmen could not buy or sell land, could not contract, could not testify in court, could not travel. Trumbull was speaking of theory when he said that "it is perhaps difficult to draw the precise line, to say where freedom ceases and slavery begins"; but the same was true in practice: slave or not, the "freedmen" certainly were not "equal." A white North Carolina farmer spoke for a generation of more "enlightened" southerners when he offered that "I haven't any prejudices against 'em because they're free but you see I can't consider that they're on an equality with a white man." Or as George C. King, a former slave in South Carolina, put it, "The master he says we are all free, but it don't mean we is white. And it don't mean we is equal."

Congress was quick to respond. Bingham's original draft of the Fourteenth Amendment, reported to the House in February 1866, would have authorized Congress to enact "all laws which shall be necessary and proper to secure . . . to all persons in the several States equal protection in the rights of life, liberty, and property." But the proposal faced opposition from across the political spectrum—Republican congressman Giles Hotchkiss of New York, for example, lamented that it "is not sufficiently radical"—and Bingham joined the vote to table the amendment. Acting under the authority of the *Thirteenth* Amendment, Congress then passed, over Andrew Johnson's veto, the Civil Rights Act of 1866, which declared the citizenship of the freedmen, and guaranteed to citizens "of every race and color" the "full and equal benefit of all laws."

For the framers of the Thirteenth Amendment—who were, after all, also the crafters of the civil rights bill—the abolition of slavery in the Thirteenth Amendment evidently contained the equality guarantee that Sumner desired: it was simply implicit, not explicit. The Civil Rights Act made this protection a part of the expressed law.

But protection by statute was insecure: hostile courts or subsequent congresses could nullify or repeal the provisions. A revised Fourteenth Amendment was introduced in the spring of 1866; when it was ratified, in 1868, Congress had effectively constitutionalized the Civil Rights Act. The language of section 1 of the Amendment in fact runs parallel to the Act:

> All persons born or naturalized in the United States, and subject to the jurisdiction thereof, are citizens of the United States and of the State wherein they reside. No State shall make or enforce any law which shall abridge the privileges or immunities of citizens of the United States; nor shall any State deprive any person of life, liberty, or property without due process of law; nor deny to any person within its jurisdiction the equal protection of the law.

The reasons behind the minor change in syntax in the equality guarantee—from "full and equal benefit of all laws" to "equal protection of the law"—are by no means clear: the change appears, on the one hand, to broaden the scope of the states' duty, by imposing on them an affirmative obligation to "protect"; but it may be, on the other hand, no more than Bingham's preference for a convention that he had employed a decade earlier.

But the picture, in any event, is completed in 1870, when the Civil Rights Act of 1866 is *re*enacted verbatim: now, the reasoning went, the act is authorized by the powers conferred on Congress in the Fourteenth as well as the Thirteenth Amendments. So, in effect, two constitutional amendments and two identical statutes were needed to assert the simple but vital principle of "equality under the law."

This history also captures in microcosm the second overwhelming impression generated by a review of the record: there is an omnipresent sense that the framers of Reconstruction are struggling mightily to reconcile the vast gulf between aspiration and actuality, between the real and the ideal. This meant, on the one hand, that much of their effort was designed to *realize* the guarantee of equality that they once thought was implicit in the Constitution, and that they subsequently made express. It also meant, on the other hand, that their aspirations were always informed by the real obstacles of the day: the political realities of the fragile union, the practical intransigence of the former master class, and the philosophical limitations inherent in the ideology of the natural order. They were, in general, committed to some vision of equality, but it was a vision invariably clouded by dissensus, ambivalence, and uncertainty. And, of course, by contradictions.

The opponents of Reconstruction tended to labor under the old paradoxes: they were opposed to equality, for example, even if their arguments were ultimately rooted in the concept. In 1864, Democratic Congressman McDowell voiced his opposition to the creation of a Freedmen's Bureau: "We also have a proposition to establish a Bureau of Emancipation," McDowell complained. "Why do they overlook all the interests of the white men of the nation and rush blindly to the negro, and think nothing and do nothing but what they fancy is for his welfare?" It was, apparently, an early plea for race-neutrality, for "color blindness," but it lacked something in the way of consistency. "We have a proposition also," McDowell continued,

> pending in the other branch of Congress, which declares that all laws shall be repealed which make a distinction between the races—between white and black. Sir, this is the culmination of all the hopes of these radical fanatics. Here is the goal toward which they are directing all their efforts: to debase the white man to the degraded level of the African negro.

Reconstruction's defenders had their own difficulties with the concept of equality. Bingham insisted, on the one hand, that "[t]his Government rests upon the absolute equality of natural rights amongst men." Then again, on the other hand, "[t]here is not, and cannot be, any equality in the enjoyment of political or conventional rights, because that is impossible." Clarifying—in a fashion—Bingham explained that "Nobody proposes or dreams of political equality any more than of physical or mental equality. It is as impossible for men to establish equality in these respects as it is for 'the Ethiopian to change his skin.'" What then was the "equality" guaranteed by our constitutional democracy? "The equality of all to the right to live; to the right to know; to argue and to utter, according to conscience; to work and enjoy the product of their toil, is the rock on which that Constitution rests—its sure foundation and defense."

The ambiguity was contagious. Thaddeus Stevens of Pennsylvania was perhaps the most radical of Republicans. But in June 1864, Stevens was moved to address Democratic Congressman Samuel S. Cox of Ohio: "The gentleman will allow me to say that I never held to the doctrine of negro equality."

"Then," asked Cox, "I understand the gentleman from Pennsylvania not to hold that all men are created equal?"

"Yes, sir," Stevens replied, "but not equality in all things—simply before the laws, nothing else."

Years later, speaking in support of the "equal protection" guarantee of the Fourteenth Amendment, Stevens would explain his understanding of "equality . . . before the laws":

> the law which operates upon one man shall operate *equally* upon all. Whatever law punishes a white man for a crime shall punish the black man precisely in the same way and to the same degree. Whatever law protects the white man shall afford 'equal' protection to the black man. Whatever means of redress is afforded to one shall be afforded to all. Whatever law allows the white man to testify in court shall allow the man of color to do the same.

But Stevens's Pennsylvania colleague, Democratic congressman Samuel J. Randall, thought the guarantee went further: "The first section proposes to make an equality in every respect between the two races . . . I feel it, in consequence, my imperative duty to oppose this section."

What the Democrats ostensibly feared—and what they seemed to detect in virtually every Reconstruction measure—was a movement to destroy the "natural" distinctions between the races, to ensure not merely "legal equality," but "political equality" and "social equality" as well. But what did these terms mean?

Roughly, "legal equality" embraced "legal" or "civil" rights: those rights, according to English jurist William Blackstone, that were enjoyed by all citizens, subject only to general restriction for the public good. The rights to buy and sell property and labor, and to sue to enforce these rights, were perhaps the most prominent "legal" rights. There was a widespread consensus that, almost by tautology, the Fourteenth Amendment guaranteed "legal equality" to the freedmen.

"Political equality," meanwhile, embraced the privileges of self-governance. These "political" rights—the rights to vote and to hold office, and, depending on one's view, the right to serve as jurors (a "legal" right in some eyes)—could be limited by the terms of the democratic compact, as it had been in America, the home of the "white man's government." The question of "political equality" for the freedmen was much debated during Reconstruction, but largely settled in 1870 with the ratification of the Fifteenth Amendment.

"Social equality," however, was quite another matter. It was the most inclusive concept, embracing those aspects of social life inherent in economic class and social rank. "Social equality" was the most direct challenge to the natural order: it even threatened—through what was variously referred to as "amalgamation" or "miscegenation"—to destroy the very biological distinctions on which the order was based. For Democrats, every Reconstruction measure was a misguided attempt to ensure "social equality," and most would lead ultimately to the "mongrelization" of the races through intermarriage. It was a painfully constant refrain; as Tennessee Republican James Mullins put it in 1869,

> Sir, it is alarming that the Democratic party should be so much alarmed about their "social rights." In the name of common sense and justice and truth what need they be alarmed about? I see nothing in the world alarming. But they are dreadfully alarmed about "social rights" and "social equality." They seem at least to be dreadfully alarmed lest somebody will marry a negro or a negro will marry somebody else.

Taken individually, each of the various concepts—"legal," "political," and "social" equality—admitted of its own ambiguities; collectively, they made most discussions of "equality" nearly incoherent. Consider, as one early example, the debate in 1864 over the use of railcars in the District of Columbia. Charles Sumner had introduced a resolution guaranteeing to all persons of any race the "equal enjoyment of all railroad privileges." Thomas A. Hendricks of Indiana objected: "I do not understand from the Senator who has introduced this resolution that any negro has been denied the right to ride in the cars which, at the expense of the company, have been provided for their accommodation."

Sumner responded that "[t]here may be here and there, now and then, once in a long interval of time, a car which colored persons may enter, but any person who traverses the avenue must see that those cars come very rarely." Henry Wilson added this anecdote:

> The other day a friend of mine came up from the Army, and with him two colored men, and they were forced to ride in a cattle car while he

rode alone in a freight car . . . In this case these persons were forced into the cattle car, and the gentleman told me he rode nearly all the way alone, when there was room for a large number of other persons in the car. He inquired about it of two officers, and the answer was that the cattle cars were for "the niggers."

Hendricks was sure that he now saw the Republican plan:

I am satisfied, sir, that the Senators have now declared the end to which we are to come, and that by the action of the Federal Government the social as well as the political equality of the negro is to be forced upon the white race. If that be the judgment of the country we shall have to accept it. The people that I represent in this Chamber have not yet adopted that sentiment. The distinction between the two races is yet maintained in Indiana. How much longer it will be maintained I am not able to say.

Daniel Clark of New Hampshire now intervened: "I think the Senator from Indiana has mistaken the resolution. I understand him to characterize this as a resolution to force the negro into the cars. I understand it to be a resolution to prevent you from forcing him out—not to force social equality, but to prevent an outrage upon him."

Wilson tried to explain his vision of the "equality" behind Sumner's resolution:

I do not want to force on the Senator from Indiana or anybody else any class of men with whom he does not choose to associate, but I think the true policy is to let men stand equally before the law, to let men win their own positions, let them have the privilege of making out of themselves all that God and nature intended that they should be.

The resolution passed in the Senate by a vote of thirty to ten. One week later, the Senate debates caught the attention of Democratic congressman Samuel S. Cox of Ohio. He, too, was certain he had detected the Republicans' motives:

The Senate of the United States is discussing African equality in street cars. We have the negro at every moment and in every bill in Congress. All these things, in connection with the African policies of confiscation and emancipation in their various shapes for the past three years, culminating in this grand plunder scheme of a department for freedmen, ought to convince us that that party is moving steadily forward to perfect social equality of black and white, and can only end in this detestable doctrine of—miscegenation!

Maintaining—or even detecting—the distinction between "legal equality" and "social equality" was no simple task, but as these debates suggest, it was in some minds a terribly important one. For the Democrats, the Republicans were always crossing the line; for the Republicans, it was all Democratic paranoia; both sides agreed that there was a line; and neither side had any idea where or how to draw it.

This is one of the reasons that even the equality they agreed on—"legal equality"—was itself so ambiguous: increasingly, its meaning was defined by negative reference to terms that had little independent integrity and that could not be easily distinguished. Legal equality was not social equality, and the consensus ended there.

But this generated another dilemma, one that the framers of Reconstruction could not avoid and yet did not resolve. Divorced from the theoretical realms of the "political" and the "social," "equality" was to do its work in the realm of "law." But that can be a decidedly abstract realm: securing "legal equality" can be an exercise in mere rhetoric or form; measuring conformity to the mandate becomes a matter of deductive fiat. "Legal equality" might require, for example, the desegregation of railcars, or, for that matter, the end of antimiscegenation laws; then again, it might not, depending entirely on the frame of reference.

Consider one final colloquy. In January 1866, during the debates over the civil rights bill, Democratic senator Reverdy Johnson of Maryland charged that the guarantee of "equal benefit of all laws" was a guarantee of the right of miscegenation. Under the proposed law, Johnson maintained, "it will be admitted that the black man has the same right to enter into a contract of marriage with a white woman as a white man has." Laws prohibiting interracial marriages would thus operate unequally and would be void.

But Republican William P. Fessenden of Maine saw it differently; he utilized a different point of comparison. The black man, according to Fessenden, "has the same right to make a contract of marriage with a white woman that a white man has with a black woman." Laws prohibiting all interracial marriages would thus operate equally, and would be valid.

It was impossible—it is still impossible—to say who is correct; as Johnson put it, "whether I am wrong or not, upon a careful and correct interpretation [of the bill], I suppose all the Senate will admit that the error is not so gross a one that the courts may not fall into it."

This was the hopeless conundrum of legal equality. Separated from "social" life—separated from the "real" world—equality under law too easily devolves into empty form. "Legal" equality becomes wholly dependent on an abstract frame of reference, and that reference—the relevant comparison—is utterly arbitrary. There is thus no way to measure "legal equality": it exists—or not—only by proclamation.

"Legal equality" is a profoundly problematic concept. At its best, it is ambiguous and indeterminate; at its worst, it dissolves into empty form. Many of the framers of Reconstruction recognized its problems at the time. But it was all they could agree on.

What, then, is a fair verdict on the Reconstruction effort? On the one hand, it might be said that the framers of Reconstruction lacked the resolve to provide practical redress to the problems of the freedmen, and the foresight to see how their general remedy—the guarantee of legal equality—could be so easily perverted by subsequent generations. Their inability, or unwillingness, to enter the realm of "social equality" meant that the only economic justice they could secure was through the same formal liberty bequeathed them by the original framers. But extending that liberty to the freedmen did very little to disturb the real-world hierarchy of race.

They might have done more. Land reform had been a part of the antislavery reform movement as far back as 1821. As Thaddeus Stevens put it, in the midst of Reconstruction, "Forty acres of land and a hut would be more valuable to [the freedmen] than the immediate right to vote. Unless we give them this we shall receive the censure of mankind and the curse of Heaven." But they did not divide the slave plantations, nor give to the freedmen more than an "equal opportunity" to succeed on their own. In failing to ensure an equality that was real, the framers of Reconstruction earned, perhaps, mankind's censure, and Heaven's curse.

On the other hand, it might also be said that they provided the greatest measure of redress possible within the constraints of their day, that they crafted mandates broad enough to serve the visions of future generations, generations unencumbered, they hoped, by the political and epistemological obstacles of the mid-nineteenth century. Some of them, indeed, thought the equality they were providing was very real, and they had fought hard to secure it. Republican senator Thomas W. Tipton of Nebraska, for one, saw Reconstruction as the real vindication of the promise of freedom:

> To grant a man his freedom from slavery and yet not secure to him the full and fair protection of law is only a mockery and insult. To allow him to amass property and then let others govern it by law, to allow him to seek liberty but deny him the power of preserving it by legislation, to allow him the claim to life but refuse him a jury of his peers, would be to rob him of the substance and cheat him with the shadow.

Stevens thought it was at least a noble start. Speaking of the Fourteenth Amendment, he said: "I will take all that I can get in the cause of humanity and leave it to be perfected by better men in better times. It may be that that time will not come while I am here to enjoy the glorious triumph; but that it will come is as certain as that there is a just God." Of course, that "glorious triumph"—of perfect equality—did not come during Reconstruction, nor, as the effort wound to its conclusion, did it appear on the horizon. Stevens knew it: "But men in pursuit of justice must never despair."

The Old Resolution: Redeeming the Natural Order

Abolitionists convened in New York City in 1870 to celebrate the passage of the Fifteenth Amendment and to dissolve their various societies. Their work, however, was far from done. They reconstituted their groups as the National Reform League and dedicated their new organization to the struggle against the "social prosecution of men on account of their color." Of necessity, their chief target was the comprehensive scheme of legal, quasi-legal, and extralegal measures that segregated and subordinated black Americans, a scheme known widely as Jim Crow.

Jim Crow had, as C. Vann Woodward famously put it, a "strange career," and harbored some contradictions of its own. Racial segregation, after all, had not been the rule in the antebellum South: close contact had been a necessary part of slave-master relations; the fear of slave rebellions had dictated that slave communities be maintained under watchful eyes on the plantations, and the ideology of racial supremacy had mandated the exclusion of black southerners—not merely their separation—from public accommodations, courthouses, and schools. In the North, on the other hand, the influx of white European immigrants in the first quarter of the nineteenth century meant a loss of black job opportunity and, with the eventual spread of universal white suffrage, a concomitant loss of political power. White-initiated segregation then became common in schools and churches; black northerners countered with the creation of formal black religious sects and black schools.

The situation very nearly reversed after the war. In the North, the post-war migration and the elimination of racial restrictions on the franchise meant that the black vote was suddenly critical to electoral success. This created at least a sympathetic political environment for the neo-abolitionist crusade: the result throughout the North was state civil rights legislation formally eliminating racial discrimination, including the racial segregation of public accommodations and schools. Even the miscegenation laws were repealed.[20]

In the South, the effort to maintain racial hierarchy without the formal restraints of the peculiar institution took one of two forms. In those realms of life in which there had been, and still needed to be, interracial contacts—the great bulk of what might be described as social and economic life—the white South determined to replicate the old hierarchy of the master-slave relationship through devices that made no pretense to equality. Landowners joined together in refusing to sell to the freedmen, offering instead only absurdly exploitative sharecropping arrangements. The freedmen were refused jobs and places to live, then jailed for vagrancy and impressed into labor for the same planters who refused to employ them. Such overt discrimination was nonetheless claimed to be beyond the reach of federal constitutional and legislative guarantees: the imposed inequalities were said to be "social."

In many of those realms of life from which black southerners were previously excluded—the courts, for example, and the schools—the white struggle against equality was eventually lost. So-called legal equality and political equality were explicitly guaranteed by the Reconstruction amendments; but since interracial contacts here were in no sense necessary, the obvious recourse was to segregation, to "separate but equal." Separate judicial systems and school systems thus became the norm throughout the South; only in New Orleans, in fact, were public schools integrated. Even in South Carolina—where the predominantly black legislature became the first in the nation to offer universal, free public education—the Reconstruction government accepted schools that were segregated by custom.[21]

The two realms, of course, were not mutually exclusive, as the case of public accommodations demonstrates. Such accommodations—inns, theaters, conveyances, and the like—were sometimes said to be "social" and beyond the equality mandate, and at other times were segregated under the doctrine of "separate but equal." Both arguments, however, were apparently rejected by the Reconstruction Congress: in 1875, it outlawed racial discrimination in public accommodations.

The Civil Rights Cases. The Civil Rights Act of 1875 was the climax of the neo-abolitionist struggle against Jim Crow. The bill had been introduced by Charles Sumner in the summer of 1870; as originally drafted, it prohibited discrimination in public accommodations, juries, and schools. The bill drifted uncertainly in and out of committee for four years, leaving Sumner to plead from his deathbed in March 1874: "My bill, the civil rights bill—don't let it fail." Shortly thereafter, the bill passed the Senate, but the House recessed without action.

Democrats controlled the House of Representatives after the elections of 1874, and the Republicans, in their lame duck session, finally passed the bill. Its managers, however, deleted the schools provision, though not before considering a provision that would have imposed a requirement that separate schools be "equal." The provision was rejected by opponents and advocates of equality alike. "If we once establish a discrimination of this kind, we know not where it will end," Congressman James Monroe explained; the freedmen and their advocates "think their chances for good schools will be better under the Constitution with the protection of the courts than under a bill containing such provisions as this."

The bill, without any schools provision, became law in 1875. It guaranteed to all citizens, regardless of "race or color," the "full and equal enjoyment of the accommodations, advantages, facilities, and privileges of inns, public conveyances on land or water, theaters, and other places of public amusement." Claims of discrimination soon arose in inns, restaurants, steamboats, theaters, saloons, and—in a case that tested the statutory limits of "place of public amusement"—a Philadelphia cemetery. The defense to nearly every claim was that the statute—and the constitutional guarantee of equality that the statute was designed to advance—was not violated by separate but equal facilities. A series of cases arising in October 1876 found their way to the Supreme Court's docket and, incredibly, lingered there for seven years.

The delay was not accidental. The Civil Rights Act of 1875 proved to be the last major act of Reconstruction. Ulysses S. Grant's second term as president had been plagued by scandal, and the presidential election of 1876 promised a Democratic win. But Democrat Samuel B. Tilden was in ill health and an unenthusiastic candidate, while Republican Rutherford B. Hayes waged a vigorous campaign, resurrecting the "bloody shirt" of the Union soldier. Still, Tilden won the popular election by over a quarter million votes. But disputed elections in four states left Tilden one electoral vote shy of a majority; the election thus went to the House, which deadlocked. A fifteen-man Electoral Commission was appointed to arbitrate the disputed elections; by a vote of eight to seven, the Commission declared Hayes the victor. The House convened to confirm the Commission's findings, but southern Democrats threatened a filibuster. A deal was struck. The terms of the Compromise of 1877 remain a subject of considerable controversy, but the net effect seems clear: the Republicans received the White House, and the Democrats secured an end to the federal effort at Reconstruction.

After 1877, the Redeemer governments in the South turned the guarantee of equality into a cruel hoax. Black Americans were disenfranchised by overt discrimination and by the unsubtle facades of poll taxes and literacy tests. Customary discriminations in public facilities became mandated by law. "Separate but equal" became only separate: forced segregation into inferior facilities served the dual purpose of limiting black opportunities and convincing poor whites that race was more important than economic class. Attempts to secure equalization were met by official hostility, in the form of racist political rhetoric and ever greater disparities in funding. Attempts by the black community itself to equalize were met by violence: churches and schools were burned; pastors, teachers, and successful businessmen or professionals were threatened, beaten, and sometimes killed. There was no more Freedmen's Bureau to offer counsel, no federal garrison to offer protection; the old order was indeed redeemed.

The end of the federal resolve meant that the Civil Rights Act of 1875 would be only weakly enforced. But it was a thorn in the side of the South, a symbolic reminder of federal control and the challenge to the old ways. In the summer of 1882, with the civil rights cases still sitting on the Court's docket, Chief Justice Morris J. Waite concluded an extraordinary series of correspondence with Hayes: "I agree with you entirely," the chief justice wrote, "as to the necessity of keeping public sentiment at the south in our favor." Waite then assigned the opinion in the *Civil Rights Cases* of 1883 to his most trusted aide, Justice Joseph P. Bradley, the man who, coincidentally, had cast the deciding vote in Hayes's favor as a member of the 1876 electoral commission.

Bradley, who made the Compromise of 1877 possible, confirmed the deal in his decision. But he did not determine whether "separate but equal" was in compliance with the Civil Rights Act. Instead, Bradley ruled that the Civil Rights Act of 1875 was unconstitutional, because Congress lacked the authority to enact it.[22] In reaching his decision, Bradley drew three vital distinctions:

First, slavery was distinct from racial discrimination. Congress had relied in part on the Thirteenth Amendment, but that amendment only prohibited slavery. There was a distinction, Bradley insisted, between slavery and racial discrimination. "It would be running the slavery argument into the ground," Bradley concluded, "to make it apply to every act of discrimination which a person may see fit to make as to the guests he will entertain."

Second, public action was distinct from private action. Congress had also relied on the Fourteenth Amendment's guarantee of equality to justify its actions, but that guarantee, Bradley insisted, applied only to actions of state officials. There was a necessary distinction between public and private action; the discriminations of inn and theater operators were merely the latter. "[C]ivil rights," Bradley concluded, "such as are guarantied by the constitution against state aggression, cannot be impaired by the wrongful acts of individuals, unsupported by state authority in the shape of laws, customs, or judicial or executive proceedings. . . . The wrongful act of an individual, unsupported by any such authority, is simply a private wrong."

Finally, the redress of action was distinct from primary measures in the face of inaction. The public-private dichotomy led to Bradley's final distinction: under the Fourteenth Amendment, Congress had only the power to respond to the wrongful actions of the states, it could not act affirmatively, in the face of, for example, state inaction. "[U]ntil some state law has been passed," Bradley wrote,

> or some state action through its officers or agents has been taken, adverse to the rights of citizens sought to be protected by the fourteenth amendment, no legislation of the United States under said amendment, nor any proceeding under such legislation, can be called into activity, for the prohibitions of the amendment are against state laws and acts done under state authority.

The Civil Rights Act of 1875 was thus void: "This is not corrective legislation; it is primary and direct."

Bradley concluded his opinion with a critique of the late Reconstruction effort: "When a man has emerged from slavery, and by the aid of beneficent legislation has shaken off the inseparable concomitants of that state, there must be some stage in the progress of his elevation when he takes the rank of a mere citizen, and ceases to be the special favorite of the laws."

Only John Marshall Harlan of Kentucky, the last Supreme Court justice to have been a slaveholder, dissented from Bradley's opinion. Driven to Republicanism by racist violence in his home state, Harlan rose to Republicanism's defense. "The opinion in these cases proceeds, as it seems to me, upon grounds entirely too narrow and artificial," he wrote. "The substance and spirit of the recent amendments of the constitution have been sacrificed by a subtle and ingenious verbal criticism."

Harlan was unconvinced by any of Bradley's distinctions. As for the distinction between slavery and racial discrimination, which Bradley used to make the Thirteenth Amendment inapplicable, Harlan wrote,

> since slavery, as the court has repeatedly declared, was the moving or principal cause of the adoption of that amendment, and since that institution rested wholly upon the inferiority, as a race, of those held

in bondage, their freedom necessarily involved immunity from, and protection against, all discrimination against them, because of their race, in respect of such civil rights as belong to freemen of other races.

As for the distinction between public and private action, it was, whatever its theoretical integrity, of no avail in this case: "In every material sense applicable to the practical enforcement of the fourteenth amendment, railroad corporations, keepers of inns, and managers of places of public amusement are agents of the state."

Harlan could not see why congressional power under the Fourteenth Amendment should be restricted to remedial measures. Before the war, he noted, the Supreme Court had given Congress expansive powers to enforce the fugitive slave clause: "I venture, with all respect for the opinion of others, to insist that the national legislature may, without transcending the limits of the constitution, do for human liberty and the fundamental rights of American citizenship, what it did, with the sanction of this court, for the protection of slavery and the rights of the masters of fugitive slaves."

In response to Bradley's broader critique, Harlan was properly incredulous: "It is, I submit, scarcely just to say that the colored race has been the special favorite of the laws."

Harlan's dissent was echoed in Congress. In December, Senator James F. Wilson of Iowa proposed a constitutional amendment designed to overturn Bradley's decision in the *Civil Rights Cases*. The amendment read: "Congress shall have power, by appropriate legislation, to protect citizens of the United States in the exercise and enjoyment of their rights, privileges, and immunities, and to assure to them the equal protection of the laws."

Wilson too was unpersuaded by Bradley's distinctions. Slavery and discrimination were interrelated phenomena: the freedmen "were freighted down with the crushing burdens of ignorance, prejudice, race distinctions, lines of caste, and disabilities evolved by two centuries of slavery." The public and private were also interrelated: private behavior was shaped by public law.

It was not expected that [the Civil Rights] act would at once dispel the race antagonism which centuries of slavery had intensified. But it was expected that by supplementing the kindly and humanizing offices of passing years with a protective law of the character of the one enacted the right end would come in time. This because most men are readily affected by the conservative influences of time, while the many not thus affected yield, more or less implicitly, to the commands of definite laws, especially if they are supported by penal sanctions. . . . It is not an easy thing to eradicate the prejudices of two centuries.

Congress could act affirmatively in the face of state inaction, because action and inaction could amount to the same thing: "non-action is a denial. Permitting things to be done in violation of a duty or obligation is a denial of both. A failure to enact laws for the equal protection of citizens is a denial of such protection. . . . The extremist oppression may result from inaction."

Wilson's efforts, of course, were to no avail. His amendment was not passed, and the *Civil Rights Cases* remained the measure of constitutional equality.

But there is one more dissenting voice worth considering; it provides perhaps the most effective rebuttal to Bradley's artificial distinctions.

As for the claim that Congress's power under the Thirteenth Amendment does not apply to racial discrimination, but extends only to the abolition of slavery, consider this 1871 judicial opinion:

Slavery, when it existed, extended its influence in every direction, depressing and disenfranchising the slave and his race in every possible way. Hence, in order to give full effect to the National will in abolishing slavery, it was necessary in some way to counteract these various disabilities and the effects flowing from them. Merely striking off the fetters of the slave, without removing the incidents and consequences of slavery, would hardly have been a boon to the colored race. Hence, also the amendment abolishing slavery was supplemented by a clause giving Congress power to enforce it by appropriate legislation. No law was necessary to abolish slavery; the amendment did that. The power to enforce the amendment by appropriate legislation must be a power to do away with the incidents and consequences of slavery, and to instate the freedmen in the full enjoyment of that civil liberty and equality which the abolition of slavery meant.

As for the contention that Congress's powers under the Fourteenth Amendment are purely remedial and cannot be exercised affirmatively in the face of state inaction, consider this view, also recorded in 1871:

> [The Fourteenth Amendment] not only prohibits the making or enforcing of laws which shall abridge the privileges or immunities of the citizen; but prohibits the states from denying to all persons within its jurisdiction the equal protection of the laws. [Denying] includes inaction as well as action. And denying the equal protection of the laws includes the omission to protect, as well as the omission to pass laws for protection.

Finally, as for the distinction between the public and private spheres, consider this speech delivered at the University of Pennsylvania Law School on October 1, 1884, one year after the decision in the *Civil Rights Cases*:

> At first view when we walk amongst our fellowmen, we may not observe the omnipotent influence and controlling effect of the law. Its power is so subtle and all-pervading that everything seems to take place as the spontaneous result of existing conditions and circumstances. . . . [But the law] is over, under, in and around, every action, that takes place. Its silent reign is seen in the order preserved, the persons and property protected, the sense of security manifested. . . . The mighty river of things generally moves on with an undisturbed current; but only because it is kept in its banks and regulated in its course by the power of law.

"[S]ociety and law are so intimately connected," the speaker concluded, "that the hypothesis of one is the hypothesis of the other." The speaker, and author of each of these passages, was Supreme Court Justice Joseph P. Bradley.[23]

But neither Harlan's protests, nor Wilson's proposals, nor Bradley's own inconsistencies could change the fundamental truth confirmed by the *Civil Rights Cases*: Reconstruction was over. As a result of the Supreme Court's decision, the *Nation* magazine opined, "the negro will disappear from the field of national politics. Henceforth the nation, as a nation, will have nothing to do with him." It would be worse than benign neglect.

Plessy v. Ferguson. From 1882 to 1901, over one hundred lynchings were reported annually. In 1892 alone, there were 230 recorded lynchings, 161 of black Americans. For black victims, lynching meant not merely a rope, but fire, torture, and dismemberment, often in a festive atmosphere, with tickets sold, and body parts of the victims distributed as souvenirs. All of it was done with official acquiescence, and sometimes official encouragement. This was America in 1896, when the Supreme Court announced its opinion on the constitutionality of segregation laws, of "separate but equal." Americans were looking for guidance from the highest court in the land; some of them, in C. Vann Woodward's phrase, were looking for "permission to hate."

They got it. In *Plessy v. Ferguson*, the Supreme Court rejected Homer Plessy's challenge to a Louisiana law requiring segregated rail facilities: Louisiana's "equal but separate" law did not violate the equal protection guarantee of the Fourteenth Amendment. Henry Billings Brown of Massachusetts wrote the opinion for the Court. He created some dichotomies of his own.[24]

A legal "distinction," such as that between black and white, was not the same as a legal "inequality":

> A statute which implies merely a legal distinction between the white and colored races—a distinction which is founded in the color of the two races, and which must always exist so long as white men are distinguished from the other race by color—has no tendency to destroy the legal equality of the two races.

There was an argument, Brown acknowledged, that the legal distinction tended to connote the inferiority of the distinguished race. But it was an argument Brown rejected:

> We consider the underlying fallacy of the plaintiff's argument to consist in the assumption that the enforced separation of the two races stamps the colored race with a badge of inferiority. If this be so, it is not by reason of anything found in the act, but solely because the colored race chooses to put that construction upon it.

Moreover, the equality that Plessy sought transcended the guarantees of the Constitution; that document ensured only a "legal equality," not a "social" one:

> The object of the amendment was undoubtedly to enforce the absolute equality of the two races before the law, but, in the nature of things, it could not have been intended to abolish distinctions based upon color,

or to enforce social, as distinguished from political, equality, or a commingling of the two races upon terms unsatisfactory to either.

And, Brown reasoned, it could be no other way—the Constitution was powerless to affect the natural order:

> The argument also assumes that social prejudices may be overcome by legislation, and that equal rights cannot be secured to the negro except by an enforced commingling of the two races. We cannot accept this proposition. If the two races are to meet upon terms of social equality, it must be the result of natural affinities, a mutual appreciation of each other's merits, and a voluntary consent of individuals. Legislation is powerless to eradicate racial instincts, or to abolish distinctions based upon physical differences, and the attempt to do so can only result in accentuating the difficulties of the present situation. If the civil and political rights of both races be equal, one cannot be inferior to the other civilly or politically. If one race be inferior to the other socially, the constitution of the United States cannot put them upon the same plane.

The only limitation on segregation laws was that they be "reasonable, and extend only to such laws as are enacted in good faith for the promotion of the public good." "In determining the question of reasonableness," Brown explained, the legislature "is at liberty to act with reference to the established usages, customs, and traditions of the people, and with a view to the promotion of their comfort, and the preservation of the public peace and good order." It is an effective measure of the myopia of the opinion that, under this standard, the Louisiana law was upheld.

Plessy v. Ferguson was, like the *Civil Rights Cases*, an eight-to-one decision; again, it was left to Justice Harlan to state equality's case. Harlan avoided, at the outset, the conundrum of formal equality—mere abstract symmetry could not hide the real inequality:

> It was said in argument that the statute of Louisiana does not discriminate against either race, but prescribes a rule applicable alike to white and colored citizens. But this argument does not meet the difficulty. Everyone knows that the statute in question had its origin in the purpose, not so much to exclude white persons from railroad cars occupied by blacks, as to exclude colored people from coaches occupied by or assigned to white persons.

The message behind the Louisiana law was unmistakable, and it was these laws and their implicit lessons—not "racial instincts"—that were the root of racial animosity:

> What can more certainly arouse race hate, what more certainly create and perpetuate a feeling of distrust between these races, than state enactments which, in fact, proceed on the ground that colored citizens are so inferior and degraded that they cannot be allowed to sit in public coaches occupied by white citizens? That, as all will admit, is the real meaning of such legislation as was enacted in Louisiana.

Harlan did not accede to Brown's myopic vision of "reasonableness": there was nothing "good" about the "order" maintained by such laws, and the "comfort" they secured was certainly not universal. In Harlan's more communal vision, there were two perspectives worth considering—black and white: "The destinies of the two races, in this country, are indissolubly linked together, and the interests of both require that the common government of all shall not permit the seeds of race hate to be planted under the sanction of law."

There was, Harlan conceded, a social order in America. But it was not a natural one, and it was not one that the Constitution could tolerate:

> The white race deems itself to be the dominant race in this country. And so it is, in prestige, in achievements, in education, in wealth, and in power. So, I doubt not, it will continue to be for all time, if it remains true to its great heritage, and holds fast to the principles of constitutional liberty. But in view of the constitution, in the eye of the law, there is in this country no superior, dominant, ruling class of citizens. There is no caste here. Our constitution is color-blind, and neither knows nor tolerates classes among citizens. In respect of civil rights, all citizens are equal before the law.

Harlan's analysis reached its climax with an assertion that was oxymoronic except as a statement of protest, as a refusal to permit constitutional aspirations to yield to the reality of inequality: "The humblest," Harlan insisted, "is the peer of the most powerful."

Harlan concluded his opinion by pointing out the lingering contradiction of American life:

We boast of the freedom enjoyed by our people above all other peoples. But it is difficult to reconcile that boast with a state of the law which, practically, puts the brand of servitude and degradation upon a large class of our fellow citizens,—our equals before the law. The thin disguise of "equal" accommodations for passengers in railroad coaches will not mislead any one, nor atone for the wrong this day done.

Plessy v. Ferguson made clear that, after civil war and reconstruction, there had been, fundamentally, no change. The natural order that slavery had converted into a racial one remained very much intact; Reconstruction's guarantee of equality under law had not changed the order because, quite simply, it could not. And the premises of that order were now firmly established. "Race" was biological. Racism was natural. The constitutional guarantee of equality was merely formal. Real inequality was inevitable. The Constitution was powerless to change the natural order. These would remain the official views till the middle of the twentieth century.

The Second Reconstruction

Living Truths

The stories of the massive grassroots civil rights movement of the mid-twentieth century and of the NAACP's concurrent legal struggles have been told masterfully elsewhere. The aim here is to briefly examine the radical revision of the official epistemology of inequality that took place in that time period, a revolution in thought inherent in the Supreme Court's decision in *Brown v. Board of Education*.[25]

Two cases presaged *Brown* and perhaps made that decision inevitable: the 1948 case of *Shelley v. Kraemer* and the 1950 case *Sweatt v. Painter*.

Shelley v. Kraemer. Racial segregation was still very much the norm in America after the Second World War. Educational segregation was somewhat more pronounced in the South, where it was mandated by law, but residential segregation was pervasive throughout the country. The NAACP targeted both: it sought a declaration that racial segregation, in schools and in housing, violated the equal protection guarantee of the Fourteenth Amendment.

The problem with residential segregation was that it appeared to be completely beyond the reach of the Fourteenth Amendment. There was some public housing in post-war America, but most housing was privately owned and most residential segregation was, accordingly, the result of private discrimination. After Justice Bradley's opinion in the 1883 *Civil Rights Cases*, such discrimination did not even implicate the Fourteenth Amendment: only through "state action"—through discrimination by public officials, not private individuals—could Americans be deprived of the "equal protection of the laws."

The discrimination in *Shelley v. Kraemer* was, under Bradley's artificial dichotomy, apparently "private": individual homeowners had agreed that they would not sell to "non-Caucasians," and had memorialized their agreements in restrictive covenants in their deeds. But the Supreme Court, in an opinion written by Chief Justice Fred Vinson, ruled that those covenants had been effectuated only through the actions of state judicial officials, and judicial enforcement of the covenants—without which the restrictions would be meaningless—was "state action" for purposes of the Fourteenth Amendment. It was, on the one hand, merely common sense: of course judges are public officers, and of course their actions are state actions. But it exposed, on the other hand, the deep conceptual problems with Bradley's public-private dichotomy: no action or decision, and certainly no agreement, is purely private, since all are shaped by and implicitly conditioned on the existence, or absence, of legal sanctions. Or, as Bradley himself had put it, the law "is over, under, in and around, every action, that takes place."

But there was another problem in *Shelley*: the state courts were not discriminating; they would enforce all restrictive covenants. The argument was in part that it was the private parties, not the courts, who harbored the racial animus. That did not matter, Vinson insisted, because "the effect" of state action was the denial of constitutional rights.

The argument was also in part the argument of symmetry that had prevailed in *Plessy v. Ferguson*: there was no legal inequality when the state merely makes a distinction, but otherwise treats all parties, black and white, the same. The state courts, the argument went, would enforce all racially restrictive covenants, separately but equally. But

Chief Justice Vinson refused to be lured into the conundrum. There was, first of all, no *real* evidence that restrictive covenants were being enforced against white home buyers. Moreover, symmetrical application would not cure the constitutional defect: "Equal protection of the laws is not achieved through indiscriminate imposition of inequalities." This last was conceptually unsatisfying and rhetorically oxymoronic: it is difficult to find discrimination in indiscriminate behavior. Still, at an intuitive level, Vinson had come closer to the truth: there was something quite unequal going on here, and the state was clearly complicit.[26]

Sweatt v. Painter. Two years later, the Court struck another blow against the formalist conception of equality. Hemann Sweatt had been denied admission to the University of Texas Law School because of his race; under the separate but equal rule, Texas offered to start a new law school for Sweatt and other black Texans. By the time the case of *Sweatt v. Painter* found its way to the Supreme Court, the new "black" school was in fact open and operating.

But it was not enough. "We cannot find," Vinson again wrote for the Court, "substantial equality in the educational opportunities afforded white and Negro law students by the State." The Court examined both "tangible and intangible factors" to reach its conclusion: resources and facilities on the one hand; reputation and "practical" opportunities on the other. It was precisely the sort of realistic inquiry foreclosed by *Plessy*'s formalism, and it was certain to expose the "thin disguise" of most separate but equal schemes.[27]

Brown v. Board of Education (Brown I). Four years later, of course, the Supreme Court found in *Brown v. Board of Education* that "separate but equal" public education was not in fact "equal" at all. The assault on formalism implicit in *Shelley* and *Sweatt* nearly demanded this result: *Shelley* had suggested that racial distinctions were, somehow, unequal, even when they were applied across the board, while *Sweatt* had demonstrated how this inequality could be manifest in both tangible and intangible ways. *Brown*, in a sense, simply filled in the blanks. And yet, for at least two reasons, the decision was remarkable all the same.

Part of it was the context. These were not restrictive covenants or law schools; these were public schools, primary and secondary, and changes here would be far-reaching. And these were not revolutionary times: Rosa Parks refused to give up her seat on a Montgomery bus to a white man in December 1955, a full year and a half after the first *Brown* decision. Whatever the state of legal thought, then, *Brown* was not, in a practical sense, merely conventional at all.

And, for that matter, it was not conventional in purely legal terms. Chief Justice Earl Warren did in *Brown* what Vinson had declined to do in *Sweatt*: he explicitly rejected the "separate but equal" rule of *Plessy*, in part by rejecting *Plessy*'s absurd suggestion that the badge of racial inferiority is self-imposed. Simultaneously, Warren did in *Brown* what Vinson had been unable to do in *Shelley*: he identified the inequality that inhered even in "indiscriminate" racial segregation. Compulsory segregation, Warren concluded, generated a stigma of racial inferiority: this was the inequality, and it inhered in the very fact of segregation, and it was why—whatever the "tangible" differences between the schools—the segregation of public school students was *inherently* unequal.

Moreover, Warren sought to prove it, and his efforts took him outside the insular realm of the law, beyond legal abstraction and vacuous form, and into the world of experience. It was common sense, in part—as for Harlan, "everyone knows" the real message of Jim Crow—but it was also evidence from the social sciences: a short footnote provided a cursory summary of the evidence establishing the connection between racial segregation and self-concept, and between self-concept and achievement. A brief full of evidence had been submitted to the Court by a coalition of social scientists; to them, Warren's footnote seemed almost perfunctory. But to conventional legal thinkers, this brief acknowledgement of other disciplines—even the suggestion that there was a social world in which equality might be measured—was revolutionary; and for many of them, it was also wrong.[28]

Brown v. Board of Education (Brown II). *Brown I* declared that segregation was unconstitutional, but it did not determine the appropriate remedy. That decision it postponed for a year, till the reprise of the case in *Brown II*. The Court there seemed to retreat: it remanded control of the cases to the local district courts and ordered desegregation to proceed "with all deliberate speed." It seemed a recipe for disaster. The local federal judges were, after all, a part of the segregated community—"steeped in the same traditions that I am" rejoiced Georgia Lieutenant Governor Ernest Vandiver—and the Court's ambiguous rhetoric hardly gave them a decisive mandate. But their performance surprised: district courts decided nineteen desegregation cases within a year of *Brown II*, and the plaintiff NAACP prevailed in every case. Typical was the decision of Louisiana district court judge J. Skelly Wright: "The magnitude of the problem may not nullify the principle. And that principle is that we are, all of us, Americans, with a right to make our way unfettered by sanctions imposed by man because of the work of God."

As for the Supreme Court, it is hard to say what happened between *Brown I* and *Brown II*. For some, *Brown II* was proof that white America was not serious about racial equality. NAACP attorney Lewis Steel wrote that "Never in the history of the Supreme Court had the implementation of a constitutional right been so delayed or the creation of it put in such vague terms. The Court thereby made clear that it was a white court which would protect the interests of white America in the maintenance of stable institutions." Years later, Professor Derrick Bell would survey the law and reach the same result: the Cold War gave white America a reason to declare segregation unconstitutional in *Brown I*, but white America had no interest in achieving real integration. *Brown II* merely demonstrates Bell's "interest convergence" thesis: the Supreme Court grants equality to black Americans only when, and to the extent that, it converges with the interests of white America.

For others, *Brown II* was more a strategic retreat. The reaction to *Brown I* was stronger, perhaps, than the Court had anticipated, and official support for the Court's position was undoubtedly much weaker. Warren waited in vain for an expression of support from the White House; Eisenhower, personally conflicted over the matter, remained resolutely silent. "If Mr. Eisenhower had come through," Associate Justice Tom Clark would later say, "it might have changed things a lot." But Eisenhower was noncommittal. The president of the newly formed Southern Christian Leadership Conference made repeated attempts to coax a statement of public support for the *Brown* decision, but always Dr. Martin Luther King's efforts were to no avail. After a fruitless meeting with Eisenhower, King reported, "I fear that future historians will have to record that when America came to its most progressive moment of creative fulfillment in the area of human relations, it was temporarily held back by a chief executive who refused to make a strong positive statement morally condemning segregation." Interestingly, Dr. King did find one friend in the administration, one official who publicly said: "There is a vital need for America to recognize that this is basically a moral problem." "If he's not sincere," King said of Vice President Nixon, "he is the most dangerous man in America."[29]

Cooper v. Aaron. Eisenhower's hand, meanwhile, had been forced to some extent by the events in Little Rock, Arkansas. The all-white Central High School was to be desegregated by nine black students at the beginning of the 1957 school year, and despite the incendiary rhetoric of state officials, the effort was expected to proceed peacefully. But on the appointed day, Governor Orval Faubus sent the Arkansas National Guard to Little Rock, ostensibly to maintain the peace, but effectively to block the admission of the students. After a two-week stalemate, and a private meeting with President Eisenhower, Faubus called off the guard. But by now, the guard was genuinely needed: an angry white mob was assembling at the school each morning; desegregation would be impossible without protection. Melba Pattilo Beals was one of the nine students; she described what happened on Monday, September 23:

> The first day I was able to enter Central High School, what I felt inside was terrible, wrenching, awful fear. On the car radio I could hear that there was a mob. I knew what a mob meant and I knew that the sounds that came from the crowd were very angry. So we entered the side of the building, very, very fast. Even as we entered there were people running after us, people tripping other people. Once we got into the school, it was very dark; it was like a deep, dark castle. And my eyesight had to adjust to the fact that there were people all around me. We were met by a local officials and very quickly dispersed our separate ways. There has never been in my life any stark terror or any fear akin to that.
>
>   I'd only been in the school a couple of hours and by that time it was apparent that the mob was just overrunning the school. Policemen were throwing down their badges and the mob was getting past the wooden sawhorses because the police would no longer fight their own in order to protect us. So we were all called into the principal's office, and there was great fear that we would not get out of this building. We

were trapped. And I thought, Okay, so I'm going to die here, in school. And I remember thinking back to what I'd been told, to understand the realities of where you are and pray. Even the adults, the school officials, were panicked, feeling like there was no protection. A couple of kids, the black kids that were with me were crying, and someone made a suggestion that if they allowed the mob to hang one kid, they could then get the rest out.

On Wednesday, September 25, a frustrated Eisenhower recognized that the costs of inaction outweighed those of acting; he sent the 101st Airborne to Little Rock to secure the safety of the nine black students. That day, Beals would later recall, "I went in not through the side doors, but up the front stairs, and there was a feeling of pride and hope that yes, this is the United States, yes, there is a reason I salute the flag, and it's going to be okay."

For the Supreme Court, however, the dispute in Little Rock was just beginning. The school board requested a two-year hiatus from the desegregation effort; the federal courts refused to grant it. The dispute went to the Supreme Court, which convened an extraordinary special session in September 1958.

What made the dispute in *Cooper v. Aaron* so remarkable was its subtext. The explicit premise of most of the resistance to *Brown* had been the contention that the case was wrongly decided and that, accordingly, state authorities were not bound by the Supreme Court decision. Implicit here was an important shift in the argument against equality.

For almost two centuries, the argument had been that the Constitution *cannot* secure equality: even the expressed guarantee of equality under law was said to be powerless to redress the inequality inherent in the natural order. But the "natural order" was on shaky grounds in 1950s America: its "science" had been discredited by the revolution in the social sciences, on the one hand, and advances in genetics and the "hard" sciences, on the other, and its politics had been rendered increasingly untenable, first, by a devastating Depression, and then, by the horrors of the Holocaust. The Supreme Court's decision in *Brown* demonstrated that the law would no longer embrace the order's central premise: racial inferiority was a product not of nature, but of state action. Races were not created unequal, they were re-created that way by discrimination.

So the argument, of necessity, was modified: it was not so much that the Constitution *cannot* secure equality, but rather, the new claim went, that the Constitution simply *does not* secure equality because of the enduring principles that inhere in it. The Constitution might in theory have contained a leveling principle, but it in fact does not: the fundamental precepts of our Constitution—states' rights, local authority, private freedom, individual liberty—reflect a very different set of choices. *Brown*, the argument went, was wrong not because it attempted to do the impossible, but because it attempted to do the forbidden: in the name of equality, it violated not the natural order, but our constitutional one. *Plessy v. Ferguson* was the law; *Brown* violated it.

But what the argument assumed was a Constitution with a fixed meaning. It assumed that the document embodied an uncontested set of principles; that those principles would yield just one answer to constitutional questions; that this one right answer could be determined; and that the answer was absolute and constant. It assumed away the compromises that produced the document, both originally and in its reconstruction; it assumed away the ambiguities—some conscious, some not—that inhere in the grand terms of the text; it assumed away the indeterminacy that attends the interpretive process, an indeterminacy that is heightened with the level of abstraction; and it assumed away the unavoidable influences of context—of individual perspective and historical setting. And it assumed, as a consequence, that yesterday's tradition would be tomorrow's norm: as the governor of Alabama would put it, "segregation today, segregation tomorrow, segregation forever."

For the Supreme Court, what was at stake was nothing less than its institutional authority: its ability—its power—to declare what the law is. On this score, the Court had to be unequivocal. In an opinion separately signed by all nine justices—the first and only such opinion in Supreme Court history—the Court emphatically declared that "the interpretation of the Fourteenth Amendment enunciated by this Court in the *Brown* case is the supreme law of the land, and Art. VI of the Constitution makes it of binding effect on the States 'any Thing in the Constitution or Laws of any State to the Contrary notwithstanding.'"

The rest followed easily, but was important all the same. The school board argued that the delay was necessitated not by its misconduct, but by private actions: private threats, private violence, private unrest, private uncertainty. But, the Court responded, those conditions were directly traceable to official actions. Eroding still further Bradley's dichotomy, the Court ruled that private behaviors brought about by public action were within the reach of the Fourteenth Amendment. The board also argued that it had acted in good faith, a not untenable claim; regardless, the Court responded, the rights of the schoolchildren to attend desegregated schools could not be frustrated by state action, "whether attempted 'ingeniously or ingenuously.'" Nothing less than compliance with the constitutional mandate would satisfy the Court: "Our constitutional ideal of equal justice under law is thus made a living truth."[30]

Loving v. Virginia. A decade later, the Court finally completed the dismantling of Jim Crow. Virginia's antimiscegenation statute prohibited interracial marriages involving its white citizens; a minor exception permitted white Virginians to marry persons with some "Indian blood," a tribute to the descendants of Pocahontas. The statute was part of a 1924 law entitled An Act to Preserve Racial Integrity, but it was clear that Virginia was interested in preserving the "integrity" of just one race.

The law was hardly an anomaly. In 1952, thirty-one states prohibited interracial marriages; fifteen years later, Virginia was one of sixteen states that still prohibited "miscegenation." These were not anachronisms: Hollywood's Motion Picture Code banned portrayals of interracial marriages until 1956, and it was not until late 1967 that Sydney Poitier interrupted Spencer Tracy's quiet evening in *Guess Who's Coming to Dinner*. The Supreme Court's decision in *Loving v. Virginia* was announced five months before the release of that film.

Chief Justice Warren again announced the decision of a unanimous Court: the Virginia law was unconstitutional. Virginia argued that the law did not implicate the type of equality guaranteed by the Fourteenth Amendment; had not its framers disavowed an attempt to protect miscegenation? There were such statements, Warren conceded, but they were inconclusive; what mattered was the "clear and central purpose" of the amendment, to eliminate "invidious racial discrimination."

Virginia also argued, of course, that the law was symmetrical: it prohibited black Virginians from marrying white ones neither more nor less than it prohibited white Virginians from marrying black ones.

True, Warren conceded, demurring to the conundrum of formal equality, but that made the law no less "invidious."

Virginia argued, finally, that its racial restriction was justified, that the Court should defer to its legislative judgment that interracial marriages were different from other marriages, inasmuch as, on this score, "the scientific evidence is substantially in doubt." But no deference, Warren responded, was due legislation like this: only a compelling interest could justify the use of invidious racial classifications, and this law, patently an attempt to promote white supremacy, served no such interest. On the "scientific evidence," Warren refrained from comment.[31]

Green v. New Kent County School Board. The following year, the Supreme Court reached the apex of the second Reconstruction. On behalf of the NAACP, Thurgood Marshall had argued before the Court in the cases of *Shelley*, *Sweatt*, *Brown*, and *Cooper*; now Marshall was *on* the Court. In the intervening years, school desegregation efforts had been hindered by a wide variety of bureaucratic schemes. The most common, by 1968, was the "freedom of choice" plan.

Under "freedom of choice" plans, students were assigned to the school they last attended, unless they chose to attend a new school. Such plans conformed to the requirements of *Brown* under the interpretation of that case announced by federal judge John Parker in 1955. "Nothing in the Constitution or in the decision of the Supreme Court takes away from the people freedom to choose the schools they intend," Parker had written. "The Constitution, in other words, does not require integration. It merely forbids discrimination." Under the so-called Parker doctrine, the state's obligations were fulfilled once it eliminated its segregative laws. If students subsequently chose not to integrate, then there was simply nothing the state could do.

In *Green v. New Kent County School Board*, the Court—again unanimously—rejected the Parker doctrine. The state was responsible for segregation, and it would be responsible as well for redressing segregation's harms. Equality was not symmetry, and neither was it neutrality: the state was charged "with the affirmative duty to take whatever steps might be necessary" to eliminate segregation "root and branch." "The burden on the school board today," Justice William Brennan wrote, "is to come forward with a plan that promises realistically to work, and promises realistically to work now."

Little was left now of the old formalism. "Race" had been reconstructed: racial inferiority and supremacy were products of the culture. Racial discrimination and segregation were neither natural nor purely private; they were both shaped and sanctioned by the state. Equality was now real; it was practical and it was measurable. Inequality was not inevitable, and neither was it tolerable. The Constitution was not powerless; it could, and it did, require that equality be made "a living truth."

Green was argued before the Supreme Court on April 3, 1968. The next day, Dr. Martin Luther King, Jr., was shot and killed in Memphis, Tennessee. Robert Kennedy fell to an assassin's bullet less than two months later. In August, the Democratic Party's nominating convention in Chicago was marred by turmoil within the convention hall and violence outside it. Richard Nixon narrowly won the White House, relying in part on a "southern strategy" that positioned him just to the left of Independent Party candidate George Wallace, the segregationist governor of Alabama. Earl Warren had submitted his resignation in the closing days of Johnson's presidency; Johnson's failure to secure Associate Justice Abe Fortas's confirmation as the next Chief Justice meant that Nixon would immediately have two vacancies to fill on the Supreme Court.[32] A second Redemption was at hand.

The Contemporary Resolve

Thurgood Marshall, a descendant of slaves, chose to celebrate not the founding document of 1787, but instead the evolving, living Constitution. As Marshall put it, "'We the People' no longer enslave, but the credit does not belong to the framers. It belongs to those who refused to acquiesce in outdated notions of 'liberty,' 'justice,' and 'equality,' and who strived to better them."

As Marshall knew, the framers left a mixed legacy, of obstacles to overcome, and of promises to fulfill. And the difficult work of reconciling that legacy was, and is, far from done. Traditions, after all, die hard, and so too the myths on which they are based. The natural order lingers in the consciousness; the powerless Constitution is just one bad choice away.

In 1972 the Supreme Court examined state school funding schemes through which wealthy districts received much more funding than poor ones. "The need is apparent for reform," Justice Lewis F. Powell wrote for the Court; the system, Justice Potter Stewart concurred, "can be fairly described as chaotic and unjust." But it was not, they agreed, unconstitutional: it did not deny the "equal protection of the law." Justice Marshall was one of four dissenters.

The following year, the Court considered the first desegregation case from the North. Even northern schools, the Court concluded, will need to desegregate, where their segregation is the result of state action. But the longstanding unanimity of the desegregation cases was broken: in a dissenting opinion, Justice William Rehnquist argued that,

> To require that a genuinely "dual" school system be disestablished, in the sense that the assignment of a child to a particular school is not made to depend on his race, is one thing. To require that school boards affirmatively undertake to achieve racial mixing in schools where such mixing is not achieved in sufficient degree by neutrally drawn boundary lines is quite obviously something else.

The next year, Rehnquist would be in the majority, when the Supreme Court ruled that desegregation orders could not ordinarily transcend school district boundary lines. Detroit's virtually all-black city schools could not be combined with the virtually all-white suburban schools, Chief Justice Warren Burger concluded, even if that was the only way to avoid one-race schools. "No single tradition in public education is more deeply rooted than local control over the operation of schools," he reasoned. As for the rights of the students: "The constitutional right of the Negro respondents residing in Detroit is to attend a unitary school system in that district." Justice Marshall, once again, was one of four dissenters:

> Desegregation is not and was never expected to be an easy task. Racial attitudes ingrained in our Nation's childhood and adolescence are not quickly thrown aside in its middle years. But just as the inconvenience of some cannot be allowed to stand in the way of the rights of others, so public opposition, no matter how strident, cannot be permitted to divert this Court from the constitutional principles at issue in this case. Today's holding, I fear, is more a reflection of a perceived public mood that we have gone far enough in enforcing the Constitution's guarantee of equal justice than it is the product of neutral principles of law. In the short run, it may seem to be the easier course to allow our great

metropolitan areas to be divided up each into two cities—one white, the other black—but it is a course, I predict, our people will ultimately regret.[33]

The Warren Court had, alas, become the Burger Court, and within a decade, the Burger Court would become the Rehnquist Court. In 1991, Chief Justice Rehnquist wrote for the Court that racially segregated schools might be relieved from the "indefinite judicial tutelage" of a desegregation decree where the segregation was the product of "private decision-making and economics." Marshall again dissented: "In a district with a history of state-sponsored school segregation, racial separation, in my view, remains inherently unequal."

It was his last official statement on desegregation. Justice Marshall left the Court at the end of the term; he was replaced by federal judge Clarence Thomas. In a 1995 opinion, Marshall's successor joined in overturning a desegregation order:

> The point of the Equal Protection Clause is not to enforce strict race-mixing, but to ensure that blacks and whites are treated equally by the State without regard to their skin color. The lower courts should not be swayed by the easy answers of social science, nor should they accept the findings, and the assumptions, of sociology and psychology at the price of constitutional principle.

That same year, Thomas expressed his reasons for opposing affirmative action: "Government," Justice Thomas proclaimed, "cannot make us equal."[34]

Just a few months before, Murray and Herrnstein had published *The Bell Curve*.

The tenets of *The Bell Curve* are neither unusual nor original; in their most fundamental sense, they can be traced at least to the founding of the American Republic. Madison professed fully two centuries ago his belief in the inherent inequality of men; it was, he proclaimed, the "first object" of government to protect those inequalities from the leveling tendencies of the masses. Hamilton concurred, and worked at every turn to protect the ruling elite from the debasing effects of egalitarianism. The political sphere was in fact the exclusive province of a distinct minority: the body politic conceived by the founding fathers comprised, in the main, only white male freeholders.

The founders explicitly embraced a hierarchy: not of royalty, not of caste, but of right, a natural hierarchy rooted in liberty and its just deserts. A nascent political science demonstrated the propriety—indeed the inevitability—of a governing elite, and in the same fashion, found refuge in natural law and science to justify social class. But the generation that proclaimed the self-evident truths of equality and universal rights could not explain the contradiction that inhered in their acquiescence to America's most severe expression of hierarchy, the institution of chattel slavery. They deferred to later generations, who found their resolution in the color of the bondsman's skin. By the mid-nineteenth century, the natural order was a racial one.

The union grounded in the paradox of liberty and slavery could not hold, and the generation charged with reconstructing the nation after its civil war struggled to resolve its fundamental contradiction. They found their resolution in the proclamation of equality under law: only unfettered could all men take their place in the natural order.

But the equality they promised was elusive, both in theory and in practice. They pledged a "legal equality," separately guaranteed a "political equality," but were forced to disavow a "social equality"; they sought the eradication of slavery and its vestiges, but had to reassure their anxious critics that the white man's dominion was secure.

The freedmen's plight, meanwhile, did not respect their neat categories and careful caveats, and the responsive legislation of the Reconstruction congresses frequently blurred the theoretical distinctions the membership struggled so mightily to maintain. In the end, the nation's second set of founders succeeded less in resolving the central paradox of American political theory than in restating it: they insisted, simultaneously, that the black man was the legal equal of the white, but that the white man was destined to predominate.

The official conventions, in short, had changed, but the underlying mythology remained the same. A nation committed now to equality remained fundamentally convinced that its people were, by nature, unequal.

If this brief historical synopsis confirms that works like *The Bell Curve* are unoriginal, it would at the same time seem to grant such works an undeniable legitimacy: this is, by most reckonings, a rather noble lineage these works are following. But it is not quite that simple. The founders of the Republic—and those who reconstructed it—bequeathed, after all, a mixed legacy.

If the framers of the Constitution acquiesced in the reality of black bondage, they also afforded guarantees both implicit and explicit for the liberty of all persons; determined that in the competition between these forces liberty would ultimately prevail, the framers deliberately withheld constitutional sanction for slavery, carefully excluding the very term from the written document. A half century later, American abolitionists would insist that this carefully crafted Constitution authorized if it did not demand the end of slavery; in the famous Dred Scott case, the Supreme Court ultimately disagreed, but there was nothing in the historical record that compelled this result, and much that recommended against it.

If the Reconstruction congresses failed to ensure the real equality—social, political, economic—of black and white Americans, they also used no language and adopted no measures that were inconsistent with that end. Within a generation, advocates for equality would in fact contend that the Fourteenth Amendment demanded more than the formal symmetry of "separate but equal," that compulsory segregation created a stigma of social inferiority, a real inequality. In the case of *Plessy v. Ferguson*, the Supreme Court disagreed, but again, there was nothing in the historical record that compelled this result, and much that recommended against it.

It would take another three generations, but the natural order would finally yield. A century after the first Reconstruction, the second would make its promises real: it was not nature, we finally learned, that made us unequal, it was we who did that to ourselves. And we resolved at long last that the culture that made us unequal would redress its harms: we could be—we must be—made equal after all.

In short, then, our political legacy includes more than a commitment to hierarchy; it includes as well a demand for hierarchy's end. The advocates of the natural order choose just one of these visions to pursue, but an alternative vision competes for our loyalty. It is a vision of a community characterized by a genuine equality, and we have, in rare moments, struggled for its realization.

It is in their pretense to science more than in their politics that Murray and Herrnstein and their various allies can make an uncontestable claim to the intellectual legacy of the two generations of founders. The framers of 1787 and the reconstructors of 1868 generally shared a belief in the integrity of biological categories as determinants of social fate: they believed in a natural order, and it was this belief above all that blinded them to the possibilities inherent in their proclamations of universal liberty and equality. The contemporary advocates of the natural order share this belief as well as its premises: for them, as for their eighteenth- and nineteenth-century predecessors, the social order is the natural one.

But there is one vital difference: the founders were constrained by the epistemology of their day; the modern "natural order" crowd ought to know better. The rest of this book aims to show why.

3

In the Nature of Things
Myths of Race and Racism

The natural order presupposes natural differences, as well as natural processes for differentiating. Accordingly, it embraces two sets of myths: first, that identity—race, gender, or disability—is biological (and thus inherent, immutable, and essential); and second, that discrimination—racism or other forms of prejudice—is innate (and thus instinctive, inevitable, and rooted in the individual). Together, they suggest that social hierarchies are biologically determined: hence, a natural order.

But these are merely myths. The salient aspects of group identity are products not of nature, but of politics: identity, that is to say, is politically constructed. "Race," for example, has very little biological integrity, but it may carry a great deal of ideological weight and social meaning. It depends entirely on the political culture: its history of "race" and its contemporary realities of "race."

Discrimination is the same. The response to the construction of identity—for example, the "racist" response to "race"—is hardly instinctive; it is instead the product of the same historical forces and cultural choices—the same politics—that shape the object of its contempt. Racism is simply a way to describe the culture's pathological ideology of "race," an ideology that simultaneously makes of "race" something it is not—something biological—and denies to "race" what it actually is—for better or worse, a meaningful social variable. Race and racism are thus barely distinct aspects of the same cultural forces: "race" is incomprehensible except as a product of racism; "racism" impossible without the construction of race.

The task confronting us is to reconstruct "race" without racism—and "gender" without sexism, and "disability" without handicaps. It is the task of reconstituting difference without hierarchy, of creating a community without a "natural" order.

Prologue

I grew up in an integrated neighborhood. Some of the kids were Irish, some were Polish, some were Italian, and one kid was Greek. There was also a kid who was part Indian (the "American" kind), and a whole bunch of kids like me who were a lot of different things, sort of integrated all by themselves. There were, on the other hand, no black kids in my neighborhood, or Asian kids or Latino kids; it was only when I looked back, many years later, that their absence seemed conspicuous to me.

We had our own gang in that neighborhood, and we were pretty serious about protecting our turf. We let kids from outside the neighborhood—kids from "across the park," as we knew them—play with us, but generally at a price. In whiffle ball, the price was literal: we charged the kids a fee. This, I should note, was not our idea, but the brainstorm of one of the guys who ran the corner store, a guy to whom we routinely went for advice (though, for some kids, just as a way to distract him while they swiped stuff, which, I think, was an idea they had in turn picked up from the guy who ran the other corner store a few blocks away).

In most of the games we played, the price we exacted was slightly less literal, but only slightly. I was reminded of this not that long ago, when I was rummaging through a box of my old toys. Mostly the box was filled with G.I. Joes, more than a dozen of them. There was no surprise in this; we played war games with the G.I. Joes all the time in my neighborhood. But three things about this collection seemed to me rather odd.

First, there were a fair number of Barbie dolls mixed in with the G.I. Joes. That was strange enough, but this was even stranger: none of the Barbies had any clothes, and many of them were headless. There is no pleasant explanation for this phenomenon, and some accounts are a good deal more disturbing than others, and while I am certain that it was the G.I. Joes who were somehow responsible for the Barbies' condition, their precise behaviors—our behaviors—remain a deeply repressed mystery (I guess, in any event, this is something I will eventually have to discuss with my wife).

Second, the G.I. Joes came in a surprising variety. There was a German G.I. Joe, who had distinctly Aryan features; and a Japanese G.I. Joe, who had distinctly Asian features; and an Australian G.I. Joe, who looked, to all accounts, just like an American G.I. Joe, except in shorts. There was also a "black" G.I. Joe, and he too was indistinguishable from the other American G.I. Joes, except that he was molded in a somewhat more deeply tinted plastic. Finally, there was a G.I Joe with circles drawn around his eyes: this I instantly recognized as my favorite G.I. Joe; I had given him glasses to look more like me. I don't know if that is particularly strange or not; I tend to think that there are a lot of kids who did that, or otherwise wished that their G.I. Joes, or their Barbies, could somehow be made to look more like them.

But it is the third oddity that is most immediately relevant to the point of this story. Some of the G.I. Joes in this box I simply did not recognize at all. It dawned on me gradually that they were in fact not mine: I remembered playing G.I. Joe war games with the kids in my neighborhood, and remembered that we sometimes let kids from outside the neighborhood play, and we always set the terms of engagement, and not surprisingly, we always won the wars. Except we never killed the other kids' G.I. Joes, we merely took them as prisoners of war, and I realized, as I rummaged through the box, that we never gave them back. As I surveyed this bounty, I recall thinking that this was not a good thing, but that it could have been worse—and then I remembered that we once took one of the actual kids as a prisoner of war, and held him hostage in my friend Dicky's basement, and even made him late for dinner, which caused the kid's mom to call one of our moms, and her to call the other moms, and most of us to get some kind of licking, which ended that version of our war games (and any aspirations we may have had to be terrorists). At least, on the other hand, we gave *him* back.

But the lickings did not dampen our enthusiasm for maintaining the integrity of our gang (and this, alas, is the point of the story). Our territorial imperative gradually spilled over into the school, where, in the second grade, we established exclusive dominion over our own table in the cafeteria. The table we staked out was right by the milk cooler in the back of the room; this was prime turf for the kids like us who could not—or would not—buy their meals through the cafeteria line at the front of the room. Each day we'd march to the back, spend our five cents for a half-pint of chocolate milk, and plop right down at our conveniently located table, with our milk and our lunch—usually a bologna sandwich with potato chips, each wrapped in wax paper, separated by our moms, but shortly to be combined by us, and all contained in a second-grader's paper bag, and most definitely not in a first-grader's lunch-box. It was our own little paradise, disturbed only briefly by the civil unrest of the spring of 1964, when runaway inflation boosted chocolate milk prices to seven cents for a half-pint, causing some kids to stage a sit-in directly in front of the milk counter, and the vice principal to call their parents, who had to leave work to come to the cafeteria to get them, which produced, I would warrant, more lickings, and an end to their civil disobedience (and any aspirations they may have had to be activists). At least the kids, on the other hand, were nonviolent.

And so too were we. We guarded our table jealously; our gang, and only our gang, was allowed to sit there, but we were altogether reasonable about the matter. Occasionally kids from outside the gang would be invited as guests, and sometimes kids from adjoining neighborhoods would, after a suitable probationary period, become honorary members of the gang, and get their own seats at the table. Strangers, however, were not otherwise allowed, and, remarkably enough, hardly any had the temerity to challenge our rule. When they did, we'd ask who their sponsor was, and if they didn't have one, we'd tell them they needed one, and they would have no idea what the hell we were talking about, and would usually just walk away. Sometimes, some kid would seem intrigued by the idea, and so he'd get a sponsor from the gang—who also, truth be told, had no idea what the hell we were talking about—and the new kid would get a shot at joining the gang. It was all very peaceful and orderly, and I don't remember there ever being any problems.

Except for one day, when a kid didn't know any better, and he found out, as I did, what it really meant to be part of a gang.

I was coming out of the milk line that day and heading toward my seat, when I saw a kid that I didn't recognize sitting at the end of our table. There was no one sitting next to him and no one across from him; he appeared to be on his own. I set down my lunch next to him and was getting ready to put him through the routine when I heard a voice from across the table.

"No, Bobby."

It was my friend Louis. I gave him a blank look.

"No, Bobby. You don't want to sit there." Louis took a drink of chocolate milk. "He's a Jew."

I continued to look blankly at Louis. Then I looked at the kid. I grabbed my lunch. And I moved.

Nobody else took that seat. Twice more, some kid from the gang started to sit there, and each time Louis explained the situation, and each time, they moved. The kid ate his lunch alone.

I don't know who had gotten to my friend Louis. I don't know who had taught him what he thought he knew, or who had taught *them*. I would have thought that his parents would have set him straight, even, I guess, if it took some kind of licking. I worry that they didn't, and I worry about what Louis is teaching his kids, or his grandkids, about who to sit next to, and who not.

The thing is, I could have set him straight. I should have known better: I was raised better. But I didn't say a word; I just moved.

Years later, my mother told me a story from her childhood. She was just a little girl, taking a walk with her dad in her neighborhood, when her mother's brothers appeared up the block, walking in their direction. Her dad gripped her hand tightly as the uncles approached; she could not imagine why. They stopped just a yard away, spit at her father's feet, and crossed to the other side. Her mother was a German Jew; she had married a man who was Italian and Irish. The family would never forgive them.

It's doubly ironic: under certain traditions, I am told, if your mother is Jewish, then so too are you. And I had moved to avoid sitting next to a Jew.

The kid did not come back to our table the next day. In fact, I never saw him again. I don't know if he found some other kids to have lunch with, or if there were more lunches that he had to eat alone. I'll suspect the worst, but imagine the best. Maybe he got into a gang; I just wish it had been ours.

Race, Racism, and Reconstruction

In April 1864, Democratic Senator James A. McDougall of California announced the reasons for his opposition to the Thirteenth Amendment. American slaves, he explained,

> can never commingle with us. It may not be within the reading of some learned Senators, and yet it belongs to demonstrated science, that

the African race and the Europeans are different, and I here now say it as a fact established by science that the eighth generation of the mixed race formed by the union of the African and European cannot continue their species. Quadroons have few children; with octoroons reproduction is impossible. It establishes as a law of nature that the African has no proper relation to the European, caucasian blood.

McDougall concluded his exposition on a conciliatory note: "I would have them kindly treated." McDougall was, in the end, one of six senators to vote against the amendment abolishing slavery; thirty-eight voted in its favor.

The differences—the *natural* differences—between the races provided the cornerstone for the opposition to every act of Reconstruction. House Democrat John L. Dawson of Pennsylvania opposed the Civil Rights Act of 1866; the bill's advocates, he explained, championed an untenable doctrine:

> They hold that the white and black race are equal. This they maintain involves and demands social equality; that negroes should be received on an equality in white families, should be admitted to the same tables at hotels, should be permitted to occupy the same seats in railroad cars and the same pews in churches; that they should be allowed to hold offices, to sit on juries, to vote . . . Their children are to attend the same schools with white children, and to sit side by side with them. Following close upon this will, of course, be marriages between the races, when, according to these philanthropic theorists, the prejudices of caste will at length have been overcome, and the negro, with the privilege of free miscegenation accorded him, will be in the enjoyment of his true status.

"We have to remember, on the other hand," Dawson observed, "that negro equality does not exist in nature."

As Dawson's comments suggest, the specter of "miscegenation" often loomed behind the objections to racial equality. Senator Garrett Davis of Kentucky was one of many Democrats to complain that the civil rights bill would authorize miscegenation or "amalgamation"; in Kentucky, Davis noted, miscegenation was and should remain a penal offense. Lyman Trumbull, chair of the Senate Judiciary Committee, found some irony in the sixty-five-year-old Davis's protests:

He also brings up the question of marriage between whites and negroes. He is troubled about amalgamation, and becomes excited and vehement in talking about it. I should have supposed that at his time of life he would feel protected against it without any law to put him in the penitentiary if he should commit it.

Andrew Johnson vetoed Trumbull's civil rights bill; his message to Congress also raised the question of miscegenation, though, the president noted, "I do not say this bill repeals State laws on the subject of marriage between the two races." This too prompted a response from Trumbull, one that, characteristically, went quite to the heart of the matter: "Then for what purpose," Trumbull asked, "is [the subject] introduced into the message?"

Opposition to the Fourteenth Amendment was also rooted in the claimed desire to preserve the "natural" distinctions between the races. Andrew J. Rogers, Democratic congressman from New Jersey, insisted that

under this amendment a negro might be allowed to marry a white woman. I will not go for an amendment of the Constitution to give a power so dangerous, so likely to degrade the white men and women of this country, which would put it in the power of fanaticism in times of excitement and civil war to allow the people of any State to mingle and mix themselves by marriage with negroes so as to run the pure white blood of the Anglo-Saxon people of this country into the black blood of the negro or the copper blood of the Indian.

As Rogers explained, it was not merely the corruption of blood that concerned him. The natural order was threatened in other ways by the Fourteenth Amendment, for "Congress would have power to compel the State to provide for white children and black children to attend the same school, upon the principle that all people in the several states shall have equal protection in all the rights of life, liberty, and property."

Congressman John A. Nicholson of Delaware also opposed the Fourteenth Amendment. He too feared that it would obliterate the legal distinctions between the races, distinctions that were in turn rooted in nature:

Now, the negro race in this country constitutes such a class which is easily and well defined . . . the radical difference between them and the white race should be recognized by legislation . . . For the negro is not actuated by the same motives as the white man, nor is he deterred from crime except by punishments adapted to the brutal, sensual nature which characterizes him.

Interestingly, when the "black race" did evidence the same motives as the "white race," Nicholson did not approve:

The negro's idea of freedom is to do nothing but bask in the sunshine. The negro woman now disdains to pick cotton, and her present ambition is to "send her daughter to boarding school, and keep a piano." And they are assisted very much in these mischievous notions by such legislation as the Freedmen's Bureau and civil rights bill.

Indiana congressman William E. Niblack reminded his colleagues that the "black race" was not the only one beneath the white man in the natural order; proclamations of equality were futile for the "Chinese race" as well:

The Chinese are nothing but a pagan race. They are an enigma to me. . . . You cannot make good citizens of them; they do not learn the language of the country. . . . They buy and sell their women like cattle, and the trade is mostly for the purpose of prostitution. That is their character. You cannot make citizens of them.

Attitudes did not much change as Reconstruction progressed; "race" itself was, after all, immutable. In 1868 Garrett Davis observed for his Senate colleagues that the freedmen "are as fixed in their ignorance and barbarism as though they were fossils under the face of the earth." The following year, Senator George Vickers of Maryland cited the fixed inferiority of the "black man" as the basis for his opposition to the Fifteenth Amendment:

[T]here are five races of man. These are the red man, the yellow man, the white man, the black man, and the brown man. . . . And because here is a distinct race, an inferior race, and because this race has color, the race is disqualified. It is not altogether on account of the color of the skin. That is only one of the indications and marks by which you distinguish the race.

Vickers's subsequent exposition of the differences between the races was just one among many in the history of the Reconstruction debates. To support his opposition to black suffrage, Garrett Davis had engaged in one of the more exhaustive exercises in amateur physical anthropology. It prompted a response from Henry Wilson of Massachusetts. "If the black man votes for the men who are just and humane," Wilson offered, "I shall not upbraid him. I do not believe the negro is to be any party's slave if you put the ballot in his hands. I want to call the attention of my Democratic friends especially to that point."

This last comment prompted laughter among Wilson's Republican colleagues. The laughter grew at the Democrats' expense as Wilson continued his defense of black suffrage and offered, in the process, one of the first political critiques of "race." If suffrage is extended, Wilson predicted,

> These negroes will then be just as sweet as anybody else. I do not think the Senator from Kentucky will be examining their pelvis or shins, or making speeches about the formation of their lips or the angle of their foreheads on the floor of the Senate. You will then see the Democracy, with the keen scent that always distinguishes that party, on the hunt after the votes of these black men; and if they treat them better than the Republicans do they will probably get their votes, and I hope they will.

On July 16, 1862, the House Select Committee on Emancipation issued its report. The committee had been charged with considering the practical obstacles to manumission; it concluded that the surest means for overcoming those obstacles was through the colonization of the emancipated slaves. The report explained,

> Much of the objection to emancipation arises from the opposition of a large portion of our people to the intermixture of the races, and from the association of white and black labor. The committee would do nothing to favor such a policy; apart from the antipathy which nature has ordained, the presence of a race among us who cannot, and ought not to, be admitted to our social and political privileges, will be a perpetual source of injury and inequitude to both. This is a question of color, and is unaffected by the relation of master and slave.
>
> It is useless, now, to enter upon any philosophical inquiry whether nature has or has not made the negro inferior to the Caucasian. The

belief is indelibly fixed upon the public mind that such inequality does exist. There are irreconcilable differences between the two races which separate them, as with a wall of fire. There is no instance afforded us in history where liberated slaves, even of the same race, have lived in any considerable period in harmony with their former masters when denied equality with them in social and political privileges. But the Anglo-American never will give his consent that the negro, no matter how free, shall be elevated to such equality. It matters not how wealthy, how intelligent, or how morally meritorious the negro may become, so long as he remains among us the recollection of the former relation of master and slave will be perpetuated by the changeless color of the Ethiop's skin, and that color will alike be perpetuated by the degrading tradition of his former bondage. Without this equality of political and social privileges, and without the hope of a home and government of their own, the emancipation of the slaves of the south will be but adding a new burden to their wretchedness. . . . To appreciate and understand this difficulty, it is only necessary for one to observe that, in proportion as the legal barriers established by slavery have been removed by emancipation, the prejudice of caste becomes stronger, and public opinion more intolerant to the negro race.

The report found many sympathetic ears. That same year, Democratic senator Joseph A. Wright of Indiana opposed emancipation in the District of Columbia for similar reasons: there *would* be no equality, because there *could* be no equality:

We tell you that the black population shall not mingle with the white population in our States. . . . We intend that our children shall be raised where their equals are, and not in a population partly white and partly black; that they shall see those around them who are on an equality, and we know that equality never can exist between the two races.

It was a bipartisan view. Republican Orville Browning of Illinois explained that the black race could never live as the equal of the white:

It is not legal and political equality and emancipation alone that can do much for the elevation of the character of these people. We may confer upon them all the legal and political rights we ourselves enjoy, they will still be in our midst a debased and degraded race, incapable of making progress, because they want that best element and best incentive to progress—social equality—which they never can have here. There are repugnances between the two races that forbid, and will forever forbid, their admission to social equality; and without social equality they never can attain to a full development of their mental and moral natures, or lift themselves to any tolerable degree of respectable social *status*.

For Browning, the futility of the egalitarian project made it worth reconsidering the wisdom of emancipation. "Mr. President," Browning continued,

> I may be mistaken in my view of this subject, but I do not believe that the races can ever live together in harmony and with mutual advantage to each other; and, hostile as every feeling and sentiment of my nature is to a system of human bondage, I am by no means sure, while the races do continue together, that it is not better for them both to continue together in the relation of master and slave. . . . There are many negroes whose intellectual and moral worth far transcends that of the white men around them, and yet they do not take a position in society that is accorded unhesitatingly to the white man who is in no respect their equal. It is because, I apprehend, of the repugnance of the races that the Almighty has implanted in our bosoms, and the strong instinct which we cannot eradicate.

Senator Waitman T. Willey, Republican of West Virginia, concurred:

> The negro, whatever we may say about the natural rights of that race, must be in this country forever an inferior race. He can never be socially equal, and, after all, that is the distinguishing characteristic of equality. He is under the ban of social inferiority in this country. Never can he rise to the dignity of a freeman or to the enjoyment of all the rights of a freeman. The two races cannot live together and prosper.

But not everyone was convinced. Senator John P. Hale of New Hampshire insisted:

> We are working out to-day some of the greatest problems that have ever been wrought in the world, and this rebellion is not the greatest. It is the ultimate result that is to grow out of the juxtaposition, in some respects antagonistic, and in some respects social and friendly, of these two races here together; and I tell you, sir, that here together they have got to work out this destiny.

Hale's view ultimately prevailed. The slaves of the nation's capital were emancipated, and by 1863, with Lincoln's Emancipation Proclamation, so too were the slaves of the Confederacy. Throughout 1862, Lincoln had suggested that emancipation must be tied to a scheme of compensation and colonization. But Lincoln's great proclamation was silent on the matter, and the colonization scheme gradually died. The two races, as Hale put it, would have to work out their problems "here together."

Some persisted in the belief that it was impossible. They would state their claims throughout the Reconstruction era and beyond: the races were, by nature, unequal, and so peace between them was, naturally, impossible. Racial oppression, in short, was as much a part of nature's plan as the color of a man's skin.

For some, the natural hostility of the races provided the best rationale for opposing black suffrage. In 1866 Democratic congressman Benjamin Boyer of Pennsylvania explained,

> It is argued that suffrage is necessary to the black man to enable him to protect himself against the oppression of the whites. . . . I am satisfied that in those localities where such prejudice is allowed to corrupt the streams of justice you would only add force and acrimony to its operation by establishing a political rivalship between the races. The true friends of the negro race should save them from the fate which would be sure to follow.

Green C. Smith of Kentucky opposed the civil rights bill on the same basis:

> [B]y such attempts you but irritate and excite the two races, the one against the other. . . . the effort to bestow the right of suffrage upon negroes throughout the country is not calculated to promote their advancement or secure their best interests. In my own state, I have never met more than two or three of these people who ever asked to be endowed with the right of suffrage. I received the other day a letter from a negro who in 1862 was my property; and in that letter he urges me to resist this effort because of the prejudice prevailing in this country against his race. I go further, and reiterate the sentiment . . . that I am utterly and entirely opposed to this doctrine of negro suffrage. I believe that God almighty never intended the white people and the black, two distinct and antagonistic races, should be copartners in the

management of civil government. . . . It is useless for man to attempt to accomplish what nature has determined shall not exist.

Boyer's Pennsylvania colleague, Democrat John L. Dawson, concurred: "It is impossible that the two races should exist harmoniously in the same country, on the same footing of equality by the law." And so, Dawson explained,

> We have, then, to insist upon it that this Government was made for the white race. It is our mission to maintain it. Negro suffrage and equality are incompatible with that mission. We must make our own laws and shape our own destiny. Negro suffrage will . . . result inevitably in amalgamation and deterioration of our race. The proud spirit of our people will revolt at such certain degradation, while American women, the models of beauty and superiority, will indignantly execrate the men who advise and dictate the policy.

The logic was echoed in the Senate. Garrett Davis explained his opposition to the civil rights bill as follows:

> The passage of such a bill as this is designed to produce interference between, and disturbance of, the relations of the black laborer and his white employer, to get up feuds and quarrels and contentions between them by interested and sinister persons, to alienate the white employer from the black laborer, and consequently by such vexations, to induce the employer to resort to the white instead of the black laborer to cultivate his fields, and perform his other work. If the bill is passed, it will promote feud and enmity between the white employer and the black laborer.

Andrew Johnson took up the cause in his veto messages. The bill providing for black suffrage in the District of Columbia, he insisted, "would engender a feeling of opposition and hatred between the two races, which, becoming deep-rooted and ineradicable, would prevent them from living together in a state of mutual friendliness." So too the Civil Rights Act of 1866, which "intervenes between capital and labor," and threatens "to foment discord between the two races."

The override of both vetoes hardly ended the debate. In 1866 Republican senator Edgar Cowan of Pennsylvania insisted that the proposed Fourteenth Amendment erred in conferring citizenship upon the inferior races. Citizenship, Cowan explained, depends upon the inherent character of the men. Why, sir, there are nations of people with whom theft is a virtue and falsehood a merit. There are people to whom polygamy is as natural as monogamy is with us. It is utterly impossible that these people can meet together and enjoy the several rights and privileges which they suppose to be natural in the same society; and it is necessary, a part of the nature of things, that society shall be more or less exclusive. It is utterly and totally impossible to mingle all the various families of men, from the lowest form of the Hottentot up to the highest Caucasian, in the same society.

Three years later, Senator James A. Bayard of Delaware would make the same argument in opposition to the Fifteenth Amendment: there was no natural equality, and the attempt to force it could only aggravate natural animosities. "[E]quality of political power," Bayard concluded, "can only end in the conflict of races."

As always, there was another side. Congressman Glenni W. Scofield of Pennsylvania rejected the contention that black equality necessarily came at the expense of the white race. There was no racial competition, he suggested; it was not a zero-sum game: "The ignorant white people have been made to believe that the elevation of the negro is equivalent to their debasement. The reverse is true. The more we improve this unfortunate race, the higher we raise our own."

As Scofield suggested, Republicans were of the view that the hostility between the races was anything but natural; it was, on the contrary, a political invention. "Attempted prejudice against the black man," insisted Congressman George F. Miller of Pennsylvania, "is gotten up by demagogue politicians." Fernando C. Beaman of Michigan elaborated:

> These expressions—"elevation of the negro," "negro equality," "negro supremacy," "amalgamation," &c.—are mere catchwords employed to excite the prejudices of the inconsiderate and the ignorant. They were not in use in the early days of the Republic, when it was believed that slavery was a temporary institution; on the contrary, negroes were then allowed to vote. But they were brought into vogue at a later period by slaveholders.

Senator Waitman Willey of West Virginia mocked the complaints of the Democrats:

"Will you place the white man under the domination and government of the negro?" That is the cry. Why, sir; it is a senseless clamor. There is no propriety in it. It is an appeal to the passions of the unthinking multitude. It ought not to be addressed to an intelligent man. That is not the purpose of it. It is the clamor of the demagogue and nothing else,

If the problem of prejudice was in fact a political one, then so too necessarily was the solution. "One thing is certain," Senator William M. Stewart of Nevada observed, "that the negro must have the ballot or have no friends; and being poor and friendless, and surrounded as he is by his enemies, his fate is extermination. But give him the ballot, and he will have plenty of white friends, for the people of the United States love votes and office more than they hate negroes." Congressman James M. Ashley of Ohio agreed: "The prejudice of caste is strong, but the ballot will soon banish its baneful spirit."

Charles Sumner put the lie to the notion of the "white man's government." "By what title do you exclude a race?" he asked. "The Constitution gives no such title; you can only find it in yourselves." And there, too, were the roots of racial prejudice: "The fountain is pure; it is only out of yourselves that the waters of bitterness proceed."

In February 1871, Sumner's thesis received the support of Mississippi senator Hiram Rhoades Revels. "Let lawmakers cease to make the difference," insisted the nation's first black senator, "let school trustees and school boards cease to make the difference, and the people will soon forget it."

Different Races

What race are you? The question has been terribly important throughout America's history. Are you white? Are you black? Yellow, red, or brown? The answer has determined your legal status throughout much of that history, your social and probable economic status through nearly all of it.

That, in the grander scheme, is unusual. Because "what race are you?" has generally been, in the history of human civilization, not only a meaningless question but an incomprehensible one. Until quite recently, the notion of "race," as we understand it, simply did not exist; the specific notion that individuals were of some biologically determinable "race" is no more than two centuries old. The suggestion that "race" should be inexorably tied to legal or social status is still more novel: even in the United States, where "race" found, perhaps, its fullest legal and social expression, it took fully two centuries to fix the practical meaning of "race," and many of its ambiguities were never completely resolved.

That is why the question "what race are you?" somewhat misses the mark; the real question is "what 'race' are you considered to be, by the culture in which you live?" In most cultures, at most times, the answer would be, "I am considered to be of the 'human race.'"

Similarly, the question "are you white?" needs to be translated as "does your culture consider you 'white'?" at which point it begs the only questions that really matter: "What does it mean to be 'white'? Or 'black'? Or 'yellow,' 'red,' or 'brown'? *in your culture?*"

Because, in the abstract, there is no such thing as a "white" person or a "black" person, or a "yellow," "red," or "brown" person; in the abstract, there is no such thing as "race." All these terms derive their meaning from the political culture that creates and perpetuates their use; that culture determines—yesterday and today—what it means to be "white," what it means to be of a "race."

"Race," in short, is a product of our political imagination. And it is precisely because "race" is political that it has been, and continues to be, so terribly important, not, again, in the abstract, but only in the political culture that created it.

It was a "race"-ist culture that created the meaning of "race": that seized upon random human attributes, generated categories from them, ranked those categories on a hierarchical scale, and defended the whole sorry enterprise as "science." It is a "race"-ist culture still that embraces this outmoded conception of "race," as something biological, inherent, innate, and immutable, and simultaneously refuses to acknowledge the real meanings of "race"—the lived and living history of "race," its social, economic, and political consequences.

It is "race"-ism, then, that compels the denial of its own paradox: there is no such thing as "race," but "race" matters all the same. And it is "race"-ism that denies this truth: there is nothing natural about any of it.

*

The Concept of Race

That "race" and "racism" are natural creations seems to be a given, a statement of universal truth. The arguments on behalf of the natural order, in fact, rest on these twin biological presumptions. They presume, first, that differences—like "racial" differences—must be biological. Racial inferiority and superiority, then, are fixed in the biology of the racial group (and, of course, the individual within it): racial inferiority and superiority are thus inherent, innate, and immutable.

The arguments presume, second, that the processes of constructing hierarchies based on these differences—like the processes of "race"-ism—are somehow natural as well. Racial discrimination is thus due either to a natural repugnance—racial animosity—or to an innate sense of hierarchy; either way, the racial order is instinctive and inevitable.

Even arguments against the natural order sometimes accept its basic premises. Race is still presumed to be natural; racial differences, then, are at least to some extent biological; and racial inferiority and superiority therefore may be to some extent natural, though opponents of the order ardently hope that these rankings reflect more the influences of environment. Racial discrimination, meanwhile, is presumed to be an individual reaction—a psycho-pathological response either to biological difference or to social caste; it too, however, is ardently hoped to be chiefly the product of the environment, that is, conditioned.

What all of these views share is an emphasis on the biological individual. Race is a fact that defines the biological individual; reactions to "race" are the reactions *of* the biological individual. The operative concepts are thus fixed in the individual, who becomes both a natural cause and effect: "race" makes individuals and individuals make "racism." And if these are natural, if these are biological, if they are part of our individual constitution, then presumably, "race" and "racism" have always been with us.

But the history of humanity surprises. Racism, it evolves, is a recent phenomenon, and so too, for that matter, is the concept of race. As far back as 1920, W. E. B. Du Bois had canvased the history and concluded that "[t]he discovery of personal whiteness among the world's peoples is a very modern thing." Subsequent scholarship has confirmed his assessment. As Bernard Crick puts it in the foreword to Ivan Hannaford's recent study of "race," "racial conditioning is not part of the human condition."

It certainly was not a part of early human civilizations. Frank Snowden's study of the ancient Egyptians, Greek, and Romans concludes that,

> the ancient world did not make color the focus of irrational sentiments or the basis for uncritical evaluation. The ancients did accept the institution of slavery as a fact of life; they made ethnocentric judgments of other societies; they had narcissistic canons of physical beauty; the Egyptians distinguished between themselves, "the people," and outsiders; and the Greeks called foreign cultures barbarian. Yet nothing comparable to the virulent color prejudice of modern times existed in the ancient world. This is the view of most scholars who have examined the evidence and who have come to conclusions such as these: the ancients did not fall into the error of biological racism; black skin color was not a sign of inferiority; Greeks and Romans did not establish color as an obstacle to integration in society; and ancient society was one that "for all its faults and failures never made color the basis for judging a man."

Jan Nederveen Pieterse's iconographic study of the period concurs in Snowden's judgment: "The oldest representations of black Africans, dating from 2500 B.C., show them well integrated into society and intermarrying. They demonstrate also that black beauty is appreciated." "Generally," Pieterse concludes, "the world of antiquity . . . was a mixed culture, and one in which difference in skin color did not play a significant role, or rather, in which black carried a positive meaning."[1]

Snowden's study concludes that this benign attitude extended at least to sixth-century Christians:

> During the first six centuries of Christianity, blacks were summoned to salvation and were welcomed in the Christian brotherhood on the same terms as other converts. Philip's baptism of the Ethiopian was a landmark in the evangelization of the world. Origen and his exegetical disciples made it clear that all men, regardless of the color of their skin, were called to the faith, and in their interpretations they employed a deeply spiritualized black-white imagery. . . . In sum, in the early church blacks found equality in both theory and practice.

And in Western Christendom, the attitude seems to have endured well beyond. Western European Christians enslaved the pagan Slavs in the Middle Ages, and later conquered the territories of Islamic peoples, capturing the black African slaves of Muslim masters. But there is no evidence, throughout this process, of a distinctively racial animus. On the contrary, Christian Ethiopianism and the cult of the King of the Moors represent parts of a hazy awareness of black Christians south of Islamic North Africa—peoples, it was hoped, who would join the holy crusade against Islam. It was thus largely a positive image of black Africa that predominates the twelfth through fifteenth centuries, one typified by Rogier van der Weyden's 1460 rendition of the *Adoration of the Magi*, which includes, significantly, a black "wise man."

Pieterse's study suggests that the Western conception of black Africa gradually changed during the sixteenth and seventeenth centuries. Positive images persisted: in Christian Ethiopianism; in respectful diplomatic relations; in the paintings of Rubens, Rembrandt, and Van Dyck; and in the literature of the era. As late as 1688, Olfert Dapper's study of Africa was filled with praise and admiration for African courts and cities. But the period of European expansion and conquest also brought new images of Africans: condescending, denigrating images of a beastly and savage people. Africans, of course, had not suddenly devolved: it was the Western attitude that was "progressing."

After the Enlightenment, the attitude became more ideological. Ivan Hannaford's study suggests that the period from 1684 to 1815 marks the first significant stage in the evolution of the modern concept of "race": the empiricist preoccupation with classification; the emerging concept of a "natural law"; and the concurrent rise of the idea of a *volk* or culture combined to make possible the idea of discrete "races" of people. Throughout the eighteenth century, the idea of "race" remained tentative, ambiguous, and highly idiosyncratic. Montesquiou, for example, used the term to identify the stages in the development of a nation's law. But the modernist emphasis on progress gradually secured this vital point of agreement: there were "races," and some were more advanced than others. Increasingly, non-European worlds became the counterpoints to modernization; "race" became a part of the demarcation. And ultimately, "race" achieved the highest status in post-Enlightenment ideology: it became "science."

The science of race developed in Western Europe roughly between 1790 and 1840. Physical anthropologists purported to identify naturally discrete classes of people; biologists then debated their origins and natural compatibilities; cultural anthropologists matched the peoples to distinct civilizations. Of course, these were not merely "racial differences" that were being discovered; the science of race, rather, was defining "superior" and "inferior" "races." At its climax, in 1840, anatomist Robert Knox declared, "That race is everything, is simply a fact, the most remarkable, the most comprehensive which philosophy has ever announced. Race is everything: literature, science, art—in a word, civilization depends upon it."

Just fifteen years later, in France, Joseph Arthur Comte de Gobineau would fully explicate the superiority and purity of the "Aryan" race. Within a few generations, some of Gobineau's German adherents would pursue his thesis to its "logical" conclusion.[2]

The victories of nineteenth-century abolitionism were a temporary obstacle to the science of "race"; twentieth-century nationalism, on the other hand, was a major boon. In the United States, the physical anthropology of "race" was largely dormant during Reconstruction and its immediate aftermath, but revived by the early twentieth century. Xenophobia, eugenics, and America's peculiar racism were part of the backdrop for Ales Hrdlicka's 1921 lecture at American University, which included this unequivocal assertion: "There is no question that there are today already retarded peoples, retarded races, and that there are advanced and more advanced races, and that the differences between them tend rather to increase than to decrease." Harvard's Ernest Hooton was among the more prominent scholars to carry this intellectual legacy into the 1930s. By the time they were done, taxonomists would have divided us into as many as 37 different races, some, of course, more "advanced" than others.

But the horrors of the European Holocaust made the idea of "advanced races" unpalatable, and the emerging science of genetics made it untenable. English biologist Julian Huxley and American zoologist Herbert Jennings were among those who opposed the eugenics movement; they focused on a new genetic approach to race that sought, in Hannaford's words, "to distinguish the rational boundaries of science from the lunatic." In 1936, as the Law for the Protection of German Blood and German Honour was taking effect, Huxley and A. C. Haddon published *We Europeans*. Their text used genetics to demonstrate the fallacies of hereditarianism, and to debunk the concept of a biological race. "The term race," they concluded, "as applied to human groups, should be dropped from the vocabulary of science."[3]

An Interlogue on the Construction of Identity

I know people who are mentally retarded. They have been tested for it, and are now called that. I also know people who seem emotionally retarded, but nobody has tested them for it or called them that. I know people who seem socially retarded, and economically, and politically, and so on, and they've never been tested either, or called the name.

I also know people who seem mentally retarded at some times, and about some things. I'm one of them. I cannot, for example, write down a set of numbers without transposing a few; I almost never get a phone number right. But I am not called mentally retarded.

I used to think that the difference here was that mental retardation was something that you had, like a disease or an infirmity, and that the tests for mental retardation were somehow medical ones. I assumed that the reason nobody considered me mentally retarded was that, quite simply, I did not have that disorder. The other kinds of retardation—emotional, social, and so on—were just things that you said about someone, subjective judgments about their behavior, not diagnoses of real conditions.

Then I learned that, at least with "mental retardation," there was no difference between what you are and what people say about you: you are what you are called.

I knew some parents whose baby was taken from them by the state; the reason was that they were mentally retarded. They had not done anything wrong; they were just mentally retarded, which meant, everyone assumed, that they could not care for their baby.

But in fact, they could care for their baby. When, after months of delay, they were finally given tests of "home skills" and "parenting aptitudes," they did all right. They knew most of the things they needed to know; what they didn't know, they showed they could learn. It became clear to nearly everyone that they would try hard, because they cared so very much. They loved their baby boy; their tears, not the tests, proved that.

It all caused some of us to wonder whether the parents had been misdiagnosed. We asked how everyone knew that the parents were mentally retarded, and were surprised to learn that there had been just two tests: a psychologist's evaluation of their "adaptive behavior" and a standardized test of intelligence, an "IQ" test. Based on these, and these alone, the officers of the state had determined that the parents were, in the words of the petition against them, "suffering from mental retardation."

They were basically right. That's all there is to mental retardation—it's basically how you do on an IQ test. Do lousy enough, and you get called the name; whatever you might have been the day before the test, the day after, you *are* mentally retarded.

Mental retardation, like emotional, and social, and all the other forms of retardation, is not something you have, it's just something you are called. It's not a disease or a disorder, it's just a name. But unlike those other names, it's one that matters—because we have chosen to make it matter. We do, in fact, make people "suffer from" mental retardation.

The prevailing scientific construct of mental retardation for much of the late nineteenth and early twentieth centuries was in fact a medical model, a construct that placed the locus of mental disability within the biological constitution of the disabled individual. The role of science, under such a conception, was to cure or eliminate mental retardation, and the concomitant role of the state was to limit the social costs of the disability. It is this medical model that still characterizes our common misconception of mental retardation as a disease or disorder.

A more critical conception of mental retardation shifts the locus of disability from the biological makeup of the individual to the society that limits her opportunities. This social—or "cultural" or "political"—construction of mental retardation recognizes that individuals may appear to possess certain mental limitations for a wide variety of reasons, not many of which are "natural," but it is society that uses those limitations to disable her. The role of science, under this conception, is to understand the interplay between the individual's perceived limitations and the societal responses they evoke, and the proper role of the state is to limit or eliminate the disabling societal restrictions that confront the disabled person.

As this new understanding makes clear, mental retardation is highly contextual. In the decision whether any given individual is mentally retarded—indeed, when the general parameters are set for the class—the perspective and motivations of the inquisitor are critical. Individuals may move in and out of the class of mental retardation, depending on both practical contingencies (e.g., the availability of resources to meet perceived needs) and prevailing philosophies. Indeed, one of the more remarkable social achievements of twentieth-century America came in 1973, when vast numbers of people with mental retardation were instantaneously "cured" of their disability by a change in the definition of the class.

Today, the most widely accepted standard defines mental retardation as "significantly subaverage general intellectual functioning existing concurrently with deficits in adaptive behavior and manifested during the developmental period." Mental retardation is thus essentially a norm-referenced statistical creation; it reflects neither a diagnosis of an inherent condition nor an absolute judgment about "intelligence." It merely reflects the opinions, first, the labeled individual demonstrates lesser aptitudes and abilities than the norm on some standardized measure of those particular aptitudes and abilities, and second, that there is something to be gained by application of the label.

In an absolute sense, then, there is no such thing as a mentally retarded person: only culture—in setting the norms, in creating the measures, and in applying the labels—can make someone mentally retarded. The decision to label someone "mentally retarded" thus represents a series of social choices, choices laden with political values and shaped by historical contingencies. Some of these choices inhere in the conception and measurement of intelligence (the focus of chapters 5 and 6 of this book); others inhere in the very decision to separately label those people who fail to convince us of their intelligence. The label we assign them could be designed to help: to bring educational opportunities, vocational opportunities, and life choices that should come automatically to all people, but do not. But in a society that values attributes that, by definition, mentally retarded persons will not exhibit—a society that values rationality, independence, and maximized economic utility more than it values compassion, communality, and equality—the mentally retarded label tends ultimately to diminish the person who receives it. To be mentally retarded is to be inferior.

The label, sadly, makes that inferiority increasingly "real." Through the complex interactions between the society and the labeled person, the "mentally retarded" person appears "retarded" and, increasingly, tailors her behavior to accommodate the expectations of her social environment. The opportunities afforded her in that environment become increasingly limited, and so too her achievements, and on and on it goes, in a relentless, self-perpetuating cycle. And it all started with an IQ test.

Mental retardation, in the end, is not so much a product of creation, as it is a product of human re-creation. People are created as just plain people; we make them "mentally retarded" just because they need to be labeled that way for one political reason or another.

And it is politics, and politics alone, that causes people to "suffer from" mental retardation.

The same applies to other forms of "disability." The World Health Organization makes this plain with its operative definitions: it defines "impairment" as "an abnormality or loss of any physiological or anatomical structure or function"; "disability" as "the consequences of an impairment"; and "handicap" as "the social disadvantage that results from an impairment or disability." Impairments, then, may be products of creation, but they are not "disabilities" until we experience them as such, and even then, it is a socio-political decision to "handicap" people due to their impairments.[4]

I am color-blind. It is an impairment. It is not a disability, except on the mornings that I am forced to dress myself. Even then, however, it is not a handicap, except to the extent that I need to appeal to a fashion-conscious crowd (which is, thankfully, never). It would be a handicap, however, if I was a clothes salesman, or a house painter, or an interior decorator, and so on—at least it would be if my customers lived in a color-coordinated society and were bent on upholding its conventions. But it is ultimately the cultural context that is important: only it can handicap me because of who I am.

Gender is also constructed. Of course, people are created as biological males and females, but that has very little significance except in a cultural context. There is, to illustrate, an ongoing and highly visible debate about gender differences in the human brain: are the differences really important, and are the differences really, well, *real*?

The first question has assumed a certain ability to identify and quantify the differences, and has led commentators to insist that gender similarities outweigh the differences, or vice versa. But such assertions are meaningful only in a very narrow sense, as statements of some kind of physiometric fact. Even then, they assume, first, a closed set of agreed-upon criteria, that, for example, there are 120 brain characteristics; second, an agreed method of assigning weight to each variable, that, for example, each variable is of equal physiological significance; third, agreement on what constitutes "sameness" and "difference" for each variable, that, for example, variables are essentially the same if they are within a range of variation of, say, ± 20 percent; and fourth, agreement as to the findings for all measured variables, that, for example, the evidence conclusively establishes that there is sameness on one hundred of the characteristics, and difference on the remaining twenty.

This is a tall order—probably both conceptually and empirically impossible. Even if we satisfied every condition, I think we haven't come close to answering the question whether the differences are really important. Because the simple fact is that the brains could be identical in *119* of 120 characteristics, but that *120th* characteristic might just control the functions that are most critically important to the most culturally significant traits. If that is the case, if, for example, the only difference is in the discrete part of the brain that controls, say, "the ability to empathize with other human beings," and if empathy was absolutely the most culturally significant trait, then the differences, slight as they are in number, would be really quite significant. Conversely, if the differences affected functions that had little or no cultural significance—to make a point, let's say that same "ability to empathize with other human beings"—then their number would not much matter: they *were* unimportant, because we had chosen to *make* them unimportant.

That is why I think the discussion of the second question—whether the differences are "real"—is often circular. The standard responses to the question are either "yes, of course, they are real, and we can measure them objectively," or "no, they are not real, they are merely: (a) measurement artifacts; or (b) reflections of cultural forces." But these answers all assume that there is a *real* gendered individual who lives outside culture, and that the differences are "real" only if they are located in this independent individual, and not "real" if they are located in the culture.

But the individual lives in culture, and the differences are measured by and through culture: there is thus nothing "real" outside culture, and nothing un-"real" about culture's creations. Even the biological differences may be shaped by culture; after all, the human brain itself has evolved in and through culture.

And culture, of course, shapes more than physiology: it shapes the behaviors of the individual, and the perceptions of other individuals, and it is in their intersections, their cultural interactions, that "gender" really comes to be. Part of the process involves a valuation of "gendered" traits, and it is here that the social fact of gender becomes necessarily a political one. In the end, it is not biology, but politics that is, as Martha Minow so wonderfully put it, "making all the difference."

We, as a culture, have determined which differences count, and how they count, and in this important way, we, as a culture, have made gender. Gender differences, whatever their "origins," have no "real" significance until we seize upon their real-world manifestations, attribute to them some significance, and reorder our culture in ways that either exaggerate or diminish the significance of the attribution and treat it as something good or something bad.

I had a friend who was a truck driver, and we got to talking one day—for reasons that have long since escaped me—about the relative absence of women from his profession. The ostensible reason, we concluded, was that women were generally too small: their legs were too short to reach the pedals. We briefly debated the truth of this observation, and stumbled on a more important discovery: the cabs did not have to be designed such that shorter people could not function in them. We reveled briefly in our revolutionary insight before my friend observed, half-jokingly, that women were still unlikely to enter the profession, because, after all, they would not want to use the truck stops. We were left, I think, with an interesting project: trying to imagine a "feminized" truck stop.

But it is not easy to imagine a truck stop—it is not easy to imagine a world—designed equally by and for women.[5]

Disability and gender are pretty much the same. We are created with some meaningless variations; over time, we re-create these variations as meaningful. The differences that constitute disability and gender are therefore not natural: they are cultural, social, and ultimately political. We make disability and gender. The same is true of race. Only more so.

The Construction of Race

The notion that "race" is at least partly the product of social forces is almost as old as the concept itself. Early expressions of the notion tended to focus on the role of society in shaping the "racial" being. Benjamin Franklin's 1755 essay on population observed that "almost every slave" is "by nature a thief"; the evolution in his thinking is apparent in his 1769 revision of the text, which contended that "almost every slave" is "from the nature of slavery a thief." Similarly, abolitionists—and later the postbellum egalitarians—stressed the role of slavery and discrimination in suppressing the abilities of black Americans: if the black race was inferior, the argument went, it was because it had been made that way.

One aspect of the bias that inhered in the "natural order" was exposed by the romantic racialism and Ethiopianism of the mid- to late nineteenth century. Edward Blyden, for example, insisted that the soulful Africans were spiritually superior to their soulless European counterparts, the latter preoccupied with material progress. In exalting the attributes of black Africans and Americans, Blyden and others essentially inverted the racial hierarchy. But they left substantially undisturbed the prevailing conception of "race": it remained something natural.

The turn of the century brought a more radical critique, this time of the concept of "race" itself. The science had never been all that definitive. Johann Friedrich Blumenbach is often considered the founder of physical anthropology; his 1795 text introduced the term "caucasian" and substantially accelerated the process of scientizing "race." But Blumenbach asserted the unity of mankind; insisted that the racial categories he created were overlapping; observed that the defining characteristics were substantially mutable; maintained that individual Africans "differ from other Africans as much as Europeans differ from Europeans, or even more so"; and denied that physical differences could be interpreted as inferiority or superiority.

A century of racial "science" tended to obscure Blumenbach's initial insights, but "race," in the end, was too weak a concept to do what science demanded. In 1904 Oswald Garrison Villard summarized for American readers the work of German ethnologists; "race," he concluded, "is merely a pseudo-scientific or political catchword." The great bulk of racial science was, in Villard's words, "ethnological claptrap"; it was "humbug pure and simple."[6]

Perhaps no one did more to expose American readers to the deficiencies of "race" than anthropologist Franz Boas. In *Anthropology and Modern Life*, Boas began his critique by noting that "There is little clarity in regard to the term 'race.'" That was, as Boas explained, because "race" was widely misunderstood.

The process of categorizing, Boas noted, was a normal cognitive phenomenon; but it was important to remember that the categories, or "types," were only products of the human mind. "The 'type' is formed quite subjectively on the basis of our everyday experience," he wrote. And it did not always comport with the reality: "We are easily misled by general impressions," he cautioned, and "[w]e must also remember that the 'type' is more or less an abstraction."

This was true of the "types" that were called "races"; that "race" had a certain subjective resonance did not mean that it was a biological truth: "The vague impression of 'types,' abstracted from our everyday experience, does not prove that these are biologically distinct races, and the inferences that various populations are composed of individuals belonging to various races is subjectively intelligible, objectively unproved."

In fact, most biological qualities could not be assigned to discrete racial types: "The multitude of genealogical lines, the diversity of individual and family types contained in each race is so great that no race can be considered as a unit." "[F]rom a purely biological point of view," Boas concluded, "the concept of race unity breaks down."

"Race" resonated, Boas contended, precisely because we had been socially conditioned to think, and act, in terms of "race": "The formation of the racial groups in our midst must be understood on a social basis. In a community comprising two distinct types which are socially clearly separated, the social grouping is reënforced by the outer appearance of the individuals and each is at once and automatically assigned to his own group." It was a process facilitated by America's historical experience: the pretenses of "race" had helped produce socially distinct classes, and those social distinctions were easily attributed to "race." The process was not universal: "In other communities . . . where the social and racial groupings do not coincide, the result is different." But it was the American experience, and it made "race" a social reality, "not only in everyday relations but also in legislation."[7]

Boas's critique was carrying the day even before the outbreak of the Second World War. In the 1920s, Robert E. Park led the Chicago school of sociology in articulating a distinctively social understanding of race. In 1936, political scientist Ralph J. Bunche observed in *A World View of Race* that "Race is the great American shibboleth." The following year, Jacques Barzun published *Race: A Study in Superstition*: "Race theories shift their ground, alter their jargon, and mix their claims," Barzun wrote, "but they cannot obliterate the initial vice of desiring to explain much by little." A year after that, the English translation of Magnus Hirschfeld's *Racism* offered American readers an extensive critique of Nazi race theory; Hirschfeld's work also popularized the term that comprised its title.

The postwar generation completed the critique. Anthropologist Ashley Montagu was at the forefront; in 1959 he wrote that

> For two centuries anthropologists have been directing attention towards the task of establishing criteria by whose means races of man may be defined. All have taken for granted the one thing which required to be proven, namely that the concept of race corresponded with a reality which could actually be measured and verified and descriptively set out so that it could be seen to be a fact.

Montagu was among those who thought the "race" project had compromised the scientific method: "The process of averaging the characters of a given group, knocking the individuals together, giving them a good stirring, and then serving the resulting omelet as a 'race' is essentially the anthropological process of race making. It may be good cooking, but it is not science, since it serves to confuse rather than clarify."[8]

More recent work has tended to confirm the critique. The concept of "race" has, in truth, little integrity as a biological phenomenon. In most communities, any attempt to identify discrete "races" will be instantly confounded by the obvious conflation of the "racial" gene pools. In the United States, the ancestry of the current "black" population is generally estimated to be between 20 and 30 percent "white"; between 75 and 90 percent of the "black" population has some "white" ancestry. Meanwhile, the ancestry of the current "white" population is estimated to be between 1 and 5 percent "black."

But even these numbers assume the existence of demarcations of "white" and "black" that have—or at some point had—some biological integrity. But in truth, whatever else may be said for "race," it does not, as a biological matter, seem to amount to much.

R. C. Lewontin, Steven Rose, and Leon J. Kamin have examined the case for or against a genetically significant "race." There are, they report, about 150 different genetically coded proteins that have been identified and examined; 75 percent of these are monomorphic, that is, they are identical in all individuals. Just 25 percent, then, are polymorphic, that is, they vary among individuals. Fully 85 percent of the variation among these polymorphic genes occurs between individuals within local populations, groupings typically identified as "tribes" or "nations," leading the authors to conclude that "[t]he remarkable feature of human evolution and history has been the very small degree of divergence between geographical populations as compared with the genetic variation among individuals." Only 8 percent of the genetic variation is between the "tribes" or "nationalities" that collectively constitute the conventionally described "races." The smallest proportion of variation—just 7 percent (of, remember, the polymorphic genes, which are in turn just 25 percent of the overall pool)—is between groups that have conventionally been considered "races." Significantly, no polymorphic gene perfectly discriminates among the traditionally classified racial groups.

The pragmatic case for racial classifications is not much stronger. Stephen Jay Gould follows nearly a century's worth of anthropological tradition when he suggests that racial classifications have no discernable scientific value. As a general proposition, he notes, subspecies "are categories of convenience only and need never be designated." Typically, subspecies "represent a taxonomist's personal decision about the best way to report geographic variations." With modern quantitative methods permitting the numerical description of geographical variation, Gould observes, "we need no longer to construct names to describe differences that are, by definition, fleeting and changeable. Therefore, the practice of naming subspecies has largely fallen into disfavor, and few taxonomists use the category any more."

Nor are the categories justified for the human species: "[w]e are not well enough divided into distinct geographic groups, and the naming of human subspecies makes little sense." Gould identifies, in fact, three distinct problems with the notion of human subspecies: the discordance of characteristics within subspecies (e.g., variation in skin color, blood group, and so on); the fluidity and gradations of the designations; and the persistent evidence of convergence—the independent evolution of similar characters—among the designated groups (e.g., of skin color among indigenous tropical peoples). "Human variation exists," Gould concludes; "the formal designation of races is passé."

This evidence does not prove, of course, that "race" is insignificant. What it does prove is that "race" is a weak biological phenomenon and does not much matter in nature—hardly a surprise, at this stage in human evolution. It remains possible, of course, that the very slight proportion of human variation that seems attributable to "race" is nonetheless significant, and equally possible that otherwise obsolete racial classifications are still necessary to preserve distinctions that quantitative methods cannot fully express. But it is important here to note that the significance of "race" and the necessity for "race" are not then mandated by nature. If "racial" differences matter, it is because they are made to matter—not by nature, but by human beings.[9]

So it is perhaps appropriate that among the sciences, only psychology seems not to have completely broken the peculiar hold of "race." But even here, it may just be a matter of time. In a recent essay in *American Psychologist*, psychologists Albert H. Yee, Halford H. Fairchild, Frederic Weizmann, and Gail E. Wyatt called on their colleagues to follow the lead of other disciplines and to re-assess the utility of the "race" construct. They noted that there was "much to question in the definitions and applications of race by several of its exponents and their allies." It was psychologists, they observed, who were arguing for the "natural" intellectual differences between "races," but the "natural" sciences were not cooperating. Surveying the evidence, they concluded that "[n]ot only do the pertinent scholarly groups and experts . . . indicate no consensual support for the genetic deficit hypothesis, their comments are highly critical toward the spurious use of and tolerance for the term *race* in psychology."[10]

A Political History of Race in America: Part 1

The meaning of "race" has not been constant throughout American history: its "scientific" meaning has evolved—or devolved—and so too has its social meaning. Moreover, "race" has meant different things for different groups. That, above all, is the real story of "race": the various ways it has included and excluded people from the mainstream of American life.

One way to tell this story—by no means the only or "right" way—is as the story of the "white race" in America. It is, of course, far too long a story to tell in just a few pages. But perhaps even an absurdly truncated edition of the story may suffice to capture some sense of the history of "whiteness," some of the ways whiteness has been created and re-created over the span of four American centuries.

"White," of course, has been the norm through virtually all of this period: even the conventional way of describing the earlier history as "pre-Columbian" serves to emphasize the point. But the "white"- "nonwhite" dichotomy that characterizes modern American race-ism has not always been with us. This is largely because "white" only gradually emerged as the distinctive feature of America's chosen people: "white"-ness has been, at various times, far less important than nationality or the ownership of property. "White"-ness, in fact, has been of little assistance to those who, at different junctures, were not propertied, were not English, were not Protestant, were not from Northern Europe, or were not both willing and able to assimilate into the cultural mainstream.

Not all "white" people were equal in the colonial era. In the early 1700s, roughly half the English and Scottish immigrants to the American colonies came in some form of indentured servitude. Being a freeholder was no guarantee of equality either. The so-called Scotch-Irish were hardly welcomed among the English colonists; Cotton Mather lamented that they were one of "the formidable attempts of Satan and his Sons to Unsettle us." For the most part, the group retreated to the backcountry to weather the storm of English hostility.

Gradually, the colonial bondsmen became exclusively non-European and, eventually, almost exclusively African. By the antebellum era, then, there were no white slaves. But the nineteenth century saw a new form of economic oppression, and it was felt principally by northern white labor. In the South, the "low, menial" work was done by slaves; in the North, the comparable work of an increasingly industrial economy was done principally by workers of European descent. Like their enslaved counterparts, and unlike the fabled yeoman of both southern and Yankee lore, these workers were generally divorced from the land and from the ownership of productive property. For many of them, "free labor" was often experienced and denounced as "wage slavery."

In 1850 the number of wage earners exceeded the number of slaves for the first time; a decade later, on the eve of war, wage earners finally outnumbered the self-employed. Gradually, the prevailing ethos changed: wage labor—once degraded as unfit for free men, occasionally degraded as unfit for "white" men—became respectable, first as a means to acquiring productive property, later as a virtue in its own right, the counterpoint to slavery. In the end, Eric Foner notes, the positive free labor ideology was defined in part by boundaries of exclusion: it was the right and province of those who were not, in Lincoln's words, of a "dependent nature"—men, not women; and "white" men, not Indian servants, Mexican American peons, Chinese coolies, or black slaves.[11]

But the racial demarcations and, specifically, the black-white dichotomy were still far from absolute. At one end of the political spectrum, the degradation suffered by some Europeans throughout the nineteenth century had all the hallmarks of the emerging "race"-ism. Nativism flourished in the Know-Nothing movement, which briefly dominated mid-century politics, and in the Progressive movement, which ascended at the end of the century. The Irish continued to suffer some of the worst of it. In England, the 1840s brought both massive Irish immigration due to famine and mounting resistance to British domination; the English, in response, gradually recast the "wilde Irish" in biological terms. By the mid-nineteenth century, Victorian depictions of the Irish were starkly simian. The prejudice found receptive audiences across the Atlantic, where comparisons between black and Irish Americans were common. *Harper's Weekly*, "A Journal of Civilization," took to lampooning both groups simultaneously, and with equal hostility.

At the other end of the spectrum, a biracial politics also intermittently flourished: in, for example, the midcentury cooperation between some abolitionists and labor advocates, and in the populist movements of the end of the century. In 1892, Thomas E. Watson of the People's Party campaigned for an end to the racial divide:

The white tenant lives adjoining the colored tenant. Their houses are almost equally destitute of comforts. Their living is confined to bare necessities. They are equally burdened with heavy taxes. They pay the same high rent for gullied and impoverished land. . . .

Now the People's Party says to these two men, "You are kept apart that you may be separately fleeced of your earnings. You are made to hate each other because upon that hatred is rested the keystone of the arch of financial despotism which enslaves you both. You are deceived and blinded that you may not see how this race antagonism perpetuates a monetary system which beggars both."

"[L]et all this be fully realized," Watson concluded, "and the race question in the South will have settled itself through the evolution of a political movement in which both blacks and whites recognize their surest way out of wretchedness into comfort and independence." Sadly, Watson's personal history provides something of a study in microcosm of this and too many other populist movements: Watson was elected to Congress in 1890, was defeated in 1892, and defeated again as the party's vice presidential candidate in 1896. He concluded his political life as a racial segregationist.[12]

By the end of the century "new immigrants" to America, principally from Italy, Russia, Poland, and Greece, for the first time outnumbered the "old immigrants" from Britain, Ireland, Germany, and Scandinavia. The former confronted a resurgent nativism supported by the anti-Catholic, anti-immigrant, "social control" elements of political progressivism, as well as by a pseudoscientific racism. Immigrants accounted for 20 percent of American workers as the new century dawned, but 60 percent of the workers in heavy industry. Conditions there were often appalling: the nation's industrial accident rate was among the highest in the world. Employers' hiring practices, meanwhile, played on traditional ethnic divisions to help stem union growth. As a consequence, wages barely justified the risks: in 1900 an American steel-worker worked twelve-hour days, six days a week, for the sum of $450 a year; a garment worker labored the same hours for $260 a year. That same year, Andrew Carnegie enjoyed a tax-free profit of $23 million. In 1900 the wealthiest Americans—less than 2 percent of the American population—owned 60 percent of the country's wealth; the poorest Americans—65 percent of the population—owned just 5 percent.

The steady influx of immigrant labor and the massive black migration during the World War I labor shortage significantly changed the composition of both the work-force and the urban neighborhood. Race and ethnicity evolved into the principal bases for social stratification. There was some economic mobility for lower class whites, but their social standing was increasingly fixed by their ancestry.[13]

Post-war xenophobia and a eugenic fixation with the measured intelligence of racial and ethnic groups both reflected and exacerbated an almost hysterical reaction to the demographic changes in America. Madison Grant's *Passing of the Great Race* helped revive the fascination with "race" as a determinant of social fate, but Grant's racial divisions—including "Nordics," "Alpines," "Mediterraneans," and "Jews"—confirmed that this was not just a question of black and white.

As immigrants clustered into ethnic ghettos, nativists warned of the "balkanization" of the country. Henry Pratt Fairchild entitled his 1926 anti-immigrant tome *The Melting Pot Mistake*. "Why should we take the pains," Fairchild asked, "deliberately to reach out after the friendship of those to whom we are not attracted?" The inability of immigrants to satisfactorily assimilate threatened the "American nationality"; "there has already developed in the United States a distinct Polish-American society, which is," Fairchild insisted, "neither truly Polish nor truly American."

Eugenicists correlated ethnicity with intelligence, ignoring the obvious cultural explanations for their measured disparities. The Dillingham Commission on Immigration correlated ethnicity with high crime, disease, and other social indices; they were remarkably oblivious to the effects of economic status. It all culminated in the Immigration Restriction Act of 1924; "America," declared President Calvin Coolidge, "must be kept American."

The "melting pot" was a failure in some eyes, and unfair in some others; among the latter, Horace Kallen's "orchestra of mankind" provided an attractive alternative metaphor. But in truth, assimilation was the only viable option for American immigrants. And it exacted a cost. According to Roger Sanjek, "In fact, the masses of European immigrants over the nineteenth and twentieth centuries had paid the price of linguistic extinction and cultural loss for the privilege of white racial status. The outcome of Anglo-conformity for non-British European immigrants has been an opportunity to share 'race' with whites with whom we do not share 'class.'"

As Sanjek suggests, assimilation was not readily available to all. Throughout the period of twentieth-century assimilation, "black" Americans were the increasingly conspicuous counterpoint, "white" America's dichotomous referent. Thus the New Deal could indeed be that, but principally for white Americans. Among the old traditions it continued was that of racial discrimination: the Fair Housing Administration, to cite one example, simply converted segregative practices into public policy.

And so while "Irish-American" and "Italian-American" and "Polish-American" were gradually transformed into honorifics, "African-American" remained something of an oxymoron. Federal law and policy continued to play their role. Before the Second World War, restrictive covenants typically forbade home sales to Jews and Catholics as well as to black Americans. But as Karen Brodkin Sacks notes, the war "led to a more inclusive version of whiteness." Part of the change was undoubtedly ideological, the inevitable effects of a war against Aryan supremacy. But part of it was simply economics; for "Euro-ethnics," Sacks notes, "economic prosperity played a very powerful role in the whitening process." After the war, restrictive covenants were limited almost exclusively to black Americans and neither the F.H.A. nor the Veterans' Administration would guarantee loans in "redlined" neighborhoods. As a consequence, black Americans could not obtain either homes or home financing in neighborhoods now open to Americans of ethnic European descent. "Such programs," writes Sacks, "reinforced white/nonwhite racial distinctions even as intrawhite racialization was falling out of fashion."[14]

It has taken, in sum, fully four centuries for "white" folks to define their own "whiteness," and for all we know, the process is still far from complete. Only time and politics will tell.

And that is only part of the story of "race" in America; it barely addresses the story of minority races, including the story of the "black race."

A Political History of Race in America: Part 2

The history of the minority experience has been richly told in other texts, and cannot be done justice in a few pages here. But for reasons that may soon be clear, the story—at least part of it—demands retelling.

This section will principally examine the story—that is, the construction—of the "black race." This is in part because, historically, the assertion of a natural racial order has generally meant the superiority of the white race to the black, and in part because contemporary expressions of that attitude also highlight the alleged intellectual inferiority of the black race. The history made for and by the other non-white "races" is certainly distinct from the black experience, and yet it is also—almost by definition—similar. But that, alas, is for another book.[15]

Origins

The American experience with "race" reflects all the ambiguities and evolutions that characterize the term. To begin with, as M. Annette Jaimes notes, "[p]rior to the European conquest, there is no evidence that indigenous peoples of the Americas had in their societies any concept of 'race' to make differentiations within the human species." The American vision of "race" thus appears to be the distinctively European vision.

Precisely what vision they brought and how they manifested it has been the subject of considerable historical debate. Here, briefly, is what historians have had to say on the roots of American "race" and its relationship to American racism.

The consensus among historians through the early twentieth century—and perhaps still in the popular mind today—is that Africans arrived in the Americas fully enslaved and fully debased because of their "race." By midcentury, however, the historical consensus had collapsed, and two quite opposed views had emerged. On the one hand, there were those who continued to believe that racism and slavery defined the African from the outset: Wesley Frank Craven's *Southern Colonies in the Seventeenth Century* (1949) and Carl Degler's *Slavery and the Genesis of American Race Prejudice* (1959) were among the leading expositions of this view. On the other hand, there were those who saw evidence that the Africans' status was not at all fixed in the early years: W. E. B. Du Bois wrote in *Dusk of Dawn* (1940) that "the income-bearing value of race-prejudice was the cause and not the result of theories of race inferiority"; Eric Williams's *Capitalism and Slavery* (1944) similarly contended that "slavery was not born of racism; rather racism was the consequence of slavery"; while Oscar

Handlin and Mary Handlin maintained, in an influential 1950 article in the *William and Mary Quarterly*, that African servitude was initially like European servitude, and only later evolved into racial slavery.

Winthrop D. Jordan's *White over Black: American Attitudes toward the Negro, 1550-1812* (1968) launched a new generation of the debate. Jordan's central thesis was that the colonists carried an unconscious English prejudice toward "black Africa," but he maintained ambiguously that "slavery and 'prejudice' may have been equally cause and effect." Edmund S. Morgan's study of colonial Virginia concluded that slavery there "had no necessary connection with race"; he suggested that race prejudice was cultivated as slavery evolved. George M. Fredrickson detected an inchoate prejudice toward outsiders among the early colonists, but maintained that it was not until the late seventeenth century that race formed the basis of a distinct prejudice, and that racism was not made explicit until the antebellum era. Alden T. Vaughn's examination of the early Virginia censuses uncovered suggestions—in the relative anonymity accorded black Virginians—that "race" mattered quite early. Warren M. Billings, on the other hand, discerned religious bases for the differentiation, noting the early reluctance to enslave Christians, regardless of their color. *Slaves without Masters*, Ira Berlin's 1974 study of free blacks, suggested an uneven evolution of racial law and ideology through the late eighteenth and nineteenth centuries, and Judge A. Leon Higginbotham's 1978 study of colonial slave law, *In the Matter of Color*, suggested much the same about the earlier slave and race codes. T. H. Breen and Stephen Innes's *Myne Owne Ground* (1980) revealed evidence of a genuinely multiracial society in the years before Bacon's Rebellion, and concluded that "not until the end of the seventeenth century was there an inexorable hardening of racial lines." Peter Kolchin's comparative study of American slavery and Russian serfdom, *Unfree Labor* (1987), maintained that "fluid class alliances" dominated seventeenth-century America, and that in the early decades of the colonies, the "rigid dichotomy of later years between black and white, slave and servant, did not yet exist."

Finally, Barbara Jeanne Fields's essay, "Slavery, Race, and Ideology in the United States," in a 1990 issue of the *New Left Review*, contended that Americans possessed no coherent racial ideology until the revolutionary era. Vaughn, her colleague at Columbia, contends that Fields misreads the evidence, that in fact racial ideology, if not racial rhetoric, preceded independence by over a century. Vaughn maintains that

> white Virginians made permanent bondsmen of imported Africans and their descendants because it was economically advantageous to the slaveowners; because Africans were usually powerless to prevent enslavement or to discourage additional importations; and because the planters, and probably most of their white neighbors, believed that Africans were an inherently inferior branch of humankind, suited by their God-given characteristics and the circumstances of their arrival in America to be slaves forever.

In the end, the last half century of historical scholarship seems to have generated more substantial agreement than these debates might suggest. The study of American race and racism and their relationship to American slavery has yielded something of a consensus on the following six vital points.[16]

First, the early bondsmen were not only Africans, but included Europeans and Native Americans as well. In 1641 Massachusetts became the first colony to authorize slavery by legislative enactment: their statute embraced European, African, and Indian bondsmen. For many decades, Virginia maintained a fairly complex hierarchy of servitude, including tenants, servants, apprentices, and "slaves," but these tended to blur in practice and were not, in any event, rigidly divided along racial lines: Virginia, like the other colonies, impressed people of each "race." Early attitudes toward African bondsmen, meanwhile, were not always—and perhaps not generally—markedly distinct from attitudes toward European servants or, for that matter, toward the poor of every "race."[17]

Second, Africans did not become the bondsmen of choice until late in the seventeenth century, and the development seems substantially unrelated to "racial" ideology. The black population in the colonies rose sharply in the 1680s, and the locus of the slave supply shifted from the Caribbean to Africa at the same time. Dissatisfaction with both Indian and European bondsmen undoubtedly played some role, and it is probably no coincidence that the shift to African labor occurred at about the same time as Bacon's Rebellion. Still, as late as 1708, a South Carolina census revealed that of 5,500 slaves, 1,400 (or more than one-fourth) were Indians. Within a generation, however,

Britain would secure complete dominion over the slave trade, ensuring a regular supply of comparatively cheap African labor.[18]

Third, the legal status of Africans and African Americans was ambiguous until the last quarter of the seventeenth century, and perhaps beyond. This was due in part to the hazy distinctions between most forms of servitude, and due in part to the fact that many black colonists were, to one degree or another, "free." In Virginia, to take one example, there were many black freemen in 1650, perhaps more than 25 percent of the black population in some counties. In colonial New York, to take another example, the "half-freedom" status, under which indentured colonists remained "free" if they paid annual dues or performed designated labor, makes such calculations meaningless.[19]

Fourth, the racial laws and rhetoric were not constant throughout the colonies or, after independence, throughout the states. The North-South distinction is well known, though in truth only Rhode Island did not unequivocally sanction slavery by legislation or judicial decree. Still there were significant regional differences. The Dutch in New York treated their slaves more mildly than did most other colonists, and the "half-freedom" status endured there until the mid-seventeenth century, when the English took control of the colony. Colonial Pennsylvania, meanwhile, did not sanction some of slavery's more brutalizing aspects: there was, notably, no special justification for killing slaves, and they were not formally considered property. And, of course, the most significant regional differences emerged after the Revolution, when the northern states proceeded to abolish the institution.

There were also significant regional differences *within* the South. In the upper South, Republican ideology and the surplus of slaves produced hostility to the slave trade and ambivalence toward the domestic institution. Until the immediate antebellum era, slavery was generally viewed as a necessary evil. As late as 1823, Congressman Charles F. Mercer of Virginia would denounce the slave trade as "the scourge of Africa, the disgrace and affliction of both Europe and America." *Swallow Barn*, John Pendleton Kennedy's 1832 account of the fictitious slave owner Frank Meriwether, captures much of the ambivalence of its region and its day:

[A]ll organized slavery is inevitably but a temporary phase of human condition. Interest, necessity and instinct, all work to give progression to the relations of mankind, and finally to elevate each tribe or race to its maximum of refinement and power. We have no reason to suppose that the negro will be an exception to this law.

The fictional Meriwether notes that the slave is presently "parasitical in his nature" and "dependent" upon his white master. Still, he concedes, "[t]his helplessness may be the due and natural impression which two centuries of slavery have stamped upon the tribe." "What the negro is finally capable of, in the way of civilization, I am not philosopher enough to determine."

Much less ambivalence tempered racial thinking in the lower South. Part of it may have been due to the timing: the first slave did not appear in South Carolina until 1670, and slaves were not present there in large numbers until rice became a profitable staple at the very end of the century. Slave owners in the Deep South, as a consequence, may have been spared the distraction created by slavery's—and "race's"—most ambiguous period. Part of it may have been demographics: South Carolina was the only colony where blacks outnumbered whites, a circumstance likely to have at least some impression on the white master's mindset. Finally, part of it may have been economics: the cotton and rice plantations of the lower South created an incessant demand for black labor, inducing a vigorous defense of both slavery and the slave trade. The South Carolina and Georgia delegations to the Constitutional Convention, for example, defended the slave trade with an intensity that easily matched the fervor that other delegates—including Virginia's—marshaled against it.[20]

Fifth, there was apparently a considerable evolution of racial thinking. The details remain controverted, but it probably does not strain the historical consensus to suggest that "race" in America evolved in four stages.

1. *Color-Consciousness: 1619-c. 1662.* The early European colonists were undoubtedly aware of the color of the African's skin, and it assumed at some level a certain importance as a defining characteristic. "Negro" emerged as a term used by the Spanish and Portuguese to describe West Africans in nonpejorative ways, and "black" served the same purpose for English-speaking colonists. There is some evidence

that at least some English colonists viewed the Africans uneasily, and perhaps with prejudice. But the fluidity of the servile and free classes, the integration of free blacks into the social and political communities, and the as-yet impoverished conception of "race" all suggest that whatever "race"-ism may have characterized the early colonies was vague, incomplete, and far from universal.[21]

2. The Formalization of Race: c. 1662-c. 1776. The restrictions of servitude hardened in the late seventeenth century, culminating in the adoption of the first major slave codes in 1680-82. Servitude became both perpetual and inheritable, typically transferred from the mother. Race emerged in this time period as a determinant of legal status: the law gradually embraced the presumption that the "negro" was a slave and the "white" person was free. This, perhaps, was no more than a reflection of economic convenience—an apparently heritable marker certainly facilitated the notion of a hereditary slavery—and of the evolving demographic reality. It may have also reflected a very conscious effort to divide the rebel class: Edmund Morgan observes, for example, that the Virginia Assembly of the late seventeenth century "deliberately did what it could to foster the contempt of whites for blacks and Indians." Interestingly, there was no concerted effort to define either "negro" or "white" in this time frame: only the Virginia legislature made the effort, as it struggled to give meaning to the term "mulatto."

At the same time, restrictions on "free" blacks surface in this period; Georgia, for example, placed statutory limitations on the occupations open to "negroes." But as Ira Berlin notes, "Though the direction of white thought was clear, the pattern of colonial black law revealed the ambiguous, incomplete nature of their thinking." The "black codes" were laced with inconsistencies: while they often treated free blacks roughly, they left large areas of legal equality, suggesting, as Berlin notes, "a flexibility in white attitudes which would later disappear."[22]

3. The Explication of Race: c. 1776-c. 1835. There were three ways to resolve the contradiction between the ideology of the revolutionary generation and the fact of chattel slavery. One way was to cure it through the abolition of slavery; this indeed was the response of those states where slavery was not an economic imperative. A second way was to demur: concede the philosophical inconsistency, but tolerate the contradiction on practical grounds; this was the initial response, at least, in the upper South, where slavery was assumed to be but a passing phase. A third way was to modify the ideology to incorporate what was by then a racial slavery, to carve out, in effect, a racial exception to the rules of liberty and equality. This, of course, would be the response wherever slavery needed more than an embarrassed defense—and that would be, eventually, throughout the American South.

"Race," in this sense, was born with the new nation. The Columbia colleagues Fields and Vaughn appear to find common ground on this score. The former has written: "American racial ideology is as original an invention of the Founders as is the United States itself. Those holding liberty to be inalienable and holding African-Americans as slaves were bound to end by holding race to be a self-evident truth." The latter notes that: "Not until the era of the American Revolution did a substantial body of literature emerge in defense of slavery and in derogation of the Negro 'race'—i.e., a racist literature . . . it marked a new stage in the ideology's development, as did, in the antebellum era, the emergence of 'scientific' explanations of 'racial' differences."

As Vaughn suggests, this early ideology of "race" was not rooted in science. At times, during this period, defenders of slavery do assert that the racial condition is "natural," in keeping with either "natural law" or the design of the creator. George McDuffie, governor of South Carolina in 1835, maintained, for example, that "[t]he African Negro is destined by Providence to occupy this condition of servile dependence." John Calhoun would make his reputation as slavery's great defender on similarly styled assertions. But this was not yet biological.

Just as often, moreover, the defense of slavery, or other discriminations against black Americans, would continue to find refuge in purely pragmatic rationales. When North Carolina and Tennessee disenfranchised free blacks in 1834-35, it was without any "race"-ist justification at all; free blacks were simply too great a political threat. A review of the *Congressional Record* over three randomly selected years from this period, 1821-24, also illustrates the point. Slavery is frequently the topic of discussion, but entirely missing are the gratuitous denigrations of the "African race" that would soon characterize the discourse. The incapacities of the "race" arise only in the context of debates on the tariff; the slave South, it is argued, cannot compete with northern manufacturers, due principally to the disabilities of slave labor. And even this racial disability is not "natural"; it is simply that "[t]he circumstance of its degradation unfits it for the manufacturing arts."[23]

4. *The Scientization of Race: c. 1835-?* The nascent "science" of "race" found a receptive audience in the antebellum South, where a besieged practice was in desperate need of some ideological foundations. "Science," of course, furnished the very best kind of post-Enlightenment foundations: "truths" that were not merely "self-evident," but "proved." Samuel Morton's *Crania Americana*, an 1839 exercise in racial craniometry, helped launch a tradition that would persist through emancipation, two Reconstructions, and beyond. Throughout, whenever "race" has been really needed, some "science" has been at hand to provide it.[24]

Sixth, the final point of historical consensus: the commitments to the divisions of "race" were never universal. Edmund Morgan notes the persistence in colonial Virginia of black-white, slave-servant alliances—personal, social, and occasionally, in the form of rebellions, political. Peter Kolchin concurs, noting that these early rebellions were class-based, not racial. Even after the fluid continuum of servitude evolved into the slave-freeman dichotomy, the presence of free blacks frustrated division along purely racial lines. As Ira Berlin notes, "[u]nder the pressure of common conditions, poor blacks and whites became one." In urban areas, an "easy intimacy" joined free blacks and whites; interracial fraternization extended to all aspects of working-class life and even into the upper classes. "Against these ties," Berlin writes, "Southern leaders arrayed an ideology and a social system which asserted the supremacy of all whites over all blacks." Only with great persistence, much ingenuity, and the control of the legal apparatus was the white master class able to confine egalitarian relations to the margins of society and ensure that their reign—what they misleadingly called "white supremacy"—would remain secure.[25]

Slavery: 1619-1863

It is important to know where the idea of a "black race" came from, but that is, of course, just a small part of the story. It is at least as important to know what was done with the idea, what history was made for—and within constraints, *by*—the "black race" in America.

The account offered here is pathetically short of comprehensive. It intentionally omits the more well-known features of "black" history, and inevitably—and sometimes unintentionally—omits significant portions of the less well-known features. It is, in sum, a decidedly partial account, but one that is, hopefully, instructive all the same.

The account begins with slavery, and with some statistics that may defy comprehension. The best estimates today are that nearly twelve million African slaves were shipped across the ocean during the Atlantic slave trade; roughly ten million survived the journey. The larger figure likely represents just half of those who were impressed in Africa: another twelve million died during their capture or transport to slave ships. Of those who made the voyage, roughly two-thirds were male; throughout the seventeenth and eighteenth centuries, the overwhelming majority were adults. During the nineteenth century, however, the demographics somewhat changed: in the end, over 41 percent of the newly impressed slaves were children under the age of fifteen.

The first African servants—again, they may have been "slaves," but both the record and terminology are ambiguous—arrived in Virginia in 1619. Georgia, chartered in 1732, was the last American colony, and the last to receive slaves. By a law of 1735, Georgia prohibited the importation and use of slaves; its de facto governor, James Oglethorpe, declared slavery "against the Gospel, as well as the fundamental law of England." But the prohibition was likely designed merely to further the objectives of the colony as a haven for poor whites and a military buffer for southern colonies. The law was largely ignored, and in any event it was repealed in 1750.

According to the 1790 census, there were seven hundred thousand slaves, of a total national population of roughly four million; by 1830, despite the end of the slave trade, the number of slaves had escalated to two million; by 1860 it was nearly four million. In the immediate antebellum era, roughly one-fourth of all southern whites owned slaves; in the Deep South—Mississippi and South Carolina—fully half the whites were slaveholders.[26]

Leon Litwack reports that the "education acquired by each slave was remarkably uniform, consisting largely of lessons in survival and accommodation—the uses of humility, the virtues of ignorance, the arts of evasion, the subtleties of verbal intonation, the techniques by which feelings and emotions were marked, and the occasions that demanded the flattering of white egos and the placating of white fears." Most slaves were illiterate, but almost all neighborhoods had some literate slaves, unknown to their masters.

The widespread assumption among slaveholders was of the slave's "contentment, docility, or indifference," an assumption not much challenged by the abolitionist imagery of the black supplicant. The assumptions generated what Peter Parish has identified as one of slavery's internal paradoxes: black acquiescence was demanded by white slaveholders, but then offered as a sign of black inferiority. Compounding the paradox, slave resistance was equally a sign of inferiority, confirming the impossibility of civilizing the "race."

And there was much resistance. Its more subtle forms included work slowdowns and stoppages; less subtle was the "theft" of consumable goods and the destruction of personal property, often through arson. More obvious still were outright rebellions. This last both provoked a genuine fear among the master class and provided a compelling rationale for "white" unity; accordingly, the fear of insurrection—and later of abolition—was deliberately propagated throughout the white population. Of somewhat less concern was an equally radical form of resistance: there is no way to ascertain the exact number, but it is clear that from the beginning, substantial numbers of slaves committed suicide.

Runaways presented their own peculiar problems for slaveholders, some of which were patently ideological. Henry Bibb was a Kentucky slave who escaped from his master, one Albert G. Sibley, sometime in the 1830s. In 1852 Bibb wrote the slaveholder, "It has now been about sixteen years since we saw each other face to face, and at which time you doubtless considered me inferior to yourself." But Bibb was now prepared to challenge the notion of racial inferiority and the standard argument that slavery was best for the race. "I have often heard you say that a slave . . . was better off than a 'free negro,'" Bibb wrote, but "in answer to this proslavery logic," Bibb suggested that "the slave who can take care of himself and master can certainly take care of himself alone." Bibb was living proof of his claim, and, like all "free blacks," an obvious challenge to the idea of the natural order.[27]

The number of free blacks had increased manifold after independence. Revolutionary ideology and Christian evangelicalism each played a role, and so too did the bondsmen's own efforts, as they manumitted themselves informally by escaping, as well as formally by spending their modest savings to purchase the freedom of their loved ones. By 1810 there were over one hundred thousand free blacks in the South, accounting for 5 percent of the free population and nearly 9 percent of all blacks. But slaves turned free at decreasing rates in each succeeding decade. By 1840, with most states requiring judicial or legislative permission to manumit slaves, the number of free blacks was increasing at a slower rate than the number of whites or slaves. By 1860 free blacks accounted for just 3 percent of the free southern population and 3 percent of all blacks.

Free blacks and some sympathetic whites were moved to establish integrated schools in the post-Revolution era, but by the turn of the century, a change in white attitudes forced most of the schools to close or segregate. Next to the church, the school became and remained the most important institution in the African American community; in fact, nearly every African church had a Sunday school, and most supported day schools. Over time, the black commitment to education only hardened white opposition to the potentially subversive enterprise; "whites," Berlin records, "moved quickly to stamp out many of the most promising black schools." Berlin recalls the story of one Christopher McPherson, a free black "of considerable talent and modest wealth," who in 1811 opened a night school in Richmond for free blacks and slaves whose masters would consent. After a flurry of educational success, Richmond officials moved to declare the school a nuisance, jailed McPherson, and shipped him off to the Williamsburg Lunatic Asylum.

As the nineteenth century progressed, the oppression of free blacks became more systematic and more extreme. Black workers were channeled by law and trade practices into marginal, stigmatized occupations, and even there they met racial discrimination and increasing competition from white wage laborers and slaves. Many made a comfortable living, but most were pushed into abject poverty. The distinction between slave and freeman became increasingly hazy, as "free" blacks were forced into debt peonage, cajoled into oppressive sharecropping schemes, impressed into servitude for failures to pay fines, taxes, fees, or even private debts, or simply kidnapped and sold into bondage. Free blacks—once, in Berlin's words, "slaves without masters"—found themselves increasingly the slaves of the state.

The North was no haven. Civil rights there were the exception, not the rule: only three states permitted black suffrage on terms equal with whites, and only one state, Massachusetts, permitted black jurors. The discrimination not accomplished by law was achieved through custom and official encouragement or indifference: segregation was the norm in public conveyances, accommodations, and schools, and exclusion the convention in many occupations. The Jim Crow South of the late nineteenth century in fact had a working model in the antebellum North.

For free blacks in the South, meanwhile, the worst came in the antebellum era. The forces that in the same era had tempered slavery's more brutal aspects were of little benefit to free blacks. The slave's welfare was of real economic interest to the slaveholder; the free black was an economic threat. The black slave merely exemplified the natural order; the free black contradicted it. "The danger," Berlin writes, "was not only that slaves would learn this from the freemen's example, but that whites would." "Southerners," Berlin continues, "willing to defend to the death a society based on Negro slavery had no desire to live alongside blacks who were free." So they sought briefly to resolve the contradiction by enslaving the free black population. Between 1858 and 1860, nearly every southern legislature entertained measures providing for the forcible removal or enslavement of all free blacks. Interestingly, the proposals encountered significant opposition from many southerners—some on theoretical grounds, others for practical or personal reasons. The impending defeat of the Georgia proposal prompted a Savannah paper to issue this ironic plea: "Every day we hear our slaves pronounced the happiest people in the world. Why then this lamentation over putting the free negro in his only proper . . . condition?" The measures were gradually withdrawn; civil war, in any event, was at hand.[28]

Reconstruction: 1863-1877

The *Cincinnati Enquirer* offered its own lament in 1863, in response to the Emancipation Proclamation: "Slavery is dead, the negro is not, there is the misfortune."

As the paper explained, the misfortune was for all. For the slaveholders, Leon Litwack writes, "war and emancipation played upon and exacerbated white fears and fantasies that were as old as slavery itself." White slave owners, distressed by the wartime behavior of slaves, decried the "numerous instances of ingratitude evinced in the African character"; "those we esteemed the most have been the first to desert us." The occasional report of violence by the slaves, or "former slaves"—the distinction was not often clear—aroused paranoid fears of mass insurrection and retribution; generally, slaveholders blamed the Yankees for stimulating "the foulest demoniac passions of the negro, hitherto so peaceful and happy." Even the many instances of slave fidelity, as slaves defended both the lives and property of their masters from Yankee harm, confused the white mind. Slaveholders puzzled over the "contradictory" behavior of their (former) bondsmen; "I am beginning," a Virginia woman sighed, "to lose confidence in the whole race." Only occasionally did the slaveholders perceive what might have been obvious to all; James Alcorn, a Mississippi planter, responded to the flight of his slave Hadley by recording in his journal, "I feel that had I been in his place I should have gone, so good bye Hadley, you have heretofore been faithful, that you should espouse your liberty but shows your sense." Most slaveholders reacted to such circumstances with outrage and contempt. Their attitudes toward the "freed slaves" were perhaps best summarized by the query of one southern woman: "If they don't belong to me," she puzzled, "whose are they?"

Emancipation elicited much ambivalence from the slaves, for whom, frankly, the proclamation often mattered little. In the absence of Union occupation, slavery remained very much a practical fact; those slaves who dared to assert their manumission experienced much oppression and retaliation for their "betrayals." Not until after Appomattox, when federal officials and soldiers were available to enforce emancipation, could the freedmen confidently celebrate in jubilees. Even then, it was not clear that it was time to celebrate. Toby Jones, a South Carolina slave, worked for years after emancipation under his master's command before fleeing to Texas with his bride-to-be. "I don't know as I 'spected nothing from freedom," Jones recalled, "but they turned us out like a bunch of stray dogs, no homes, no clothing, no nothing, not 'nough food to last us one meal."

Often, it was worse than that. Assisted by the "Black Codes," the southern master class was able to maintain a system of virtual slavery, this time unrestrained by economic concern for the welfare of the labor force. Violence against the freedmen was as much the rule as the exception. The precise numbers "beaten, flogged, mutilated, and murdered in the first years of emancipation will never be known," Litwack reports. "Nor could any accurate body count or statistical breakdown reveal the barbaric savagery and depravity that character- ized the assaults made on freedmen in the name of restraining their savagery and depravity." A mass assault on the black population of Memphis in 1866 cost the lives of forty-six black citizens and two white. The Memphis newspaper editorialized, "The negroes now know, to their sorrow, that it is best not to arouse the fury of the white man."

The Reconstruction state legislatures and federal government provided some measure of relief, and briefly suggested a move to a genuinely multi-racial community. Under Republican control, the Arkansas, Louisiana, Mississippi, and South Carolina legislatures repealed their antimiscegenation laws. The South Carolina legislature, the only one composed of a black majority, made that state the first in the nation to offer a free public education to all its citizens. Other Reconstruction legislatures moved to equalize their schemes of taxation and improve the bargaining power of agrarian labor. At the federal level, three constitutional amendments and a series of enforcement acts were designed to pursue legal, political, and—in the Civil Rights Act of 1875—what Democrats universally denounced as "social" equality.[29]

The most progressive Republicans of the Reconstruction era were indeed "Radicals" in one limited but vital sense: they sought to erase the color line. They did not broadly pursue the radical egalitarian goal of "social equality," nor did they pursue the radical democratic goal of universal suffrage. Many of them, after all, quite likely believed that people were not, as individuals, all that equal; "social" and "political" equality were, in this sense, unattainable. Many did not believe, on the other hand, that the "races" were necessarily unequal. What they sought was the elimination of artificial "racial" constraints on individual merit; from this "equality under law," a real justice, a natural justice, would then follow. But they miscalculated: the roots of "race" were deeper than they perceived, and their own time was much shorter.

For Reconstruction was not to last. By the time the federal garrison was withdrawn in 1877, most southern legislatures were already controlled by Bourbon Democrats. The old order would be shortly "redeemed"; the color line was secure.

Jim Crow: 1877-1941

In 1877 the Republicans traded the freedmen's security for the White House; southern Democrats were thrilled by the deal. Democratic control of the new southern legislatures was not, however, a given, thus the Bourbons actively courted the black vote during the early years of Redemption. Once they had secured power, they quickly moved to disenfranchise the black population. In the 1890s a biracial populism emerged throughout the South, but the ruling Democrats, with the assistance of Northern Republicans, stemmed the tide of rebellion. Frustrated by political failure and economic depression, the white Populists—with no little encouragement from their former adversaries—turned, in John Egerton's words, with "reactionary fury" against their black compatriots. Thus, in the span of a generation, Republicans, Democrats, and Populists had each in succession courted, exploited, and then abandoned black southerners.

The limited gains of Reconstruction were systematically undone. The case of Berea College offers a study in microcosm. The school's formal mission was "to break down the caste of race," and in the 1880s it was thoroughly integrated. Its president, Edward H. Fairchild, reported of the school's black students that there was "no essential difference, other things being equal, between their standing and that of the white students." But Fairchild died in 1889, and his successor was determined to increase Berea's white enrollment, even if it meant occasionally catering to white racial prejudice. The result was an increasingly white, and increasingly segregated, school. In spite of this change, or perhaps because of it, the Kentucky legislature determined in 1904 to formally segregate all of its private institutions of learning; Berea was its obvious target. Ridiculing the Berea mission statement, one Kentucky legislator declared, "If there is one thing clear about the designs of Providence it is that the 'caste of race' shall be preserved." The bill became law, and the college challenged it all the way to the Supreme Court.

In 1908 the Court sustained the law; the college, Justice David Brewer wrote, "had no natural right to teach at all," and hence was subject to whatever conditions the state should impose. Kentuckian John Marshall Harlan dissented:

If pupils, of whatever race . . . choose, with the consent of their parents, or voluntarily, to sit together in a private institution of learning while receiving instruction which is not in its nature harmful or dangerous to the public, no government, whether Federal or state, can legally forbid their coming together, or being together temporarily, for such an innocent purpose.

Harlan decried the "mischievous, not to say cruel, character of the statute in question." "Have we become," he asked, "so inoculated with prejudice of race that an American government, professedly based on the principles of freedom, and charged with the protection of all citizens alike, can make distinctions between such citizens in the matter of their voluntary meeting for innocent purposes, simply because of their respective races?" It was intended to be a rhetorical question, but the obvious answer was not the one Harlan had hoped for.[30]

Black Americans continued their struggle for equality. "Historians," George M. Fredrickson writes, "have only recently begun to uncover the record of black assertiveness after Reconstruction that made state action necessary to guarantee white prerogatives." But the boycotts and protests brought only more oppression, some of it through the law, some of it outside the law, much of it in forms that defied the distinction. Jim Crow was all-pervasive, the white commitment to it passionate, and in the absence of federal intervention, it was quite secure.

In the face of such relentless hostility, some black Americans resigned themselves to "separate," but determined to achieve at least some form of "equal." The New England–style classical education offered by the black missionary colleges throughout the South seemed futile to some, in light of the practical and legal obstacles confronting black Americans. Samuel C. Armstrong at Hampton had pioneered the idea of an industrial education for black Americans, and it was soon championed by his protégé, Booker T. Washington of Tuskegee. In an 1895 speech at the Cotton States Exposition of Industry and Arts in Atlanta, Washington assured the white members of his audience that, just as in the past, "in the future, in our humble way, we shall stand by you." "In all things that are purely social," he offered, "we can be as separate as the fingers, yet one as the hand in all things essential to human progress."

Washington became, by white acclamation, the "voice of his people." Behind the scenes, his reform efforts often went considerably beyond the very moderate public positions he staked out for his white audiences. Still, those positions mattered, and the line between moderation and accommodation seemed to some critics a very fine one, and that between accommodation and surrender a finer one still.

The most significant response to Washington came in 1905. The Niagara Movement Address demanded "political rights" and "civil rights" for black Americans, protested the "denial of equal opportunities . . . in economic life," and advocated reforms in both educational policy and labor practices. W. E. B. Du Bois emerged as the movement's leader and the more radical counterpoint to Washington. Du Bois denounced accommodation, insisted that the black race was capable of its own greatness, and promoted the notion of a black intellectual vanguard (he adopted Henry L. Morehouse's term, the "talented tenth") to help lead the way.

Each approach had its pitfalls. Du Bois's own form of romantic racialism was easily perverted by white supremacists, who saw in his work a glorification of racial attributes rather than a celebration of cultural achievements. Even Du Bois himself was, in those early years, unable to completely escape the biological determinism of his day: Du Bois's vanguard was composed of a very natural elite. We must acknowledge, he insisted in a 1900 speech, "the fact of human inequality and differences of capacity"; "there are men born to rule, born to think, born to contrive, born to persuade." Only later in his career would Du Bois emphasize that "comparatively few have, under our present economic and social organization, had a chance to show their capabilities."[31]

But the hazards of accommodation were much greater. "Separate" was never "equal," but served only, as Fredrickson writes, to "mystify the process of racial domination and permit the illusion of justice and fairness." That illusion was a thin one. In 1909 the southern states spent an average of 2.5 times as much on the per capita education of white children as they did on black children; in 1915, after six more years of accommodation, they were spending 3.5 times as much. In 1932 North Carolina, widely reputed to be among the most progressive southern states in matters of education, maintained white schools with a per capita value five times as great as that of the black schools. As late as 1946, the state was spending three times as much for the education of its white children as it spent on the education of its black children.

The "black" schools compensated in other ways. Vanessa Siddle Walker's study of North Carolina's Caswell County Training School notes that educators there "forged a system of schooling that emphasized the importance of teacher/student relationships, valued activities as a key means of developing the students' many talents, and believed in the children's ability to learn and their own ability to teach." The community donated resources, and "caring adults gave individual concern, [and] personal time." Throughout the segregation era, Caswell County and the other black schools would lag well behind the white schools in material resources; but there was here, Walker notes, no "poverty of spirit."[32]

Reconstruction Reborn: 1941-1948

As George Fredrickson suggests, A. Philip Randolph's 1941 March on Washington Movement was in many respects the first significant national political movement of black Americans. Randolph made a conscious decision to exclude whites from the movement, in part due to his fear of white communist control (Randolph had disassociated himself from that movement in 1940), but also to ensure black solidarity. Black control, Randolph insisted, "helps break down the slave psychology and inferiority complex in Negroes which comes with Negroes relying on white people for direction and support."

The movement achieved little in the way of material success, but it brought prominence to Randolph and to a new generation of civil rights advocacy and advocates. In 1944 the University of North Carolina Press published *What the Negro Wants*, a collection of essays by a cross-section of these advocates: it featured contributions from, among others, Randolph, Mary McLeod Bethune, and Langston Hughes. Representative was the essay by the still vital Du Bois; what the "negro" wants, Du Bois advised, was nothing less than "full economic, political, and social equality."

That these were still a great distance away was made plain by another work published that year, Gunnar Myrdal's *American Dilemma*. The Swedish social scientist, working with a research team of over one hundred scholars (including Ralph Bunche, E. Franklin

Frazier, Guy Johnson, and, as a consultant, Du Bois), painstakingly documented the details of American racial discrimination. Myrdal described a "vicious circle" of racism, in which perceived inferiority justified discrimination, which in turn perpetuated the inferiority (both "real" and perceived, to whatever extent these differ). Significantly, Myrdal noted that the justifications for racial caste—that blacks like to be separate, that segregation avoids friction, that separation is natural—were now clearly disingenuous; racial oppression was rarely defended for what it was, a way to preserve white interests. Myrdal exposed the shallowness of the centuries-old cry "no social equality": "the term," he noted, "is kept vague and elusive, and the theory loose and ambiguous." "The very lack of precision," he concluded, "allows the notion of 'social equality' to rationalize the rather illogical and wavering system of color caste in America."

Not everyone perceived the same problems: according to a 1946 survey, two-thirds of all white Americans believed that blacks were "treated fairly" in American society.

In 1947 John Hope Franklin published his remarkable social history, *From Slavery to Freedom: A History of Negro Americans*. Like Du Bois's history of Reconstruction, or Carter Woodson's history "from the ground up," Franklin determinedly demonstrated the accomplishments of a people who were denied the opportunity "to make significant achievements in the usual sense of the word." Echoing Du Bois and confirming Myrdal, Franklin vividly described the separate and unequal "two worlds of race." "In a nation dedicated to the idea of the essential equality of mankind," Franklin concluded, the continued existence of a segregated black community constituted "one of the remarkable social anomalies of the twentieth century."

In June of that same year, the president of the United States addressed the annual meeting of the National Association for the Advancement of Colored People from the steps of the Lincoln Memorial. To a crowd of ten thousand, Harry Truman promised protection not only from government, but by the government. In October the President's Committee on Civil Rights explicitly called for an end to segregation, denouncing separate but equal as "one of the outstanding myths of American history." In December the President's Commission on Higher Education issued its report, "Higher Education for American Democracy." Segregation, the report concluded, "contravenes the equalitarian spirit of the American heritage." Just three of the twenty-seven members dissented: the efforts to ensure equality, they insisted, must "be made within the established patterns of social relations, which require separate educational institutions for whites and Negroes." In 1948, as Congress was contemplating a peacetime draft, A. Philip Randolph testified before that body against the continuance of racial segregation in the military. Randolph did not need to wait for a congressional response; Truman ordered the desegregation of the military shortly before the presidential election.

Truman's overtures were too much for many southern Democrats. The Dixiecrats bolted the party and formed their own. The keynote address at the States' Rights Party convention denounced Truman's initiatives, which threatened "to reduce us to the state of a mongrel, inferior race." The party nominated South Carolina governor Strom Thurmond to be its flagbearer. Throughout his campaign, Thurmond defended racial segregation as a matter of principle: it was merely a question of "state's rights." Everyone knew, of course, that it was much more than that. Some things, it seemed, would never change.

Truman barely eked out his upset victory over his Republican opponent, Thomas Dewey. But in the South, Truman defeated both Dewey and Thurmond by margins in excess of two to one. And it was not merely the "black" vote that provided the margin: barely 10 percent of the voting-age black southerners were permitted to cast ballots in the 1948 presidential election. Not everything had changed, but some things clearly had, and there was more to come.[33]

Contemporary Meanings

There are many signs of continued change. The percentage of white Americans between the ages of twenty-five and twenty-nine who had completed at least twelve years of education increased from 40 percent in 1940 to 65 percent in 1965 to 86 percent in 1987; the percentage of black Americans in the same category increased from only 12 percent in 1940 to 50 percent in 1965 to 83 percent in 1987, nearly at parity with whites.

Within the schools, the achievement gap between black and white Americans, as measured by standardized tests of achievement, has narrowed substantially: the math gap was reduced 25 to 40 percent during the seventies and eighties alone, the science gap 15 to 25 percent, and the reading gap by half. Regional analyses suggest that the achievement gap has seen particularly significant reduction in the Southeast, due in part, no doubt, to desegregation. As Martin Carnoy observes, these advances are all the more impressive since they occurred: first, when the percentage of black Americans graduating from high school was increasing; and second, during a time when the demands on public education—due to increasing poverty, and reduced parental and public support—have reached near-crisis proportions.[34]

Some of the signs are, on the surface, ambiguous. In 1967, 34.5 percent of white Americans between the ages of eighteen and twenty-four were in institutions of higher education, as compared to just 23.3 percent of black Americans; by 1977, however, near parity had been achieved: 32.3 percent of those white Americans were in college, and so too were 31.3 percent of black Americans. By 1991, however, the gap had ballooned: fully 41.0 percent of those white young adults were in college, but just 28.2 percent of the black young adults. Despite the increase in the number of black high school graduates during the eighties, that decade also saw a decline in the absolute number of black recipients of bachelor's degrees. By 1994, then, about 23 percent of all eighteen- to twenty-four-year-old high school graduates were American Indian, Latino, or African American, but students from those groups constituted just 16 percent of all students at four-year colleges, and just 12 percent of all students at colleges that were not historically black or Latino.[35]

Some signs are distressingly familiar. The black-white economic gap closed substantially during the mid century, but the gap stabilized in the mid-seventies and has now again widened. Today, one in seven white Americans lives in poverty, but so too does one in three black Americans. The poverty rate among white children is a distressing 13 percent; among black children it is an unconscionable 46 percent. America's white citizens average roughly twice the income of its black citizens; its black citizens are unemployed at over twice the rate. The median net worth of white Americans is more than ten times that of black Americans. Black Americans account for 12 percent of the population, but just 10 percent of the labor force; they constitute 31 percent of all nursing aides but just 1.5 percent of all dentists; 30 percent of all domestic servants but just 2.6 percent of all lawyers; 28 percent of all postal clerks but just 1.5 percent of all pilots; 21 percent of all janitors but just 2.1 percent of all architects.[36]

Part of the gap may be due to an emerging college barrier. The percentage of black high school graduates from families with annual incomes under $10,000 rose from 27 percent in 1968-73 to 35 percent in 1980-85; for white graduates it remained constant at 9-10 percent. Black graduates unable to attend college but able to find work are almost invariably consigned to positions where wages are declining: wages, on the whole, have fallen more than 15 percent for black Americans since the early 1970s.[37]

Part of the gap may be due to continuing disparities in the delivery of education. Substantial funding disparities between "poor" and "wealthy" districts have been documented by the courts, by the United States Congress, and, in a narrative that conveys the tragedy behind the numbers, Jonathan Kozol's *Savage Inequalities*. Not surprisingly, the "poor" districts are disproportionately populated by racial minorities. Economists David Card and Alan Krueger have demonstrated the connection between education and income: spending per pupil translates into future earnings for the student. Meanwhile, total spending on public education increased 70 percent—5.4 percent annually—from 1960 to 1970, but during the next two decades, growth fell by half, to 35 percent, or roughly 3 percent annually. It is a compound irony: the schools that need the most get the least, when they need it most.

Part of the gap may be due to a resurgence in conventional racial discrimination. Carnoy estimates that wage discrimination was roughly halved in the quarter century 1959-84, but is now on the rise again. The expanded wage differential remains even after non-racial variables—economic sector, region, education and work experience, marital status, and hours and weeks of labor—are controlled for. A 1991 study by the Urban Institute also suggests that old-fashioned racial bias is very much alive: among carefully controlled and matched job applicants, white applicants were three times more likely to advance through the screening stages of the hiring process, and three times more likely to be offered jobs.

Part of the gap may be due to governmental "downsizing." The reduction in governmental services and payrolls reduces not merely a source of public benefits, which are disproportionately needed by black Americans, but also reduces a significant source of wages. As Carnoy notes, a higher percentage of black Americans are employed in the public sector than are whites, and black Americans encounter less discrimination—and thus higher pay—in government jobs than they do in the private sector.

Part of the gap is deeply structural: a racialized division of education and labor perpetually limits advancement. Sharon M. Collins's examination of black executives in Chicago is illustrative. She describes a circular relationship between occupational aptitudes and experience—"human capital"—and the structure of management positions: "A race-based system of job allocation creates a deficit in on-the-job training and experience, and this structurally imposed deficit, in turn, leads to human capital deficits that create barriers to black advancement."[38]

There are other disturbing signs. A recent study of excess mortality rates notes that "[d]eath rates for those between the ages of 5 and 65 were worse in Harlem than in Bangladesh." The root causes of this mortality rate, the study concluded, were "vicious poverty and inadequate access to the basic health care that is the right of all Americans." Harlem's population is 96 percent black. The situation in Harlem is not an isolated phenomenon: researchers found "strikingly higher rates of death and disease in Philadelphia's poorer communities," communities that, coincidentally, had the highest concentrations of nonwhite residents. Nationally, mortality among black women between the ages of fifteen and sixty is 79 percent higher than among white women. American white men have a 16 percent probability of dying between the ages of fifteen and sixty; American black men have a 30.3 percent probability, a level in excess of the mortality rates among men in some of the poorest developing nations in the world. The infant mortality rate is twice as high for black Americans as for whites.

Racial ghettos are yet another sign that some things have yet to change. Approximately one-third of all poor black Americans live in substandard housing, roughly 2.5 times the proportion of poor white Americans living in such conditions. A recent analysis of the 1990 census concludes that "the majority of the nation's 30 million black people are as segregated now as they were at the height of the civil rights movement in the '60s."

George Fredrickson's comparative study of the "Black Liberation" movements in South Africa and the United States concludes this way:

Despite the problems that remain, black South Africans have thrown off the shackles of white domination and have achieved genuine self-determination, while African-Americans remain at the mercy of a white majority that remains racist—not in the old-fashioned sense of openly advocating the legal subordination of blacks, but in the new sense of denying the palpable fact that blacks as a group suffer from real disadvantages in American society and will continue to do so unless radical action is taken.[39]

One vital part of this radical action might be to accept Fredrickson's premise: to acknowledge the continuing truth of racial advantage and disadvantage, and to abandon the pretense that it is inevitable, acceptable, or natural.   Merely to do so is to comprehend—and overcome—the "new" racism.

"Racism" in America

Recognizing the political nature of "race" suggests this ultimate conclusion: in America, "race" and "racism" are one and the same. "Race" is the history constructed by racism; "racism" is simply a convenient name to give the process of construction.

The story of race in America, then, is substantially a story of racism. But not racism, it must be emphasized, in the conventional sense, as overt racial animus and bigotry. There has been, of course, plenty of that. But the politics of race goes beyond overt acts of hatred and personal psychopathology. The process of race-making—"race"-ism—transcends the individual, even as it partly constitutes him.

Racism is the distorted way we perceive race and the distorted perceptions of us as racial beings. It is the systematic and systematized failure to recognize the realities of "race," in ourselves as well as others. Racism thus embraces not only the continued tendency to make of race what it is not, something biological, immutable, and inferior; racism embraces as well the refusal to recognize what race is, a powerfully significant social and political reality. These have predominated at different times, but they are flip sides of the same coin. The rhetoric of natural racial inferiority has yielded to a rhetoric of "color blindness" and "race-neutrality," but these separate assertions are equally deluded, equally unrealistic, and equally harmful. Both explicitly deny what "race" is, and inevitably deceive us into believing that "race" is something that it is not. Both are equally race-ist.

Our conventional understanding of racism, like our understanding of race, has tended to obscure these points. At first, we believed that racism, like race, was natural: it was something instinctive, something normal, something inevitable. Later we saw that racism was not natural at all: it was learned, it was pathological, and it could be changed. But even this later conception was preoccupied with the individual, with curing his psychopathology. But psychology is no more adequate to fully comprehend racism than was the biology that preceded it. Racism, after all, is not something that is *in* some of us; racism, rather, is something that partly *defines* all of us. We are all, as Du Bois put it, "entombed" in race.[40]

Racism rewards some of us with advantages; it burdens some of us with disadvantages. And racism makes it hard to see them both.

Rejecting the Naturalistic Conception

Louisiana's "separate but equal" law, the Supreme Court told us in *Plessy v. Ferguson*, was no more than the codification of our innate racial animosity. To insist on integration—or "social equality"—was to defy nature: "If the two races are to meet upon terms of social equality, it must be the result of natural affinities, a mutual appreciation of each other's merits, and a voluntary consent of individuals. Legislation is powerless to eradicate racial instincts, or to abolish distinctions based upon physical differences." Nothing in the Fourteenth Amendment's guarantee of equality could change this biological truth. Only Justice Harlan saw what now seems obvious: the compulsory segregation of the races did not simply recognize the natural racial order, it created an artificial one. Racism was not natural, it was generated—by laws such as this.

Thomas Pearce Bailey was among the first prominent southerners to concur. In 1914 the former Memphis superintendent of schools, and then dean of the Education Department at the University of Mississippi, published *Race Orthodoxy in the Old South*. "The real problem is not the negro," Bailey wrote, "but the white man's attitude toward the negro."[41]

And this was not natural either. Franz Boas made this clear: in undermining the concept of "race," Boas also exposed the myth of racism. "The differences of cultural outlook and of bodily appearance," Boas observed, "have given rise to antagonisms that are rationalized as due to instinctive racial antipathies." But without "race" there could be no such "racism": "The basis of race consciousness and race antipathies is the dogmatic belief in the existence of well-defined races all the members of which possess the same fundamental bodily and mental characters."

Moreover, Boas observed that "race antipathy among different groups of mankind takes distinctive forms and expresses itself with varying intensity"; "we may doubt," he thus concluded, "whether we are dealing with instinctive phenomena."

What, then, was the explanation for "racism"? For Boas, it was to be found in the coincidence—carefully perpetuated—of two factors: visible difference and attendant social consequences. As Boas explained, "The first view of an entirely foreign type is likely to impress us with consciousness of contrast, that may well take the form of antipathy." But this did not necessarily persist: "Constant familiarity with strange types modifies our standards to such an extent that the consciousness of contrast becomes very slight."

The great difficulty arose only when the apparent differences coincided with social differences. "When social divisions follow racial lines, as they do among ourselves, the degree of difference between racial forms is an important element in establishing racial groups and in accentuating racial conflicts." "As long as the social groups are racial groups," Boas concluded, "we shall also encounter the desire for racial purity."

If racism was the product of the coincidence of differences in appearance and social status, then disrupting that coincidence—through, for example, the social integration of the different "races"—would seem to end racism. As Boas wrote,

> It follows that the 'instinctive' race antipathy can be broken down, if we succeed in creating among young children social groups that are not divided according to the principles of race and which have principles of cohesion that weld the group into a whole. Under the pressure of present popular feeling it will not be easy to establish such groups. Nevertheless, cultural coöperation cannot be reached without it.[42]

Boas's work was in fact part of an evolving tradition. The abolitionists had argued that prejudice was the result of status or condition, and so too had many of the advocates of congressional Reconstruction. In 1884 T. Thomas Fortune's *Black and White: Land, Labor, and Capital in the South* urged both a biracial labor coalition and an independent black economic effort, in the belief that the economic elevation of black Americans would end racial prejudice. Booker Washington was essentially following the same logic in urging an independent black capitalism: when blacks can demonstrate a prosperity comparable to whites, he reasoned, they will be treated by whites as equals.

But racism was more than simply prejudice against status or condition, more than just another manifestation of contempt for the poor. Racism, after all, added another feature, "race," and that feature, over time, had acquired extraordinary significance, if only as an unconscious proxy for class. William I. Thomas of the University of Chicago wrote in 1904 that "race" prejudice itself was prompted "primarily by the physical aspect of an unfamiliar people," and, as such, it was not a terribly significant phenomenon. "When not complicated by caste-feeling," Thomas wrote, "race prejudice is after all very impermanent, of no more stability, perhaps, than fashion." The difficulty, as Boas saw, was that race prejudice *was* now complicated by "caste-feeling"; what he might have seen, in fact, was that "race" was now incomprehensible without caste.

The stubborn persistence of racial prejudice through the first half of the twentieth century presented a superficial challenge to those who had insisted that prejudice would disintegrate with the elevation of black America's status or condition. Of course, the short answer was that black America's status had not changed all that much; even today, it takes more than just "color blindness" not to see the reality of racial caste. But the deeper answer was that it was becoming almost impossible to achieve Boas's project of disengaging "race" and "caste": the coincidence of "race" and "caste" was now being reproduced by American society without much conscious effort. Gunnar Myrdal's *American Dilemma* made the point: "We consider the social differentiation between Negroes and Whites as based on tradition." And tradition, like nature before it, seemed both normal and inevitable. It was difficult, as a consequence, to see tradition's bias, to see the color of tradition. But some could see it, even then: "The Negro problem,"

Myrdal concluded, echoing Thomas Pearce Bailey, "is primarily a white man's problem."[43]

Rejecting the Individualistic Conception

Even today the persistence of racism remains something of a mystery. If racism is neither innate nor inevitable, why—after emancipation, Reconstruction, and yet a second Reconstruction—does the color line persist?

The initial response is that, in some sense, it might not: the color line that divides white and black America today is in some ways demonstrably less distinct and rigid than the one that has historically prevailed. A recent survey of the evidence on racial attitudes concludes that, at least in what they say, "white Americans are gradually becoming less prejudiced and more egalitarian." Over the past four decades, negative stereotypes of black Americans have consistently faded, while pro-integration sentiments have consistently risen. By 1980 over 90 percent of white northerners and 75 percent of white southerners supported school integration; by 1982 the support for integration was at 90 percent for the entire national sample. A slightly earlier survey, done in 1978, indicated that roughly three-quarters of the general white population had no objection to their child being in a school where half the children were black; over 40 percent had no objection if a majority of the children were black. In a 1988 survey, more whites reported that they would prefer to live in a neighborhood racially mixed "half and half" than in a neighborhood with "mostly whites."

But there are reasons to be cautious. The surveys consistently reveal that a significant minority in the white population—roughly 20 percent—continues to exhibit traditional racial prejudice, either embracing the old, invidious stereotypes or declaring an overt hostility. Moreover, there are undeniable indications of ambivalence in the surveys, indications that racial prejudice persists among white Americans, but in more subtle forms, what some have called a "new" racism.[44]

Today, of course, it is easy to invoke race without being explicit: such is the undeniable cultural power of the construction. Strom Thurmond avoided references to "race" in his presidential campaign of

1948, but the meaning of "states' rights" and "tradition" were clear enough. Richard Nixon could be more subtle in his "Southern Strategy" twenty years later: "busing" and "crime" did the trick for him. Ronald Reagan evoked the specter of a "welfare queen" and George Bush flashed the actual image of one, Willie Horton and neither had to mention race to get their message across. The text of Jesse Helms's "white hands" ad—which showed merely a pair of white hands crumbling a job rejection letter—was "race-neutral": "quota bills" are bad because they punish the folks who deserve the jobs. Racial competition was merely the subtext, racial hierarchy the context, and lingering just below the surface was the imperfect image of the undeserving black—unqualified, incompetent, inferior. No one has to use the "r" word: it's just about being fair to the individual.

But it is important to recognize in all events that racism, old or new, is not fairly attributable merely to individual pathology. The cognitive processes that provide the foundation for individual racial prejudice—the ability to differentiate—is, as Boas noted, both normal and quite benign. But while the individual may have an innate ability to differentiate based on "race," it is principally the work of cultural influences that makes "race" salient in particularized contexts. Thus "race," itself a social construction, evokes principally the attitudes and attributes developed for "race" by social processes. These may be, as Boas suggested, not so much based on "race" itself, but rather the attitudes and attributes that are otherwise associated with social "class" or "caste"; but since, as Boas knew, we made "race" *as* a social caste, the distinction is unknowable and practically insignificant.

Social processes are vital in an additional way: it is social norms that make specific differentiating behaviors either more or less acceptable. The norm, for example, that permits a preference for persons who are subjectively similar need not be accompanied by a comparable norm for disliking persons who are "different"; indeed, research indicates that biased positive attitudes (by, for example, whites in favor of whites) are not invariably accompanied by equally biased negative attitudes (by, for example, whites against blacks). Specific negative responses to differentiating characteristics seem to find expression where they appear to enjoy social sanction. "Racism" is perpetuated, in this sense, by its own long-standing tradition.

Consistent with these understandings, evidence suggests that racism can be "unlearned" through the meaningful engagement of countervailing truths. The epistemological premises for racist behavior, for example, can be refuted, as Boas predicted, through interracial learning: when it is clear that the real meanings of "race" are social and not biological, the negative racial schema is substantially undone. Significantly, such a result cannot be obtained merely through the insistence on "color blindness." Rather, the insistence that "race" has no contemporary meaning resolves the impossible dissonance between the reality of racial caste and society's egalitarian ideals only through denial. "Race," after all, does not lose its salience through mere proclamation; one unfortunate consequence of such inauthentic attempts to resolve the dissonance may actually be the entrenchment of racist beliefs. "So today more than ever," write Michael Omi and Howard Winant, "opposing racism requires that we notice race, not ignore it, that we afford it the recognition it deserves and the subtlety it embodies."

The proclamation of competing *moral* truths can also counter racist attitudes, but, at this normative level, they must directly challenge the norms on which racism is constructed. Research suggests that appeals to the ethic of individualism do not meet the moral challenge; on the contrary, this ethic seems positively correlated with negative racial attitudes and behavior, including a failure of interracial empathy and a tendency to discount the effects of racial discrimination. The reinforcement of the individualist ethos may actually exacerbate negative race-related tendencies. As Michael L. Blakey writes, "Individualism contributes to ahistorical and social context-free explanations of inequality, to overly narrow definitions of racial discrimination (as merely racial epithets or other openly racist personal acts), to victim blame, and to the denial of institutional racism and racially linked class barriers."

The set of norms that does appear to provide an effective counter to racist tendencies is that which includes principles of fairness and equality. But these norms are comparatively abstract and complex and, perhaps as a consequence, apparently fragile. Modern racism, in fact, does not so much confront these norms as elude them. The effectiveness of egalitarian norms thus apparently depends on their presentation in clear and unambiguous terms; when the divorce between the norm and the racist behavior is made clear, the modern subject, who may not recognize the behavior as racist, can and does reject the behavior in favor of the egalitarian norm.[45]

It is worth reiterating, however, that the norm and its applications must be unambiguous. The most significant feature of American racism has always been its ability to assimilate some conception of the egalitarian framework while avoiding the implications of the mandate for specific contexts. In an earlier day, this evasion typically took the form of the hideous fiction of "natural" inferiority. Today, it is more likely to take the form of the equally hideous fiction of the "color-blind" society. The assumptions, in either case, are essentially the same: "we"—the government, society, the white race, me and mine—are not responsible for the inequality. We are "neutral"; the inequality must be "natural."

Inherent here is the final deficiency of the individualistic model of "racism": it assumes that all racist behavior is the result of deliberate, conscious, willful hostility. But these behaviors are merely the tip of the iceberg. Much contemporary "racism" can barely be captured by the concept, so much of it is sub- or unconscious, structural or institutional, that it hardly seems "racist" at all. But in its pretenses to neutrality, in its blindness—willful or otherwise—to its biases, it is racist indeed.

So what is race? "The truth is," Anthony Appiah has written, "that there are no races: there is nothing in the world that can do all we ask 'race' to do for us." But if there can be no "race," there nonetheless are, as Appiah notes, "civilizations where we now speak of races." It is in that context that "race" demands definition, or rather, definitions: definitions that reflect insight into the forces that construct "race" without blindly perpetuating the need for it. "Race," after all, is, in Edward Said's words, "the product of human work." It is made; it can be re-made.

We do not talk enough about the way that we—as Americans—have made "race." If we ignore the story of its origins, the color line between us becomes an evolutionary truth, rooted in some undiscoverable primal moment, shaped perhaps by unalterable tribal instincts. Forged this way by the mysterious forces of creation, the story of racism becomes at once too profound and too elusive to tell. The story, in some important ways, also becomes irrelevant, and the sense of relief is compounded by the realization that the otherwise painful history is not one of "our" making: it just happened, it's nobody's fault, and it's nobody's responsibility.

But there is a story to tell, and it contains some embarrassing truths for those who today deny its relevance. And if the story is painful to hear, it is nonetheless an ultimately empowering one, for it suggests that the racism that pervades America's soul is no less an artifact than the laws that formalize it; and that the promises of Reconstruction—challenged as they have been by nullification and interposition, by obstinacy and avoidance, and now by the resanctification of "private" decision making and economics—remain today both viable and fully realizable. As Frederick Douglass said of slavery over a century ago, "[W]hat man can make, man can unmake"; "race"-ism, the history suggests, is for us now to unmake.[46]

We might begin by rejecting its myths: that "race" is natural; that the processes of responding to race "differences" are natural. And this myth as well: that the resultant hierarchy reflects not merely "natural" differences, but "neutral" valuations of human worth. That is the myth of merit.

4

A Neutral Qualification
Myths of the Market

Two explanations are typically offered for the extraordinary divorce between the ideal of equality and the reality of widespread inequity. The first, the "official" explanation, is that inequality is rooted in the disruption of market forces caused by malicious acts of discrimination; the second, the "unofficial" explanation, is that inequality is rooted in the natural inferiority or superiority of individuals or groups. The two explanations are really more complementary than they are alternative: both suppose that people, as individuals or as groups, are either more or less deserving of some reward based on their "merits," and both contend that inequity—a wrongful inequality—exists only where those "merits" are not duly rewarded. The explanations differ primarily in their focus: in the official view, merit is something that bad people refuse to recognize in others; in the unofficial view, merit is something that unfortunate people just don't have very much of.

This chapter is about the "official" explanation. It is about the attempt to confront the contradictions of equality—or rather, the attempt to elude them—through the fiction of equal opportunity. It is about the contention that inequality is not simply caused by the malicious denial of equal opportunity, but rather that inequality should be defined as that denial. It is about the feeble attempt to guarantee equality by eradicating "intentional" discrimination, as if a market "freed" from discrimination would be equally open to all. It is thus about the naive faith in the ability of the "free" market to produce just results, the blind faith in the fairness and neutrality of the market's schemes. It is, in fact, about our congenital blindness to the realities of contemporary discrimination: the unconscious assumptions and structural biases that pervade social, economic, and political life. It is about the "official" myth of merit, the myth of the market.

Prologue

We used to play whiffle ball in the alley behind the row houses on my block. Everybody played: the boys, the girls, the men, the women; Mr. Marsinison, who had just one arm and was the steady pitcher and could strike anyone out anytime he wanted to, which was, fortunately for all of us, really never; and me. I was little and skinny and despite my very thick glasses, was pretty much blind in one eye, but these things somehow didn't matter in whiffle ball, and from the age of five on I played nearly all the time, and I think I was actually pretty good.

We moved when I was eleven to a neighborhood without row houses, without alleys and without games of whiffle ball. The kids there in fact played none of the games I had grown up with: not whiffle ball, not Wall-Ball, not Rundown, not kick-the-can. The kids played other games in this new neighborhood, games called two-square and four-square and a somewhat more violent game called, quite misleadingly, medicine ball.

The strangest game of all was somewhat less violent than it sounded. In the game that I thought the kids were calling "sock-her," you neither got to "sock" anybody nor, for that matter, play with any "hers": at my new school, the girls dutifully stood on the sidelines while the boys played the game.

Which made even less than no sense, since the boys did not play the game particularly well. Or that, at least, was my considered view after five minutes of my first recess. My new classmates seemed completely unable to control the black-and-white ball: they kicked at it, kneed at it, had it bounce off their torsos and, most ridiculously, off the tops of their silly little heads.

Not a single kid seemed able to catch the ball. Except me. It was still fairly early in the game, and I think I was trying to make a good impression—maybe show off a little, maybe just fit in. The ball was sailing toward my team's end of the field, and I ran under it, jumped in the air as it floated down toward my teammates, and caught it just before it conked yet another hapless soul in the noggin. I cradled the ball securely in both hands and barreled toward the opposing end zone.

But no one tried to stop me. The rest of the kids all just stopped. Something was wrong. I looped around the stunned opposition and began running back toward the other goal. Still the kids didn't move.

I was lost. I kept running, past my motionless classmates, searching each face for some clue. But there was nothing there.

I was still sprinting at midfield when, for no apparent reason, I threw the ball high in the air, as high as I could, and the effort caused me to fall awkwardly to the ground. I felt like I was hurt, but I got up quickly and kept on running, back to my end of the field, to my original position, where I stood in place for the rest of the recess.

I only moved once after that, when a ball was kicked right at me. I raised my hands to catch it, but managed only to knock it to the ground, and a bunch of the other kids yelled, "Hands! Hands!" and pointed at me, and they ran up and snatched the ball from where it had landed at my feet. I was left standing there feeling very little and very skinny and very stupid and oddly ashamed. I did not say a word to anyone as we filed back into school when recess was over. And nobody said a word to me.

A few days later we played softball at recess. Except I didn't play. I didn't get picked to be on a team. So I sat behind the backstop and watched, along with all the girls in the class and one very pale boy who wore glasses even thicker than mine. The class played softball almost every day after that, and I never got picked, and neither did any of the girls or the very pale boy, who always brought a book out during recess, which started to make some sense.

Sometime during the second or third week of school, after yet another miserable recess, our teacher asked us which baseball team was going to win the National League pennant. He went around the room asking the kids, except he didn't ask every kid, only the boys, and each boy would say a team, almost always the Phillies, and the girls would all yell, "Yea!" cheering the kid for picking the Phillies, despite the fact that the Phillies were twenty games out of first place with just ten games left to play. Around the room he went, and the boys would say, "the Phillies," and the girls would say, "Yea!" until he got to some kid named Brad, who said he thought the Reds would win the pennant, because they led by two games and they had the pitching needed to hold on down the stretch, and the other kids oohed and ahhed at Brad's superior knowledge. The teacher called on the next boy, who quickly said, "the Phillies" and the girls again said, "Yea!"

Then the teacher got to me.

"Bobby, who do you think will win the pennant?"

I had not said a word since I had arrived there, whether I had been called on or not, and I was not about to start now. So I sat there once again in silence, looking down at my desk.

He asked again. "Bobby, who do you think will win the pennant?"

I really did not want any part of this.

"Bobby?"

I could feel my face turning red. I kept looking down.

Then I guess he felt like he had some insight. "Or don't you really care?"

So that was it: I was the little, skinny, clumsy kid who can't play sports and probably doesn't know anything about sports and probably doesn't care. Suddenly there was very much at stake here, and I could feel my face getting redder, and the need to say something grew more urgent, and still I looked down at my desk and my mouth did not move.

"Okay, Bobby. Terry, who do you think . . ."

"I don't know who will win the pennant."

It was me.

"I don't know who will win the pennant, but I don't think it will be the Reds, because all they have is Nuxhall and McDowell and then their pitching is really pretty weak, and their bullpen has struggled all year, and I know Pinson and Robinson are having really great years, but the Reds still aren't scoring that many runs. So I don't think it will be the Reds."

There was a long silence.

"I think it will be the Phillies."

The girls all said, "Yea!" The boys all nodded. And the teacher moved on.

The next day we played softball and I got picked and I was put in left field. Late in the game some kid hit a high fly ball and I took off after it, and I ran down the hill that they used as the left field foul line, and I kept running and running and at the bottom of the hill I stuck out my glove and the ball landed in it and I held on tightly, and a couple of kids at the top of the hill started yelling, "he caught it! he caught it!" As I jogged up the hill I could hear the excited chatter, and a bunch of kids said, "great catch!" and some patted me on the back, and I heard the teacher ask some kid whether I really caught the ball, and the kid said yes, he saw it, and I heard the teacher say something about how he hadn't figured me to be much of a ballplayer.

The next spring when we formed our official team for the sixth-grade softball competition, I was picked to play third base. I wasn't very good as a third baseman; second base was really my position. But Jean Thompson was picked to play second base, and Jean Thompson turned out to be one of our best players, which was kind of a big deal, because Jean was a girl.

I guess the moral to the story is that it is wrong to assume that just because a kid is skinny or wears glasses or doesn't know the rules of soccer, he can't play baseball. Also, I guess, that no kid will ever seem to be much of a ballplayer if he—or she—never gets the chance to play.

The Myth of the Market

In America we have forsworn assumptions about people's talents or aptitudes based on their race, gender, or apparent disability. Everyone is presumed to possess equal ability; each individual is afforded the same benefit of the doubt.

In America we have abolished attempts to exclude people from social, political, or economic life based on their race, gender, or apparent disability. Everyone is afforded an equal opportunity; each individual rises or falls on her merits.

There are occasional transgressions: a few individuals apparently haven't gotten the word. They still make assumptions, they still exclude. We punish these acts of malicious discrimination; we seek their elimination. They are all that stand in the way of true equality.

This is our vision of equality: equality as equal opportunity. This is the root of inequality: malicious denials of equal opportunity. This is the myth of the market, the "official" myth of merit.

Reconstructing the Market: Guaranteeing Equal Opportunity

Will equal opportunity produce a genuine equality? The question was in the forefront of much of the debate surrounding the Reconstruction effort. Some argued that it would, that the complete liberation of black Americans would permit them to assume an equal position—legally, politically, socially—with white Americans. They opposed liberation for that reason.

Others argued that it would not, that even complete liberation would leave black Americans in an inferior position—perhaps not legally, but probably politically, and certainly socially—to white Americans. This they offered in support of the case for liberation.

From this perverse transposition of logic emerged our limited ideal of equality: equality under law. Freedom from formal caste. Freedom from formal barriers to success. Equal opportunity.

There were to be no guarantees of equal outcomes. This reflected, in part, the epistemology of the day: those who believed in a natural order—white over red, white over yellow, white over brown, and above all, white over black—were not about to defy the laws of creation. It reflected, in equal part, the politics of the day: southerners, Democrats, white men in general, were not about to surrender their privilege and power.

So slavery was abolished, and later discrimination, to ensure equal opportunity. Equal opportunity, a truly free market, would be the crowning achievement of the Reconstruction effort.

Even this was hard won. At first, the objections were expressed in terms of concerns for the black man. He was not fit for equal opportunity; he was not fit for freedom.

In 1837 John C. Calhoun of South Carolina had stood on the Senate floor and offered the conventional defense of slavery: the Central African race, he insisted, "had never existed in so comfortable, so respectable, so civilized a condition, as that which it now enjoyed in the Southern States."

The Civil War had not necessarily changed this view. Congressman Robert Mallory, Democrat from Kentucky, reasserted the position in May of 1862. "I have made the declaration upon this floor that the condition of slavery is the very best condition in which you can place the African race. That is my deliberate conviction."

His compatriot in the upper chamber, Senator Garrett Davis, explained the futility of emancipation: "A negro's idea of freedom is freedom from work, as a general rule. . . . [I]n, I may say, ninety-nine cases out of one hundred, after they were liberated and acquired their freedom, they became lazy, indolent, thievish vagabonds."

Republican Henry Wilson of Massachusetts responded to Davis with the evidence from the nation's capital:

As a class, the free colored people of this District are not worthless, vicious, thriftless, indolent, vagabonds, criminals, paupers, nor are they a charge and a pest upon society. The Senator from Kentucky, sir, has no right to apply to them these disparaging epithets. Do they not support themselves by their industry and thrift? Do they not support their own churches? Do they not support their own schools? Do they not also support schools for the education of white children, from which their own are excluded?

But the question remained, if their fetters were removed, what would happen to black Americans? And what would happen to the white man?

"What do you intend to do with the slaves when they are freed?" asked Congressman Mallory. "Where will you give them a tarrying place?" He addressed his inquiry to John Bingham:

> I know that the gentleman from Ohio does not intend that this exodus from the South shall find its way into the State of Ohio . . . No; he has too much regard for that State . . . ever to be willing that the blacks shall go there and be the competitors of the free white men for the rewards of labor.

Bingham knew that, even outside the South, emancipation had been no guarantee of equal opportunity: Massachusetts, by law of 1787, had made it unlawful for an "African or negro" to "tarry" within the state for more than two months; more recently, Kansas had prohibited the entry of free black Americans, as had Illinois, Indiana, and Oregon, through its state constitution; even Ohio, Bingham's home state, had maintained—over the congressman's objections—its own set of "black laws" designed to discourage black emigration. But Bingham denied that he would acquiesce; he would never, he insisted, "consent that any man born upon the soil of this republic, by any vote or word of mine, shall be excluded from the limits of any state, my own included."

He was true to his word: just a few years later, Bingham was the principal draftsman of the first section of the Fourteenth Amendment, with its guarantee of the "equal protection of the laws."

In the interim, the debates continued over the opportunities to be afforded black Americans. An 1864 dispute in the Senate over the use of railcars injected, quite typically, the fear that equal access would lead to "social equality." "If there were not a slave within our state," declared Senator Eli Saulsbury of Delaware, "I still should want a slave code to keep out your intermeddling negroes who wish to associate on terms of equality and to ride in railroad cars and other public conveyances with white people."

Senator Lot M. Morrill, Republican from Maine, responded that the question was not one of social equality, but of equal opportunity, that is, black freedom:

> Sir, it is not a question of social or political equality, or the fear of it, that offends the Senator and those of whom he speaks; it is not a real apprehension that the negroes will be made equal in these respects. It is a question of freedom, which puts the *slave out of the power* of the master and beyond his control, that fills this Chamber with the lamentations of the Senator when questions of this sort arise.

Early the next year, in the debates over the Thirteenth Amendment in the House, Thomas T. Davis of New York made the explicit merito-cratic argument for emancipation:

> I am not, sir, one of those who believe that the emancipation of the black race is of itself to elevate them to an equality with the white race. I believe in the distinction of races as existing in the providence of God for his wise and beneficent designs to man; but I would make every race free and equal before the law, permitting to each the elevation to which its own capacity and culture should entitle it, and securing to each the fruits of its own progression.
>
> This we can do only by removing every vestige of African slavery from the American Republic.

The clear understanding, then, was that emancipation would produce only equal opportunity, not necessarily a political, social, or economic equality. Senator James W. Patterson, Republican of New Hampshire, echoed these sentiments in the upper chamber:

> Some gentlemen . . . seem to fear a fair competition between free white and black labor. Now, if the black man belongs to a more intellectual and vigorous race than we, then he ought to triumph in the conflict, and will. But if the white man has a larger brain, stronger and more enduring muscles, and a more active temperament than the black, then he will conquer in this legitimate conflict, and will gradually push the

weaker race from the continent, leaving the heritage of liberties to our children after us to the latest generation.

Freedom, then, was to include the freedom to fail. Even freedom's advocates insisted that failure was, inevitably, the black man's fate.

After emancipation, meritocracy afforded the rationale for both sides in the debate over equality. For advocates of Reconstruction, the argument was that the southern states afforded no real equal opportunity. Republican congressman Ignatius Donnelly reviewed the various "black codes": "All this," he concluded, "means simply the reestablishment of slavery."

The Freedmen's Bureau bill of 1866 was part of the response. It extended the federal government's protection of freed black Americans; as Donnelly explained in support of the bill, "it is as plain to my mind as the sun at noonday, that we must make all the citizens of the country equal before the law; that we must break down all walls of caste; that we must offer equal opportunities to all men."

But equal opportunity—deference to the market—was the argument on the other side as well. The Freedmen's Bureau bill was vetoed by President Andrew Johnson. As Johnson explained in his veto message of February 29, 1866, the freedmen needed no help:

> The laws that regulate supply and demand will maintain their force, and the wages of the laborer will be regulated thereby. There is no danger that the exceedingly great demand for labor will not operate in favor of the laborer.
>
> It is earnestly hoped that instead of wasting away, [the freedmen] will, by their own efforts, establish for themselves a condition of respect, ability, and prosperity. It is certain that they can attain to that condition only through their own merit and exertions.

The Senate vote to override the veto fell two votes short of the needed two-thirds, but in July, a second version of the bill was enacted over Johnson's veto.

The same dialogue was repeated for the Civil Rights Act of 1866, the ideological and rhetorical precursor to the Fourteenth Amendment. The bill provided that

> all persons born in the United States . . . are hereby declared to be citizens of the United States . . . and such citizens, of every race and

color, and without regard to any previous condition of slavery or involuntary servitude . . . shall have the same right . . . to make and enforce contracts, to sue . . . and to full and equal benefit of all laws and proceedings for the security of person and property, as is enjoyed by white citizens . . . any law, statute, ordinance, regulation, or custom, to the contrary notwithstanding.

Explaining his support for the bill, Representative Henry J. Raymond, Republican of New York, insisted that emancipation could only be the beginning: "Having gone this far, I desire to go on by successive steps still farther, and to elevate them in all respects, so far as their faculties will allow and our power will permit us to do, to an equality with the other persons and races in this country."

Again, Johnson vetoed. Again, his vision of meritocracy provided the rationale:

The white race and the black race of the South have hitherto lived together under the relation of master and slave—capital owning labor. Now, suddenly, that relation is changed, and as to the ownership, capital and labor are divorced. They stand now each master of itself. In this new relationship, one being necessary to the other, there will be a new adjustment, which both are deeply interested in making harmonious. Each has equal power in settling the terms, and if left to the laws that regulate capital and labor, it is confidently believed that they will satisfactorily work out the problem. Capital, it is true, has more intelligence; but labor is never so ignorant as not to understand its own interests, not to know its own value, and not to see that capital must pay that value. This bill frustrates this adjustment.

On April 6 the Senate voted to override 33 to 15; the next day, the House voted to override 122 to 41. It was the first time in American history that Congress enacted a major piece of legislation over the president's veto.

And so it went. For each new measure, equality's friends insisted that intervention was needed to provide a true equality of opportunity to the freedman; only then could he succeed—or, as many claimed, fail—on his merits. And for each new measure, equality's opponents insisted that there had been too much intervention already; nature had already decreed the black man's status, and she should now run her inevitable course.

Subsequent debates often focused on the critical predicates to equal opportunity. For many, education was the key. As Senator Oliver H. P. T. Morton, Republican from Indiana, explained:

> Intelligence has always prevailed against numbers, and always will, . . . the present educated classes of the people of the South will control the new governments, and they will continue to do so until you educate all the other classes of the southern people. . . . the only way we can take control of the colored people of the South out of the hands of their late masters is by educating them.

"I regard it as a fundamental condition," Morton concluded. "Education is essential to reconstruction."

Charles Sumner agreed, and his amendment to the supplementary Reconstruction bill of 1867 promised an "open public education": "Without education," Sumner argued, "your beneficent legislation may be a failure. . . . In a republic Education is indispensable."

Senator George H. Williams of Oregon inquired, "Does this proposition mean that each school shall be equally open to persons without distinction of race or color, that there shall not be such a thing as a school for white children and a school for black children, but that each and every school shall be open to both races?"

Sumner's commitment to a genuine equality of opportunity then became clear: "If I should have my way, according to the true principle, it would be that schools, precisely like the ballot-box or the rail cars, should be open to all." But Sumner knew the political realities: "But the proposition is necessarily general in character; it does not go into details." Even at that, Sumner's amendment was defeated when the forty votes were evenly divided; equality of opportunity had its limits.

Equal opportunity often informed the debates over suffrage, over "political equality." Opponents insisted that political equality would lead ultimately to the political subordination of the white man; that was not the kind of equal opportunity they were willing to concede. Senator Thomas A. Hendricks, Democrat of Indiana, explained his opposition to black suffrage in the District of Columbia:

> [I]n the District of Columbia, the negro population almost equals, I believe, the white population, and I think at some election recently the negro vote was larger than the white vote. . . . It is a very different and

important question in the District of Columbia whether the negroes shall have the political power than it is in the State of Ohio, where the white race, notwithstanding this privilege might be extended to the negroes, would maintain its supremacy.

"I am opposed to this policy," Hendricks concluded, "which subjugates the white race to the colored race."

Senator James Patterson responded to the claim that black suffrage established "negro supremacy":

I repel the charge. It simply recognizes the political equality of the races according to the dogma of the fathers, and leaves both black and white at liberty to work out their position in society according to their capacities. Is not that right judged by any law, human or divine? If the white man complains of such legislation, he exhibits a cowardly want of confidence in his own abilities.

Patterson then made clear the meritocratic defense:

The social status of men is determined by original capacity, and cannot be fixed or safely tampered with by legislation. A fair chance for all, leaving the rest to God and nature, is the fundamental axiom of free governments.

We cannot level the earth while its internal forces are at work; neither can we bring society to a social equality while the original forces of character are unequally distributed; but social and intellectual differences cannot be made an excuse for any class monopoly of political power. Equality before the law is the groundwork of our civil fabric.

Senator Oliver H. P. T. Morton echoed these views in the debates over suffrage in the southern states, a precursor to the introduction of the Fifteenth Amendment:

It is a little remarkable, Mr. President, that whenever any allusion is made to placing the negro upon a political equality with the white man, they call it placing him over the white man; thereby conceding, as they do, that if he is made equal to the white man in political rights he will become his superior. I have never insulted the white race that way. I have always supposed they were capable of taking care of themselves; especially when their numbers were equal and certainly when they were superior.

Congressman John H. Broomall of Pennsylvania was, in a sense, more sympathetic to the claims of the Democratic opponents of black suffrage. "I am willing to concede of late," he told the House, "that if the Democrats are to be kept above the negroes in the social scale there must be some discriminating legislation in their favor."

"[P]olitical rights are needed for the preservation of our civil rights," Broomall explained on another occasion, "and the man who is poor and ignorant and low has more necessity for political rights than the man who is learned and wealthy and elevated." His argument then took another derisive turn. "If the negro gets so far above the Democrat that he can read and write while the Democrat cannot, I will refuse to exclude the Democrat's vote on that account." Laughter filled the Republican side of the chambers. "Though he may be poor and ignorant, I will give him a vote."

In the end, the argument for equal opportunity was certain to win the day; both sides, after all, were advancing it. The question ultimately was a qualitative one: how genuine would the equality be? For those opposed to Reconstruction, the empty formalism of neutrality would suffice. For those who framed congressional Reconstruction, a real effort was needed to secure a practical equality. As Senator Henry Wilson explained:

> Our great purpose is to make the citizens of the United States equal in rights and privileges; to make the Declaration of Independence the living faith, the practical policy of the nation. When that great work is completed—and the great struggle will go on until it is completed—intellect, character, and worth will win their proper places and wield their legitimate influences.

Black Americans largely accepted this limited conception of equality. In the statewide freedmen's conventions of the immediate postwar era—the beginning of black America's organized political movement—convention delegates generally pursued equality before the law: legal rights essential to the protection of their lives and their family, and to the acquisition of property. Conspicuously absent from the conventions were calls for social or economic equality, for reparations, or redistributions of wealth. Equality of opportunity appeared sufficient.

Perhaps this reflected only the political realities. "Social equality" was the Democrats' bogeyman: behind every attempt to break down the walls of caste loomed the specter of "amalgamation," and white America insisted that it was not ready for that. Black Americans, meanwhile, had experienced plenty of "amalgamation," and it was rarely voluntary; a people who had already experienced "social equality with a vengeance" were unlikely to make it a continuing objective.

Economic equality, as it had been conventionally understood, had been almost entirely absent from the Reconstruction projects of both the state and federal governments: "forty acres and a mule" was William T. Sherman's field order and nothing more. Indeed, the very idea of economic equality was transformed by the ideology of equal opportunity: "Reconstruction," Eric Foner writes, "may be seen as a decisive moment in fixing the dominant understanding of free labor as freedom of contract in the labor market, rather than ownership of productive property." For the most part, black Americans could hope only to escape slave labor for the uncertain future of wage labor, and even that aspiration was easily subverted by apprenticeship, sharecropping, and tenancy schemes. Through it all, the white stranglehold on property remained secure.

In part, too, the acceptance of "equal opportunity" likely reflected the black leadership's own conception of the natural order. They knew the falseness of the myth of natural inferiority; surely equal opportunity, genuinely equal opportunity, was all that was needed for racial hierarchy's demise. They knew—and of course they were right—that it would take more than "nature" to keep black Americans in their place.

The problem was, white America knew it too. Why else enact the "black codes," perpetuating a "virtual slavery"? Why else oppose the basic guarantees of civil rights, of equality under law? Why else decry a "social equality," why lament black "competitors ... for the rewards of labor," why portend the end of white political "supremacy"?

For all the overblown rhetoric of congressional debates, it may have been a North Carolina farmer who said it most succinctly: "If we let a nigger git equal with us, the next thing we know he'll be ahead of us."[1]

So white America made sure he'd never really get the chance.

*

A century and a half later, the debate over equal opportunity is fully resolved: we are committed to equal opportunity for all. Still, our commitment begs the question: will equal opportunity produce equality?

Consider this simple dilemma. Presumably we have seized on the nobler sentiments of the Reconstruction framers, and we celebrate today not their racism, but their commitment to equal opportunity. But a discomforting picture emerges. If we no longer believe in racial or gender superiority, and if our commitment to meritocracy is genuine, then why is our society marked by such grotesque inequalities, inequalities that conform with frightening precision to the natural hierarchy we no longer accept?

There are two typical answers. One is that meritocracy is still handicapped by invidious discrimination, the marketplace still distorted by the inefficient prejudices of malicious individuals. Our governmental efforts to promote equality remain premised on this notion: when maliciously constructed barriers to equal opportunity are removed, we are assured, equality will be attained.

But from time to time, pseudoscientific works like *The Bell Curve* surface to remind us of a second explanation for our social inequities: we are not truly equal after all. The epistemology that shaped much of the Reconstruction effort remains the unofficial cultural understanding over a century later: inequality cannot be eliminated because it inheres in the natural order.

Of course, the overtly racist rhetoric of natural inferiority has largely disappeared from our public discourse. But it is an oddly uneasy understanding that we have achieved. Today even comparatively mild inferences of racial inferiority are apt to provoke an angst-filled public rebuke; at the same time, however, this rebuke in turn is certain to stimulate an even more angst-filled public hand-wringing over the "politically correct" suppression of "ideas." We are of two minds, it seems, about these notions of natural inferiority: we are no longer willing to give public sanction to these views, but we are not quite prepared to say that they so lack legitimacy as to be beyond our marketplace of "ideas." In short, we cannot approve of those who say it, but neither can we fault those who persist in believing it.

In fact, more folks believe it than we are prepared to admit. It is as if there are two versions of the story of natural inferiority: the official understanding reflected in our public discourse, which professes unequivocally to reject all such notions, and the unofficial version that in fact constitutes our current cultural conception, which is not merely open to the possibility of a natural hierarchy, but which in fact implicitly embraces it.

So we maintain, really, two explanations for the persistence of inequality: the official view, which blames it on the malicious acts of individual discrimination, and the unofficial view, which attributes inequality to the inherent inferiority of groups and individuals. On the surface, the two explanations would not appear to share much in common. The official view locates inequality in the heart of a malicious oppressor; the unofficial one locates it in the natural disabilities of the unfortunate oppressed. The official view posits an end to inequality with the suppression of group-directed malice; the unofficial one suggests that inequality can be ended only by suppressing merit. In the one view, inequality is an aberration; in the other, inequality is only natural.

But the two views share this: they both define equality in meritocratic terms, as the opportunity to succeed according to one's merits. In the official version, those opportunities are artificially limited by malicious discrimination; in the unofficial view, they are inherently limited by natural differences. Both views, however, share the central commitment to meritocracy as the measure of equality.

The two views share this as well: they are both wrong. Both remain tied to the untenable notion of a "natural order" in two significant ways. Both are still rooted in an outmoded science: they conceive of people in essentially naturalistic terms, and thus fail to appreciate the significance of cultural forces in shaping both identity and behavior. Moreover, they both conceive of the social order—of "merit"—in naturalistic terms, as something innate and immutable. They thus fail to recognize that the meritocracy they seek to vindicate is itself contingent, and inevitable only in the sense that it inevitably expresses the preferences, biases, and increasingly entrenched inequities of the culture. Our criteria of merit, after all, are not universal; our schemes for assessing merit are not neutral; even the processes we use for evaluating the validity of our schemes are closed and exclusive. Our meritocratic schemes were constructed to the exclusion of many of us, and function today without the conscious deliberation of hardly any of us; our meritocracy, in short, is not truly "ours" at all.

This is why neither the official nor the unofficial version offers an adequate account of our existing inequities: both are blind to the structural nature of inequality. Any effort to promote equality that accepts as a given the fairness of our meritocracy is doomed merely to replicate the existing patterns of inequity. Because meritocracy is not the cure for inequality; it is the cause. And it is not fair.

The Official Explanation: Intentional Discrimination

Will equal opportunity produce equality?

The official mythology barely comprehends this question. The official myth of merit defines equality in market terms: equality, in the official myth, *is* "equal opportunity," equal opportunity, that is, to compete in the social, political, or economic marketplace. Inequality is thus the distortion of the marketplace caused by individual acts of malicious discrimination. The cure for such market imperfections—the cure for inequality—is to purge the market of these individual acts of discrimination. Thus the market is made free, and when the market is free, everyone enjoys an equal opportunity to succeed. In the myth of the market, that is the measure of equality.

Like all myths, the myth of the market is elegant enough to be believable and familiar enough to seem indisputable. But in fact it rests on one very shaky assumption. It assumes, above all, that the relevant markets are governed by neutral forces, that they are free from biases that would impair the efforts of distinct cultural groups. So, in theory, minority cultural groups—racial minorities, women, people with disabilities—would be disadvantaged neither by their long history of exclusion from the markets nor by their contemporary position at the bottom of the hierarchy of market resources.

The assumption, of course, is every bit as preposterous as it sounds. The historical exclusion of minority cultural groups ensures that the markets are not, in relevant respects, "neutral" at all; on the contrary, that exclusion has produced a significant divorce between the abilities of these groups—both "real" and perceived—and the abilities rewarded by the market. The standing assumption behind centuries of discrimination was that the excluded people lacked the ability to play the game; their long-standing exclusion ensured that this was so. Needless to say, dropping the formal barriers to the marketplace does not automatically remove these disadvantages: in a competitive game, the newcomer might not even get picked to play.

Thus the real bias that confronts cultural minorities is not to be found in the conscious acts of malicious individuals. Rather, it is to be found in the effects of centuries of exclusion from market participation: the structural disadvantages created by a complex network of unconscious assumptions and material differences. This is the real discrimination.

The Myth of Intentional Discrimination

Here is how discrimination works, according to the official mythology.

A white able-bodied man is in charge of hiring to fill a government position. There are four applicants for the position. One is a white able-bodied man. One is a black able-bodied man. One is a white able-bodied woman. One is a white man with a disability.

In one scenario, the white able-bodied man gets the job. When asked to explain his choice, the man in charge of hiring says, "The man I hired was the best qualified for the job." This is not discrimination.

In a second scenario, the white able-bodied man again gets the job. When asked to explain his choice, the man in charge of hiring says, "I hate blacks, women, and people with disabilities." This is discrimination.

It is fairly easy to tell these scenarios apart: the first decision was motivated by an assessment of neutral qualifications, the second by group-based animus. This is precisely the distinction embraced by the official mythology: the decision motivated by animus distorts the market, the decision motivated by merit simply *is* the market.

It is also the distinction embraced by the Supreme Court, which tells us that the "equal protection of the law" can be denied only by "purposeful" or "intentional" discrimination.

It lets a lot get by.

The stories of George Harley and John Sellers were told in Chapter 1. To briefly reiterate, Harley and Sellers wanted to be police officers in the District of Columbia. But they failed to attain a score of forty, a passing score, on Test 21, the civil service exam used to screen applicants to the D.C. Police Department's training program.

Test 21 was a multiple choice test. It tested "verbal ability." As the excerpt in the introductory chapter indicates, it required applicants to identify the "correct" definition of words like "bounty" and "promontory"; "correct" analogies involving concepts like "because," "reason," and "therefore"; and the "correct" meaning of quoted passages, parables, and assertions of conventional wisdom.

No one had ever determined whether Test 21 bore any relationship to the substance of the department's training program. No one had ever determined whether Test 21 bore any relationship to the qualities needed to be a good police officer. But Harley and Sellers were excluded from the training program because of their scores on Test 21. They weren't alone. Other black candidates failed Test 21. They failed it, in fact, at four times the rate of white candidates.

But in 1976 the Supreme Court insisted that reliance on Test 21 evidenced no racial discrimination, at least, not for purposes of the Fourteenth Amendment's guarantee of the "equal protection of the laws." The only discrimination that mattered, the Court ruled, was "intentional" or "purposeful" discrimination; disparate racial impacts, even at a ratio of better than four to one, did not prove unconstitutional inequality.

"As an initial matter," Justice White wrote for the Court in *Washington v. Davis,* "we have difficulty understanding how a law establishing a racially neutral qualification for employment is nevertheless racially discriminatory and denies 'any person . . . equal protection of the laws' simply because a greater proportion of Negroes fail to qualify than members of other racial or ethnic groups."[2]

He never explained how he knew that a score of forty on Test 21 was "a racially neutral qualification." The statistics might have suggested otherwise. But the statistics did not matter.

A "passing score" on Test 21 was a neutral qualification. It was not biased. The D.C. police department did not have any malice toward black applicants. It was not discriminating. Black folks, for some darned reason, just couldn't pass the test.

Thus was the requirement of "purposeful discrimination" made a part of equal protection law. From that point forward, the only discrimination that mattered was the discrimination that was "intentional"—or more accurately, only the discrimination that the complaining party might somehow *prove* was "intentional." Subsequent cases made clear precisely how difficult this would be.

In 1970 the Clerics of St. Viator, a religious order, leased a fifteen acre site in Arlington Heights, Illinois, to the Metropolitan Housing Development Corporation for the purpose of building 190 federally assisted townhouses for low- and moderate-income families. About 40 percent of the eligible families in the area would be black.

Construction on the site required rezoning by the village of Arlington Heights from a single-family zone to a multi-family zone. Only twenty-seven of the village's sixty-four thousand residents (roughly .04 percent) were black. The village denied the rezoning.

The corporation sued. The U.S. Court of Appeals ruled that the actions of the village were unconstitutionally discriminatory; the area, it noted, exhibited a high degree of residential segregation, and the village was "exploiting" the situation by allowing itself to become and remain a nearly all-white community.

The Supreme Court reversed: there was no "purposeful discrimination." Justice Lewis Powell ruled that the plaintiffs "simply failed to carry their burden of proving that discriminatory purpose was a motivating factor in the Village's decision." This was so despite the fact that public testimony at the rezoning hearings "might have been motivated by opposition to minority groups"; despite evidence that the village's rationale for its decision—to limit multi-family uses to "buffer zones" between single family and non-residential—was not consistently applied; and despite the fact that the Village Planner, whose primary responsibility includes zoning and planning matters, was never consulted for a written or oral opinion on the rezoning, an omission Powell found "curious," but evidently not terribly suspicious.[3]

The village's planning process was neutral. It was not biased. The village had no malice toward black folks. It was not discriminating. Black folks, for some darned reason, just could not seem to find suitable housing in the village of Arlington Heights.

Helen B. Feeney entered the Massachusetts civil service in 1963. Eight years later, she was forty-nine years old, widowed and with three children, earning $11,000 as a federal funds coordinator. In 1971, 1973, and again in 1974, Feeney took the Massachusetts civil service exam for the post of assistant secretary of the board of dental examiners. She did well each time: her score was the second highest in 1971 and the third highest in 1973. Each time, however, she was bumped way down the eligibility list, replaced in each case by male applicants. The reason: a Massachusetts law that grants an absolute, life-time preference to veterans applying for civil service positions.

Feeney sued in 1975, contending that she was denied the equal protection of the law. At the time of her suit, 98 percent of Massachusetts's veterans were male. This was no coincidence: until 1975 only 2 percent of noncombat armed forces could be female, a limit set by federal law.

Feeney's suit noted that in her first decade of employment, from 1963 to 1973, 43 percent of the people hired for the Massachusetts civil service were women, but nearly all were hired for low-level slots. This also was no coincidence: until 1971 the Massachusetts veterans preference law contained an exemption for jobs—nearly all low paying ones—"especially calling for women."

Judge Joseph L. Tauro held that the Massachusetts's veterans preference law was unconstitutional. It "permanently prevents a nonveteran from achieving a place on the civil service appointment test," and because "few women will ever become veterans . . . few, if any, will ever achieve a top position on a civil service eligibility list for other than positions traditionally held by women." The state, Tauro concluded, was "intentionally sacrificing the career opportunities" of Massachusetts women.

Judge Levin H. Campbell agreed. The Supreme Court's decision in *Washington v. Davis*, he acknowledged, required proof of intentional discrimination; that requirement was met here. "[T]he cutting off of women's opportunities was an inevitable concomitant of the chosen scheme," he wrote, "as inevitable as the proposition that if tails is up, heads must be down. Where a law's consequences are that inevitable, can they be meaningfully described as unintended?" To rule otherwise, Campbell concluded, would mean that the guarantee of equal protection was, "in this area of employment, little more than a hollow pretense."

But in 1979 the Supreme Court ruled otherwise. "'Discriminatory purpose,'" Justice Potter Stewart wrote for the Court, "implies more than intent as volition or intent as awareness of consequences. It implies that the decisionmaker, in this case a state legislature, selected or reaffirmed a particular course of action at least in part 'because of,' not merely 'in spite of,' its adverse effects upon an identifiable group." That was not the case here, he concluded: "nothing in the record demonstrates that this preference for veterans was originally devised or subsequently re-enacted because it would accomplish the collateral goal of keeping women in a stereotypic and predefined place in the Massachusetts Civil Service."

Justice Thurgood Marshall, joined by Justice William Brennan, dissented. "Although neutral in form," he wrote, "the statute is anything but neutral in application." The veterans preference, Marshall noted, reserved a major sector of public employment for a group that was over 98 percent male; the historic exception for jobs "especially calling for women" merely compounded the problem:

> In practice, this exemption, coupled with the absolute preference for veterans, has created a gender-based civil service hierarchy, with women occupying low-grade clerical and secretarial jobs and men holding more responsible and remunerative positions. . . . Such a statutory scheme both reflects and perpetuates precisely the kind of archaic assumptions about women's roles which we have previously held invalid.[4]

But the veterans preference statute was neutral. It was not biased. The state of Massachusetts harbored no malice toward women like Helen Feeney. It was not discriminating. Women, for some darned reason, just could not seem to get ahead in the civil service system.

Warren McCleskey, a black factory worker, was convicted in 1978 by an all-white Georgia jury of two counts of armed robbery and one count of murder for his participation in the robbery of a furniture store and the killing of a white police officer. The trial court followed the jury's recommendation and sentenced McCleskey to death. On petition for a federal writ of habeas corpus, McCleskey claimed that the Georgia death penalty scheme was administered in a racially discriminatory manner in violation of the guarantee of the equal protection of the law.

In support of his claim, McCleskey introduced a statistical analysis of over two thousand murder cases prosecuted in Georgia during the 1970s. The "Baldus study" indicated that prosecutors sought the death penalty in 70 percent of the cases involving black defendants and white victims, but only 19 percent of the cases involving white defendants and black victims. The study also indicated that the death penalty was assessed in 22 percent of the cases involving black defendants and white victims, but just 3 percent of the cases involving white defendants and black victims. Overall, the study revealed that those convicted of killing white victims were eleven times more likely to be sentenced to death than those convicted of killing black victims. When it controlled for "nonracial" variables, the study indicated that black defendants were 1.1 times more likely to be sentenced to death than white defendants and that defendants charged with killing white victims were 4.3 times more likely to be sentenced to death than those charged with killing black victims. Defendants like McCleskey, black defendants charged with killing white victims, had the greatest likelihood of receiving the death penalty.

The federal trial court assumed the validity of the study but concluded that it did not "contribute anything of value" to the constitutional inquiry. A divided Court of Appeals affirmed.

So too did the Supreme Court. Justice Lewis Powell wrote the opinion for the Court: "Our analysis begins with the basic principle that a defendant who alleges an equal protection violation has the burden of proving 'the existence of purposeful discrimination.'" "A corollary to this principle," Powell continued, "is that a criminal defendant must prove that the purposeful discrimination 'had a discriminatory effect' on him." Powell then made clear the implications of this "corollary": "Thus, to prevail under the Equal Protection Clause, McCleskey must prove that the decision-makers in *his* case acted with discriminatory purpose." And that McCleskey had not done—and almost certainly could never do. As Powell put it, McCleskey "offers no evidence specific to his own case that would support an inference that racial considerations played a part in his sentence."

But how could he? How would such evidence be available? What more could he offer than the pattern of discrimination, what more could he prove than the probability that his case fit the pattern? How much more individualized does proof ever get? As the authors of the Baldus study would later explain,

> As proof of classwide discrimination, the persistence of a statistically significant racial disparity of the magnitude estimated in *McCleskey*—after adjusting for all plausible background variables that would be expected to be an influence in the system—is commonly accepted as proof that race is an influence in a highly discretionary selection-process system and that race was the decisive factor in some decisions. Moreover, it is

possible with the *McCleskey* data to estimate how many fewer death sentences would have been imposed if all of the white-victim cases had been processed in the same manner as the black-victim cases, or how many more death sentences there would have been if the black-victim cases had been treated like the white-victim cases. The same logic and methodology has been used not only to establish the now generally accepted fact that cigarette smoking causes cancer, but also to quantify the number of lung cancer deaths that are the product of cigarette smoking.

But the evidence was not enough for the Supreme Court. Prove, they told McCleskey, discrimination in *your* case.

But McCleskey also argued that the entire Georgia statutory scheme was discriminatory, and that the legislature should be obliged under the Constitution to fix it. Failure to cure the obvious discrimination violated McCleskey's right to the equal protection of the laws.

But the disposition of Helen Feeney's claim precluded this argument: "For this claim to prevail," Powell wrote, "McCleskey would have to prove that the Georgia legislature enacted or maintained the death penalty statute *because of* an anticipated racially discriminatory effect." Ignorance or indifference was again insufficient; only evidence of racial malice would suffice.

Following Justice White's lead in *Washington v. Davis*, Justice Powell was candid about the factors that informed his decision:

> McCleskey's claim, taken to its logical conclusion, throws into serious question the principles that underlie our entire criminal justice system. . . . [I]f we accepted McCleskey's claim that racial bias had impermissibly tainted the capital sentencing decision, we could soon be faced with similar claims as to other types of penalties . . . [as well as] claims based on unexplained discrepancies that correlate to membership in other minority groups, and even to gender. . . . [T]here is no limiting principle to the type of challenge brought by McCleskey.

It was left to Justice Brennan, writing in dissent, to point out the obvious difficulty with this response: "The Court . . . states that its unwillingness to regard petitioner's evidence as sufficient is based in part on the fear that recognition of McCleskey's claim would open the door to widespread challenges to all aspects of criminal sentencing.

Taken on its face, such a statement seems to suggest a fear of too much justice."

Brennan's dissenting opinion, joined by Justices Marshall, Blackmun, and Stevens, protested the simple unreality of the decision: did the majority really believe that there was no discrimination in the Georgia death penalty scheme? The numbers alone were convincing, but, as Justice Brennan pointed out, "Evaluation of McCleskey's evidence cannot rest solely on the numbers themselves. We must also ask whether the conclusion suggested by those numbers is consonant with our understanding of history and human experience. . . . For many years, Georgia operated openly and formally precisely the type of dual system the evidence shows is still effectively in place."

But the most convincing proof was the most practical:

> The Court's decision today will not change what attorneys in Georgia tell other Warren McCleskeys about their chances of execution. Nothing will soften the harsh message they must convey, nor alter the prospect that race undoubtedly will continue to be a topic of discussion. McCleskey's evidence will not have obtained judicial acceptance, but that will not affect what is said on death row. However many criticisms of today's decision may be rendered, these painful conversations will serve as the most eloquent dissents of all.

But Georgia's death penalty scheme was neutral. It was not biased. The Georgia legislature, judges, prosecutors, and juries harbored no special malice toward people like Warren McCleskey. They did not discriminate. People like McCleskey, for some darned reason, just kept getting sentenced to death.

Warren McCleskey consistently maintained that he was innocent of the charge of murder. In July 1987, a change in Georgia's open records law produced new evidence for McCleskey's defense. That evidence established that the principal witness against McCleskey was in fact a jailhouse plant who had been offered a favorable deal by prosecutors in return for incriminating testimony. Prosecutors had not revealed this arrangement at McCleskey's trial; at least two jurors indicated that they would not have voted for the death sentence if they had known of the arrangement. Upon a second application for habeas corpus, a federal district court judge reprimanded the prosecution and ordered a new trial. Ultimately the Supreme Court ruled, by a vote of six to three, that McCleskey's arguments could be properly raised only in an initial habeas corpus petition. "In refusing to grant a stay to fully review McCleskey's claims, the court values expediency over human life," Justice Marshall wrote in dissent. "Repeatedly denying Warren McCleskey his constitutional rights is unacceptable. Executing him is inexcusable."

Nelson Mandela, president of the African National Congress, joined in the effort to commute McCleskey's sentence. In a September 1991 letter to the Georgia Board of Pardons and Paroles, Mandela wrote: "As a person who practiced law as a lawyer before my imprisonment, I appreciate fully the concept of 'beyond a reasonable doubt.' To my mind there is far more than reasonable doubt in the case of Warren McCleskey, and I believe that his execution would be a tragic miscarriage of justice."

Support for McCleskey's original claim was published at about the same time. A 1990 analysis by the U.S. General Accounting Office revealed "a pattern of evidence indicating racial disparities in the charging, sentencing, and imposition of the death penalty" throughout the nation. The GAO identified twenty-eight independent studies confirming the existence of statewide or nationwide racial disparities.

Early in the morning of September 25, 1991, Warren McCleskey was strapped into the electric chair at the Georgia state prison in Jackson. Shortly after three o'clock in the morning, he was dead. A candlelight vigil was held outside the prison walls in protest; not far away, a man in Ku Klux Klan regalia held a sign reading, "We Support the Death Penalty."

Earlier that summer, Justice Powell's biographer asked him whether he would change his vote in any case. "Yes," he replied, "*McCleskey v. Kemp*. . . . I have come to think that capital punishment should be abolished."[5]

Briefly reconsider our discrimination hypothetical, the white able-bodied male employer who hires another white able-bodied man for a government job. When asked to explain his choice, the man in charge of hiring may say, "The man I hired was the best qualified for the job." Or he may say, "I hate blacks, women, and people with disabilities." Only the latter would give rise to a claim under the Constitution; the first would not be discrimination.

It would not be discrimination even where our employer over and over, again and again, hires white able-bodied men, explaining each time that they are the "best qualified for the job." The statistical disparities would not matter; what is needed is proof of *intentional* discrimination.

It would not be discrimination even if our employer is aware that his hiring practices have produced this disparity, and even if he knows that his particular practices inevitably will continue to produce the disparity. "I know," he may say, "but I do not care." His awareness and indifference do not matter; what is needed is proof that he *desired* the disparate results.

It would not be discrimination even if our employer's "neutral" explanations leave much of the disparity unexplained, if, for example, when the "neutral" criteria are factored out—if we account for the variables of education, experience, and so on—our employer is still four times more likely to hire a white able-bodied man than a similarly situated woman, minority, or person with a disability. These probabilities do not matter; what is needed is proof of discrimination in the *individual* case.

So, indeed, a lot gets by. Even more, in fact, than this exercise suggests. For the truth is, the requirement of "intentional" discrimination is plagued by problems that transcend the distinctions among these various scenarios, problems so fundamental that they undermine the integrity of the very concept of "intentional discrimination" in any case, no matter what the facts.

There are three such problems. First, the bare insistence on proof of intent suggests a rather odd preoccupation with the mindset of the discriminator and a concomitant disregard of the impact on the victim. For a constitutional provision meant to protect people from the pain of discrimination—not "benign" discriminators from the inconvenience of lawsuits—this preoccupation is at least slightly perverse.

Second, proof of intent is not easy to come by, in part because it may not be all that real a phenomenon, and in part because, however real it may be, it is not easy to discern but is very easy to hide. Determining an individual's "intent" is difficult; getting a fix on the "intent" of a legislature or a state agency is more difficult still; finding proof of that "intent" in the "no-comment," attorney-reviewed, double-speak world of modern bureaucracy is all but impossible.

Third, and by far the most important problem, the insistence on proof of intent seriously misunderstands the nature of contemporary discrimination: it is more unconscious than conscious, more structural than individual. People—including state actors—generally don't "intend" to discriminate, at least not in the usual sense of that word; they simply do what they are told, do what they have always done, do what the law, or the regulations, or the market seems to demand. The built-in biases of the schemes they implement guarantee disparate results; their own unconscious assumptions reinforce the biases and prevent them from re-appraising the outcomes. It all just happens. Requiring proof of intentional discrimination simply lets most discrimination be.

The Problem of Perspective: Who Cares? There are at least two distinct perspectives to consider in defining what counts as "discrimination."

Consider, first, the perspective of the victim of the allegedly discriminatory conduct. Imagine being excluded from an educational program, being denied a job or promotion, receiving a harsh criminal sentence, and knowing—as certainly as such things can be known—that more likely than not, the outcome would have been different were it not for your race, your gender, or your disability. Imagine the disappointment, the frustration, the bitterness, the sadness, the anger. Then imagine being told that you were not the victim of discrimination.

This is so, you are told, because you must consider the other perspective. This second perspective—the state's perspective—is what matters. And the program, the agency, the court did not *mean* to hurt you. It would be unfair to penalize them for your misfortune; without malice in their hearts directed at you, we cannot say that they have done wrong. You feel aggrieved, but they are innocent.

And you wonder, "Who cares?"

Why does their "innocence" matter? This is not, after all, a criminal proceeding, the "rights" at stake are not those of the state actors. What difference does it make whether their hearts are pure or evil? The effect of their actions is the same, the harm they have done is the same, and you—and the people like you—will continue to feel the hurt. Is this what it means to receive the "equal protection of the laws"? Should a constitutional provision designed to protect people from discrimination be so indifferent to those people's perspective? Should it be so utterly absorbed with the psyches of those in power?

They may be good, bad, or indifferent—it does not change what they have done, it does not change what they will do, and it does not change the way you feel.

So they didn't mean to hurt you; who cares?

My Cousin Vinny is a funny movie. Joe Pesci plays this streetwise but courtroom-dumb novice New York lawyer, Vinny Gambini, who is called on to defend his innocent cousin from a murder rap in a small Alabama town. Pesci arranges to go hunting with the local district attorney; in his hotel room, he tries to decide what to wear. Marisa Tomei plays Pesci's girlfriend, Mona Lisa Vito; she does not see fashion as a priority. The scene goes like this:

Vinny: What am I gonna wear?
Lisa: What are you going to hunt?
Vinny: I don't know. He's got a . . . he's got a lot of stuffed heads in his office.
Lisa: Heads?! What kinda heads?
Vinny: I don't know. He's got a boar, a bear, a couple o' deer.
Lisa: Whoa! You're gonna shoot a dear?!
Vinny: I don't know. I suppose. I mean, I'm a man's man; I could go deer huntin'.
Lisa: A sweet, innocent, harmless, leaf-eatin', doe-eyed little deer.
Vinny: Hey, Lisa. I'm not gonna go out there just to wimp out, ya know? I mean, the guy'll lose respect for me; would you rather have that?
(Lisa stomps into the bathroom and slams the door)
Vinny: What about these pants I got on? You think they're okay?
(No response)
Vinny: Oh.
(Lisa comes out of the bathroom)
Lisa: Imagine you're a deer. You're prancin' along, ya get thirsty, ya spot a little brook. You put your little deer lips down to the cool, clear water. Bam!! A fuckin' bullet rips off part of your head! Your brains are layin' on the ground in little bloody pieces! Now I aks ya, would ya give a fuck what kinda pants the sonovabitch who shot ya was wearin'?![6]

That's about it. When you're always under the gun, and somebody keeps pulling the trigger, you don't much care about their fashion sense, their state of mind, or how their day has been. Their actions have consequences; you can feel that reality; the rest is strictly for the lawyers.

The Problem of Proof: Who Knows? Our hypothetical employer swears he hires only the "most qualified" candidates, regardless of their race, gender, or disability.

The big question: "Is he telling the truth?" In almost every case, there is only one honest answer: "Who knows?" Probably not even him.

My sister has a little boy named Stephen, who is the most wonderful little boy in the world, and this would be true whether he was my godson or not. He has a mischievous streak, or at least I think it is a mischievous streak, but I can't really be sure, which is kind of the point. Consider these two honest-to-goodness stories.

At the age of four, Stephen still liked to have his pacifier, which he called—after the manufacturer, I think—his "binky." My sister thought that four was beyond the binky age, and she tried a variety of rhetorical appeals, persuasive means, and plain sneaky schemes to get Stephen to abandon his binky. None of them worked.

My mother tried her luck one evening as she was tucking Stephen into bed. "Stephen," she asked, "have you ever heard of the Binky Fairy?"

Stephen looked at her suspiciously. He did not answer.

"You know about the Tooth Fairy, don't you, Stephen?"

His eyes narrowed. He nodded.

"Well, the Binky Fairy is just like the Tooth Fairy. If you leave your binky under your pillow tonight, the Binky Fairy will come and take it, and give you a present in return."

"What kind of present?"

"Anything you want."

Stephen mulled this over. My mom sensed her opportunity.

"What do you want from the Binky Fairy, Stephen?"

"Something."

"Well what kind of something, Stephen?"

"A gun."

"A Power Ranger's morphing gun?" My mom knows the lingo.
"No."
"A water gun?"
"No."
"What kind of gun, Stephen?"
"A real gun."
"Stephen, what are you going to do with a real gun?"
Stephen did not hesitate.
"Shoot the Binky Fairy."
It was quick thinking for a four-year-old. But Stephen outdid himself a few months later, during Thanksgiving dinner at my parents' house. My sister was shepherding her son through his safety lessons for the benefit of the rest of the family.
"Stephen," she asked, "what will you do if a stranger offers you candy?"
"I won't take it," Stephen replied, and the aunts, uncles, cousins, and grandparents assembled around the table all smiled and clapped their approval.
"And what will you do if the stranger tries to make you take the candy?"
"I'll run away." More clapping, a little louder.
"Stephen, what will you do if a stranger offers you a ride?"
"I won't take it." Stephen is now smiling with pride as the family cheers him on.
"And what if the stranger tries to make you take a ride?"
"I'll run away!" The applause builds.
"And Stephen," my sister continues, "what will you do if someone offers you drugs?"
"I won't take 'em!" Now the crowd goes wild.
"And what if someone tries to make you take drugs?"
"I'll run away!"
"Stephen, will you ever take drugs?"
"No!"
"Never?"
"Never!"
The table erupts with one final loud cheer. Stephen is positively beaming. It is, in all, a very wonderful moment.
As the dinner winds to a close, Stephen politely asks my mother if he may be excused from the table. My sister surveys his plate.

"Stephen, you didn't eat any of your lima beans."

Stephen looks down at his plate, as if to verify. He looks back up, but doesn't say a word.

"You should eat your lima beans first, then you can be excused."

Stephen looks back down at his plate. He isn't budging.

"Come on, Stephen, you like lima beans."

Nothing. My mom intervenes.

"What's wrong, honey, why didn't you eat your lima beans?"

Stephen gives my mother a sideways glance.

"I thought they was drugs."

Now I don't know if Stephen really thought his beans were drugs. In context, I tend to doubt it, but I can't be sure. And I don't know if Stephen really plans on shooting the Binky Fairy. Knowing him as I do, I tend to doubt it, but I can't be sure. Kids are tough to figure out; sometimes they just say stuff.

But *why* they say stuff—why they *do* stuff—is darned near impossible to say. Was Stephen just playing to his audience? I don't know. Was he just looking to get his way? I don't know. Was he just mimicking what he had been taught? Or was he using what he had been taught to get what he wanted? Or was he using what he had been taught to get what he had been taught to want?

It's a little easier with adults. An adult doesn't threaten to shoot the Binky Fairy; he knows better. An adult doesn't mistake lima beans for drugs; he knows better. And when, in either case, the adult claims not to know better, *we* know better ourselves—we know, that is, that he is lying.

But sometimes adults are even tougher to figure out; they may be less impulsive than kids, and perhaps what they say is more suspect. Did our hypothetical employer really think the white guy was the most qualified? Or was he just saying that? Was it just an excuse to conceal his bias? Was he, in effect, using what he had been taught to get what he wanted?

How will we know what is in our employer's head? How will we know what he was really thinking, unless he is foolish enough to admit, as in our alternative hypothetical, that he hates the groups he does not hire? The problem with proving intentional discrimination is precisely that adults *do* know better than to say such foolish things. And we credit their alternative explanations because we don't find them incredible. When someone keeps saying that the white man is the "most qualified," we, sadly, act as if we do *not* yet know better.

There is an even more profound difficulty with this concept: How does the employer himself know what was really in his head? Is there a deeply conditioned animus that he does not recognize? A distrust? A suspicion of inferiority? Or perhaps he just acts from habit, perhaps hiring able-bodied white men is as conditioned, or as impulsive, as avoiding drugs and beans and defending binkys from Binky Fairies. Was our employer, when you really get down to it, using what he had been taught to get what he had been taught to want?

Human behavior is complex stuff, complex enough to make most talk of "intent" seem pointless. Do we "intentionally" choose our friends? Do we "intend" to make enemies? Do we "purposefully" favor our friends over our enemies?

So what does it mean to say that someone "intentionally" discriminated? Does it mean that their choices were entirely volitional, unaffected by social, or professional, expectations? That is impossible; it never happens. Does it mean that their choices were entirely deliberative, unaffected by unconscious assumption, impulse, or desire? That too is impossible; that never happens. We are simply not autonomous beings in the ways that this talk of "intent" presupposes; we almost never—in the narrow sense required by law—intentionally do anything, including discriminate. So proving "intent" is something of a pickle.

The law, to its credit, has accounted for this problem of proof in most situations: it makes the actor responsible for the foreseeable consequences of his action. It admits, in effect, that this "intent" is largely unknowable, so it imputes the intent—it assigns it—based on the likely results of an individual's behavior.

Imagine a young man confronting some other person—an intruder, an acquaintance, the Binky Fairy, whomever; imagine the young man has a gun, a real gun; imagine the young man points the gun at this other person and squeezes the trigger, and this other person drops wounded to the floor.

Our young man claims later that he did not intend to shoot this other person. Yes, he aimed the gun; yes, he pulled the trigger; but no, he did not intend to shoot the other person. He swears that this is so, swears it on a stack of Bibles. How do we prove that he is lying?

There is more. We learn that the young man has been taught that this other person—or other persons in general—is evil. He has been conditioned to point guns at other persons and pull the trigger. He does it reflexively. Does he do it intentionally?

As a matter of law, these are not difficult problems: the actor intends the foreseeable consequences of his actions. A shot other person is the foreseeable consequence of pointing the gun and shooting; our young man "intended" to shoot the other person. We do not care what he swears and we do not care what he has been taught; "intent," as a legal concept, means less than that.

As Justice Stevens noted in his concurring opinion in *Washington v. Davis*, this rule of the foreseeable consequences is a rather fundamental principle of law. There is no reason it should not apply in cases of discrimination. Yet it does not. So strong is the commitment to the free market that the ordinary rules are waived: the law insists that the public employer, school, or state legislature that knows, beyond any doubt, that the consequences of its actions will advantage one racial or gender group and disadvantage another somehow does not "intend" those consequences when it acknowledges the expected disparity and goes ahead anyway. Ignorance of the discriminatory effects is an excuse, and so too is indifference. Only proof of malice will suffice.

So the victim of discrimination is forced to search for that elusive evidence of a hostile purpose. Needless to say, that is hard to find. Only the most naive actors, or the most uninhibited, or the ones whose actions are unfiltered by legal counsel, are apt to provide the necessary "smoking gun." The rest all know better. And we pretend that we do not.

The Problem of the Premise: What Is Discrimination? The third problem with the concept of "intentional discrimination"—and by far the most fundamental—is really the simplest: it's just not the way things work. This is true not merely on the level of individual psychology, where the whole idea of "intent" is problematic enough. It is also true on a societal level, where the fundamental assumption behind the idea is wrong. "Intentional discrimination" assumes a neutral free marketplace distorted only by the occasional malicious, conscious discrimination of individual actors. That is not the way of our world.

The decisions of the Supreme Court make explicit the assumption that informs most of our dialogue about equality: the unquestioned belief in the neutrality of our meritocratic schemes. Its requirement that the complaining party prove "intentional discrimination" is in many respects the inevitable product of this assumption. If all is neutral, then disparate impacts can be explained only by one of two phenomena: either real difference in merit or measurement schemes distorted by the malicious interference of biased individuals. If it is the former, then meritocracy simply has its day; if the latter, then the law demands redress. Merit or malice, one right, one wrong.

But of course, it's more complicated than that, more complex than the elegant either/or of "merit"/"malice." In fact, the range of inequalities quite likely reflects a little of both.

Yet there is something deeper going on here, and it is this something that unites the reconceptions of identity and discrimination—of, for example, race and racism—and dissolves this simple dichotomy of merit and malice, revealing them to be the flip sides of the same coin.

That something is the simple recognition that our schemes of meritocracy are not neutral; rather, the criteria, the standards, the instruments, the systems are all systematically biased in favor of the dominant cultural group. And the biases run so deep—are so constitutive—that it is nearly impossible to escape them long enough to perceive the ways they constrain us.

Group identities are faithfully reproduced, and discriminatory behaviors consistently replicated, precisely because they do not depend anymore on conscious, deliberative decisions. Our habits, our traditions, our systems, our institutions do the job—they make all the differences—for us.

The Reality of Unconscious Bias

It is difficult to reconstruct race and gender and disability on more equal terms—maddeningly, agonizingly difficult. But it is not because we are fighting the natural inferiority of subordinate groups, nor because there are too many malicious individuals resisting the effort. It is rather because our systems of reward and punishment, after centuries, perhaps millennia, of cultural domination, are premised on some decidedly non-neutral assumptions about the cultural value of certain human attributes. The people who work within those systems—which is to say, all of us—necessarily share those same assumptions, and rarely if ever think about them at all. What is more, the same history of cultural domination has led us—all of us—to embrace certain assumptions about group attributes, to assume that some groups have either more or less of what our culture values. Again, we rarely think about these assumptions at all. But we act on them. The assumptions become, in effect, the reality.

Consider an abstract example. There are two jobs, one requiring talent A and the other talent F. Talent A is very highly valued; talent F not highly valued at all. We work for a company that seeks people with talent A; our job is to find such people. We do not stop to wonder why talent A is so highly valued, or why talent F is so devalued. It is not our job.

There are two cultural groups: group 1 has many people working in jobs that require talent A; group 2 does not, but labors largely in jobs requiring talent F. The reasons for the discrepancy are largely historical, having to do with a combination of false assumptions about the unfitness of group 2 for talent A tasks, overt attempts by group 1 to horde talent A jobs for itself, and the perhaps significant fact that it was group 1 who defined the relative worth of the talents. But we only vaguely understand this history. What we know is that group 2 generally does not do talent A jobs; and we assume, without malice, that it is because they are, generally and relatively, without talent A. So we assume that our employees will come from group 1; and so they do. We have done our job.

As we keep doing our job, for years, and decades, and generations, our cultural divisions become more and more firmly entrenched. Group 1 does talent A work; group 2 does talent F work. Group 1 receives all the social, economic, and political benefits that attend their position; group 2 gets less. And when at some point group 2 begins to complain that it too has talent A, we—who are mostly group 1—devise schemes and tests to measure talent A, and they reveal that group 2 does indeed have Talent A, just not as much of it as group 1. A voice deep inside us tells us that maybe our ancestors were right all along about group 2, and our bosses tell us they need a few people with talent A and a bunch more with talent F, and we set out to find them, and we know right where to look.

In the abstract, it is perhaps easy to identify the critical questions and expose the assumptions and biases in this scheme:

- Are the individuals who work in this system really neutral, or do they harbor assumptions and biases that favor group 1?
- Are the tests for talent A really neutral, or do they reflect assumptions and biases that favor group 1?
- Does group 2 have "less" talent A because it is innately inferior to group 1, or because it has been denied access to the resources needed to develop talent A?
- Is talent A really more valuable than talent F, or was it just made that way by group 1, which, at that historical moment, happened to have more of it?

But these questions are much easier to raise in the abstract than they are in the real world. Because in the real world, we operate in the same culture that constrains us with its assumptions and biases; it is very difficult—and in one sense impossible—to "transcend" this culture for the purpose of critiquing it. At its most general level, this is the postmodern quandary: modernity's all-pervasive rationality leaves us with no tools of cultural criticism beyond the very rationality we might otherwise critique. We can never, in this sense, move "beyond" our culture. But at a more specific level—the terrain, thankfully, of this critique—the quandary is slightly less severe: the cultural precepts we seek to critique are not so universal; they are, rather, merely the *dominant* precepts. Of course, that is obstacle enough. The difficulty with the assumptions and biases that shape our schemes of "merit" with unconscious, subconscious, institutional, or structural discrimination—is precisely their pervasiveness: they are so dominant, so much a part of our culture, that they hardly seem like assumptions or biases at all.

Eraser, a film starring Arnold Schwarzenegger, was released in June 1996. It was, not too surprisingly, an action movie, with a reported cost of around $100 million. The script called for a female lead, a character whom Schwarzenegger could save. The part was eventually landed by actress, singer, and former Miss America Vanessa Williams.

The choice actually surprised the man who made it, the movie's producer, Arnold Kopelson. As Kopelson explains, "I wasn't considering Vanessa. It just didn't occur to me. She's not mainstream. She's a singer."

There are many reasons, perhaps, why Vanessa Williams would just not "occur" to a producer looking to cast a female lead; there are many reasons, perhaps, why Williams might be considered outside the "mainstream"; and there are many reasons, perhaps, why Williams, unlike other female performing artists, might be thought of as a "singer" rather than an actress, despite her Broadway, television, and film experience. Had producer Kopelson ended his explanation there, most of us would assume that these reasons had nothing to do with Williams's race. Producer Kopelson's mindset (what "occurs" to him), his conception of public tastes (the "mainstream"), his categorization of performing artists (as "singers," not actresses), are all, we would assume, altogether "race-neutral."

But Kopelson did not end his explanation there.

"And we weren't thinking about going black."[7]

His candor is both refreshing and depressing. Refreshing because he was both insightful and honest enough to acknowledge the truth: that the female lead was presumptively the province of a white actress, and that only an affirmative decision to "go black" would disturb that norm. Depressing because that *is* the truth, and that mindset—that of Kopelson and every producer and every other powerful decision maker like him—is so viciously self-perpetuating, both reflecting and shaping public tastes, defining the entertainment "mainstream," reinforcing our cultural sense of what is normal and natural and, yes, "race-neutral."

Heroes and heroines are white. Unless somebody decides to go black.

Imagine walking down a long dark hall. At the end of the hall is a door. You walk to the door. You open it. The light from the room briefly blinds you. Gradually you regain your vision. You see that you have walked into a room full of lawyers.

What do you see?

What you probably see are briefcases and haircuts and suits. And mostly men. And most of them, maybe all of them, are white.

In this limited respect, Hollywood and the real world are one and the same: their assumptions are identical; indeed, they are mutually reconstitutive. The Hollywood image of hero and heroine, of lawyer and doctor, of prostitute and thief—these *are* the realities, of both yesterday and tomorrow.

Delaware Today is my home state's unofficial magazine. It recently polled the state bar to identify the "seventy best lawyers," by specialty, in the state. It noted, somewhat apologetically, that the winners shared "a similar demographic profile." Small wonder. There were no women lawyers in Delaware until 1923. There were no black lawyers in Delaware until 1929, and Louis L. Redding would be the only minority member of the bar until 1956.[8]

Lawyers are white men. They look like white men. They talk like white men. They think like white men. And if the way that someone looks, talks, and thinks is different, then she is not a lawyer, or at least, not a very good one.

This doesn't even surprise us, because we all know that—perhaps through no fault of their own—people who aren't white men just aren't as good at being lawyers.

So go hire a lawyer, and try not to hire a white man. It takes an effort.

I have seen firsthand the hiring process at more than one law school. A minority applicant for a law school teaching position is denied the job because his scholarship is "unconventional"; a white applicant with no record of scholarship at all is then hired.

A minority teacher—a good teacher, with good scholarship, whose substantive expertise meets perfectly the law school's needs—is rejected for a job because he is not a "good fit"; a white teacher, not superior by any "objective" measure, is hired the same day.

A minority litigator with unsurpassed experience and unequaled communication skills is dismissed from serious consideration for a law school teaching position out of concern that the students—virtually all white—might not be able to "relate" to him.

None of these things are said with malice, and all the decision makers would be properly appalled by the suggestion that they are "racist" or "biased." They are just following "convention," just looking for the good "fit," just looking for someone that people could "relate" to. They are looking for someone who fit the mold. They are doing what had always been done. They aren't ready to "go black."

The Reality of Structural Bias

Sometimes—rarely—discrimination results from a malicious prejudice buried deep in our souls.

Sometimes—much more often—it results from unconscious biases, the assumptions of competence or incompetence, aptitude or ineptitude, a "fit" that is good or not.

But sometimes—perhaps most often—discrimination is not rooted in the biases of any individual at all. Discrimination results simply from bureaucratic practices, from the unthinking repetition of the ordinary ways of operating in the world. Most of the practices seem altogether neutral. In the abstract, perhaps, they are. But in the real world, they are not.

Consider the simple example of government contracting. The city lets a competitive bid; the low bidder gets the prime contract. The low bidder, it turns out in a particular case, is a white contractor, but the process can hardly be considered racially biased. Low bid wins; it is hard to imagine a scheme more neutral than that.

But an odd statistical pattern emerges. White citizens constitute barely half the city's population, but white contractors get 99.3 percent of the city's prime contracts. White citizens, then, are seventy-five times more likely to get a prime contract than their minority counterparts.

Why? Are white folks better bidders?

Even the most cursory review of the city's history reveals a relentless pattern of public and private discrimination. And, it turns out, the contracting industry has been plagued by a nationwide pattern of racial discrimination.

Are white folks "better" bidders for a reason?

Bidding possibilities, it emerges, are limited by certain economic realities: bonding requirements, insurance premiums, credit approvals, the economies of scale, and pervasive networks of business connections—economic realities forged in the long history of racial oppression.

White folks are "better" bidders because they have monopolized for centuries all the resources required to bid.

These are precisely the facts that confronted the city of Richmond, Virginia, when it enacted its affirmative action plan for city contracting. The Supreme Court invalidated that plan; Justice Sandra Day

O'Connor insisted that the city of Richmond could not demonstrate a need for the plan, since it did not establish "any identified discrimination in the Richmond construction industry."[9]

But minority contractors do not need the assistance of affirmative action solely to overcome the racial biases of individual officials; that is not the way discrimination works. They need affirmative action to overcome the systemic disadvantages, both "real" and perceived, created by the history of discrimination and the philosophical equation of short-term fiscal value with the public good.

In the real world, there is nothing neutral about the bidding scheme; it systematically and inevitably disadvantages minority contractors. It might save the city a few dollars, but it is not, in a deeper sense, worth the cost.

Nearly every "neutral" scheme is subject to this same critique. There are always latent advantages; there are always assumed norms; and they all just look like the ordinary course of business. It is true of the criteria for education, employment, and the full range of governmental punishments and rewards. And it is true of tests of "verbal ability," like the Civil Service Commission's Test 21.

In the Constitutional Law course that I teach, we usually begin the discussion of "purposeful discrimination" with a hypothetical problem. It is, I tell them, based on a real-life conundrum.

Let us suppose, I say, that my course in Constitutional Law is very popular, so popular, in fact, that there is a waiting list to get in. This, of course, instantly alerts the students to the fact that the hypothetical is very loosely based on reality. But let us suppose that the waiting list is so long that I must develop an entrance exam to screen students out. And so I do, and to every student applying to be in the course, I administer the same examination. And students who pass the examination are admitted into the course, and students who fail it are excluded from the course.

Are there, I ask, any problems so far?

The first time I asked the question, I assumed the answer would be "no." In my mind, at least, there were no problems so far.

But of course there are problems; I simply could not see them. The students, meanwhile, have been perfectly willing to tell me that an entrance examination to get into a course seems altogether unfair;

perhaps, they suggest, it is precisely the students who are failing the entrance exam who would most benefit from the course.

But, I have come to retort, we use entrance examinations all the time; aptitude for a pursuit is frequently one of the preconditions for receiving the privilege of the pursuit.

We all nod together; yes, we agree, it is after all the way things are done.

But, I continue, a strange phenomenon has developed over the years with my entrance exam. Preoccupied as I am with demographics and statistics, I have always requested a great deal of biographical data as a part of the entrance exam. I collect it on a separate form and grade the exams anonymously, so the data do not in any way influence my judgment. But in subsequently correlating the exam scores with the biographical data, I discovered an odd trend: 13 percent of the applicant students who self-identified as Democrats failed the entrance examination; of the applicants who self-identified as Republicans, 47 percent failed.

What, I wondered, was the cause of that?

The hypotheses I receive are sometimes very elegant, sometimes extraordinarily complex, and sometimes quite fantastic: one of my favorites has been the suggestion that Democrats and Republicans have distinctive handwriting styles, that I have either studied these differences (the conspiracy theory) or am at some deep level aware of them (the unconscious discrimination theory), and that handwriting thus becomes the proxy for my anti-Republican bias. This is just one variation on a theme that runs through most of the hypotheses: essentially, it is that my exam is biased. The bias hypothesis is one of the two major accounts for the disparate results; probably 90 percent of the hypotheses center around the possibility of bias.

But, I tell them, it is a multiple-choice exam, and I do not grade it myself, but have it scanned by computer. This effectively refutes the handwriting theories, and, a bit to my dismay, quiets most other objections as well. For most of us, the only palpable bias remains the malicious bias of a decision-maker, and once we control for that—as, for example, in providing that the exams will be graded by a computer and not by me—the possibility for tainted results disappears.

But some of the bias theorists persist: maybe the problem is not with the grading of the exam, but with the examination itself. Maybe the examination is biased.

I assure them that it is not.

Some persistent souls want proof.

I offer them this: I have run a separate correlation study to determine whether the entrance examination is valid and reliable. Indeed it is. There is a consistent correlation between scores on the entrance examination and success on my final examination; specifically, there is a significant positive correlation between scores on the entrance examination and a score of eighty on the final examination, a score that usually translates to a B. So, it evolves, the entrance examination does in fact validly and reliably measure aptitude for the study of constitutional law.

For just about everyone, this modest statistical assault ends the effort to prove bias. They revert to the second of the two major accounts for the disparate results:

Republicans are stupid.

I don't believe this hypothesis has ever been offered in earnest, and yet we attempt to explore it with a sobriety appropriate to the subject matter: it is, after all, rather a disturbing claim. We have developed some fairly credible explanations to support it.

Intelligence, we submit, may be properly defined as the ability to adapt to one's environment. Ashley Montagu once said this, and that's good enough for us. Intelligence is also a dynamic process, not a fixed entity; lots of scientists have said this, and we believe them all. People who must regularly solve problems and adapt to the demands of their environment are getting more opportunity to develop their intelligence; this follows ipso facto, which is Latin and therefore quite irrefutable. Wealthy people pretty much create their own environments; they have fewer problems to solve and less need to adapt to their environment than do poor people, and therefore have fewer opportunities to develop their intelligence; more Latin is appropriate here. Republicans are comparatively wealthy; we think this can be proved statistically, which is even more irrefutable than Latin. Republicans are, only comparatively of course, stupid; Q. E. D.

So my entrance exam simply confirms a larger sociological phenomenon. Or maybe it is a biological one: it will take more research (or maybe more Latin) to make this determination. But in either event, we can be confident now that Republicans are disproportionately failing my exams because they are disproportionately unintelligent.

Even in jest, it makes me uncomfortable to talk like this. And although we laugh, there is a bit of an edge to our discussion, an uneasiness that runs through the class. I suspect, but cannot prove, that the discomfort is particularly keen among folks who think of themselves as Republicans and who probably are not accustomed to listening to accounts of their intellectual deficiencies, especially not hypotheses developed by folks who are themselves not Republicans and who may seem to derive a certain venal pleasure from the whole debasing affair.

We are usually saved at this point by a question. It comes from a student—maybe a "Republican," maybe not—and it precipitates a dialogue that goes something like this:

"Professor, what's on the test?"

"Which test?"

"Well, either test? I guess start with the entrance exam."

"It's basically a history test."

"Why a history test?"

"Because, as you know by now, I think history is vital to an understanding of constitutional law. Most cases can't be understood outside their historical context, and if you don't know the history, you can't understand the cases."

"But you seem to teach the history."

"Well, I try."

"Then do you really need to know the history *before* the course begins?"

"Well, it helps. I mean, evidently it helps, because the folks who do well on that history test also do well on my final exam."

"Professor, can you tell us in general terms what's on the final exam? In the hypothetical, of course."

"In the hypothetical—of course—the final exam is mostly history."

"But you don't teach mostly history."

"I guess not."

"And as lawyers, we won't need to know mostly history."

"That's probably true. What are you thinking?"

"That your entrance test is pretty worthless, except to find out if people are any good at multiple-choice history tests."

I could put up more resistance; I could argue about the importance of history to law and lawyering, the transferability of the skills tested on my history exam, and the general aptitudes that are captured by this specific measurement scheme. But the point is unavoidable: in the final analysis, what my entrance exam measures is not general intelligence, not an aptitude for lawyering, and not even an aptitude for the study of my idiosyncratic vision of constitutional law: what it measures is the ability to perform well on it and similar tests.

The claim of bias gains a renewed vitality. My neutral criteria of aptitude suddenly look very ad hoc; and, students begin to wonder, what precisely is this "history" that I purport to test? I share with them just one item from the entrance exam:

The effort to desegregate America's public schools was principally thwarted by:
   a. its inherently flawed premise, that law can make people equal.
   b. the unwillingness of the Warren Court to take a firm stand.
   c. the failure of the Eisenhower administration to support the effort.
   d. the failure of Congress to support the effort.
   e. all of the above.

The correct answer is (c); (a) is not true at all; (b) is only partly true, since in some cases the Warren Court took a quite definitive stand; (d) is only partly true, since Congress did eventually condition educational funding on compliance with desegregation decrees; and (e) is incorrect since (a) is untrue, (b) and (d) are partly untrue, and the questions calls, in any event, for the designation of a "principal" cause. That leaves (c), which is completely true, as Martin Luther King, Jr, insisted at the time, and as Earl Warren himself observed in his memoirs.

That's the hypothetical. I don't know, really, whether there is a right answer to this question, and I certainly am not sure that it is captured by the options listed here. I am fairly confident, in fact, that the designation of a "correct" answer will tend to reflect a certain political bias, and I would not be at all surprised if that bias inures to the benefit of the affiliates of one or the other of our two main political parties. This item, in short, is "biased," and it would not take too many items like this—some perhaps more subtle, perhaps some much less so—before we could confidently conclude that the entire test was "biased." Not, again, in any malicious sense, and maybe not even in a conscious sense, but just in presupposing as universally known or believed that which is in fact not universally "true" at all.

I always ask, as the penultimate question, whether anyone still believes that Republicans are dumb. I always get a few raised hands. I think they're just kidding.

I then conclude by asking whether they think I should change my scheme. Everyone says yes. If there is nothing essential about this test, or about the knowledge and skills that it purports to measure, if in fact it is altogether ad hoc, and there is a substantial likelihood that its built-in assumptions operate to the detriment of an identifiable group, then why in the world would I persist in using it?

The facts of the hypothetical, they learn, are indistinguishable from those of *Washington v. Davis*.

Was a passing score of forty on Test 21 "a racially neutral qualification" as Justice White claimed in *Washington v. Davis*?

In the abstract, of course, it was. To a people conditioned to equate the knowledge and skills that Test 21 measured with "verbal ability"—and conditioned to believe that multiple choice tests can validly and reliably capture that ability—nothing in the test itself would arouse suspicion. So why did black applicants fail the test at four times the rate of white applicants?

Again, to a people conditioned to expect white success and black failure on tests like Test 21—and conditioned to believe that those successes and failures are not merely predictable, but positively normal—nothing in the statistical disparity would arouse suspicion.

Justice White was a cultural spokesman when he proclaimed Test 21 "racially neutral" without the benefit of any critical inquiry. Test 21 was consistent with our assumptions, the outcomes consistent with our norms; in a very meaningful sense, then, it *was* neutral, and we did not need any inquiry to prove it.

That, of course, is precisely the difficulty: practices that embrace our cultural assumptions and perpetuate our cultural norms are said to be neutral, even if those assumptions and norms are not neutral at all. The uncritical endorsement of Test 21 reflects this difficulty, for there was nothing neutral about the instrument, its use, or the outcomes it so predictably generated.

Consider: Reliance on Test 21 presupposes that "verbal ability" is a valuable aptitude. This, perhaps, is fair enough as a general proposition. But the dispositive role played by Test 21 in the case of the D.C. police department presupposes something more: it assumes not merely that "verbal ability" is generally valuable, but also that "verbal ability" is specifically valuable to police officers, and, further, that it is of such preeminent value to police officers that no combination of other aptitudes can ever compensate for its deficit.

This last proposition is not a universal truth; it is a choice. For cultures and people who value other aptitudes more than "verbal ability"—interrelational aptitudes, for example, like patience, empathy, and compassion—the sanctification of "verbal ability" is not neutral at all.

Consider: Reliance on Test 21 presupposes that "verbal ability" comprises a discrete set of skills. This, perhaps, is fair enough, if only as a definitional exercise. But Test 21 actually presupposes something more: it assumes not merely that "verbal ability" comprises a discrete set of skills, but that those skills are exclusively limited to written communication.

This last proposition is not a universal truth; it is a choice. For cultures and people who value other forms of "verbal ability"—who value, for example, oral traditions and inter-personal communications—the privileging of written "verbal ability" is not neutral at all.

Consider: Reliance on Test 21 presupposes that "verbal ability" is measurable in some valid and reliable way. This, perhaps, is fair enough, if only as a necessary artifact of any testing procedure. But Test 21 actually presupposes something more: it assumes not merely that "verbal ability" is measurable, but that it can be captured by a single multiple-choice examination with determinate "correct" answers.

This last proposition is not a universal truth; it is a choice. For cultures and people who value forms of "verbal ability" that cannot be reduced to "right" and "wrong" answers—for example, rhetorical abilities, persuasion, listening skills, and moderation—the exclusive reward of "correct" information is not neutral at all.

Consider: Reliance on Test 21 presupposes that "verbal ability" includes knowledge of words and phrases. This, perhaps, is fair enough, as a general assertion. But Test 21 actually presupposes something more: it assumes not merely that "verbal ability" includes knowledge of words and phrases, but that it includes certain specific words and phrases, not their synonyms or functional equivalents.

This last proposition is not a universal truth; it is a choice. It is a choice that works to the distinct disadvantage of cultures and people who have not been indoctrinated in the value of the specified words and phrases. This is not merely a claim that specific items on Test 21 may reflect a "white male middle-class bias," although it certainly seems true that some cultural groups, almost by definition, will be at a disadvantage in defining words like "promontory" or explaining the origins of hunting laws. The more important claim is that the formal and informal educational experiences of Americans are not uniform; that among the ways they will vary is in the significance they attach to an expanded repertory of words and phrases; and that this variance is likely to occur along racial lines.

Let it be said plainly: we, as a nation, teach white kids more words. We always have, and we still do.

These are just some of the ways Test 21 is not at all neutral. And they do not even include the many biases that inhere in the very attempt to quantify the intellectual aptitudes of Americans, the bias, that is, that inheres in our construction of "smartness." That broader critique is the point of the next two chapters.[10]

Will equal opportunity produce equality?

There is no reason to think not. The historical record is perhaps not very reassuring, but neither is it dispositive. What it discloses above all is that we have never had anything resembling equal opportunity.

Our antidiscrimination laws have not changed this central truth: opportunity still is not equal. Individuals and groups, defined by race, gender, and disability, still enjoy or labor under a pervasive set of advantages and disadvantages in playing the social, economic, and political games. Moreover, the games themselves harbor their own biases, their own sets of assumptions and norms that reinforce the disadvantages of cultural outsiders. And it is all very hard to see.

It is difficult for someone who accepts the assumptions to see that they are not natural; difficult for someone who fits the norm to see that it is not inevitable; difficult for someone who shares the truths to see that they are not universal.

Sometimes these are comparatively small truths, like the truths of Test 21. But sometimes they are very large truths, like the truth of intelligence.

Creating the Smart Culture
Myths of Inferiority

The official explanation for America's inequality is supplemented by an unofficial understanding: the elimination of all purposeful discrimination will not result in social, economic, and political equality. The reason: the natural inferiority of some groups and individuals. America's hierarchies reflect an enduring natural meritocracy: some people just are, by nature, better than others.

This chapter begins the examination of America's unofficial understanding, the mythology of the natural order. It reviews the history of this mythology: the history of racial and gender inferiority, the construction of mental deficiency, and the invention of IQ. It notes that while the myth of a natural intellectual order has permeated American social life—infecting its arts, its sciences, its religion, and its politics—it has never been able to fully suppress the dissenting voice, a voice that rejects scientist hypotheses in favor of experiential truths. That voice, it observes, had won the day by the midpoint of the twentieth century, when the science of the natural order was exposed as a sham and the politics of hierarchy rejected in favor of a more egalitarian vision. There were, it evolved, no inferior people—just bad science, and worse ideas.

Prologue

We used to have a crippled dog. Alice got him from a dog pound in Kansas City when he was a few weeks old. He was a birthday present for me. I named him Buddy. I thought that up all by myself.

On my second effort. Truth is, Buddy's name used to be Spike. That's what I first called him anyway, though to no great effect. "Come here, Spike," I'd say, "let's go, Spike . . . *now*, Spike," and he wouldn't do a damned thing. "Aw, c'mon, buddy, please," I would say in mild exasperation, and at that he would come bounding over, cheerfully scramble into my hands and, after chewing my thumb long enough to draw blood, fall asleep.

So eventually I skipped the preludes, and he just became Buddy instead of Spike. Which I reckon makes one of us, either him or me, pretty stupid for not knowing the dog's real name. I vote for the dog, for reasons I will now explain.

The folks at the pound said Buddy was a "Border Collie mix," and what he was mixed with, we discovered, was an Australian Cattle Dog, which is in reality just a dingo with, on the whole, slightly better manners. Unfortunately, the gentility trait appears to be recessive, or maybe it skipped Buddy's generation, because our dog, at least as a puppy, was indistinguishable from his aboriginal ancestors. For Buddy, every inanimate object was meant to be chewed and every moving object was meant to be subdued for chewing ease. He chewed our rugs, our furniture, our clothes, our briefcases, and even, I swear, a stack of my students' research assignments (causing me to beg lamely for their indulgence, as my dog had eaten their homework). Our feet were victims in waiting, and so too were our hands and our ears and Alice's hair and my nose. He either did not comprehend or simply ignored our every command: "no" meant chew and "stop" meant chew and "*ouch!*" meant chew really hard. He was the canine equivalent of a delinquent youth, a rebel with furry paws. So when people would inquire about his breed, we would respond earnestly that he was, to the best of our knowledge, an Australian Cattle Punk, or, after his second most notable skill, a Missouri Fart-hound, neither of which, I should acknowledge, is a breed currently recognized by the American Kennel Club, which appears to take such things far too seriously, and would undoubtedly be all in a tizzy over the appropriate breed specifications.

But Buddy was more than just wild or ornery or odoriferous. Buddy was an impossibly stupid dog. This we believed not merely because Buddy could not or would not heed our commands. Rather, we based our conclusion largely on his eating habits: specifically, that he wouldn't. The only thing in the entire house that escaped his manic chewing was, in fact, his food, which interested him only to the extent that it was conveniently surrounded by a plastic bowl that was in itself eminently chewable. It apparently did not occur to Buddy that the ingestion of food was related quite directly to his health, but fortunately, it did occur to us—we being less stupid—and so once a day we would gather as a family by the food bowl and feed Buddy his dog crunchies by hand, amusing him between servings—as his minimal attention span necessitated—with games of catch or tug-of-war. To prevent his starvation, we were forced to continue this practice throughout both his adolescence and his adult life. So, long after he was fully grown, you could find me outside on snowy evenings with our impossibly stupid dog, a hockey stick, a ball, and our impossibly stupid dog's food bowl, and I'd shoot him a few, and he'd eat a little, and I'd shoot him a few more, and he'd eat a little more, and so it would go through five or six rounds, and always our impossibly stupid dog would leave at least one crunchie in his bowl—the lure for one more round.

Yes, it eventually occurred to us that Buddy had impossibly stupid owners. It also eventually occurred to us—indeed, we became positively convinced of it—that Buddy was in actuality a genius dog.

Which he proved, over time, by mastering quite an impressive vocabulary: he learned how to go "upstairs," "downstairs," "outside," and to the "basement"; where to go to get the "mail," the "papers," a "bath," and "a ride"; how to "sit," "stay," "heel," and "spin"; and how to retrieve his "towel" (usually dragged upstairs onto the bed), his "rawhide" (usually buried in the backyard), his "treats" (usually stored under a sofa cushion), and his "mother" (that would be Alice, not usually in any place in particular). Eventually, he even learned the approximate meaning of "no," which, in his translation, meant "okay, but only if you do it sheepishly."

So we knew, beyond all doubt, that we were raising a genius dog. Proving this to other people was a trickier business, and yet proving it mattered to us immensely all the same. Evidently, we were not alone in feeling this way. Some fellow named Stanley Coren wrote a best-selling book about genius dogs, *The Intelligence of Dogs*, and we, of course, were among the proud parents who bought the book, thrilled by the promise of intelligence rankings and canine IQ tests and everything you would apparently need for determining whether your four-legged prodigy was indeed a genius or merely a dolt. But there were, according to the book, different *kinds* of canine intelligence ("instinctive," "adaptive," and "working" intelligence, if anybody cares), and the "Canine IQ" test was an hours-long ordeal that ended up measuring only one measly kind of intelligence, and even then, that test had to be supplemented by a whole other test for something called "personality." The entire genius business proved way too complicated: all we wanted was a number, preferably a really high one. The author did, well, toss us a bone, by ranking some one hundred breeds according to their "working" intelligence, and we took some pleasure in finding Australian Cattle Dogs ranked tenth and Border Collies at the very top spot on the list. Still, of course, it was an incomplete vindication: the list purported to be comprehensive, but in truth, Cattle Punks and Fart-hounds were nowhere to be found.

So it had to suffice that *we* knew that Buddy was a genius. We settled for our own forms of validation, which, of course, we easily found, as when Buddy would play his version of catch with our two-year-old nephew Stephen, and drop the tennis ball at young Stephen's feet, and then sometimes snatch the ball away at the precise moment Stephen reached for it, leaving the little boy waving at air and giggling with delight. *Our* son, we thought proudly, was outsmarting my sister's. Within a year, admittedly, the tables would turn, and Stephen would be playing keep-away from Buddy, and we would have to acknowledge that Stephen had, alas, passed Buddy on the learning curve, and yet, on the other hand, my sister's boy never did learn to catch the tennis ball with his teeth.

But Buddy did, and that really is the heart of his story. Buddy's genius and his passion—what truly made his heart sing—was play. With a tennis ball, a frisbee, a football, or a hockey puck, it didn't matter: what Buddy loved to hear most, the phrase he cherished above all others, was "let's go frolic." He was forty-some lean pounds of pure playing brilliance, and he could play forever, at any time of the day, and he never seemed to tire and he never slowed down.

And that's why it broke our hearts when he couldn't play anymore.

We first became suspicious when Buddy was about four: his hind legs would give out, for no apparent reason, as if they had been dislocated. It happened only rarely, and we largely ignored it, but then he started to seem stiff and sore after strenuous frolics, and then after milder plays, and soon he was limping throughout the evenings. By the time he was five, even the briefest, lightest frolic in the yard would bring him hours of anguish.

He was lame. Buddy, it turned out, had been born with a congenital hip defect, and as his sixth birthday approached, the dysplasia was already so severe that nonintrusive therapies like drugs and rest were of no use. Surgery was his only hope.

The opinions were not encouraging. He was too old for surgery, we were told, and the operations in any event are not all that helpful. The risks of surgery outweigh the benefits, it was said, and besides, it's a lot of money to spend on a mongrel. Even the most optimistic appraisal seemed gloomy: in the best-case scenario, Buddy might walk without pain, but he might not run again, and he certainly would never again jump. He was then—and would forever be—a crippled dog, surgery or not.

Buddy had his operation anyway, a "bilateral femoral head and neck excision," which, roughly translated, meant the elimination of Buddy's hip joint through the removal of the tops of his hind leg bones. It sounded horrible from the start, and after it was done, it seemed a terrible mistake. Buddy could not stand and he could not walk. He lay immobile in a makeshift bed, helpless and despondent. After weeks of in-home therapy, his hind legs just hung limply at his side, like the useless appendages of a stuffed toy.

But we persevered, all of us. Buddy started to stand, and then to take steps. He stumbled out of his bed and around the room, and later out of the room and into another. He was walking.

He took himself outside through his dog door one evening, and down the back steps and into the yard. The journey back up the steps, though, was too much, and we found him lying in the grass the next morning. He struggled to his feet when he saw us, and his tail wagged furiously, and I swear he smiled, and our hearts soared.

In a few days, he started to trot. And then to run. Soon he was climbing steps, and eventually, with great effort, scrambling—half-jumping and half-climbing—onto our bed. Then there was no halfway about it, and he was *jumping* onto our bed, and into our car, and up after tennis balls and frisbees. And at the end of a year, he was playing like he was a puppy again, and he was doing it effortlessly, and he was doing it all without pain.

Because he had no hip joint, he still had his difficulties, especially indoors. He would move too fast when he was summoned to frolic, and his legs would give out on the slippery hardwood surfaces of our house, and he'd crash down hard onto the floor. It was a painful reminder that Buddy was not quite an ordinary dog. So we got carpet, and were never reminded of it again. And "let's go frolic," once more, meant nothing but joy.

So that's the story of Buddy, the crippled dog we used to have. Yes, "used to have." Oh, we still have Buddy. He's just not a crippled dog any more. Just like he's not impossibly stupid any more. And he's not named "Spike."

Some dogs are smarter than others. That, at least, is what the book says, though only sort of. And the book doesn't say what the smarter dogs get on account of being so doggone smart. I guess they get to be in charge, but I'm not sure of what.

Some people are smarter than others. That's what some other books say, and more than sort of. And as for smarter people, well, we know what they get on account of being so smart. They get good grades, get into good colleges, get good jobs, and make lots of money. And they get to be in charge—of everything. Some of them become corporate CEOs, some of them become legislators, some of them become judges, and it's all because they are so smart.

Most of the CEOs and legislators and judges—quite a disproportionate number, in fact—are white men without disabilities. So too are most of the folks who make lots of money. White men without disabilities, it seems, are almost always in charge of everything. They must be really smart. Smarter, on average, than black folks or other racial minorities. Smarter, on average, than women. Smarter, on average, than people with disabilities.

This is the thesis of books like *The Bell Curve*. It is the thesis of a natural hierarchy: of inherent intellectual differences between biologically defined groups, differences that can be ordered as "inferiority" and "superiority" and that inevitably manifest themselves in social rank.

It is an elegant thesis: the smarter they are, the higher they climb. It is a verifiable thesis: statistics prove it. It is a thesis with great explanatory power: all the apparent inequities of social, political, and economic life suddenly make sense—explained, no less, by the very best kind of explanation, a scientific one. It is an altogether positively splendidly wonderful thesis.

It is plagued by only two shortcomings: part of it is false; and the rest of it is nonsense.

Because, it turns out, not all *kinds* of smart people get to be in charge—just some kinds.

And, it turns out, not all *groups* of people have the same chance to *get* smart in the way that will enable them to be in charge. Some groups get more chance than others.

And, it turns out, the groups who have the *best* chance to get smart in the way that will enable them to be in charge are the groups who *already were* in charge. They were in a position to give themselves the best chances.

And, it turns out, they got in that superior position and maintained it in part through physical violence, in part through laws that they enacted and brutally enforced, and in part through simply insisting, loudly and relentlessly, that they were the very smartest people in the land.

They are still insisting it. "Everyone has the same chance *now*," they say. "And look," they say, "we are *still* the best kind of smart, truly the smartest of the smart."

And my dog is smarter than your dog.

Partly false. Partly nonsense. Completely wrong.

A brief review of the history helps to explain why.

Reconstructing Hierarchy: The Natural Order

Alexander Pope posited the existence of a "great chain of being" in his 1734 *Essay on Man*, defining an intellectual tradition that would, perhaps, reach its pinnacle—or nadir—in a 1799 treatise by Charles White bearing the marvelously descriptive title, *An Account of the Regular Gradation in Man, and in Different Animals and Vegetables*. In between came Thomas Jefferson's *Notes on the State of Virginia*, written in 1781 and revised the following year. *Query 14* of the *Notes* includes Jefferson's reflections on slavery, and it is clear that the author of the Declaration's stirring proclamation of equality—"that all men are created equal"—uneasily embraced the tradition of the natural order.

Query 14 contains an extensive discussion of the differences between the white race and "the negro." At the outset, it is apparent that the differences are to be hierarchically ordered. Even the difference in "colour" can be understood in ordered terms, as Jefferson exalts the "superior beauty" of whites, insisting that the "fine mixtures of red and white," permitting the "expressions of every passion," are "preferable to that eternal monotony, which reigns in the countenances, that immovable veil of black which covers all the emotions of the other race." That veil notwithstanding, Jefferson observes in the "other race" certain emotional peculiarities: "love seems with them to be more an eager desire, than a tender delicate mixture of sentiment and sensation. Their griefs are transient." The race suffers as well from certain intellectual disadvantages: "it appears to me, that in memory they are equal to the whites, in reason much inferior . . . , and that in imagination they are dull, tasteless, and anomalous." Ironically, the traits in which the race is deficient—sentimentality, imagination—provide a partial foundation for Jefferson's judgment that the race is culturally inferior; the works of Ignatius Sancho, Jefferson notes by way of example, "do more honour to the heart than the head . . . ; his imagination is wild and extravagant, escapes incessantly from every restraint of reason and taste . . . ; we find him always substituting sentiment for demonstration."

Yet Jefferson was only tentative in hypothesizing that black Americans were, by nature, the intellectual inferior of whites. "To justify a general conclusion," he wrote, "requires many observations":

> How much more then where it is a faculty, not a substance, we are examining; where it eludes the research of all the senses; where the conditions of its existence are various and various combined; where the effects of those which are present or absent bid defiance to calculation; let me add too, as a circumstance of great tenderness, where our conclusion would degrade a whole race of men from the rank in the scale of beings which their Creator may perhaps have given them.

So he was not sure. "I advance it therefore as a suspicion only," he concluded, "that the blacks, whether originally a distinct race or made distinct by time and circumstances, are inferior to the whites in the endowments both of body and mind." His persistent doubts would reemerge in Query 18, when he pondered the contingencies and perhaps the ultimate legacy of American slavery:

> Indeed I tremble for my country when I reflect that God is just: that his justice cannot sleep for ever: that considering numbers, nature and natural means only, a revolution of the wheel of fortune, an exchange of situation, is among possible events: that it may become probable by

supernatural interference! The Almighty has no attribute which can take side with us in such a contest.[1]

But the ambivalence of men like Jefferson would become increasingly rare as the movement toward abolition intensified, yielding to a certainty that black slavery was Creation's plan. James Henry Hammond of South Carolina was one of slavery's most vigorous defenders. On February 1, 1836, Representative Hammond offered Congress the increasingly typical defense of slavery: it was part of Creation's plan. "The doom of Ham has been branded on the form and features of his African descendants," Hammond explained. "The hand of fate has united his color and his destiny. Man cannot separate what God hath joined."

And Creation's plan was a benevolent one. In January 1840, William Cost Johnson, a Whig congressman from Maryland, informed the House that it was "a blessing to the colored race to keep them in slavery. . . . In [Africa], they were little more intelligent than the *ourang outang* species; but now they had become a civilized and Christianized people."

The attitudes grew hardened, the racism more intense, as the sectional rift pointed increasingly toward dissolution. By the time it came, black inferiority was at the fulcrum. Alexander Stephens, vice president of the Confederate States of America, declared in March 1861 that the Confederacy "rests upon the great truth that the negro is not equal to the white man; that slavery—subordination to the superior race—is his natural and normal condition."

The failure of that government to secure its cause did not change the attitudes of its constituents. Thus a prominent Virginian could still proclaim of slavery in June 1865 that "for the slave it is the best condition in every way that has been devised." Henry W. Ravenel, South Carolina's great "benevolent" master, would still insist that slavery "had received the divine sanction & was the best condition in which the two races could live together for mutual benefit."[2]

It is unsurprising, perhaps, that neither civil war nor emancipation settled the question of the black man's rank in the natural order. But neither, really, did Reconstruction. Many of the founders of modern equality—the framers of the Reconstruction effort—professed their belief in the inherent superiority of the white race to all other races, and of men to women. In guaranteeing the "equal protection of the laws," they purported to do no more than free the natural hierarchy from unnecessary constraints. They contended that, quite aside from the advantages secured by discriminatory laws, the white race would be forever superior, and white men in particular would always have their dominion.

At least on this score, the rhetoric of the Reconstruction debates must be viewed with a certain skepticism: Republicans often exaggerated their belief in white supremacy to assure their moderate and conservative colleagues that the white man's status was secure; Democrats, meanwhile, frequently exaggerated their fears of black ascendancy to make the case for restrictive laws. But this perverse posturing was not universal: some Republicans argued that the inherent equality of all men made discriminatory laws immoral and unnatural; some Democrats, meanwhile, argued that the inherent superiority of white men meant that *anti*discriminatory laws were abominations against God and nature.

What they really thought is, of course, nearly impossible to know. But what they *said* typified a debate that, incredibly, still rages over a century later.

A substantial part of the opposition to the Reconstruction effort—initially to emancipation, subsequently to the protection of the freedmen's civil rights—was rooted in the belief that equality was contrary to nature. In 1864 Senator Thomas A. Hendricks, Democrat from Indiana, explained his opposition to the effort to ensure civil equality for black Americans:

> You may say here that the negro is the equal of the white man; but you cannot make him such. You may say that he shall be trusted as the white man is trusted; but you cannot give him the qualities that inspire confidence among white men toward each other. . . . This is a proposition based upon the idea that the negro is the equal in law, socially, and politically, of the white man. I say it is an unfortunate step. . . . It may be done; they may be forced upon society in all its relations as the equal of the white race; but that legislation will not make them equals.

As Hendricks made plain, the inherent inequality of the races was all-pervasive: they were created unequal socially, politically, and economically as well. "I do not believe," Hendricks insisted, that "negroes" "are our equals in the Army, in the courts, or anywhere else; and for that reason I voted against the bill proposing that they should have the same pay in the Army as white men." "Their services are not worth so much," he explained; "They cannot command so much at home for their labor, because they lack those qualities that secure a high rate of compensation to the white man."

Racial inferiority provided the primary justification for the political exclusion of black Americans. For some, the freedmen simply were not ready for suffrage. In January 1867, President Andrew Johnson vetoed a bill providing for black suffrage in the District of Columbia: "we may well pause to inquire whether, after so brief a probation, they are as a class capable of an intelligent exercise of the right of suffrage." "The people who are daily witnesses of their mode of living," his veto message continued, "and who have become familiar with their habits of thought, have expressed the conviction that they are not yet competent." "Hardly yet capable of forming correct judgment upon the important questions that often make the issues of a political contest," he concluded, "they could readily be made subservient to the purposes of designing persons."

Senator James R. Doolittle of Wisconsin was one of Johnson's few Republican supporters. He concurred in the president's verdict on black suffrage: "as a general rule the African race are incompetent to do it. It is not so with the white race." Another Republican ally, Senator Lafayette Foster of Connecticut, later a professor of law at Yale, offered the following thesis for excluding the black vote: that governments rest on intelligence and morality; that intelligence comes through knowledge; that knowledge comes through history; that history is recorded in books; and that books require reading. Literacy, therefore, was the true test of intelligence: "Now, where a man, no matter from what cause, cannot thus become acquainted, through books, by reading, with the wisdom of past ages, nor with the events and occurrences of the day, I say he is not and cannot be intelligent, and is not therefore a safe voter."

For others, the thesis was slightly less complex. Democratic congressman Benjamin M. Boyer of Pennsylvania explained the nature of black inferiority in explicitly biological terms. "It is not the complexion of the negro that degrades him," he explained, nor was it the long litany of other physical distinctions, including the "significant" "fact" that "the bones of his cranium are thick and inclose a brain averaging by measurement fewer cubic inches in volume than the skulls of white Americans." Nor was it "because his facial outline does not conform to our ideals of beautiful humanity."   "All these considerations," Boyer explained, "I am willing to discard from the argument,"

> But if the peculiarities I have mentioned are the outward badges of a race by nature inferior in mental caliber, and lacking that vim, pluck, and poise of character which give force and direction to human enterprise, and which are essential to the safety and progress of popular institutions, then the negroes are not the equals of white Americans, and are not entitled by any right, natural or acquired, to participate in the Government of this country.

Senator Garrett Davis emphasized the cultural inferiority of the black race. No nation or tribe of the black race, he insisted, "has ever established a polity that could be denominated a Government, or has elaborated for itself any sciences or literature or arts or even an alphabet, or characters to represent numbers, or been capable of preserving those achievements of intellect when it has received them from a superior race." For this reason, Davis concluded, black suffrage was "revolting to reason."

Democratic congressman Michael C. Kerr of Indiana concurred. "Is it statesmanship," he wondered, "to introduce into the body of electors, the governing and law-making classes, the most inferior, ignorant, and corruptible races on earth?"

Still others insisted that the political exclusion of black Americans was a more pragmatic necessity, but one justified, nonetheless, by the fact of inferiority. George W. Woodward of Pennsylvania had failed to win confirmation when nominated by James Polk to the U.S. Supreme Court; he did, however, serve for fifteen years on the Pennsylvania Supreme Court, the last three as Chief Justice. He left the bench for Congress in 1867; the following year, he explained his opposition to black suffrage:

> I do not place my objections on ethnological distinctions of races, nor on the denial which is sometimes made, but which I am always pained to hear, that they are human beings, having a common God and Father of us all and a common destiny with ourselves; but I place it on those high considerations of expediency which always prevailed with the founders of our Government. It is not best for the common interests

of both races that the inferior should share political privileges with the superior.

The arguments against black equality were not limited, of course, to the issue of suffrage. In 1866 Indiana Democrat William E. Niblack defended his state's exclusion of free blacks. The inferiority of black Americans, he insisted, was a fundamental political tenet:

> I have always maintained, and certainly a very large majority of the people of Indiana have, heretofore at least, that in the grand scale of humanity the negro race is inferior to the white race, and that anything like social or political equality between the two races is neither practicable nor desirable. Our whole system of laws in relation to the negro, from the first organization of the State to the present time, has been based on that theory.

Senator Peter G. Van Winkle, a Unionist from West Virginia, explicated the threat to the white man posed by contravening the laws of nature:

> I do not believe that a superior race is bound to receive among it those of an inferior race if the mingling of them can only tend to the detriment of the mass. I do not mean strict miscegenation, but I mean the mingling of the two races in society, associating from time to time with one another.

Van Winkle made clear that his concern was not limited to the freedmen; rather, it "involves not only the negro race, but other inferior races . . . those whose mixture with our race, whether they are white or black, could only tend to the deterioration of the mass."

But there was another side to the debate. The inferiority of black Americans was, in a certain sense, an undeniable fact: the white population was more literate, more knowledgeable, and, perhaps, more intellectually "advanced." But not everyone was willing to concede that this was the natural state of affairs.

Frederick Douglass had offered an alternative understanding in 1854:

> Ignorance and depravity, and the inability to rise from degradation to civilization and respectability, are the most usual allegations against the oppressed. The evils most fostered by slavery and oppression are precisely those which slaveholders and oppressors would transfer from

their system to the inherent character of their victims. Thus the very crimes of slavery become slavery's best defense.

Douglass's view animated many voices during the Reconstruction debates: each claim of black inferiority was met with the simple response, "yes—but you have made it so, and it need not be." Republican congressman Glenni W. Scofield of Pennsylvania argued for black suffrage in the District of Columbia early in 1866. He responded to the claim that the freedmen were inherently incapable of participating in self-governance: "We are again told that their average ability is below that of the white race. How do you know that? The colored man has never exhibited equal ability, to be sure, but he has never had equal opportunities."

Late in the year, the upper chamber was still debating the issue. Henry Wilson of Massachusetts was explicit: if the freedman was in a sense "inferior," it was not by creation's design, but by the slave-holder's. "They kept the colored man in ignorance to keep him in slavery," Wilson noted; "they will continue to keep him in ignorance to prevent his becoming a voter."

The arguments must have had a certain resonance: both chambers passed the bill providing for black suffrage in the nation's capital, and in the first weeks of 1867, the Senate voted to override President Johnson's veto of that bill by a vote of 29 to 10, the House by a vote of 113 to 38.

But suffrage in the District of Columbia was just a small step toward black empowerment, and the debate over the freedmen's intellectual abilities and political disabilities would continue through the adoption of the Fifteenth Amendment and its enforcement acts. In 1868 Republican congressman Carman A. Newcomb of Missouri vehemently denounced the repetitive refrain of black inferiority: "It is criminal, it is wicked on the part of a Government to hold a people in ignorance against their will and then disfranchise them or deny them the right to vote because they are ignorant." Later that same year, Congressman Oliver H. P. T. Morton of Indiana rose to observe that, "it ill becomes the southern people now to slander and traduce the negro. If he is degraded, they have made him so; slavery has made him so. If he is ignorant, they have made him so by making it a crime to teach him to read and write."

Congressman James M. Ashley, Republican of Ohio, may have offered the most far-reaching critique of the "natural" order: no social arrangement could be understood apart from the educational system that sustained it. Standing in support of a guarantee of open public schools, Ashley insisted that "civilization and education are inseparable." "Without the maintenance of free public schools in this country," he explained, "the people could not long be secure in civil or religious liberty."

"Knowledge," he concluded, "is power."

The History of Natural Inferiority

In its review of *The Bell Curve*, the *National Review* observed that Murray and Herrnstein's text "confirms ordinary citizens' reasonable intuition that trying to engineer racial equality in the distribution of occupations and social positions runs against not racist prejudice but nature, which shows no such egalitarian distribution of talents." The irony, as the *National Review* would have it, was that equality was the brainstorm of an elite class of liberal social engineers. Ordinary people, meanwhile, knew better: their "reasonable intuition" was that some folks—and some races—are plain smarter than others.[3]

But here lies the real irony: the "reasonable intuition" of "ordinary citizens" is in fact none of these things: it is the carefully crafted product of centuries of cultural propaganda, a myth of natural inequality perpetuated by men in power—a political, economic, and intellectual elite. Ordinary citizens actually know better: throughout history, the better judgment of many has been to reject the vicious lies of natural inferiority. But the lies have been relentless.

The Myths of Inferiority: Race

The men who framed the Constitution in the late eighteenth century, and those who reframed it three generations later, were by no means the last to promote the myth of the natural superiority of the white race. Just as the overtly racist defenses of slavery increased as abolition intensified, so too did the overtly racist defenses of privilege increase as legal equality blossomed. By the turn of the twentieth century, notions of racial supremacy were as firmly rooted as ever in American epistemology.

Racial supremacy was a truth in national politics. The great Progressive Theodore Roosevelt had invited Booker Washington to the White House, but he assured white Americans that blacks "as a race and in the mass, are altogether inferior to the whites." Woodrow Wilson shared the Progressive mantle and secured the support of the egalitarians Oswald Garrison Villard, W. E. B. Du Bois, and William Monroe Trotter in his 1912 election bid; he repaid them by formally segregating the departments and services of the federal government, the first official federal segregation since the Civil War. And while Villard, Du Bois, and Trotter were denouncing D. W. Griffith's negrophobic, pro-Klan vision of Reconstruction, *The Birth of a Nation*, Wilson was giving the film a private screening at the White House, lamenting that its tale was "all so terribly true."

Racial supremacy was a truth among historians. Ulrich B. Phillips's *American Negro Slavery* appeared in 1918; his landmark history was premised on the notion of black inferiority, and his central thesis, that slavery was a largely benevolent and unprofitable institution, would define mainstream scholarship on slavery for the next forty years. Reconstruction, meanwhile, has been described as the historian's chief whipping boy during the era of new nationalism. William Dunning's 1907 account, *Reconstruction, Political and Economic*, established a tradition that embraced, as one of his adherents put it, the central belief in "negro incapacity." Writing in this tradition, John W. Burgess of Columbia pronounced Reconstruction the "nadir of national disgrace" and a "soul-sickening spectacle." These views too would hold sway till midcentury, culminating with E. Merlton Coulter's 1947 publication of *The South during Reconstruction*; for Coulter, "negro rule" was a "diabolical" development to be "remembered, shuddered at, and execrated."

Racial supremacy was a truth in American religion. The "modern view" of twentieth-century "polygenecists," that the several races had separately evolved from distinct genetic origins, had been defeated by the biblical tradition of a single act of creation and a common origin for all mankind. But the prevailing view was not an egalitarian one: science and religion combined for the "monogenecists" in a theory of black racial degeneration under the "curse of Ham." The theological conception of black peoples as a cursed people found its most benevolent expression in a certain pity for the unfortunate race; its more malevolent manifestations included a vicious racial hatred and, ultimately, racist violence. The American religious tradition that produced Christian abolitionism thus also produced the missionary message of resignation, urging black Christians to accept their lot first under slavery, and later under racial hierarchy. It produced too a fierce opposition to social integration: to cite but one extreme example, the Ku Klux Klan revival of the early twentieth century was explicitly a "white Christian" movement.[4]

Racial supremacy was also a truth in the sciences, both hard and soft. In 1896 the Supreme Court ruled in the case of *Plessy v. Ferguson* that the compulsory segregation of the races into "equal but separate" rail accommodations was not unconstitutional, but was in keeping with the "comfort and traditions of the people." If there was any "badge of inferiority" implicit in the forced segregation, the Court insisted, it was because "the colored race chooses to place that construction upon it."

But scientists in that year made clear what the Supreme Court would not: the colored races felt inferior because, in fact, they were. Franklin Giddings's *Principles of Sociology* surveyed the accomplishments of the various "races": the Chinese and the American Indians, he concluded, "have been in existence . . . much longer than the European race, and have accomplished immeasurably less. We are therefore warranted in saying that they have not the same inherent abilities." Darwinian principles of evolution were now firmly grounded throughout the sciences and led inexorably to scientific theories of a natural racial order. *American Anthropologist* reported unequivocally in 1896 that the "Caucasian stands at the head of the racial scale and the Negro at bottom."

Stephen Jay Gould has noted that "all leading scientists followed social conventions"; the founders of the modern scientific tradition—Linnaeus, Georges Cuivier, Charles Lyell, Louis Agassiz—largely accepted the ideological commitment to white supremacy. As Gould explains,

> white leaders of western nations did not question the propriety of racial thinking during the eighteenth and nineteenth centuries. In this context, the pervasive assent given by scientists to conventional rankings arose from shared belief, not from objective data gathered to test an

open question. Yet, in a curious case of reversed causality, these pronouncements were read as an independent support for the political context.

This did not change with the turn of the century; if anything, the "science" of racism grew more strident. In 1901 William H. Thomas, a mulatto sociologist, insisted in *The American Negro* that the black man was in essence a lazy, immoral savage, rational only in proportion to his admixture of white blood. Edward A. Ross, a liberal populist sociologist, derided the "equality fallacy," positing instead the obvious differences in "moral and intellectual traits." Robert Bennett Bean, writing in *American Medicine* in April 1907, revealed "the anatomical basis for the complete failure of the negro schools to impart the higher studies—the brain cannot comprehend them any more than a horse can understand the rule of three." "Leaders in all political parties," Bean insisted, "now acknowledge the error of human equality." Writing in the dawn of the age of eugenics, Bean cheerfully concluded that at long last "[i]t may be practicable to rectify the error and remove a menace to our prosperity—a large electorate without brains."

If the "cure" for black inferiority was becoming more clear to scientists, the "cause" of it still was not. Some hypothesized that it was "recapitulation": adults of inferior races, they said, had regressed to a permanent immaturity, and as adults were like the children of superior races. Others hypothesized a form of "neoteny": it was the superior races, they insisted, that retained their childlike character throughout maturity, while the inferior races devolved toward apishness. The hypotheses were, of course, diametrically opposed, and in this sense, the science of the early twentieth century failed even to offer, let alone substantiate, a unified theory of racial supremacy. But if the specifics were in doubt, the general assumptions were not: white people were superior to black people, and this was, somehow, natural.

In the second decade of the twentieth century, the assumptions were apparently bolstered by empirical proof. Lewis M. Terman of Stanford University had adapted French psychologist Alfred Binet's test of "intelligence" for use in the United States. But Binet's test, designed to identify schoolchildren in need of special educational services, was modified in Terman's revised scale. The Stanford-Binet differed from the original in two significant respects: first, it included adults as well as children; and second, it calculated the ratio between chronological age and the tested "mental age" and called that ratio the "intelligence quotient," or IQ. Terman, then, could describe the "intelligence" of an individual with a single number, and individuals could be ordered—highest to lowest, most smart to least—on an intelligence scale. He could do the same with groups, including groups defined by race. So, of course, he did.

In 1916 Terman reported that low intellect was "very common among Spanish-Indian and Mexican families of the South-West and also among negroes." "Their dullness," he concluded, "seems to be racial." Easing effortlessly from scientific fact to policy prescription and back again, Terman opined that "[c]hildren of this group should be segregated in special classes. . . . They cannot master abstractions, but they can often be made efficient workers." But segregation was not the ideal solution to the problem of inferior races, only the most practical: "There is no possibility at present of convincing society that they should not be allowed to reproduce, although from a eugenic point of view they constitute a grave problem because of their unusually prolific breeding."[5]

There is another story to tell.

Not every politician accepted the truth of racial supremacy. Franklin Roosevelt at least harbored some doubts on the subject, and while he might not have been the friend of black Americans in particular—here, he seemed to value expedience over principle, choosing, for example, to abandon federal antilynching legislation in return for Southern support of the New Deal—much of the New Deal was of at least incidental benefit to the working classes of all races. Moreover, the Roosevelt White House contained at least one genuine friend of racial equality in the person of Eleanor Roosevelt; in 1944, her efforts helped secure the first significant step toward desegregation—of public transit for American soldiers. Never, observed William Hastie at the time, "have I seen so much enthusiasm and goodwill generated by a particular bit of official action." FDR's successor, meanwhile, manifested no ambivalence on the subject; Harry Truman, of course, completed the desegregation of the military but also, less famously, pledged his administration's support to the NAACP at their 1948 convention and indeed, the Truman Justice Department supported their cause in the major civil rights cases argued before the Supreme Court.

Not every historian accepted the truth of racial supremacy. Ulrich Phillips's interpretation of the slave experience always had its critics; Carter Woodson, for example, offered his own critique and assembled a core of young historians dedicated to re-writing the history "from the bottom up." By 1956, with the publication of Kenneth Stampp's work *The Peculiar Institution,* Phillips's depiction of slavery as a largely benevolent and inefficient institution was supplanted by the view that the institution was both very harsh and very profitable. Three years later, Stanley Elkins's *Slavery: A Problem in American Institutional and Intellectual Life* ushered in a new era of mainstream slavery scholarship: the "discovery" of the slaves' humanity would eventually facilitate an appreciation of their economic, cultural, intellectual, and moral achievements.

The Dunning school of Reconstruction scholarship, which insisted that Reconstruction was both a failure and a moral disgrace, also had its critics, including W. E. B. Du Bois, whose 1935 *Black Reconstruction in America* not only rejected the conclusions of his contemporaries but explicitly denounced the racism that informed them. Within a decade, Howard K. Beale was urging all white historians to reassess Reconstruction without the working assumption that "their race must bar Negroes from social and economic equality." The next two generations of Reconstruction historians would assume these challenges, and while they produced neither consensus nor coherence, they did reject black subordination as the necessary precondition of their assessment.

Not every religion and religious leader embraced the truth of racial supremacy. Christian evangelicals had been at the forefront of the egalitarian crusade, and religion had supplied abolitionism's most powerful arguments. In 1835 William Slade of Vermont had quoted Revelations to his congressional colleagues: "God hath made of one blood all nations of men, to dwell on the face of the earth." "Now, sir," Slade intoned, "let gentlemen show me that Africans are not 'men', and I will give up the argument." In 1865 Congressman James M. Ashley of Ohio denounced the hypocrisy of the pro-slavery contingent: "Under the plea of Christianizing them it has enslaved, beaten, maimed, and robbed millions of men for whose salvation the Man of sorrows died." Christian neo-abolitionists continued the crusade and contributed mightily to the refutation of biological theories of racial inferiority; it was, they said, environment, or "social heredity," that shaped the differences between white and black

Americans. Harlan Paul Douglas both described and spoke for many generations of Christian reformers in his 1909 text *Christian Reconstruction in the South*. His work included an elegant exegesis of the "environmental thesis": "average capacities are socially suppressed, partly through undernourishment and other environmental handicaps . . . and partly through paralyzing beliefs in natural inferiority which forbid them to hope for themselves and prevent society from doing its best on their behalf."[6]

Not every scientist accepted the truth of racial supremacy. Charles Darwin's theory of natural selection had made the science of the natural racial order possible and, perhaps, even inevitable. But Darwin himself was no racist: natural selection, he explained in *The Descent of Man*, could not account for the differences between the races; "race" seemed outside the evolutionary process. Alfred Wallace had shared the discovery of natural selection with Darwin; Wallace specifically insisted on the intellectual equality of the races.

This was not the typical assumption, but it would become that, due in large part to the work of Franz Boas. Boas emigrated from Germany to the United States in 1885 and brought with him a unique critical perspective. Writing in 1894, Boas commented that scientists "are always liable to interpret as racial characters what is only an effect of social surroundings." Later in the decade, Boas became the first social scientist to speak of cultures in the plural, not merely as a single hierarchical system. He celebrated the achievements of African culture; his rebuttal of the myth of black cultural inferiority left Du Bois "astonished."

In his 1911 text, *The Mind of Primitive Man*, Boas argued that there were no innate intellectual differences, just different histories. For Boas, "social conditions," a lack of truly "equal opportunities," explained black failures in America. He pioneered a theory of prejudice, a "consciousness of the outsider," the "tendency of the human mind to merge the individual in the class to which he belongs, and to ascribe to him all the characteristics of his class." His was, in sum, the first comprehensive cultural theory of racial inferiority: what made white folks superior, in Boas's view, was no more than their tendency to see themselves as superior and their ability to convert that belief into cultural fact.

Boas's impact was felt throughout the American academy. Sociologists Charles W. Ellwood of the University of Missouri and

Carl Kelsey of the University of Pennsylvania both rejected the racist hypothesis after Boas, as did Howard Odum of the University of Georgia. Low achievement, Odum posited, "may be due only to environment"; "there is thus far," he noted, "no evidence to contradict such a claim." In 1917 Alfred L. Kroeber of Columbia published "The Superorganic" in *American Anthropologist*; it was the classic argument against biological notions of inferiority. Following Boas, Kroeber was explicit about the assumption of "absolute equality"; students of culture, he warned, must assume this equality to avoid the conflation of history and biology.

And so it went. Boas had effectively shifted the burden of proof to the scientific racists. From then on, it would not do simply to allege the natural inferiority of the black race; after Boas, the racists would have to prove it.

They could not. Lewis Terman himself recanted in 1937: he had become, he said, more interested in the environmental hypotheses.

That might have been the end of it. The victory over Nazi Germany might then have been the exclamation point to this simple declaration: racial supremacy is just a lie—an evil, hateful lie.

But in 1969 psychologist Arthur R. Jensen called for a re-examination of the assumption of racial genetic equality in intelligence. In 1971 H. J. Eysenck revived neoteny as an explanation of black inferiority. In 1989 J. Phillipe Rushton announced that black craniums were, on average, smaller than white craniums, and black people were, as a consequence, less intelligent. And in 1994, Murray and Herrnstein published *The Bell Curve*.[7]

The Myths of Inferiority: Gender

Race, of course, has not provided the exclusive "biological" explanation for the natural order. The theory of gender inferiority has a legacy that is in some ways just as rich, though it proved, in the end, slightly less durable.

The critical element in theories of gender inferiority has been the idea of a "woman's nature," a nature that "unfitted" her for, among other things, political life. It was an idea shared by the "founding fathers"—women, Thomas Jefferson observed, "are too wise to wrinkle their forehead with politics"—and by their successors. In 1838

Congressman Benjamin C. Howard objected that abolitionist petitions to Congress were being offered by women. "He always felt regret," the *Congressional Globe* reported, "when petitions thus signed were presented to the House relating to political matters." The *Globe* continued,

> He thought that these females could have a sufficient field for the exercise of their influence in the discharge of their duties to their fathers, their husbands, or their children, cheering the domestic circle, and shedding over it the mild radiance of the social virtues, instead of rushing into the fierce struggles of political life. He felt sorrow at this departure from their proper sphere.

"I say," John Quincy Adams retorted, "that the correct principle is, that women are not only justified, but exhibit the most exalted virtue when they do depart from the domestic sphere, and enter the concerns of their country, of humanity, and of their God."[8]

Many of the "fathers" of Reconstruction were prepared to follow Adams's lead; they could conceive neither of a political hierarchy rooted in race nor one rooted in gender. But they proved to be a minority; efforts to extend suffrage to women were premature. Typical of the prevailing view was that offered in 1866 by Republican Lot M. Morrill of Maine, an advocate of black suffrage:

> Now, sir, in practice its extension to women would contravene all notions of the family; "put asunder" husband and wife, and subvert the fundamental principles of family government, in which the husband is, by all usage and law, human and divine, the representative head. Besides, it ignores woman, womanhood, and all that is womanly; all those distinctions of sex whose objects are apparent in creation, essential in character, and vital to society; these all disappear in the manly and impressive demonstrations of balloting at a popular election. . . . Moreover, it associates the wife and mother with policies of state, with public affairs, with making, interpreting, and executing the laws, with police and war, and necessarily disservates her from purely domestic affairs, peculiar care for and duties of the family; and, worst of all, assigns her duties revolting to her nature and constitution, and wholly incompatible with those which spring from womanhood.

Three years later, when Congress approved the Fifteenth Amendment, women's suffrage was scarcely worth debating. Among the altogether proper exceptions to general suffrage, insisted Senator James A. Bayard, Jr., "is that of sex. I will not argue this question either with communists or socialists, nor with the woman's right party, because the folly of this species of fanaticism, though it has made great progress lately, is not sufficiently widespread to need an elaborate refutation."

The initial "scientific" support for the idea of a woman's nature, and a woman's inferiority, came from anatomical studies. Typical was the 1869 report of anthropologist McGrigor Allan, concluding that "The type of the female skull approaches in many respects that of the infant, and still more that of the lower races."

But the strongest "evidence" was to be found in the theory of natural selection. Charles Darwin had not offered any direct support for the belief in natural racial supremacy, but he was unambiguous on the subject of gender differences: men were, in many important respects, naturally superior. In *The Descent of Man* he explained, "The chief distinction in the intellectual powers of the two races, is shewn by man's attaining to a higher eminence, in whatever he takes up, than can woman—whether requiring deep thought, reason, or imagination, or merely the uses of the senses and hands." Darwin elaborated at length on the idea of a woman's nature: while men were competitive and ambitious, women were more intuitive, more perceptive, and more tender, exhibiting characteristics, Darwin noted, "of a past and lower stage of civilization." By the end of the nineteenth century, Darwin's theory of natural difference reached its logical conclusion in the suggestion that men were "katabolic" or animal-like, while women were, in essence, "anabolic" or plant-like.

Ironically, the concept of a distinctive "woman's nature" would provide the initial basis for rebutting the thesis of male superiority. Eliza Burt Gamble's *Evolution of Women*, published in 1894, drew heavily on Darwin, but argued that the traits he associated with women in fact established their superiority. Lester Frank Ward's *Pure Sociology*, published in 1903, maintained that only force, not moral or intellectual superiority, achieves woman's subordination and hides the real truth of her superiority. The cooperative, caring nature of women, Ward argued, made society possible, and evolution made these traits increasingly vital.

But the idea of woman's nature, either inferior or superior, was met with skepticism in some quarters. In 1896 Amy Tanner, a graduate student at the University of Chicago, offered a compelling critique of the various theories of inherent difference. In rejecting the "natural" gender differences purportedly demonstrated by disparate performances on word-association tests, Tanner maintained that it was not nature, but "habit [that] determines the association of ideas." "[T]he real tendencies of women," she wrote, "cannot be known until they are free to choose, any more than those of a tied up dog." In 1903 Helen Bradford Thompson of the University of Chicago examined gender differences in rearing, education, socialization, and perception: the differences in interests and aptitudes, she concluded, were "socially stimulated"; the "woman's sphere" was the result not of nature, but of the "necessities of social organization." Four years later, her colleague William I. Thomas would observe that "[t]he world of modern intellectual life is in reality a white man's world"; differences in achievement, he therefore concluded, "are no greater than they should be in view of the existing differences in opportunity."

The so-called social feminists continued to emphasize the woman's inherent caring, nurturant nature, and they found a receptive audience in circles not yet prepared to accept women in the "manly" spheres. The famous "Brandeis brief" submitted to the Supreme Court in the 1908 case of *Muller v. Oregon* argued that laws designed to limit the maximum working hours of women, and only women, were permissible in a way that general labor laws applicable to men and women alike were not. The difference was to be found in the special biological needs of women: their relative frailty, their need for masculine protection, and their maternal roles.[9]

Progressive legislation had not fared well with the conservative Court; laissez faire had dictated the invalidation of scores of reform measures. But this law struck a responsive chord. Justice David Brewer, perhaps the Court's staunchest protector of the "free market," wrote the opinion sustaining the law. Mindful, perhaps, that the influx of women had been accompanied by a decline in the birthrate: "as healthy mothers are essential to vigorous offspring, the physical well-being of woman becomes an object of public interest and care in order to preserve the strength and vigor of the race." History, Brewer wrote, "discloses the fact that woman has always been dependent upon man," and while women now had secured many of the same legal rights as men, "there is that in her disposition and habits of life which will operate against a full assertion on those rights." Thus Brewer found his rationale for the law "in the inherent difference between the two sexes, and in the different functions in life which they perform."[10]

But in the scientific community, such views were increasingly anachronistic. By 1927 the cultural approach to gender predominated in the psychological literature: gender differences—and most assuredly gender "inferiority"—were products of social choices. Margaret Mead's *Sex and Temperament in Three Primitive Societies*, published in 1935, offered anthropological support for the cultural thesis. Gender roles, Mead noted, were very much institutionalized, but varied across the studied cultures. No particular temperament seemed inevitably correlated with gender; "human nature," she concluded, "is almost unbelievably malleable."

Mead herself would acknowledge that some gender roles might be rooted in reproductive functions; later she would allow for other biological bases. But always she would stress the role of culture in shaping and sustaining the realms of possibility: the woman's sphere was, in the final analysis, culturally defined.

The relative roles of "nature" and "culture" in shaping gender attributes remain subjects of vigorous debate. But for the past half century, almost no one has argued that gender differences, whatever their "origins," must inevitably translate into inferior and superior social ranks.

Almost no one. In 1974 Steven Goldberg argued for *The Inevitability of Patriarchy*: male domination, Goldberg insists, results from the "psychophysiological" inability of women to challenge it. Regardless of the cultural conditions, the struggle for dominance runs counter to the woman's "nurturative tendency"; it is against her "nature," contrary to her "own juices."

The following year, E. O. Wilson observed that "In hunter-gatherer societies men hunt and women stay at home." Such remains the case, he insisted, in "most agricultural and industrial societies"; the gender caste, consequently, "appears to have a genetic origin."

In 1994 Murray and Herrnstein published *The Bell Curve*. It is largely silent on gender issues: the data, after all, do not well serve their hypothesis, since women lag behind men in every significant social measure, even though testing reveals no significant gender disparity in IQ. Thus the "intelligence" of women merits discussion in but one instance: when the authors discuss male mating propensities, that is, the "man's marriage calculus." Thanks to feminism, evidently, smart men now are willing to reject the view that brains are not "sexy" in a woman. She's come a long way . . . [11]

The Myths of Inferiority: Mental Deficiency

At the beginning of the twentieth century, H. H. Goddard was the director of research at the Vineland Training School for Feeble-Minded Girls and Boys in New Jersey. It was Goddard who brought the Binet scale to America, and Goddard who reified Binet's test scores as "intelligence." It was Goddard too who took the Greek word for "foolish" and invented from it a new English word to describe "high-grade" mental defectives: for Goddard and succeeding generations, such people would be known as "morons."

And it was H. H. Goddard, above all, who sought to establish the meaning of mental deficiency. At his Vineland School, Goddard traced the pedigrees of the "feeble-minded" and determined that they followed the Mendelian rules of inheritance. Among his most notable case studies was the pseudonymous Kallikak family, a multigenerational collection of criminals, misfits, and above all, morons who would grace the pages of psychology textbooks for decades to come. Their past, Goddard determined, was also to be their future: visiting a Kallikak home in 1912, Goddard ruefully observed that "In this house of abject poverty, only one sure prospect was ahead, that it would produce more feeble-minded children with which to clog the wheels of human progress."

"We know what feeble-mindedness is," Goddard wrote in 1914, "and we have come to suspect all persons who are incapable of adapting themselves to their environment and living up to the conventions of society or acting sensibly, of being feeble-minded." It was a sweeping definition with broad implications: to be struggling socially or economically, to be unconventional psychologically or culturally, was to be feebleminded. And Goddard meant it. Indeed, Goddard was convinced that social rank was, at every level, merely a reflection of the "mental levels," and those levels were of a "fixed character."

Lecturing at Princeton in 1919, Goddard asked, "How can there be such thing as social equality with this wide range of mental capacity?" His answer is worth quoting at length:

These men in their ultra altruistic and humane attitude, their desire to be fair to the workman, maintain that the great inequalities in social life are wrong and unjust. For example, here is a man who says "I am wearing $12.00 shoes, there is a laborer who is wearing $3.00 shoes; why should I spend $12.00 while he can afford only $3.00? I live in a home that is artistically decorated, carpets, high-priced furniture, expensive pictures and other luxuries; there is a laborer that lives in a hovel with no carpets, no pictures, and the coarsest kind of furniture. It is not right, it is unjust." . . . As we have said, the argument is fallacious. It assumes that the laborer is on the same mental level with the man who is defending him.

Now the fact is, that workman may have a ten year intelligence while you have a twenty. To demand for him such a home as you may enjoy is as absurd as it would be to insist that every laborer should receive a graduate fellowship. . . . The different levels of intelligence have different interests and require different treatment to make them happy.

As for an equal distribution of the wealth of the world that is equally absurd. The man of intelligence has spent his money wisely, has saved until he has enough to provide for his needs in case of sickness, while the man of low intelligence, no matter how much money he would have earned, would have spent much of it foolishly and would never have anything ahead. It is said that during the past year, the coal miners in certain parts of the country have earned more money than the operators and yet today when the mines shut down for a time, those people are the first to suffer. They did not save anything, although their whole life has taught them that mining is an irregular thing and that when they have plenty of work they should save against the days when they do not have work. . . .

These facts are appreciated. But it is not so fully appreciated that the cause is to be found in the fixed character of mental levels. In our ignorance we have said let us give these people one more chance—always one more chance.[12]

But Goddard was not prepared to give the feebleminded one more chance. Left alone, the feebleminded would replicate their degenerative trait in increasingly feebleminded offspring; without intervention, civilization might drown in a sea of incompetence. Goddard would have none of it; he would become perhaps the nation's foremost spokesman for the eugenics movement.

In 1898 the Michigan legislature had been the first in the United States to consider a bill providing for the compulsory sterilization of people with mental disabilities; it was not passed. In 1905 the Pennsylvania legislature passed such a bill but failed to override the governor's veto. Two years later, Indiana produced the first sterilization bill signed into law; it was followed shortly by Goddard's home state of New Jersey, and then Washington and California. By the early 1930s over thirty states had sterilization laws, and by January 1935, some twenty thousand Americans had been involuntarily sterilized in the name of a better humanity.

The eugenics movement enjoyed considerable scientific acceptance. In her 1926 text *Gifted Children*, Leta Hollingworth had argued against the natural inferiority of women; there were, she insisted, "powerful determinants of eminence besides intellect," including bias and social controls. But Hollingworth was also a doctrinaire eugenicist: "economic reward," she maintained, "is positively correlated with intellect," and inevitably so. Her conclusions echoed Goddard's: "The immemorial division of mankind into 'lower' 'middle' and 'upper' classes, economically speaking, rests on a biological foundation which guarantees the stubborn permanence with which it persists in spite of all efforts to abolish it by artifice."[13]

Others were not so sure; they began the systematic examination of eugenics theory. In 1915, William Healy challenged one of the eugenicists' most visible claims, that "[e]very imbecile is a potential criminal." In *The Individual Delinquent*, Healy found no link between mental deficiency and criminality; the only way to comprehend criminal tendencies, Healy argued, was to examine the life experience of the individual. Healy's central conclusion found support in Carl Murchison's 1926 *Criminal Intelligence*: convicted criminals, Murchison reported, attained an average score on the army intelligence test that was 75 percent higher than their prison guards.

As early as 1916, W. Wallace Wallin was expressing doubts that feeblemindedness was a true psychological phenomenon: "How many non-feeble-minded children committed to state institutions are permanently retarded by the limitations of the institutional routine no one can say." Others, like Irene Case and Kate Lewis, challenged the contention that feeblemindedness, whatever its scientific integrity, was the product of genetics. Writing in 1918 in the *American Journal of Sociology*, Case and Lewis reported that parental alcoholism and poverty were identifiable factors in the generation of "feeble-minded-ness."

In 1923 Princeton biologist Edwin Grant Conklin warned that intellect and morality, unlike physical characteristics, were complex phenomena, the occurrence of which it will "probably never be possible to predict." In 1927—the same year that Justice Holmes blessed the sterilization of Carrie Buck with the ringing declaration, "Three generations of imbeciles are enough"—Raymond Pearl of Johns Hopkins University denounced eugenics in an article in *American Mercury* magazine: "The literature of eugenics has largely become a mingled mass of ill-grounded and uncritical sociology, economics, anthropology, and politics, full of emotional appeals to class and race prejudices, solemnly put forth as science and unfortunately acknowledged as such by the general public." Conklin's Princeton colleague Herbert S. Jennings joined in the critique; eugenics, he wrote was the manifestation of "both racial arrogance and the desire to justify present social systems."[14]

But the most damning critique of all came from the most unlikely of sources. Goddard's Kallikak family turned out to be a myth: feeblemindedness among the clan, it evolved, was diagnosed either through visual assessments by Goddard's assistants or through inferences based on second-hand descriptions, and the whole shoddy enterprise was sullied further by the deliberate alteration of photographic evidence. But even before the sham was exposed, Goddard himself had second thoughts. His focus gradually shifted to the environmental causes of feeblemindedness, and his goals became the educability and self-sufficiency of his subjects. By 1928 he was prepared to recant. "It may still be objected," he wrote in that year, "that moron parents are likely to have imbecile or idiot children. There is not much evidence that this is the case. The danger is probably negligible." He offered two conclusions:

1. Feeble-mindedness (the moron) is *not incurable.*
2. The feebleminded do not generally need to be segregated in institutions.

Through the 1930s, eugenics rapidly declined both popularly and in the scientific disciplines. In the end, the "science" of eugenics, both its biological foundations and its findings, were thoroughly discredited by scientific inquiry; and the politics of eugenics, its odd conflation of

Social Darwinism and a hyper-active racism, was made untenable initially by the Great Depression, and finally by the revealed horrors of Nazism. The biological model of mental deficiency gradually yielded to a sociological construct that recognized both the socioeconomic "causes" of mental deficiency and the critical role of culture in defining the criteria of deficiency. The surest way to ameliorate the effects of mental deficiency, it emerged, was through inclusion and accommodation—through the creation, that is, of societies in which differences were not disabilities.

Some learning comes hard. In 1980 Dr. K. Ray Nelson, Director of Lynchburg Hospital, examined the records of his institution. Carrie Buck had been sterilized there in October 1927; she was not the last. The sterilizations had continued at least through 1972. There were four thousand in all.[15]

The Myths of Inferiority: IQ

Throughout much of the nineteenth century, scientific assessments of mental and moral traits were largely anatomical ones. For Paul Broca, the dimensions of the skull were the ultimate measures of intellectual capacity. Craniometry confirmed the conventional rankings of the races, the mental deficiency of criminals, and the intellectual superiority of men over women. Never mind that the data had to be carefully culled to support these conclusions—all nonconforming results dismissed as anomalous; each confounding variable like class, health, age, and body size either discounted or heavily factored at the whim of the investigator—in the final analysis, the evidence proved what was suspected all along.

For Cesare Lombroso, the presence in human beings of anatomical stigmata associated with primitive creatures—a simian forehead, rodent-like teeth, or a facial asymmetry suggestive of flatfishes—indicated not merely a physical atavism but a mental one as well. By mere physical examination, Lombroso could identify those individuals—and, of course, those races—that were in fact living primitives, devolved toward apishness, mentally and morally degenerate. Lombroso founded a new discipline, criminal anthropology, rooted in the discovery of the born criminal, *homo delinquens*, the "criminal man."[16]

Alfred Binet began his investigations of intelligence as a craniometrist. But he lost faith in his discipline as he recognized both the pervasiveness of the investigator's unconscious bias and the extraordinary malleability of the data. "The idea of measuring intelligence by measuring heads," he wrote, "seemed ridiculous." He gradually shifted his attention from what people *were* to what they *could do*—from anatomy to psychometrics.

In 1904 Binet received a commission from the French minister of public education to perform a study to identify children in need of special educational services. Binet developed a test designed to correspond to teachers' a priori notions of ability; student achievement, after all, would ultimately be measured against the teacher's expectations. Thus the success of Binet's test and its subsequent revisions would be found in its ability to predict school performance; every educational test since has been adjusted and standardized to afford this prediction.[17]

Binet's psychometric project had a specific, practical purpose: the identification of students in need of special assistance. It measured "intelligence," he insisted, only in this limited way, and he warned repeatedly against its mischaracterization and misuse. But the translators and interpreters of Binet's test, particularly those who brought it to America, embraced an ideology completely at odds with Binet's. They believed everything that he did not: that his tests could be used to measure a general intelligence; that this intelligence could be described by a single ordinal number; and that this intelligence was an innate, unchangeable quantity fixed by genetic inheritance.

The three American pioneers of hereditarian theories of intelligence were Lewis Terman of Stanford, H. H. Goddard of the Vineland Training School, and R. M. Yerkes of Harvard. As America prepared for entry into the Great War, it was Yerkes who persuaded the U.S. government to authorize the intelligence testing of its army recruits. Armed with a military commission and working in collaboration with Goddard and Terman, "Colonel" Yerkes prepared intelligence tests—or "IQ tests," following Terman's Stanford-Binet model—and administered them to roughly 1.75 million recruits.

After the war, Yerkes and E. G. Boring selected over one hundred thousand cases from the pool for a detailed statistical analysis. Two major conclusions emerged, one predictable, and one something of a shock.

The first conclusion was that IQ was correlated with race and nationality. This, of course, surprised no one. The intellectual inferiority of black Americans was commonly assumed, and so too were the deficiencies of some immigrant stocks. Just a few years earlier, in fact, Goddard had supervised a study of immigrants at Ellis Island; his assessment—based, admittedly, only on "trained" observation—was that 80 percent or more of all Jewish, Hungarian, Italian, and Russian immigrants were feebleminded.

The Yerkes army tests confirmed these impressions, but this time with hard data. The analysis of nationality concluded that "[t]he range of differences between the countries is a very wide one." The report ordered the countries from top to bottom: "[i]n general," the report summarized, "the Scandinavian and English countries stand high in the list, while the Slavic and Latin countries stand low." The low countries, in fact, stood very low. For each nationality, Yerkes and Boring calculated a mean mental age: the average mental age of the Russian recruits was 11.34, of the Italians 11.01, and of the Poles 10.74. Still, all of these fared better than the black recruits; their average mental age was 10.41. These numbers take on an added significance when it is noted that, under the prevailing standards, anyone with a mental age of twelve or below was a "moron."

This is why the second conclusion came as something of a shock. Lewis Terman had determined that the classic distribution of intelligence—the Stanford-Binet "bell curve"—fixed a mean mental age of sixteen. Yerkes and Boring painstakingly calculated the mean mental age of the white recruits: it was about thirteen years. Unless the recruits were somehow atypical, it appeared that America was fast devolving into a nation of morons. This became, for many, the received message, and it added fuel to the fires of the eugenics movement as well as the postwar effort to curb the immigration of undesirable peoples.

Of course, what the tests more likely revealed was the folly of the prevailing mental age construct—this, indeed, appeared to be Yerkes's view—and the latent malevolence of the psychometric enterprise. In 1922 eugenicist Lothrop Stoddard was popularizing the Yerkes analysis in his book *The Revolt against Civilization*; "[t]he average mental age of Americans," he had ominously reported, "is only about fourteen." As journalist Walter Lippman put it,

It is quite impossible for honest statistics to show that the average adult intelligence of a representative sample of the nation is that of an immature child in that same nation. The average adult intelligence cannot be less than the average adult intelligence, and to anyone who knows what the words "mental age" mean, Mr. Stoddard's remark is precisely as silly as if he had written that the average mile was three-quarters of a mile long. . . . But instead of pausing to realize that the army tests had knocked the Stanford-Binet measure of intelligence into a cocked hat, [Stoddard] wrote his book in the belief that the Stanford measure is as good as it ever was. This is not intelligent. . . . It leads one to suspect, after such a beginning, that the real promise and value of the investigation which Binet started is in danger of gross perversion by muddleheaded and prejudiced men.

"[T]he statement that the average mental age of Americans is only about fourteen is not inaccurate," Lippman concluded. "It is not incorrect. It is nonsense."[18]

The next year saw the publication of the classic exegesis of the army tests, Carl C. Brigham's *Study of American Intelligence.* Brigham, a Princeton psychologist, reanalyzed Yerkes's data: "These army data," he wrote, "constitute the first really significant contribution to the study of race differences in mental traits. They give us a scientific basis for our conclusions." Brigham's conclusions were unequivocal: American intelligence was in decline, and it was declining due to three factors: "the change in the races migrating to this country, . . . the sending of lower and lower representatives of each race . . . [and] the most sinister development in the history of this continent, the importation of the negro."

Brigham's analysis of the army data used the average score of the black recruits as the baseline, a certain benchmark for low intelligence. He then calculated that 46 percent of the Polish recruits, 42.3 percent of the Italians, and 39 percent of the Russians scored at or below the black average. This established, ipso facto, the deficiencies in these European stocks. He went on to note the "very remarkable fact" that measured intelligence generally increased with the years spent in the country: immigrants with less than five years in the country were essentially feebleminded, while those in America twenty years or longer were intellectually indistinguishable from native-born Americans. This might have served as a tip-off to the cultural biases of the tests, but it did not. Instead, Brigham concluded that "the curve indicates a gradual deterioration in the class of immigrants examined in the army, who came to this country in each succeeding five year period since 1902."

Brigham did not shy away from the political implications of his findings. He concluded his work with the following assessment:

> The decline of American intelligence will be more rapid than the decline of the intelligence of European national groups, owing to the presence here of the negro. These are the plain, if somewhat ugly, facts that our study shows. The deterioration of American intelligence is not inevitable, however, if public action can be aroused to prevent it. . . . The steps that should be taken to preserve or increase our present intellectual capacity must of course be dictated by science and not by political expediency. Immigration should not only be restrictive but highly selective. And the revision of the immigration and naturalization laws will only afford a slight relief from our present difficulty. The really important steps are those looking toward the prevention of the continued propagation of defective strains in the present population.[19]

With the publication of Brigham's tract, the IQ phenomenon was in full swing. "We have learned once and for all," wrote Henry Fairfield Osborn, president of the American Museum of Natural History, in 1923, "that the negro is not like us. So in regard to many races and subraces in Europe we learned that some which we had believed possessed of an order of intelligence perhaps superior to ours were far inferior." A 1926 publication titled *Genetic Studies of Genius* featured the IQs of history's most famous personages, based largely on anecdotes about their youthful achievements. Charles Spearman, meanwhile, was busy calculating the first principal component of a factor analysis of IQ tests; he called it g, and claimed that it represented the general intelligence underlying all cognitive activity. In 1927, Spearman announced that black inferiority was most pronounced on tests "known to be most saturated with g." Cyril Burt chimed in with a hereditarian argument for g, and a concomitant argument for the innateness and immutability of IQ. "Capacity must obviously limit content," Burt wrote. "It is impossible for a pint jug to hold more than a pint of milk; and it is equally impossible for a child's educational attainments to rise higher than his educable capacity permits."[20]

But already there were voices urging caution: IQ was not necessarily intelligence; and what it measured was not necessarily innate. In 1914

Josiah Morse had reported the Binet differences between black and white school-children in *Popular Science Monthly*; these results, he claimed, suggested the hereditary superiority of whites over blacks. But that same year, Oswald Garrison Villard's *Evening Post* published a rebuttal, citing Morse's failure to adequately control for the quality of schools, interactions with the community, and the social history of the respective families. Villard was joined by the majority of his white neo-abolitionist peers in echoing William Hayes Ward's declaration that innate racial inferiority was "false in science, ruinous in government, and intolerable in morals."

In 1921 Ada Arlitt of Bryn Mawr examined the social status of IQ testees and found that social status was more positively correlated with IQ than was race. There is, she reported, "more likeness between children of the same social status but of different race than between children of the same race but different social status."

Franz Boas offered his own exegesis of the army tests, noting, among other things, that northern blacks outperformed many southern whites. Yerkes posited selective migration as the explanation; Boas suggested that the relative oppression faced by blacks was the primary racial variable. Otto Klienburg of the University of Colorado tested Yerkes's selective migration theory by systematically examining the school records of the draftees; they offered no support for Yerkes's view. The IQ tests, Klienburg concluded, reflect differences in environment, not race; his life's work was thereafter dedicated to rebutting all contrary assertions.

J. R. Kantor, a psychologist at Indiana University, rejected the conception of "intelligence" inherent in the prevailing IQ construct. Intelligence, Kantor insisted, was a concrete activity, not an innate capacity; accordingly, it could not be reduced to a fixed, immutable quantity.

By 1930 most psychologists were no longer willing to assume innate intellectual differences between races or nationalities, and many, like Kantor, were questioning the conception of intelligence behind the psychometric project. Whatever its value, the IQ test surely did not measure innate group difference in intelligence. As one prominent psychologist observed that year, Americans of different races and nationalities are not afforded "equal opportunities to acquire the vernacular of the test"; accordingly, "comparative studies of various national and racial groups may not be made with existing tests."

"[O]ne of the most pretentious of these comparative racial studies," wrote Carl Brigham, "the writer's own—was without foundation."[21]

The natural order of intelligence was on shaky ground by midcentury. Its first casualty had been its science: genetic theory, it evolved, could not account for most instances of "mental deficiency"; no biological theory offered an effective rebuttal to the obvious environmental explanations for racial and gender disparities in achievement and measured intelligence; and IQ tests—the last best chance for empirical proof of the order—merely confirmed the existence of well-known social disadvantages. Stripped of the veneer of scientific certainty, what was left of the natural order was mostly its politics, and all of this too gradually collapsed: social Darwinism under the weight of the Great Depression, eugenic racism after the revelations of the Holocaust, and the central inegalitarian premise in the wake of the Cold War.

But the decisive blow to the natural order was neither distinctly scientific nor political: it was an epistemological one, and it revealed, among other things, that science and politics were often the same. Truth and ideology, it emerged, tend to overlap: there is not always a certain distinction between what we know and what we choose to believe. All knowledge, "scientific" and "political," is both facilitated and constrained by culture, a culture that we make and that in turn remakes us.

The implications for the natural order were staggering, as each term of the biological inequation came under a new form of scrutiny. The previously unremarkable assertion "This group is intellectually superior to that group" now seemed not only scientifically inaccurate or politically misguided, but philosophically out of date. The immutable truths that had once informed such statements were now revealed to be quite contingent: "intellectual superiority" was not an inevitable fact, but inevitably a reflection of cultural choice. The same was equally true for the apparently immutable term of the inequation: "group" identity—"race," "gender," and "disability"—was itself a product not merely of creation, but substantially of cultural re-creation.

What ultimately had changed, then, was the *meaning* of assertions like "This group is intellectually superior to that group." The contemporary thinker re-cognized that assertion to mean "Some of the differences that we have constructed between these groups can now be reduced to a single variable, quantified and ordered, and labeled as 'intelligence,' if that is the sort of thing we are determined to do." It becomes, in effect, an assertion only of cultural possibilities, which is to say, in the final analysis, that the assertion becomes merely tautological (we can conceivably do, of course, anything that we are determined to do) and thus by many measures—including most "scientific" ones—utterly meaning*less*.

Yet it is good to be reminded of the choices, and also—and this is the other great contribution of contemporary thought—of the forces that constrain them. We *can* make some groups intellectually superior to other groups, and indeed we have chosen to do so. We *can* make some groups the intellectual equals of other groups, and indeed we have chosen to do this as well. And all of the choices that we have already made invariably constrain the choices that now confront us. The history we have constructed makes the choices more or less difficult: some equality is now fairly easy to realize, some is not very easy at all.

Superiority and inferiority, then, are self-perpetuating. But only, ironically, if we make them that way.

6

The Smart Culture
Myths of Intelligence

The natural order is a product partly of science fiction and partly of political malevolence, yet it remains a cultural truth for many Americans. This chapter seeks to offer an account of its extraordinary resiliency. It examines the contemporary attempt to place the concept of merit—of "superior" and "inferior"—somehow beyond culture, rooted instead in a genuinely universal phenomenon called "intelligence." It examines as well the attempt to cloak that phenomenon in the garb of scientific neutrality: to fix intelligence in biology, to measure it with standardized tests, and to define it as a single quantifiable entity, IQ.

This chapter also examines the choices that inhere in the construction of an intellectual hierarchy, political choices that are obscured by the veneer of scientific neutrality. We choose which talents and attributes will count as "intelligence"; we choose our response to measures of those talents and attributes; we choose the ways we distribute the resources needed to develop those talents and attributes. We choose, in short, to believe in and to reproduce our smart culture.

This chapter concludes with an addendum, disclosing one simple but perhaps surprising truth: despite centuries of racial caste, the construction of intelligence is only poorly correlated with the construction of race. The measured differences in racial group "intelligence" are truly insignificant: we are—all of us—equally smart.

Prologue

Every eleventh-grader had a choice of electives at my high school: for the entire junior year, we could take either Auto Mechanics, Computer Science, or Home Economics. Only girls and football players took Home Economics, and that left me out, my high school football career having lasted all of two weeks, ending officially due to a knee injury, but in actuality, as I will explain, because I was no good. Computers, meanwhile, seemed alien and vaguely sinister to me, and the guy who taught Computer Science—like too many of the kids who signed up for it—had, I thought, very bad breath. Auto Mechanics, on the other hand, was taught by the football team's defensive line coach, and Coach Vass had admired my spunk if not my talent, and I liked him very much even though he generally frightened me into incoherence. Besides, all the men in my family were pretty good mechanics and I was working six nights a week in a J. C. Penney auto center. So I took Auto Mechanics.

It is important to understand, I think, that Coach Vass liked me. I suppose I had made an impression in my brief tenure as a football player: I was nominally a back, both offensive and defensive—we did not distinguish—but I was very small, and thus easily knocked over; I was very slow, and thus easily run past or caught up to; and I was very uncoordinated, which meant that there was not much point in trying to pass, lateral, or, for that matter, hand the football to me, since I was likely in any event to drop it. All of which meant that I spent most of the two weeks of football practice either holding the blocking dummies or serving as the obligatory ball carrier in tackling drills, which is to say, I spent most of the two weeks getting creamed, which I did very well.

Most of the time the backs ran their drills against other backs, but once a day, some back had to run the tackling drills against the linemen, who were always much bigger, generally much stronger, and occasionally, it seemed, much meaner. I did not much like this version of the drill.

The tackling drill itself was simple: four tackling dummies were laid out on the ground parallel to one another, spaced about four feet apart, creating three lanes to run through. About ten feet on either side of the dummies were positioned the participants: the back—with the football—facing the dummies, the lineman facing the same direction, away from both the running back and the row of dummies in between. At the sound of the whistle, the back would sprint for a lane, the lineman would spin around toward a lane and hope, through a combination of lucky guessing and instincts and agility, to hit the lane—and the running back—before the back got through. If the back was quick, it was tough to catch him without a lucky guess; if the back was big, sometimes the lineman was quite happy to guess wrong; if the back was neither, it was a field day for the linemen. Occasionally one of our starting backs would be picked for the drill, and the practice would otherwise come to a halt while we watched one of our best runners try to avoid—or run over—our best tacklers. Usually, though, the coaches picked some scrub like me, and the rest of the backs would go about their business largely oblivious to the fact that, just yards away, their defenseless brother was being massacred.

Coach Vass, it should be mentioned, professed the genetic superiority of linemen, and always took this daily occasion to prove his theory. I obliged him well, and I think he appreciated my cooperation. And I believe he tried to show his gratitude one Friday, about a half hour into the fifth and final time I ran the drill for him. I had been getting clobbered for two weeks, and was on this day enduring a particularly brutal pounding, as one lineman after another slammed me to the dry, hard ground. "Bobby," Coach Vass asked, "do you want to switch for a minute; want to tackle?"

In the spirit of things, I lied and said I did.

There was a lot of whooping and hollering and laughing and, for a second, I forgot how bad I hurt, and I had to smile myself.

Then Coach Vass gave the ball to our middle linebacker, Chick DiRocco. Chick was at least a foot taller than me, weighed at least a hundred pounds more, and was between five and ten years older; rumor had it that he had kids who were already my size. I stopped smiling.

Chick lined up across from the dummies, and I took my spot, turned around, crouched, and waited for the whistle. Under the circumstances, I was sure Chick would come up the middle, and I wanted no part of that collision, so I planned to spin as quickly as I could to my right, head for that outside lane, then dive back at Chick as he charged through the middle. I'd make a good effort of it, and might even trip him up.

Coach Vass blew the whistle. I spun to my right. Without looking up, I leapt to the right outside lane.

I had guessed right. Or wrong, depending on your perspective.

Chick, thinking he was doing the merciful thing, had bolted for the same lane.

We collided solidly, "numbers on numbers" as the coaches liked to say, and I went flying backwards. For some reason—I have no clue why—I grabbed onto Chick's shoulder pads and he tumbled down on top of me.

There was a lot of screaming and clapping, and I could hear Coach Vass hollering over and over "Way to hit, Bobby Hayman, way to hit." Chick got up, smiled, and said "nice stick." I did not say anything, on account of not being able to breathe. Coach Vass asked me if I was okay, I nodded another lie, and Coach Vass sent me back to the rest of the backs. He smacked my helmet as I jogged shakily by.

Later that day my knee began to hurt, and that night it swelled up, and on Monday I told the head coach I was through. He did not try to talk me out of it. A couple of years later, I hurt the same knee playing club football in college, and when I had arthroscopic surgery, the doctor told me that my cartilage had been torn long before, which meant that I had hurt it in high school and had played through the injury in college, which is why I am really quite proud to tell this story.

The point of which, remember, is that Coach Vass liked me. Which is, I think, important.

Back to Auto Mechanics. Each kid in Coach Vass's Auto Mechanics class had his own workstation, which was basically just a fourteen-inch plot on a mile-long workbench. At one station next to mine was a kid I knew pretty well. Barry's presence in the class was something of a mystery to me, since he was undeniably brilliant and seemed to have Computer Science written all over him. On the other hand, his personal hygiene was beyond reproach, and auto mechanics was his passion, and it turned out that he could handle himself fairly well in the shop—well enough, actually, to win the John Dickinson High School STP Trouble-Shooting Competition or some such thing, which was pretty much the highlight of the class. As for the kid on the other side of me, he appeared to be in Auto Mechanics mostly by default, and he was, in my expert opinion, basically hapless. Only one student, in fact, would ever separate that kid from the ignominy of the worst grade in the class: that would be me—I finished 116th in a class of 116.

But only because of a technicality. To be admitted into the "advanced" portion of the course, each kid had to do a set of "basic" exercises involving some sort of discrete mechanical skill, and while the exercises were probably designed to ensure some understanding of the basics of workshop safety, they were really quite perfunctory, and mostly just provided a good excuse for welding some other kid's screwdriver to some barely accessible metal surface. Only the very last exercise in "basic" Auto Mechanics involved any real auto parts, and it only required us to dismantle and rebuild a carburetor in one sixty minute class, which was not really very difficult.

At least, for most kids. Barry did the carburetor in a flash: he dismantled it, rebuilt it, modified it to ensure higher performance, and spent the last fifty minutes of the class doing his calculus homework. The other kid and I had somewhat less success. At the end of an hour, the hapless kid's carburetor was very much in shambles, and I thought Coach Vass was unnecessarily generous when he surveyed the remains scattered around the kid's workstation and pronounced it "close enough." My carburetor, meanwhile, was in relatively pristine condition, largely because, admittedly, I had no idea how to get it apart. Still, I was disappointed when Coach Vass shook his head and asked, "Do you want to try again, Bobby?" I guess the voice that responded was my own, but I don't know what the hell I meant by, "No thanks, I'm fine." Neither at first did Coach Vass, who gave me kind of a quizzical look, but then smiled, chuckled, "okay," and moved on down the line. So I became the only kid that I know of who was barred from even entering the "advanced" phase of Auto Mechanics, which, I guess, was just as well, since I am fairly certain that, in all events, I had a lock on the worst grade.

It took a few more weeks of lost parts, broken tools, and one very minor mishap with a dead battery—the kid should have stayed away when he saw me with the drill; besides, battery acid itches more than it actually hurts—but I gradually grew accustomed to the notion that even "basic" Auto Mechanics was beyond the realm of my aptitude. When I told Coach Vass that I needed to withdraw from the course, he said he understood, and said he'd do what he could to make sure I got some credit. He gave me one credit's worth of a D in Auto Mechanics, which he earnestly intended to keep me on a pace to graduate, and which in fact disqualified me from the school's chapter of the National Honor Society. For both, I was genuinely grateful, and that was what I had in mind when I saw Coach Vass in the cafeteria the next semester, and stammered, clumsily but sincerely, "Thanks, grade, for the coach." The hapless kid, meanwhile, made it through both semesters of the course, while Barry got As both semesters, and was the runner-up in the Mid-Atlantic Regional Trouble-Shooting Competition. Barry, on the other hand, had no way out of the Honor Society.

I saw Coach Vass for the last time the following year at the Senior Awards Banquet. I was the master of ceremonies, which had to have shocked Coach Vass, seeing as how he had never before associated me with a coherent sentence. But I guess he was even more shocked when I won the award as the senior class's Outstanding History Student, and I believe that he was being honest when he came up to me after the banquet, heartily shook my hand, and said, "Congratulations, Bobby; I had no idea you were so smart."

I felt good about that. I know that a lesser person might just as easily have said, "Congratulations, Bobby; they have no idea you are so dumb."

Difference Made Inferior

Consider the available options when we make intellectual superiority.

Assume, for a moment, that our tests of "intelligence" regularly yield a statistically significant performance disparity between two groups. Forget, for a moment, about the reasons for the disparity: perhaps we know the reasons or perhaps we don't know, perhaps we can never know and perhaps we do not care. Assume the statistical disparity is simply there. What remains true, in any event, is that our response to this disparity is not preordained, but may be selected from a number of viable options.

There are at least four options:

1. We can eliminate the disparity by modifying our tests.
2. We can keep our test as it is, but simply ignore the disparity.
3. We can keep our test as it is, acknowledge the disparity, but deny to that disparity any legitimate social meaning.
4. We can keep our test as it is, acknowledge the disparity, and invest that disparity with social significance.

In short, the test disparity is like any other "difference" between people or groups of people: even if the difference is "real"—in the limited sense that it may be validly and reliably measured—the salience of the difference remains very much up to us. What we make of it, in other words, is a matter of choice. And historically, we have exercised each of our options in dealing with these kinds of differences.

Consider the first option: modifying the tests. The early Stanford-Binet tests produced gender disparities in performance. But we assumed—or insisted—that intelligence was evenly distributed between the sexes. So we changed the tests, either eliminating each item that generated a disparity or balancing it with an item that was gender-biased in the opposite direction. The equality achieved through this standardization was permanent: all tests are validated by their conformity to the prevailing standards, and tests today are marketed on the basis of their agreement with Stanford-Binet norms. Today, then, there is no gender disparity in standardized measures of intelligence, because we resolutely forbid it.[1]

Consider the second option: ignoring the disparity. Intelligence tests regularly produced disparities between subgroups of white Americans. Some of these were regional: northerners outperformed rural white southerners. Some of these were intergenerational: young white Americans outperformed older white Americans. And some of these were ethnic: white Americans of Northern European or Anglo descent outperformed white Americans of Southern or Eastern European descent. Aside from the period of postwar xenophobia that culminated in the Immigration Act of 1924, our response to these differences has been, in effect, "who cares?" As Andrew Hacker notes, "For the last half-century, this country has had an unstated understanding that it would not draw genetic distinctions among Americans who have been allowed to identify themselves as white." While some English "scholars" remain bent on proving the intellectual inferiority of the Irish, we Americans have remained determinedly indifferent to intelligence differences *within* the "white race." The disparities were there—and apparently still are—but we choose not to recognize them.[2]

Consider the third option: denying the social legitimacy of the difference. Not all of the real differences between Americans are intellectual: there are spiritual, physical, and emotional differences as well. Spiritual differences—as evidenced, for example, through religion—are manifestly not valid grounds for social differentiation, and there is widespread agreement that this is good. Physical attractiveness, meanwhile, correlates positively with indices of academic, economic, and psychological success, but we seem almost universally embarrassed by this fact, and there is widespread agreement that our embarrassment is good. Emotional ability, finally, is measured only at its negative extreme, in emotional illness, and there seems to be no great desire to construct a more extensive emotional hierarchy. In short, most acknowledged differences are simply not legitimated as social factors: even when we know that differences exist, we insist that they do not, or should not, matter, and are embarrassed when they do.

Then there is the fourth option: make the differences count. Maybe lots even. And be proud of it. This is the option we have chosen for the racial disparity in measured intelligence. We have chosen not to modify our tests to eliminate racial disparities in measured intelligence. On the contrary, we have preserved largely intact the same measures of intelligence, perhaps not so much in spite of the disparities, but rather, as Lewontin, Rose, and Kamin suggest, "precisely because it is these differences that the tests are *meant* to measure."

We have chosen not to ignore the racial disparities in measured intelligence, even though willful ignorance is a courtesy routinely extended to white Americans. As Orlando Patterson notes, the main achievement of the twentieth-century civil rights movement was in making black Americans a fully constitutive part of "our" community. But not quite: in drawing distinctions between white and black Americans that we now refuse to draw within the white race, we ensure that black Americans remain outsiders.[3]

Finally, we have chosen not to deny any legitimate social meaning to these differences, even though we refuse to legitimate other forms of difference, whether they correlate with social success or not. Instead, we insist that measured intelligence matters, and that measured disparities will—and should—translate into social disparities, and that measured racial disparities are no exception to this rule.

But in fact, they are the exception: we make racial disparities count like no others. That is our choice.

The Myths of Intelligence

There are other hidden choices in the assertion of intelligence differences, choices that inhere in the construction of "intelligence." These choices, too, will determine the nature of our intellectual order.

To briefly illustrate, assume, once again, that our tests of "intelligence" regularly yield a statistically significant performance disparity between two groups. But this time, we will choose not to ignore the possible explanations for this difference. Suddenly, as a consequence of *this* choice, we recognize that there are at least three more sets of choices available to us, each of which may account, in whole or in part, for the disparity.

1. We choose what counts as intelligence. We make choices at the outset when we identify the aptitudes that we seek to measure: different choices will undoubtedly produce different types or degrees of disparity, or eliminate it altogether. If we don't like the intellectual order created by one set of criteria, we can always generate a new one or, of course, choose not to create an order at all.

2. We choose which disparities are acceptable. We make choices when we are confronted with disparities in aptitudes: if we determine that particular aptitudes do and should matter, then we must determine whether and how we will develop those aptitudes in a more equal fashion. If we don't like the intellectual order created by our current scheme of aptitude development, then we can level it with a more egalitarian plan.

3. We choose which reports of disparity are credible. We make choices when we are confronted with evidence of disparity: we can insist that the evidence represents real differences in aptitude, or we can consider the role of bias and other confounding variables. If we don't like the intellectual order reported by one set of measurements, we can always improve our measures or, of course, get out of the measuring business.

The problem with all these choices is that they are so hard to see: they are obscured by the powerful mythology of "intelligence." Historically, the aura of scientific neutrality that surrounded the concept of intelligence was so overwhelming that reports of intelligence disparities were simply assumed to reflect biological truths: the intellectual order was natural and there was no room for human choice at all. Intelligence was thus conceived as a purely scientific phenomenon: objective, immutable, and measurable.

The contemporary epistemological climate is less hospitable to the claims of the natural order. The order's a priori premises—the objectivity of the governing constructs, the immutability of identity, the measurability of discrete differences—are now very much in doubt.

Above all, a new skepticism reveals the dangers of scientism: the veil of neutrality often obscures the fact that some scientific "truths" are derived less from scientific methods and more from ideological commitments. This, indeed, is the reality of "intelligence": born of politics, it persists out of political necessity, devoid of empirical support, and otherwise without theoretical foundation. Politics aside, there is no reason today to believe in the myth of intelligence.

But it is difficult to put politics aside. The mythology of intelligence may be empirically and theoretically weak, but it is politically powerful. Thus it persists, stripped of its veil of scientific neutrality, revealed as the creation of an ideologically charged scientism, but still clouding our imagination and obscuring our vision all the same.

Freedom from its illusions thus requires more than mere critical insight—more, simply, than the recognition that science is not always neutral or that identity and difference are not only natural. What it requires is a willingness to contest the scientism of intelligence not merely as bad science, but as bad politics as well. It necessitates, in short, an equal and opposite political will: a determination to dispute the peculiar *ideology* of intelligence.

That ideology can be reduced to three assertions about the desirability, inevitability, and reality of the intellectual hierarchy, each of which simultaneously obscures and represents a choice:

1. Choosing what counts as intelligence: Because hierarchy is desirable, intelligence can and should be ordered according to a single set of characteristics.
2. Choosing which disparities are acceptable: Because hierarchy is inevitable, intelligence can and should be viewed as an immutable capacity.
3. Choosing which disparities are credible: Because hierarchy is real, intelligence can be and is reliably measured as an independent phenomenon.

For each of these assertions, there are superior alternative visions; there are, that is, better choices. These alternative visions are scientific when they can be, and their empirical premises are derived not from ideology, but from human experience. The visions are political when they must be, and their moral imperatives are derived not from a commitment to order, but from a faith in the inherent equal worth of all human beings. And they maintain that the intellectual hierarchy is neither desirable, nor inevitable, nor real:

1. Hierarchy is not desirable: There are many different kinds of intelligence; they need not—and should not—be reduced to a single-axis hierarchy.
2. Hierarchy is not inevitable: Intelligence is a dynamic process; it can be learned, and it can be taught.
3. Hierarchy is not real: Intelligence is not a discrete phenomenon; its measurement is inevitably confounded by cultural variables.

Each choice is worth examining in some detail.

Choice 1. Choosing What Counts as Intelligence

> The scale, properly speaking, does not permit the measure of the intelligence, because intellectual qualities are not superposable, and therefore cannot be measured as linear surfaces are measured.
> — Alfred Binet, *The Development of Intelligence in Children*

Alfred Binet knew what some of his American successors either don't or pretend not to: there is no single natural phenomenon that we can identify as *the* intelligence. There are, rather, many intelligences, many diverse intellectual qualities, and their graphic representation would require an almost infinite number of axes extending in as many different directions, the dimensions limited only by our own intellectual ability to identify and distinguish the intelligence types. Or by our will.[4]

We could, of course, simplify our graph by choosing to ignore the different types of intelligence: either we could insist that some kinds of intelligence do not count as "intelligence" as we choose to understand the term—and thus not plot these intelligences on our graph at all—or we could insist that the differences in kind are really ones of degree, and thus reduce our many axes to one.

In fact, the purveyors of the conventional wisdom about "intelligence" do both of these things. The various intellectual qualities that do not conform to their hypothesis of the hour are defined away: they are not "intelligence" and are not worthy of their measure. Meanwhile, the measured differences in "intelligence" are reduced to a single axis order, and the realness of the order validated by instruments that were *designed* to reduce intelligence to a single-axis: it's a question of degree, because, well, that's how it's measured. In short, measured "intelligence" becomes everything Binet insisted that it was not: complete, unitary, and plotted on a single vertical line.

Now if intelligence can really be represented this way—complete, unitary, reducible to an ordinal number—we would expect that it could be defined in fairly concrete terms. And if intelligence is purported to be a scientific phenomenon—and, more specifically, a natural scientific phenomenon—we would expect that its definition would not be dependent on either (a) some notion of cultural consensus, because then "intelligence" is partial, not complete, and is simply how we *choose* to define it; or (b) its persistence as a statistical artifact, because then "intelligence" becomes superposable, reduced to a single entity, simply because that's how we *choose* to *measure* it. We expect, in sum, a definition that vests the concept of "intelligence" with some independent integrity, independent, that is, of the commitments—the choices—of the people who are defining it.

But that's not what we get. Instead, we get scientistic mumbojumbo that only poorly obscures the precise errors that Binet had cautioned against: a partial collection of intellectual qualities re-presented as *the* intelligence, reduced to a single axis and ordered as differences of degree. And it is all a matter of choice.

Consider the case of *The Bell Curve*. What, according to Murray and Herrnstein, is "intelligence"?

We are told, initially, what it is not. It is not "musical abilities" or "kinesthetic abilities." Why not? Because, "[i]n the case of music and kinesthetics, *talent* is a word with a domain and weight of its own, and we are unclear why we gain anything by discarding it in favor of another word, *intelligence*, that has had another domain and weight." In other words, apparently, linguistic convention mandates that some abilities be "talent" rather than "intelligence," and "we" don't "gain anything" by reconceiving the terms.

Fine. Conventions can be good. But whose conventions are these? Who made them? Who was excluded from the process of making them? Who has gained from them? Who has been harmed by them? And who precisely is the "we" that does not stand to "gain anything" by revising them?

Then there are "intrapersonal and interpersonal skills." These don't count either, for the same reasons. With regard to these abilities, "words like *sensitivity, charm, persuasiveness, insight*—the list could go on and on—have accumulated over the centuries to describe them." Again, linguistic convention differentiates these skills. Why not reconceive them as "intelligence"? Because "[w]e lose precision by using the word *intelligence* to cover them all."

Again, fine—with all the appropriate caveats. Here, at least, we learn why the scope of intelligence must be limited: for the sake of precision. Precision is good. So now that we know what intelligence is not, we can learn, with precision, what intelligence is. So what is it, precisely? Well, "[h]igh intelligence has earmarks that correspond to a first approximation to the commonly understood meaning of *smart*." So intelligence, then, is what people think of when they use the word "smart." But not exactly, just sort of.

It is clearly a good thing we did not sacrifice any precision: we hadn't much to lose.

But there is more. "IQ scores match, to a first degree, whatever it is that people mean when they use the word *intelligent* or *smart* in ordinary language." So "intelligence" is "smartness," "to a first approximation," and it matches "IQ score," "to a first degree." Moreover, "IQ scores are stable, although not perfectly so"; "[p]roperly administered IQ tests are not demonstrably biased"; and "IQ tests expressly designed" to measure general intelligence "measure it most accurately."

Apparently, then, measured intelligence can be the *imperfectly* replicable *statistical representation* of the *conventional cultural image* of "smart" *if* the measures are properly designed and administered to secure that representation.

Understand what is being said here: measured intelligence is what we *choose* to measure as intelligence, and what we choose to measure as intelligence is what we *ordinarily speak of* as intelligence. But not quite. "Many people conclude that if they see someone who is sensitive, humorous and talks fluently, the person must surely have an above-average IQ." Yes, that stands to reason: if IQ measures smart, and if "ordinary" people define smart, then high IQ should be prevalent among people ordinarily thought of as "smart." But "[t]he identification of IQ with attractive human qualities in general is unfortunate and wrong." In fact, we are told, there is only a "modest correlation" between attractive human qualities ordinarily associated with smartness—sensitivity, wit, articulateness—and actual IQ.

So here it is at last: measured intelligence is what we *choose* to measure as intelligence, and what we choose to measure as intelligence is what we *ordinarily speak of* as intelligence . . . some of the time.

It does not get any more precise than this.

It is difficult to respond to this conception of intelligence, except to point out the obvious: that it is utterly bankrupt of any integrity except as a cultural and statistical construction, and that even on those terms, it is rather pathetic. Perhaps the best way to illustrate the almost limitless limitations of such a construct is by posing what should be a fairly simple problem: are "funny" people "smart"?

The Bell Curve's answer is "not necessarily": "a person can have a terrific sense of humor without giving you a clue about where he is within thirty points on the IQ scale." "Many witty people," the authors explain, "do not have unusually high test scores, but someone who regularly tosses off impromptu complex puns probably does (which does not necessarily mean that such puns are very funny, we hasten to add)." Many people, *The Bell Curve* acknowledges, will tend to equate "wit" and "intelligence," but this is one of the occasions when the "ordinary" people are wrong: people might be "funny" but still not "smart."

Which means, conversely, that people might not be "funny" and yet still might be "smart," which a cynic might suggest (after reading *The Bell Curve)* is the very possibility the authors were personally interested in preserving. But I suspect that the authors had at least two programmatic reasons for excluding humor from their conception of intelligence.

First, including wit in their definition of intelligence would almost surely embarrass their hypothesis, that is, that intelligence is directly correlated with the conventional measures of social success. There are simply too many hilariously funny people who are really quite poor, and too many rich people who are dreadfully unfunny. Wit is simply not the kind of smart that our culture has *chosen* with any consistency to reward in material ways. Given their commitment to a unitary conception of intelligence, *The Bell Curve* can deal with this cultural choice only by pretending that it is a semantic one: the witty kind of "smart" doesn't get rewarded because it isn't really "smart" at all.

Second, including wit in their definition of intelligence would instantly expose the falsity of their central premise about intelligence, that intelligence is an objective phenomenon. The *Bell Curve* conception of "intelligence" depends on the kind of unitary, determinate criteria—if not biological, then at least cultural—that simply do not exist, except as a matter of fiat, and the case of "humor" is a too obvious example. "Ordinary" people, after all, don't agree on who is "funny," and the *Bell Curve* crowd could never convince folks with divergent views on the matter that their senses of humor were either "wrong" or "inferior." So the potential debate is mooted by being rendered irrelevant: the debate over who is funny, we are told, is simply not a debate about intelligence.

But in attempting to elude the truth, *The Bell Curve* merely demonstrates it. The truth is that there is no unitary intelligence, for two principal reasons:

1. You can seem "smart" in some contexts—in some ways, or to some people—without seeming smart in all others; and
2. What counts as "smart"—which contexts, which perspectives—is invariably a matter of choice.

"Witty" is not "smart" only because the authors of *The Bell Curve* chose—for no good reason, indeed, for no reason at all—to elide humor from their conception of intelligence. In so doing, they merely aggravated the dilemma they sought to avoid. It was bad enough that "intelligence" might be no more than whatever most people choose to say it is: linguistic conventions or other cultural fiats at least have the weak claim to legitimacy afforded by crude majoritarianism. But now "intelligence" becomes whatever the authors of *The Bell Curve* choose to say it is: the "popular" wisdom is to be arbitrated by the intellectual elite. And the elite choose not to include humor in their conception of "smart."

So what happens, we might ask, to the concept of the "comic genius"?

It is conventional wisdom, I think, that Jerry Lewis is regarded as a "comic genius" in France, but has never quite achieved that status in America; is it possible that the process of exportation enhances his comic IQ? Jerry Seinfeld is a comic who is thought to be very funny by many white folks, and the Wayans brothers are comics who are thought to be very funny by many black folks, and—at least if the Nielsen demographics mean anything—the opinions are pretty much mutually exclusive; so which group gets to decide who is the "comic genius"? Then there is the matter of "comic actor" Jim Carrey, who is in fact neither according to most professional critics, but who greatly amuses a very large number of Americans, both black and white; can you in fact be very unfunny—a "comic moron"—and yet make almost everybody laugh?

My own hunch is that the "comic genius" is just one form of genius among countless others, and that it itself includes an infinite number of specific variations. My hunch is also that somebody can seem to be very much a genius in this way—a true "comic" genius, that is—and yet be decidedly un-genius in some other ways—a dunce, for example, in advanced physics or auto mechanics. Finally, it is my hunch that it would be nearly impossible to generate a consensus on the defining criteria of this or any other form of genius, and that the question whether someone is brilliantly funny—or brilliantly anything else—will be decided more by personal opinion and cultural (or "subcultural") convention than by craniometrics or standardized tests.

I think my dad is a very smart man; I think, in fact, that he is a genius. His high school teachers, however, did not share this assessment; they routinely flunked him in everything except physical education, so he dropped out of school after the tenth grade. Maybe he wasn't a born genius—there is, after all, that old saw about fathers getting a lot smarter after their sons have matured—or maybe he wasn't a genius in the narrow ways that his teachers were trained to find. But I know that he is a genius today, and in quite a few ways.

My dad is, to cite one specific way, a "comic genius": he can make anybody laugh. Or almost anybody.

Some years ago, the dean of the law school at which I was teaching graciously gave me permission to bring my parents to his annual faculty party. A few minutes into the party, I found the dean and introduced him to my folks. The dean and my father had a short but memorable exchange.

"So," the dean said, "you are from Wilmington, Delaware."

"Yes, we are." My dad was smiling very broadly, with his lips together and his eyebrows raised; it's his hopeful look, a sign that he's a little uncomfortable.

"There are a lot of corporations headquartered in Wilmington."

"Yes." My dad nodded in agreement. "A lot of banks." My dad smiled down at his beer; I took a big drink of mine.

"Oh, so you are in banking?"

"No," said my dad, "but we have a checking account."

I started to laugh, and the beer rushed up through my nose. My mother started to laugh too, partly at my dad, and partly at me, and pretty soon my eyes were watering.

But the point of the story is this: the dean didn't laugh. He carried on the pleasantries for another thirty seconds or so, then moved on to the rest of his guests, and never once gave any indication that he had just personally witnessed a comic genius in action.

And when I caught up to one of my best friends on the faculty, and told her the story—"and my dad said, 'No, but we have a checking account'—*she* didn't laugh either.

They didn't get it.

But whenever I'm home, and tell the rest of the family, or my old friends, they get it, and they laugh, and sometimes the beer comes out their noses.

Alice, my wife, laughed when I told her this story, and she also thinks my dad is a genius. She should know a little something about genius, seeing as how she is one herself. At least in some ways. Alice, you see, used to be a public defender, and she was brilliant at it—too brilliant, I sometimes worried, for the public good. She once persuaded the jury to return a "not guilty" verdict in an aggravated assault case; her defense theory was that the victim fell on the defendant's knife . . . twice. But Alice also used to be a waitress, and she was not brilliant at this at all: "If you were any slower," her boss once complained, "you'd be dead." Law, apparently, was her better career path.

Now *The Bell Curve* crowd would have us believe that a smart person like Alice would be smart in all contexts. But, to borrow a phrase, the "ordinary citizens' reasonable intuition" is that this is nonsense: people—as ordinary people know—can be very smart about some things and very unsmart about others. There is a lawyer's intelligence and a waitress's intelligence; there is also a butcher's, a baker's, and a candlestick maker's intelligence, and also a mother's intelligence and a father's intelligence, and a billion others besides. Some lousy waitresses make great lawyers and even better mothers;

some great lawyers would be lousy waiters and are, in some people's eyes, pretty lousy fathers.

Now the *Bell Curve* crowd would also have us believe that a smart person like my father seems smart to everybody. But again, ordinary people know better: they know that people disagree over the brilliance of lawyers and waitresses, and also over the relative genius of politicians, and judges, and ballplayers, and mothers, and fathers, and comics. Not everybody, after all, thinks my father is a comic genius, and I guess it's even possible that not everybody would think that my father is a genius as a father, but, really, you'd have to be pretty stupid *not* to think so.

"Intelligence" does not exist in a vacuum. Rather, "intelligence" is defined by the relevant context, principally by the demands of the environment and the perspective of the observer. Intelligence thus is not absolute, but contingent or situational; it is not general, but local or specific; and it is not abstract, but practical or experiential. Intelligence, like beauty, is truly in the eyes of the beholders: initially, as they define the governing cultural criteria, and subsequently, as they make the invariably subjective determination whether and to what extent those criteria are manifest in another human being. All of which is really only to acknowledge the obvious: there are many kinds of intellectual aptitude, and what will count as "intelligence"—and what will be perceived as "genius"—is decidedly a matter of choice. As a consequence, the only proper response to the question whether someone is "smart" is to ask, in reply, "Who wants to know, and why?"

But all the choices that inhere in the construction of "intelligence" are obscured by *The Bell Curve*'s insistence that intelligence may be reduced to some unitary essence, something they call—following Spearman and Burt—"general intelligence." But the concept of "general" intelligence ignores the invariably contextual nature of cognitive activity: it defies human experience to suggest that there is a single aptitude or even a unified set of aptitudes that underlies all intellectual pursuits.

Binet knew better right at the outset of the psychometric movement. While his message was initially lost on the early American testers, they too eventually learned. As H. H. Goddard, who brought

Binet's scale to America, would eventually acknowledge, "A man may be intelligent in one environment and unintelligent in another."

Contemporary investigations of intelligence tend to follow Binet's lead—and that of the rehabilitated Goddard—in reconceptualizing intelligence less as an absolute, general, abstract capacity and more as a contingent, specific, practical ability. Thus Robert J. Sternberg has focused on a "practical intelligence" rooted in context-specific problem-solving skills; Ralph Rosnow has investigated "social intelligence," the real-world ability to function in complex social settings; Lauren Resnick and Jean Lave have studied "on-the-scene" problem solving; and Anders Erricson and Stephen Ceci have documented a trained intelligence, that is, practical intellectual aptitudes that may be taught and learned. Interestingly, measures of these reconceptualized visions of intelligence appear in no case to be correlated with IQ, the conventional unitary measure of abstract intelligence. Moreover, these reconceptualized intelligences appear to be better predictors of task-specific success than is IQ.[5]

Which is only, well, logical. Phillip L. Ackerman notes that general intelligence testing measures a "capacity" for intelligence or a "maximal intelligence" only by artificially discounting the context, the "environmental" and "situational" variables. But expressions of intellectual ability typically do not take place in a vacuum: intelligence in fact is both contingent and malleable, varying with the context, as defined by both the individual and her environment. Ackerman thus concludes that separation of the context from "intelligence" is neither practical nor desirable; he proposes measures for "typical" intellectual performance, incorporating the "multidimensional determinants" of performance, that is, "temperamental and situational motivation and volitional factors." Reconceived this way, he notes, intelligence is in truth a "personality construct."

In similar fashion, Robert Sternberg argues against a preoccupation with "inert academic intelligence" and in favor of what he calls "successful intelligence," an intellectual ability with "analytical, creative, and practical aspects," all of which are "relatively independent of one another." "The analytical aspect," he suggests, "is used to solve problems, the creative aspect to decide what problems to solve, and the practical aspect to make solutions effective." "Conventional intelligence tests," he notes, "measure only the analytical aspect of intelligence, and they don't even measure all of that."[6]

The value of the conventional conception of intelligence—or IQ or "general intelligence" or *g*, all of which are, for *The Bell Curve*, rough equivalents—is, according to its advocates, that it accurately describes an overall and essential capacity for cognitive achievement. But if "intelligence" is indeed IQ, if it is indeed this general capacity for cognitive success, then it is at once necessarily too broad and too narrow.

It is too broad because it ignores the importance of context and is, as a consequence, inferior to more contextualized conceptions by every meaningful measure. As a scientific matter, it less accurately describes the experience of intellectual activity, and less reliably predicts success on real tasks. As a political matter, it invariably promotes the unfortunate tendency to convert specific differences—for example, in facility with specific tasks—into general notions of superiority and inferiority. Except as a tool for promoting hierarchy, it is hard to see the utility of the concept, hard to see how "we gain anything" by keeping it around.

Moreover, IQ fails even as a predictor of "general" cognitive success, and is, for this reason, also too narrow. Buried in the ambiguous rhetoric of *The Bell Curve* is their apparent acceptance of the more-or-less standard working definition of intelligence as the ability to adapt to one's environment. But *The Bell Curve* seems to narrow the scope: high intelligence—high adaptability to the culture—is demonstrated by achievement—by success within that culture. This conception of intelligence is surprisingly culture-bound, and in fact its validity is premised on universal assent to *The Bell Curve*'s conventional measures of success: people who get high-paying jobs are successful; people who collect welfare are not, and neither are people who get divorced, have children out of wedlock, or commit crimes.

But these assessments are not uncontroversial; the judgments that inhere in them certainly are not immutable or universal. And they would need to be, if the "intelligence" that they demonstrated was a truly "general" one. *The Bell Curve*'s narrow conception of success as adaptability is thus difficult to square with its simultaneous commitment to an intelligence that is both general and innate; *The Bell Curve*'s cognitive losers are, after all, adapting, just not in ways that the authors approve. *The Bell Curve*'s conception of intelligence, then, is too narrow to embrace those populations who may in fact be exhibiting the most extraordinary capacity to survive.

But there is no need to specially credit anyone's achievements: the fact is, we are all adapting to our own peculiar environments, and we are all doing it with more or less equal success. Which is, of course, as it would have to be at this stage in human evolution. As Orlando Patterson points out, if intelligence is indeed the ability to adapt to the environment, and if it is, as *The Bell Curve* maintains, innate and heritable (according to *The Bell Curve*, at a factor of .6), then variation in intelligence should by now be close to zero. Any significant variation cannot be variation in "intelligence": as Patterson concludes, "[w]hatever it is that IQ tests are measuring, whatever it is that *g* is, . . . it could have nothing whatever to do with those vitally important behavioral qualities that meaningfully account for survival in both broad evolutionary and narrower sociological terms."[7]

So if general intelligence necessarily correlates with neither specific cognitive achievements nor general human survival, what precisely is its predictive value? It appears to be this: "general intelligence"—as expressed, for example, through "IQ"—is a fairly reliable rough predictor of success on tests that measure those aptitudes that are measured by general intelligence, or IQ, tests.

Measured "general intelligence," in other words, is correlated with itself. But only imperfectly.

In fact, measures of cognitive ability are not always reliable predictors of success with other measures of cognitive ability. For example, a 1995 study of 122 academically "gifted" students, all of whom scored in the top percent on standard measures of aptitude, suggested that meaningful correlation among measures of cognitive ability required at least a three-factor solution. Success on a measure from within one of the three domains—the researchers suggested separate spheres of "linguistic," "logical-mathematical," and "social" ability—was correlated with success on other intra-domain measures, but the top scorers in one domain were not necessarily among the top scorers in other domains. The researchers also noted that while there were no group differences in global "self-concept," there were differences in domain-specific self-concept, and these were correlated with performance. The results led the researchers to conclude as follows: "Rather than working to find the best single scale to assess people as less or more intelligent, it appears to be more appropriate to think of ability as emerging from and reflecting individual and group socialization experiences, as varying individually across domains, and as interacting significantly with personality variables such as self-concept and values."[8]

Another study from 1995 tested the stability of the famed racial gap in measures of cognitive ability. The study revealed that the performance gap varied on tests even within the same domain of ability: some tests yielded a small gap, while other tests—of presumably the same cognitive processes—yielded a large gap. The researchers concluded that the gap was at least partly dependent upon the specifics of the measures: the nature of the stimuli, for example, or the called-for response. The results, according to the researchers, "raise the possibility that the differences are due to acculturation factors associated with the specific types of different cultural experiences available within the black community relative to mainstream white communities."[9]

Correlations between measures of cognitive ability, then, may vary according to both the specific ability being measured and the specific measurement instrument employed. Results like these certainly cast doubt on the idea of a "general intelligence," even as a statistical artifact. But this is no surprise: almost from the outset, we had good reason to believe that "general intelligence," or *g*, does not exist.

American psychologist L. L. Thurstone was not conceptually opposed to the idea of an essential intelligence, but his reexamination of *g* in the 1930s failed to replicate Spearman's findings. Thurstone's own factor analysis of measured intelligence actually produced several "*gs*"—he labeled them "primary mental abilities"—and laid the foundation for an important discovery: Spearman's *g* could be made to appear or disappear depending solely on the dimensions of the factor analysis. Thurstone himself remained convinced that there was an underlying reality called "intelligence" that could be faithfully represented through factor analysis, but he also believed that this reality actually consisted of multiple intelligences, that they were better described by a set of vectors than by a single number, and that the case for *g*, even as a statistical artifact, was remarkably weak.

Thurstone was either unwilling or unable to take the logical next step: he did not admit the possibility that Spearman's *g* and his own "primary mental abilities" were not naturally occurring phenomena at all, but were *only* statistical artifacts, that they represented no underlying reality, no pre-existing thing called "intelligence." But in fact, any assortment of measures will establish some correlations, and these can be factored to produce either a dominant component like "*g*" or a variety of group factors like "primary mental abilities." Neither of these analyses necessarily captures a reality that exists independent of either the initial measurement processes or their subsequent statistical manipulation: the factor analysis of "measured intelligence" invariably describes only the statistical correlations among the measurements, not some underlying reality called "intelligence." Thus "general intelligence," as F. Allan Hanson concludes, "is nothing but a social construct produced by intelligence testing."[10]

So here, at last, is what we need to believe before we can accept an intellectual hierarchy rooted in IQ or "*g*" or "general intelligence," that is, before we can accept the major proposition that "intelligence can and should be ordered according to a single set of characteristics."

First, we must believe, contrary to all evidence and our better judgments, that there is only one kind of intelligence and that differences in intelligence can therefore be conceived as ones not of kind, but of degree.

Second, we must believe, contrary to all evidence and our better judgments, that this unitary intelligence exists independently of our perceptions of it, including those perceptions that are formalized as measurements.

Third, we must believe, contrary to all evidence and our better judgments, that our perceptions of this unitary intelligence are themselves valid and reliable, such that our various representations of it will be positively correlated to a high degree.

If all these things were true—and only if all these things were true—then we would have established the major proposition . . . halfway.

But only halfway. Because all we would have really established is that we *can* now construct an intellectual hierarchy; we have said nothing yet about whether we *should*.

Even if we are confident that intelligence is real and that we can reliably describe intelligence in quantitative terms, even if we are sure that human beings can be ordered, top to bottom, from most to least intelligent, there is nothing that precludes us from declining to undertake the task: there is nothing that prevents us from insisting on a society in which all human beings are treated as equals. This would be so even if the "intelligence" that we described was absolute and essential, even if it was the intrinsic ability to perform vital social tasks. It is true that some contemporary sociobiologists suggest that hierarchy is itself innate, that the reality of intrinsic and relevant differences must invariably dispose the human animal to vertically ordered societies. But we have not always believed this, and we do not all believe it today. Theodosius Dobzhansky is one of the leading evolutionists of the twentieth century; in *Genetic Diversity and Human Equality*, he maintains that we *can* build a society in which all of us, whatever our "natural" "differences," receive equal psychic and material rewards. If we want to. It is our choice.[11]

Choice 2. Choosing Which Disparities Are Acceptable

> Never! What a momentous word. Some recent thinkers seem to have given their moral support to these deplorable verdicts by affirming that an individual's intelligence is a fixed quantity, a quantity that cannot be increased. We must protest and react against this brutal pessimism; we must try to demonstrate that it is founded upon nothing.
> — Alfred Binet, *Les Idées Modernes sur les Enfants*

When Alfred Binet wrote these words in 1909, he was recalling the university examiner who had told him that he would "never" have a "philosophical spirit." Binet would not render similar judgments about others; for the rest of his life he contested the "brutal pessimism" that limited another human being's potential. Accordingly, his tests of "intelligence" were calculated not to establish the upper-most limits of an individual's capacity, but rather to identify the most fertile bases for intellectual development. Binet was not merely a tester, he was a teacher, and his "mental orthopedics" were designed to teach students, above all, those skills and aptitudes necessary to learning. When these were mastered, when his students became better learners, Binet was satisfied that his students had become, in every meaningful sense, more "intelligent": "It is in this practical sense, the only one accessible to us, that we say the intelligence of these children has been increased. We have increased what constitutes the intelligence of a pupil: the capacity to learn and to assimilate instruction."[12]

For those committed to hierarchy, Binet's notion of a learnable intelligence is nothing less than subversive. A malleable intelligence, learnable and teachable, undermines the stable intellectual order. What happens, after all, if people get smarter? What happens, moreover, if people are especially likely to get smarter when an effort is made to teach them? Suddenly, once again, intellectual hierarchy becomes purely a matter of choice.

Binet's American successors chose not to follow his vision of intelligence. For the inventors of America's IQ, "intelligence" would be an immutable, finite capacity: individual intellectual potential was limited by individual genetic makeup. And the Americans were not unwilling to say "never." Lewis Terman, creator of the Stanford-Binet, described this scene in 1916:

> Strange to say, the mother is encouraged and hopeful because she sees that her boy is learning to read. She does not seem to realize that at his age he ought to be within three years of entering high school. The forty minute test has told more about the mental ability of this boy than the intelligent mother had been able to learn in eleven years of daily and hourly observation. For [the boy] is feeble-minded; he will never complete the grammar school; he will never be an efficient worker or a responsible citizen.

For the first three decades of the century, American psychometricians insisted that intelligence was a fixed capacity defined by individual biology, by an individual's genes. Many of them—Goddard, Brigham, Terman himself—would later recant; the eugenics movement that they championed would suffer an inglorious demise, crushed by the weight of scientific disrepute and political disfavor. But today a new generation of eugenicists— Arthur Jensen, Michael Levin, Richard Lynn, J. Phillipe Rushton, as well as Murray and Herrnstein—resurrect the claims that intelligence is immutable because intelligence is genetic. They are as wrong today as their predecessors were a century ago.

For the modern eugenicist, the case for an immutable, genetically determined intelligence is fairly simple: environmental variables fail to fully account for the intelligence differences between biological groups or the intelligence similarities along genetic lines. Only genes, then, can cause intelligence. But this is, as a general matter, a poor way to prove a scientific hypothesis—by negating, in effect, the alternative hypotheses. As the researchers behind the Minnesota Transracial Adoption Study point out, "one cannot demonstrate the validity of a scientific hypothesis by default."

This is particularly the case when the alternative hypotheses depend on variables that are easily confounded or even conflated. That is precisely the case with "intelligence": the relevant variables, both "innate" and "environmental," are complex, synergistic, and sometimes difficult to differentiate. The risk of conceptual error is therefore high.[13] In fact, the modern eugenicists are guilty of at least four:

Error 1. First, they tend to confuse "intrinsic" features with "genetic" ones, when in actuality, not all "intrinsic" or "nonenvironmental" features are genetic at all. As Lewontin, Rose, and Kamin indicate, much of the physiological and morphological variation among humans is developmental, not genetic; people may then be different—and intrinsically so—but genes may have nothing to do with it. In fact, many of those "intrinsic" differences may themselves have developed in part for environmental reasons; these, of course, are not necessarily genetic.

To briefly illustrate, assume that a child from an economically and educationally deprived background is moved into an environment that is both economically and educationally rich. But the child's IQ fails to increase in ways commensurate with the environmental gains, and fails to rise to the level of her socioeconomic peers. Does this prove that the child's intellectual capacity is genetically limited? It does not: the child's intellectual development may be intrinsically different from her peers, but genetically the same; her development may even reflect the lingering effects of her initial environment. The effects of environmental stimulation—or deprivation—on early intellectual development are well documented, and so too are the effects of prenatal conditions; all of these vary significantly with class. Lead exposure, to take just one example, is particularly likely for low-income children, both in the womb and in their homes. If there was a chance the child was exposed, and is now exhibiting the effects of exposure, then we could argue endlessly about whether her intellectual condition is "intrinsic" or "environmental," but in no case could we say with any confidence that it was "genetic."[14]

Error 2. Second, the modern eugenicists sometimes confuse the notions of "heritability" and "genetic determination," when in actuality, some characteristics can be highly heritable, but not genetically determined at all. "Heritability" refers to the percentage of variation in a given trait in a given population—phenotypical variation—that is correlated with genetic factors—with genotypical variation—as opposed to environmental ones. A perfectly heritable trait, expressed as a correlation of 1.0, is one that varies entirely with genetic factors, and not at all with environmental ones. A perfectly nonheritable trait—the heritability correlation would be 0—varies entirely with environmental factors, and not at all with genetic ones. Most traits fall somewhere between. Eye color, for example, is a highly—but not perfectly—heritable trait: the overwhelming percentage of variation in eye color in any given population is likely attributable to genetic factors, but there may be a few instances of variation due to environmental factors, like physical injuries, for example, or tinted contact lenses—which may or may not count, depending, of course, on how the trait is defined.

A trait is "genetically determined," on the other hand, when it is genetically coded for intergenerational replication. Some highly heritable traits, like eye color, are definitely genetically determined. But some are not. Consider, for example, why some Americans become nurses. There may be some marginal environmental explanations—correlations with socioeconomic class, perhaps, or proximity to nursing schools—but most of the variation will be due to a genetic factor: the biological sex of the individual. Being a nurse, then, may be highly heritable. But there is no evidence that it is genetically determined, nothing to indicate that there is a "nurse gene" passed from one generation to the next. Intelligence is similar; "[i]n fact," according to Ned Block of MIT, "IQ is a great example of a trait that is highly heritable but not genetically determined."

The difference becomes very important when the question is whether intelligence is malleable. If the claim is that intelligence is "genetically determined," then there is no room for enhancement beyond that permitted by the genes: genes "cause" intelligence. If, on the other hand, the claim is that intelligence is highly heritable, then there *is* room for enhancement: genetic factors may be correlated with intelligence variations in the population, but this sets no limit on the extent to which individual variation may be achieved or mitigated through environmental intervention.

For the most part, *The Bell Curve* is careful to limit its claim to the heritability hypothesis. Thus even if the authors are correct, and IQ is heritable to a factor of .6, it remains the case that, *in the abstract*, some 40 percent of the variation in the population is explicitly conceded to environmental factors. This alone means that virtually all intelligence differences could be explained or eliminated by the environment: with a phenomenon this contingent or malleable, the environment could account for all of the "intellectual deficit" in any given individual or group of individuals. But as Ned Block notes, *The Bell Curve*'s surviving coauthor has, in his subsequent interviews, consistently misstated *The Bell Curve*'s heritability thesis: "60 percent of the intelligence comes from heredity," Charles Murray has said, both "in any given person" and in the "human species." Murray's misrepresentations, whether through ignorance or calculation, tend to make "intelligence" seem partly (60 percent of it) genetically determined: the suggestion is that only 40 percent of any person's intelligence can be enhanced. But heritability, properly understood, means no such thing.[15]

Error 3. Third, and closely related, modern eugenicists tend to confuse "heritability" with "immutability," when in actuality, highly heritable characteristics may also be highly malleable. Again, it stems from confusion about the meaning of assertions of "heritability." Heritability establishes only the relative prominence of genetic correlations for variations in the trait. Even a trait that is perfectly heritable—one where the genetic correlations account for all the variation—may be malleable, and environmental factors may cause the change.

This is, in part, because of the peculiar meaning of the claim that the variation is correlated with a genetic trait: it does not mean *exclusively* genetic. As Block explains, "[t]he methodology used to measure heritability counts differences in characteristics as caused by genetic differences if there is a genetic difference, even if there is *also an environmental difference*, thus distorting the ways in which we normally think about causation" (emphasis in original).

It is also because genetic and environmental effects are not entirely discrete: they interact bidirectionally and sometimes in causal ways. For this reason, as Jonathan Crane explains, genes and the environment are really "nonadditive": "The proportion of variation in an observed trait (a phenotype) that is explained by genes and the proportion that is explained by environment do not sum to 1. . . . no matter how high heritability is, it sets no upper limit on the proportion of variation in a trait that is determined by environmental factors."

Consider, for example, the relationship between "race" and "intelligence." Assume that intelligence was perfectly heritable for all populations (an implausible assumption, as we will later see), and assume that there was a distinct racial variation in intelligence, an IQ gap, let's say, of 15 points. Does this mean that the racial gap in IQ is caused by genes?

The answer is unquestionably "no," and it is "no" because we simply cannot separate the "genetic" factors—the "racial" genotype—from the unique environmental responses to those factors, for example, a history and contemporary reality of racial privilege and racial oppression. The genotype may be perfectly correlated with the trait, and we still do not know whether the variation is "caused" by the genotype itself or the environmental responses to it. As a consequence, we cannot know whether the variation will be mitigated, or perhaps eliminated, by changes in the environmental responses. All we can do is guess.

Which, sadly, is what many modern eugenicists do: they assert, with far too much confidence, that the racial gap in "intelligence" is "caused" by genes and cannot be un-"caused" by changes in the environment. But they don't know this. As Ned Block points out,

> [W]ithout being able to *measure* the effect of being treated as subnormal and the effect of a legacy of slavery and discrimination from the past, how do we know whether its average effect is sufficient to lower black IQ 15 points, or less than that—or more than that? Given the social importance of this issue, *guessing* is not appropriate.

And in fact, the eugenicists' guess—that the racial gap in IQ is genetic—is certainly a bad one. Summarizing the case, Stephen Jay Gould has observed that there is a "strong circumstantial case for substantial malleability and little average genetic difference" in IQ. Indeed, the evidence suggests: first, that intelligence, however heritable it might be, can be increased; and second, that the vaunted racial gap in intelligence, however rooted in "genes" it might be, is disappearing.[16]

As to the first, there is evidence that intelligence is highly malleable, and that changes in the environment—including the cultural environment—can enhance intellectual abilities, as R. C. Lewontin notes, "by many orders of magnitude." Consider:

- Studies on the effect of early intervention show significant IQ gains among the affected children. Early intervention (at age 3) among at-risk infants, for example, produced a nine-point IQ advantage; similar interventions produced comparable gains. These studies tend to be dismissed by advocates of an immutable IQ because the gains are not always sustained when the interventions cease, that is, when the children return to unenriched environments. But the most elegant explanation for both the increase and, where it occurs, subsequent decline is rooted in the environmental change, and indeed, the IQ gains are sustained where intervention efforts are maintained.

- Adoption studies indicate that children moved from disadvantaged to middle or upper class environments show substantial IQ gains, as much as twenty points. A 1989 study by Christiane Capron and Michel Duyme of the Université Paris found significant improvement in academic performance: the "improvement in performance," the study concluded, "is clearly caused by change—low SES [socioeconomic status] versus high SES—in the postnatal environment." The most prominent interracial adoption study, the Minnesota Transracial Adoption Study by Irwin D. Waldman of Emory, Richard A. Weinberg of the University of Minnesota, and Sandra Scarr of the University of Virginia, found significant IQ gains among black children raised in relatively advantaged white households. In their 1994 follow-up study, Waldman, Weinberg, and Scarr determined that socially classified black adoptees scored ten points higher than black children raised in the black community, and as adolescents, scored at the average of the white population on school-administered tests, far above the average performance of children in the black community. The study, the researchers concluded, does afford evidence for "the malleability of IQ."

- School studies demonstrate the efficacy of remedial or enrichment programs on academic performance. James Comer of Yale University assisted in the development and implementation of remedial programs for the two schools ranked last and next-to-last in standard measures of academic achievement among New

Haven's thirty-five schools; within a few years, those schools were among the top five in achievement. The efforts are merely representative: Larry Hedges of the University of Chicago conducted a meta-analysis of studies on the effect of school funding on student performance. His conclusion—utterly unremarkable, except in our political context—was that funding has a large impact on academic achievement.

Not surprisingly, the evidence also suggests that the racial gap in measures of academic aptitude and achievement is gradually disappearing. The IQ gap between white and black test takers—historically, fifteen points, or one standard deviation—was closed in the last generation by between 20 and 50 percent. Long-term studies of standardized tests of academic aptitude all suggest that the gap was closed by between four and six points; at the same time, the number of high SAT scores by black test-takers increased by 35 percent. Current tests of "general intelligence" also document a decrease in the gap: administrations of both the Ravens Progressive Matrices Test and the Kaufman Assessment Battery for Children suggest a gap of just seven points, and two recent Stanford-Binet studies suggest that the gap has been cut by one-third, to ten points.

Interestingly, heritability estimates—by advocates of a genetic IQ—have been decreasing with the racial gap: Arthur Jensen suggested in 1969 that IQ was heritable at a factor of .80; he subsequently revised it down to .65. *The Bell Curve* suggests a heritability ratio of .60; other advocates are even more modest, suggesting heritability at .40. Keep in mind, as Jonathan Crane notes, that even if IQ were 100 percent heritable, the race gap could still be a product of the environmental disadvantages experienced by black Americans. The current heritability estimates only increase the likelihood that there is an environmental explanation for the entire racial gap in measured "intelligence."[17]

Error 4. Fourth, and finally, modern eugenicists tend to confuse the validity of within-group estimates of heritability with between-group estimates of heritability, when in actuality, the former may tell us nothing about the latter.

Recall that heritability estimates are for the proportion of variation within a given population: the integrity of the estimate necessarily assumes a population that is relatively coherent. If an attempt is made to extend the estimate to diverse populations—ones with, for example, distinct environmental experiences—the entire effort is hopelessly confounded: there is simply no way to discount the environmental factors.

To illustrate, assume that longevity is a perfectly heritable trait within two separate populations; within each population, that is, life expectancy is correlated perfectly with genotypes. Assume too that there is a significant difference in life expectancy between the two groups: one lives ten years longer than the other. Since longevity was perfectly heritable within each population, is it also perfectly heritable as between the populations? The answer is not necessarily—in fact, it might not even be the more plausible hypothesis. If, for example, the population with the shorter life span lived in a less hospitable climate or subsisted in a more violent culture, the more compelling hypothesis for the longevity differential would almost certainly be an environmental one.

The same, of course, is true for between-group estimates of the heritability of intelligence. The suggestion that the racial gap in intelligence, to whatever extent it exists in any meaningful way, is itself somehow "heritable" is simply not plausible. Even if intelligence was perfectly heritable within racial populations, the undeniable fact is that racial groups have experienced and continue to experience very different environments, and as a consequence of those differences, the assertion that the "racial gap" in "intelligence" is "genetic" is at very best a guess—a dubious, malicious guess.

Which, sadly, does not prevent some from offering it. In the beginning of a 1994 article, J. Phillipe Rushton claims that "[s]urveys show that a plurality of experts in psychological testing and behavioral genetics think that a portion of the Black/White difference in IQ scores is genetic in origin"; curiously, by the end of the article that belief is held by "a majority of the experts" (and Rushton's effort is not *that* persuasive). But it's not the numbers that really matter. Given the inherent limitations in the concept of "heritability," even the apparently modest suggestion that "a portion" of the racial gap is "genetic in origin" is specious, and Rushton's "experts" should know better. As Evan Balabam notes, "[t]he people who say intelligence is genetic are the ones with no training in genetics." But, of course, they believe what they choose to believe.[18]

*

Choice 3. Choosing Which Disparities Are Credible

> It is really too easy to discover signs of backwardness in an
> individual when one is forewarned.
> — Alfred Binet, *The Development of Intelligence in Children*

For many generations, Western scientists fully expected that their
investigations of "intelligence" would reveal racial differences. They
were rarely disappointed. This was not, however, because the evidence
they uncovered fully conformed to their working hypotheses. It was,
rather, because their predispositions were so strong that they shaped,
and at times perverted, their "scientific" methods. In fact, the history
of scientific theories of intelligence is characterized by a measurement
bias so strong that it has at times bordered on outright fraud.

Historically, the most overt forms of bias have taken four forms:

1. bias in the measurement instruments;
2. bias in data selection;
3. bias in reporting; and
4. bias in interpretation.

Louis Aggasiz, the famed Harvard zoologist, constantly insisted on
the need for scientific objectivity. His own "scientific" studies
produced the conclusion that "the brain of the negro is that of the
imperfect brain of a seven months infant in the womb of the white."
But it was a conclusion that was first formed outside the laboratory.
His first encounter with black Americans had prompted Aggasiz to
confide in his mother, "The more pity I felt at the sight of this
degraded and degenerate race, the more . . . impossible it becomes for
me to repress the feeling that they are not of the same blood as we
are." Later he would dismiss the argument for black equality as "mock
philanthropy" and fill his personal memoirs with expressions of
repugnance and antipathy toward black Americans. His deeply felt
convictions on the matter made him increasingly dogmatic; he
willingly employed, one biographer reports, "the authority of science
to support social doctrine." But his findings were all objective:
"truth," he had promised his mother, "before all."

The nineteenth-century craniometrists, the self-proclaimed "apostles
of objectivity," in fact manifested and confirmed all the prejudices of

their day. Stephen Jay Gould has revisited their works. Paul Broca, he reports, culled data selectively and manipulated it unconsciously; when correlations defied the predicted racial rankings—when they suggested, for example, caucasian inferiority—the criteria were simply abandoned, dismissed suddenly as irrelevant. The case for a racial hierarchy was built anecdotally: "Broca and his school," Gould observes, "used facts as illustrations, not as constraining documents." Samuel George Morton "was widely hailed as the objectivist of his age." But he also selectively distilled and interpreted his data. Gould does not believe it was blatant fraud: "All I can discern," he concludes, "is an *a priori* conviction about racial ranking so powerful that it directed his tabulations along preestablished lines."

At the turn of the century, physiological studies of intelligence yielded to psychometrics and brought new claims of objectivity. At least at its inception, psychometrics promised valid, reliable, and—most critically for advocates of equality—"neutral" schemes for identifying those possessed of merit or in need of assistance. Salvation from prejudice was available in the form of standardized tests.

The promise of standardized tests was, and perhaps still is, that they would eliminate bias. Accordingly, these tests found considerable favor among black social scientists in the early twentieth century. Some might have been motivated in part by self-interest—the tests, after all, tended to legitimate their own status—but many certainly believed that standardized tests were the necessary first step toward a genuine equal opportunity.

But the tests were problematic from the start. Yerkes's army studies, the scientific foundation for the twentieth century's intellectual hierarchy, were almost laughably biased. The instruments purported to measure "native intelligence," but that claim proved only to be a poor play on words. Recent immigrants fared poorly: they were not by nature intelligent enough to know, as the written test required, that John Adams was the second president, that Crisco was a food product, that Christy Mathewson was a baseball pitcher, or the number of a Kaffir's legs. The Beta version of the test, a wordless version designed to accommodate those who could not read English, managed to reduce these cultural biases to pictures: test takers were required to recognize depictions of phonographs, tennis courts, and bowling alleys and to comprehend Hindu-Arabic numbers. The tests were administered in an almost frantic rush, and the test takers themselves were often at a loss: many could not see or hear the examiner; many had never before held a pencil.

As a testament to the failure of the tests, six of eight "Alpha tests" yielded their highest mode at zero; in one test, nearly 40 percent of all scores were zero. Perhaps it was not surprising, then, that the tests led to the preposterous conclusion that the average mental age of Americans was only thirteen.[19]

Certainly the ethnic and racial hierarchy created by the tests was no surprise. Lewis Terman, co-designer of the tests, had relied on traditional racial rankings to validate his earlier intelligence tests, and there was no reason to believe that the army tests would not replicate the rankings. As it turned out, however, the natural intellectual order was vindicated by the tests only after the test results were given some surprising spins. Consider:

- Recent immigrants fared poorly compared to their second- and third-generation counterparts. The obvious, elegant explanation: recent immigrants were less familiar with the substance and vernacular of the tests. The "scientific" explanation offered in Carl Brigham's exegesis of the tests: America was receiving an increasingly degenerate stock of immigrants.
- Test takers suffering from hookworms had lower scores than those who were healthy. The obvious, elegant explanation: physical health affected test performance. The "scientific" explanation offered by Yerkes: "Low native ability may indicate such conditions of living as to result in hookworm infection."
- Test scores were highly correlated (.75) with years of schooling. The obvious, elegant explanation: the tests were measuring accumulated—and acculturated—skills, knowledge, and attitudes. The "scientific" explanation offered by Yerkes: it was not that education led to measured "intelligence," but rather that measured "intelligence" led to education. "The theory that native intelligence is one of the most important conditioning factors in continuance in school is certainly borne out by this accumulation of data."
- Black recruits reported no educational experience, according to Yerkes, in "astonishingly large proportion." The obvious, elegant explanation: education was a privilege denied to black Americans, both formally, through Jim Crow laws, and practically, through

inferior facilities, economic necessities, and acts and threats of violence. The "scientific" explanation offered by Yerkes: the high proportion of black recruits who report no schooling must reflect a disinclination based on low innate intelligence.

- The average Alpha score for black recruits was 21.31 in thirteen southern states and 39.90 in nine northern states; the mean score for black recruits in the four highest northern states exceeded the white mean for nine southern states; and, there were high correlations between a state's expenditures for education and the test performance of its recruits. The obvious, elegant explanation, fully developed in Ashley Montagu's 1945 analysis of the test data: measured "intelligence" was significantly a property of educational experience. The "scientific" explanation offered by Yerkes and later refuted by both Montagu and Otto Klienburg: only superior blacks were smart enough to move to the North. As for the performance of southern white recruits, well, this was best left unexplained.

Consistently, then, the most obvious, elegant explanation for the test data was rejected if that explanation did not support the hypothetical natural order. And always, of course, it was done under the guise of scientific objectivity.[20]

Today we have our own craniometrists and psychometricians and their tactics have not much changed. J. Phillipe Rushton attempts to prove the intellectual superiority of "Whites" to "Blacks" through various measures of "brain size." He offers a "Relative Ranking of Races on Diverse Variables," which, in part, correlates brain size with the following assessments of "Blacks" (relative to "Whites" and "Orientals"):

- "Intelligence": "decision times" are slower and "cultural achievements" are lower;
- "Maturation rate": the "age of first intercourse" is earlier and the "life span" is shorter;
- "Personality": "aggressiveness," "impulsivity," and "self-concept" are higher, while "cautiousness" is lower;
- "Social organization": "marital stability," "law abidingness," "mental health," and "administrative capacity" are lower; and

- "Reproductive effort": "size of genitalia" is larger, and "intercourse frequencies" and "permissive attitudes" are higher.

It is difficult to know where to begin a response; it hardly suffices to say that Rushton's "variables" seem at least a bit subjective, in terms of both their relevance (for the apparently quantitative variables) and their measurement (for the obviously qualitative variables). Dr. Zack Z. Cernovsky, Rushton's colleague at the University of Western Ontario, has attempted to treat Rushton as a serious scientist. Cernovsky notes, among other things, that Rushton's "scientific" sources include anonymous 1898 notes from "the French Army Surgeon," a Penthouse publication, and the works of other racialists, like Arthur Jensen, who selectively published only the data that complied with their racial hypotheses. Rushton cures weak statistical relationship by aggregation, but is himself selective in choosing the studies that he aggregates. He makes no effort to identify the criteria for his assessments, nor to secure representative samples that comport with the governing criteria. And this barely scratches the surface of the bias that inheres in Rushton's qualitative assessments. Rushton's work, Cernovsky concludes, is "methodologically incompetent."

Arthur Jensen's assertions of white intellectual superiority are substantially based on his studies of "choice reaction" time: white subjects, according to Jensen, have a faster "choice reaction" time than black subjects, evidencing a natural cognitive superiority. But as Cernovsky notes, Jensen has been somewhat selective in publishing the results of his studies. Leon J. Kamin reports that there have in fact been three "choice reaction" studies. In 1975 Jensen alleged, without publishing the supporting data, that his tests revealed a slower choice reaction time among black subjects. In 1984 Jensen repeated his study, but could not replicate the findings; Jensen ruefully reported that the results were "inexplicably inconsistent." In 1993 Jensen tried again, and the results matched the 1984 study; again, Jensen was forced to report the "apparent anomaly" of black superiority in tests of choice reaction time. Remarkably, the results have not dissuaded Jensen—or those who rely on him, like Rushton and the authors of *The Bell Curve*—from continuing to claim that white reaction time is faster. As Kamin suggests, "Two out of three is not conclusive. Why not make the series three out of five?"

It is clearly more than mere incompetence that characterizes the work of some contemporary eugenicists. Richard Lynn is described by *The Bell Curve* as "a leading scholar of racial and ethnic differences." Lynn is, in fact, a professor of psychology at the University of Ulster and the associate editor of *Mankind Quarterly*, a journal of "racial history" dedicated to the belief in the genetic superiority of the white race. Lynn claims to have established the intellectual inferiority of black Africans, but, according to Kamin, "Lynn's distortions and misrepresentations of the data constitute a truly venomous racism, combined with scandalous disregard for scientific objectivity." Michael Levin is a professor of philosophy at the City College of New York; his work is premised on the belief that some racial groups are genetically inferior in intelligence. He makes no pretense to objectivity:

I'm interested in innocence for whites, and the genetic hypothesis is evidence for the defense . . . Race differences show whites aren't at fault for blacks being down, and making whites pay for something they're not responsible for is a terrible injustice. Eliminating affirmative action is the first step. Next—please, yes, if only—eliminate the Civil Rights Act.[21]

And then there is *The Bell Curve*. Entire texts have been devoted to the sources and methodologies employed in that treatise. Among the more charitable assessments is the one from Howard Gardner: *The Bell Curve*'s science, he notes, is curiously out of date; moreover, "the science in *The Bell Curve* is more like special pleading, based on a biased reading of the data, than a carefully balanced assessment of current knowledge." Stephen Jay Gould has described it as a "rhetorical masterpiece of scientism," while John Carey views it as "a breathtakingly wrongheaded interpretation of the underlying science." Richard Nisbett notes that the authors are selective in their reporting of the evidence, and "their summary of that evidence is factually wrong"; Leon J. Kamin observes that the authors' source data are often "pathetic," their citations of that data are often inaccurate, and their tendency to confuse correlation with causation "repeatedly leads Herrnstein and Murray to draw invalid conclusions." Less charitably still, Allan Ryan has called *The Bell Curve* "intellectually, a mess"; Jeffrey Rosen and Charles Lane describe it as "a chilling synthesis of the work of disreputable race theorists and eccentric eugenicists," and Lane notes that, for all of that, *The Bell Curve* still misreports the shoddy evidence it relies on. Jacqueline Jones summarizes the case against the objective "science" of *The Bell Curve* in perhaps the strongest terms: the book is, she writes, "hate literature with foot-notes."[22]

But the most significant claim of "bias" goes far beyond the allegations that individual theorists are motivated by malice or that their scientific methods are tainted by prejudice. The most significant claim of bias goes to the very heart of the concept of scientific objectivity.

In the conventional view, science is objective: it has no a priori premises beyond those inherent in the scientific method; its processes, accordingly, are characterized by a neutral rationality. It strives, then, to discover and to test truths, truths that are elegant and fertile, falsifiable and reproducible, externally valid and internally consistent. Conceived this way, science and scientific constructs are unequivocally apolitical. Science transcends political culture: its truths are not contingent on the politics of time and place.

But the conventional view offers an incomplete picture. In truth, human comprehension cannot be so easily divided into separate spheres of knowledge, the one political, the other scientific. In truth, science and politics overlap, are mutually reconstitutive, and collective-ly define—and are defined by—the contingencies of culture. And there is no transcending culture.

Indeed, the insistence that "science" is somehow objective and apolitical, that it may be separated from culture, is itself a decidedly political suggestion. Lewontin, Rose, and Kamin make the point explicitly: "the separation of fact from value, of practice from theory, of 'science' from 'society' is itself part of the fragmentation of knowledge that reductionist thinking sustains." Moreover,

> scientists have done more than simply participate in the general objectifica-
> tion of society. They have raised that objectification to the status of an
> absolute good called "scientific objectivity." . . . But the emphasis on
> objectivity has masked the true social relations of scientists with each other
> and with the rest of the society. . . . Thus, at any historical moment, what
> pass as acceptable scientific explanations have both social determinants and
> social functions.

And Western science has very particular social functions: "'Science,'" Lewontin, Rose, and Kamin observe, "is the ultimate legitimator of bourgeois ideology."[23]

Perhaps no "scientific" construct evidences this truth more clearly than "intelligence." All the choices that inhere in this purportedly neutral term are choices that are made in accordance with the demands of the culture in which the construct subsists. Measures of "intelligence," if they validly and reliably serve their goals, must necessarily reflect these same cultural choices. The biases that inhere in standardized measures of intelligence, then, are the biases that inhere in our culture. Standardized tests merely objectify, quantify, and legitimate those biases; they do not and cannot transcend the cultures they are designed to serve; they do—and perhaps must—re-present and re-enforce the biases of those cultures with relentless precision.

The Bell Curve's major contribution to our understanding of "intelligence" is thought to be its revelation that measured "intelligence"—if the measures are valid and reliable—correlates to some degree with social success. If you do well on properly designed "intelligence" tests, that is, then you will do well in the culture that administers them. But as my young niece is wont to say, "well, du-uh." In fact, this revelation should come as a surprise only to those who know absolutely nothing about these measures. Standardized tests of aptitude are designed to predict success in some social endeavor; they are valid and reliable only to the extent that they succeed as predictors. To say that the test scores correlate with social success is only to say that "intelligence" tests measure "intelligence."

And that is critique, not criticism. In one sense, the culture-bound conception of "intelligence" is both unremarkable and unobjectionable. We live, after all, in culture; we must perform social tasks in culture; our ability to adapt is, necessarily, the ability to adapt to culture. If we need a word to describe that ability to adapt, then "intelligence" is, perhaps, as good as any. And if, finally, we are determined to measure that ability, then we might as well do it validly and reliably, even if that means validly and reliably replicating our biases. It is true, as Lewontin claims, that "IQ tests are instruments for giving an apparently objective 'scientific' gloss to the social prejudices of educational institutions." But it is also true, as Lewontin observes elsewhere, that we cannot meaningfully measure any "intelligence" outside culture: "there are no measures of 'unaided' ability, nor are we really interested in them . . . we are concerned with differences in the ability to carry out *socially constructed* tasks that are relevant to the structure of our actual social lives."[24]

In the final analysis, we might have no objection to the suggestion that, based on standardized measures, person A or group B has X amount of "intelligence," *provided* we are clear on what we mean. And what we mean is only that we have chosen, from a virtually unlimited pool, some aptitudes and skills that seem to correlate with social success as we have chosen to define it, and we have called this correlation "intelligence," and some individuals and groups may at some points in their development seem to have more of it than others—undoubtedly because we have chosen to make it more available to some than to others—and our measurements tend to confirm this because, after all, that is what we have designed our measurements to do.

The danger, of course, is that we are not always clear on what we mean by "intelligence." The danger is that we might sometimes suggest, and might seem to believe, that "intelligence" transcends culture, that it is not a matter of choice, that it is an absolute, innate, immutable capacity. We might then come to believe that when we say some people are more "intelligent" than others, this is somehow "really" the case, as if it was some kind of scientific truth, and not simply something we find useful to say for one reason or another.

There may be good reasons for saying it; it all started, after all, with a very good one. Binet thought it would be useful to identify "deficiencies" in "intelligence" so that students in need could be made academically whole. "Intelligence" thus served a perfectly useful administrative purpose: to identify students who needed to learn how to learn. We have strayed, it seems, from this goal.

We might do well, then, when we speak of "intelligence," to remember both *what* we mean by the term and *why* we find it useful to employ it—to remember, that is, that the "intelligence" construct both is made by culture and serves cultural purposes.

We would do particularly well to keep these things in mind when we speak of group differences in "intelligence." Which brings us, again, to the disparities in standardized test performance between black and white Americans. Some say, based on these disparities, that white Americans are more "intelligent" than black Americans. What, legitimately, might that mean, and why might we say it?

We might begin, following *The Bell Curve*, by noting what it cannot mean. It cannot mean that white Americans are naturally superior to black Americans; nor can it mean that white Americans innately possess more of some biologically essential aptitude than black Americans; it cannot even mean that white Americans inevitably possess more of some socially important aptitude than black Americans. Each of these assertions ignores some important aspect of the cultural construction of "intelligence": the choices that inhere in creating an order based on "intelligence," in defining "intelligence," and in giving some groups greater access to "intelligence." All the assertions ignore some important aspect of the cultural construction of "race": the culture that defined the attributes of "white" and "black" did so in ways that both posited and perpetuated an intellectual order rooted in the color of people's skin.

When we are reminded of the role of culture in simultaneously constructing both intellectual ability and group identity, we see the test disparity for what it is: a cultural one. "Intelligence," the ability to adapt to culture, is inevitably shaped by culture: there is nothing natural or inherent or inevitable about it. In America, that shaping—the cultural construction of "intelligence"—has been inextricably intertwined with the construction of "race." "Intelligence" was defined by one race and defined in racial terms; "race," in turn, was defined in substantial part through "intelligence," through intellectual inferiority and superiority. And it was more than just theory, it was a cultural reality: it was written in the "science" books, codified in the laws, and lived in the schools and workplaces. There was—there is—no escaping it.

And it is manifest today in test disparities. Keep in mind that we are not now talking about a cultural *explanation* for the "IQ gap," for that would be redundant. What we are talking about is the cultural *construction* of the "IQ gap," of the ways "race" and "intelligence" were made—and made unequal—together.

So how, precisely, has the gap been constructed? It is, of course, no easy task to unweave the complex cultural strands of race and intelligence, and we can never be certain that we have told the story exactly right. But we know enough, and we know it with enough certainty, that we can offer credible hypotheses.

So here is one: the "IQ gap" is composed of five interrelated cultural factors:

1. Educational Inequity. Writing in the *Atlantic Monthly* in 1922, Cornelia James Cannon noted that a very large percentage of black recruits had tested as "morons" in Yerkes Army tests; "the education of the whites and colored in separate schools," Cannon concluded, "may have justification other than that created by race prejudice." Thus did educational deprivation serve to limit "intelligence," and the limitations in "intelligence" subsequently serve to limit educational opportunity. Henry Louis Gates, Jr., paraphrases Frederick Douglass when he summarizes the cycle this way: "The crimes of discrimination have become discrimination's best defense."

Part of the "racial difference" in "intelligence"—probably, in this author's view, nearly all of it—may simply reflect these long-standing differences in educational opportunity. This is not merely history; it remains real today. A recent report prepared for the House Committee on Education and Labor documented substantial inequities in school financing both within and among the states, and determined that "fiscal inequity ordinarily is translated into major differences in the educational services provided by wealthy and poor school districts." It noted, not surprisingly, that the principal victims of fiscal inequity were often racial and ethnic minorities.

Today, educational inequities are manifest in a host of material ways. Poor districts must depress the salary structures for their teachers, are disproportionately plagued by teacher shortages, and are forced to rely on long-term "substitute" teachers and underqualified entrants. Poor districts lack the physical plant facilities, the computer and modern communications equipment, and the curricular materials to achieve even the most basic educational objectives. Whatever learning might be attempted must take place under physical conditions that most American workers would find utterly intolerable.

"Racial differences" are reflected as well in the school curricula. In part, perhaps, because of the disparities in resources, poorer districts do not offer the range of liberal arts or advanced science and math courses routinely available in other districts. The curricula of the poor districts, on the other hand, do have a disproportionate abundance of remedial courses and reflect much less emphasis on college preparatory courses and much more on vocational training.

Even within individual schools, research documents disturbing educational inequities. The modern preoccupation with academic "tracking," a practice that appears to afford little or no educational benefits to most students, tends to limit the educational opportunities available to black students, who find themselves assigned with uncommon frequency to low achieving tracks. A recent study of 174 school districts with at least 15,000 students and 1 percent black enrollment documented this and other trends, concluding that "[t]he sorting practices of schools are associated with racial disproportions." Specifically, the study noted that a black student is nearly three times more likely to be placed in a class for the educably mentally retarded than is a white student and is 30 percent more likely to be assigned to a trainable mentally retarded class than a white student, while "[a]t the other end of the sorting spectrum," the study observed, "a white student is 3.2 times more likely to be assigned to a gifted class than is a black student." A black student, meanwhile, is more than twice as likely as a white student to be corporally punished or suspended, and 3.5 times more likely to be expelled. Given all of this, what is remarkable about the disparity in educational outcomes—that black students are 18 percent more likely to drop out of school and 27 percent less likely to graduate—is that it is not much greater than it is.

All of which makes it difficult to avoid the conclusion that America's poor and minority citizens are being assigned their life's station at a very early age. As F. Allan Hanson concludes, the "intelligence gap" "is explicable not by any differences in largely innate cognitive potential between people of different classes (and races), but by different opportunities to learn."[25]

2. Socio-Economic Differences. To some extent, "racial" differences in "intelligence" may be no more than the predictable corollaries of poverty. Research consistently establishes the correlation between socioeconomic status and standardized measures of aptitude. There is, for example, a direct and proportional relationship between wealth and score on the Scholastic Aptitude Test (SAT) and between wealth and various measures of math aptitude and achievement. Indeed, much of the racial gap in standardized measures of aptitude disappears when socioeconomic factors are controlled. For example, a 1993 analysis of a random sample from the National Longitudinal Study of intelligence examined racial differences in IQ while controlling both for structural factors (socioeconomic status) and home environment (intellectual stimulation and emotional support as measured by the "HOME" index, except to the extent that the indexed factors were correlates of maternal IQ): there was, with these controls, no racial gap at all.

Two specific poverty factors also seem to be highly correlated with depressed academic achievement: long-term poverty and the poverty concentration of the school. Regarding the former, research indicates that for each year of student poverty, the likelihood of falling behind in grade level increases by 2 percent. Regarding the latter, academic failure is more closely correlated with schoolwide concentration of poverty than it is with individual poverty. Of course, these two poverty factors are disproportionately present for black students.

Consider, too, all the corollaries of poverty, and the ways they might depress "intelligence" or academic achievement. There are medical impediments: low birth weight, lead exposure, malnutrition, and higher incidence of nearly all diseases. There are psychological stressors: financial pressures, domestic difficulties, increased crime and violence. Any one of these might be debilitating; in combination, they seem almost insurmountable.

The Bell Curve's response to all of this is that wealth is correlated with IQ principally because "intelligence" leads to wealth. But that is not precisely the case. A child in the top IQ decile (top 10 percent) is fifty times more likely than a child in the bottom IQ decile to wind up in the top income decile. This, of course, neatly fits *The Bell Curve*'s hypothesis. However, when controlled for family background and education, that high-IQ child is only twice as likely as the low-IQ to hit that top income group. A child whose family is in the top *income* decile, meanwhile, is twenty-five times more likely to reach the top income level than is a child in the bottom income decile, even when both children have an average IQ. Clearly, then, the far superior predictor of wealth is—surprise—wealth.[26]

3. Differences in Attitudes toward Formal Education. As Richard Nisbett observes, "[t]here are systematic differences in the socialization of black and white children that begin in the cradle." Some of these differences may be reflected in attitudes toward formal education. There is, first of all, evidence suggesting that many African Americans share a distinctive attitude shaped in part by their experience as, in John U. Ogbu's terminology, "involuntary minorities." Somewhat more specifically, historical factors and contemporary realities seem to have combined to generate considerable anger and alienation regarding mainstream American institutions; these feelings clearly extend to the public schools. Historically viewed as harboring the best hope for the realization of racial justice, the public educational process may now be viewed with an increasing bitterness and sense of betrayal.

The schools, sadly, have failed to respond to the unique needs generated by this perception. "[M]ost schools," writes John Goodlad, "simply do not provide environments congenial to students who fail to adapt to the conventional expectations and regularities of schooling." For all students, such school difficulties force a choice between the school culture and the home or neighborhood culture: an inhospitable educational environment may make the choice tragically easy. For black students, the conflict may be heightened by the intensifying dissonance between the skepticism of the home culture and the increasingly illusory promises of academia, promises that may be articulated in voices that are insensitive or outright hostile. Already alienated students find themselves caught in a relentless gestalt of academic depression: failure breeds distrust breeds failure.

And attitudes do matter to achievement. Intrinsic motivation is positively correlated with educational outcomes; amotivation, meanwhile, is negatively correlated. Significantly, motivation and its consequences can be produced situationally by environmental factors as well as by the learner's predominant motivational style. People, in short, learn when they are motivated to learn, and they can become motivated.[27]

4. Differences in Root Culture. There is some evidence to suggest that learning styles reflect the attributes of the surrounding culture, and that distinct cognitive styles may reflect the distinct attributes of cultures or subcultures. The case for the existence of distinct African American cultures is a strong one, and whether they reflect the persistent influence of Western African culture, the historical discontinuity of the American experience, or some combination of these and other factors, it does not seem illogical to suggest that these distinct cultures might be reflected in distinct learning and cognitive styles for African American children.

If, then, white Americans are generally exhibiting greater facility with the criteria and processes of intellectual achievement, it may be because, in substantial part, white Americans have devised them. Moreover, white Americans have devised them largely without the participation of black Americans: the persistent segregation and exclusion of black Americans from the dominant culture has simultaneously served to insulate the dominant criteria of achievement from the influence of African American culture, and perpetuate the existence of an African American culture that is "different" from—and subordinate to—the dominant perspective. Unless American schools affirmatively accommodate "different" learning styles and kinds of intelligence, and those of black students in particular, education, academic achievement, and "intelligence" just become additional expressions of cultural hegemony.

J. Phillipe Rushton inadvertently made this point in his 1994 assault on egalitarianism, *The Equalitarian Dogma Revisited*. "The historical record shows," Rushton wrote, "that an African cultural disadvantage has existed, relative to Europeans and Asians, ever since Europeans first made contact 2,000 years ago." Rushton attributes the "cultural disadvantage" to, of course, the genetic inferiority of Africans, but we do not have to accept this assertion, or his pejorative characterization of African culture, in order to acknowledge the more basic premise: that European and African cultures are different. Moreover, we learn from Rushton—as an example, not as a teacher—that African culture has been viewed as inferior, that it has been subordinated in (North) America, and that any efforts to accommodate African or African American cultures will likely be viewed as compromises: of "educational excellence," we are likely to be told, but also, in truth, of cultural control.

Cultural differences may explain in part the results of adoption studies suggesting that IQ gains may be dependent both on the ethnicity of the adoptive family and the surrounding ethnic milieu. The exposure to "white culture" evidently influences the development of skills, attitudes, and problem-solving orientation; thus among black children adopted by black families, those adopted into white or mixed neighborhoods or into families with white friendship networks showed the largest IQ gains.

It is worth emphasizing that this issue is not unique to black Americans. Measured intelligence differences persist between rural and urban Americans—the former do not fare as well—but only among older test takers. The electronic media have helped integrate younger rural Americans into the cultural "mainstream"; they are, as a consequence, more "intelligent." Additionally, Thomas Sowell notes that "groups outside the cultural mainstream of contemporary Western society tend to do their worst on abstract questions"; as a consequence, some European immigrant groups have also been disadvantaged by the dominant conception of "intelligence." To reiterate, this conception of "intelligence" is neither inevitable nor universal; as Camile Paglia notes, "What they're calling IQ is Apollonian logic—cause and effect—that the West invented. It's Eurocentric. . . . Anyone who wants to enter the command machinery of the world, as I hope many aspiring African-Americans do, must learn that style. . . . But to identify that narrow thing with all human intelligence is madness. It is folly."

It may even be outdated. In some views, linear, objectivist epistemologies are increasingly untenable; in almost all disciplines, context now matters as it never has before. Thus we have seen the development of new histories, and divergent rationalities, and contingency in the social sciences, and even relativity—and now complexity, field theory, and systems theories—in the physical sciences, all disrupting the stable order of a fixed reality, abstract truths, and absolute governing principles. Life, it thus appears, cannot always be reduced to true and false, or even to multiple choice: it is sometimes chaotic, sometimes paradoxical, sometimes, perhaps, unknowable, at least in the sense in which we have been used to knowing things. Life is complicated, frighteningly or wonderfully so, depending, of course, on your perspective.[28]

5. Disadvantages in Assessment Processes. Finally, biases may inhere in the formal assessment process. Some of these may be found in the evaluation instruments: it should be clear by now that cultural and class biases are unavoidable in definitions and measurements of "intelligence," but at times these biases have been so patent and prejudicial that the courts have been compelled to require their redress. Standardized measures of intelligence are now purported to be class- and culturally neutral, and this is undoubtedly the case—if the "neutral" test taker is, in class terms, one with *average* access to educational resources and, in cultural terms, one who shares the norms and expressions of the *dominant* culture.

In addition, cultural beliefs and expectations may shape the behavior of both the examiners and the subjects of examination in the processes of intellectual assessment. With respect to the former, research indicates that in a variety of academic settings, black students are rated less favorably and treated less favorably than white students with comparable performances; evaluators also maintained lower academic expectations for black students than for white students with comparable credentials.   As for the test-taking subjects, studies of racial differences in test performance reveal that black students perform worse than white students only when led to believe that the test measures intellectual ability and that race is likely to matter to the outcome.   Poor performance, in effect, becomes—for both parties in the assessment process—a self-fulfilling prophecy.[29]

These five factors, collectively, tell part of the story of "race" and "intelligence" in America—but only part of it.   There can be no pretense that they offer the only, the fullest, or the best account of the cultural gap manifest in measured intelligence disparities.   But let us suppose, for a moment, that we accept at least the premise of the account.   Let us suppose that we have arrived at some agreement on the meaning of "intelligence" and the roots of the "racial gap" in intelligence.   Let us suppose that we all understand that the gap is a cultural one and that it has nothing to do with inviolable measures of immutable abilities that must invariably be described as "intelligence."   We know, in short, precisely *what* we mean when we say, "white people generally demonstrate more measured intelligence than black people."

The question remains: *Why* would we say it?   Perhaps it is because we recognize a need to change the concept of "intelligence."   Perhaps by pointing out the cultural gap, we mean to draw attention to the cultural myopia that pervades our construction of "intelligence."   Perhaps we have recognized that "intelligence" is inescapably culture-bound, but that it need not be formulated at an impossible level of abstraction.   Perhaps we mean to demonstrate the need for bringing "intelligence" down to earth, the need to reformulate it in specific, practical contexts.   Perhaps we know what research suggests, that in those specific contexts—in the real world—there is no racial gap in intelligence.

Or perhaps it is because we recognize a need to change our means of delivering access to "intelligence."   Perhaps by pointing out the cultural gap, we mean to acknowledge the shameful disparity in educational and employment opportunity—in cultural opportunity—that distinguishes black and white America. Perhaps we have recognized that "intelligence" is correlated with cultural success, but, as Anthony Appiah observes, "[i]f your way of measuring the adequacy of a test is to see how well it correlates with social success, then you're assuming the current society produces social success in a way that is just fine." Perhaps we are no longer willing to make that assumption; perhaps we want to produce success in a more equal way. Perhaps we would accept Rogers Elliot's assessment of race differences in intelligence: "they are what they are, and they say something about the society that produces them." Perhaps pointing out the racial gap in measured intelligence is one way to demonstrate the need for egalitarian reform.[30]

So there are two reasons why we might talk and write about the racial gap in measured intelligence. The natural order crowd might have their own.

"Intelligence" is no more an absolute phenomenon—no more beyond culture—than any of the other criteria of merit, and it is no more a biological phenomenon than the constructs of group identity, like "race," with which it is sometimes correlated. To talk, then, of natural intelligence is to talk in oxymorons; to say that one racial group is naturally more or less intelligent than another is, quite simply, to speak nonsense.

But it is possible to protest too much. As right as it is to say that the talk of natural hierarchies of group intelligence is nonsense, it is equally important to note that assertions of such hierarchies are, even on their own narrow terms, simply erroneous. To paraphrase Walter Lippman, then, the statement "this racial group is genetically smarter than that racial group" is not merely nonsense, it is also incorrect.

An Addendum: Equal in Intelligence

The authors of *The Bell Curve* profess a "resolute agnosticism" on the question of the genetic superiority—in intellectual terms—of white folks to black. But as Ned Block indicates, their "agnosticism ends up as agnosticism about just how genetically inferior blacks are."

There is really no avoiding *The Bell Curve*'s none-too-subtle message, and the authors' disclaimers only add an air of disingenuousness—or, as they would have it, intrigue—to an otherwise predictable pastiche of scientistic racialism. Herrnstein and Murray do, after all, resolutely report all the correlations between race, intelligence, and social success for a reason, and that reason does not appear to have much to do with a desire either to reconstruct "race" and "intelligence" or to equalize access to the instruments of social success. Indeed, their diatribe against "affirmative action," and their preposterous suggestion that American law is simply *too* egalitarian, make it altogether too clear that their central hypothesis—that genetic intelligence is correlated with social achievement—has a distinct racial component. It is precisely because the suggestion is so predictable, precisely because it is so *un*original to suggest that white folks are genetically superior, that the authors of *The Bell Curve* can be so coy about the whole sordid business: they can state their claim through innuendo, root it in next-to-nothing, and renounce what they have not said—and still everybody will know exactly what they mean.

And it is precisely because what they mean to say is so hideously wrong that it demands a response. Part of that response has filled the first six chapters of this book: it is that "race" and "intelligence" are correlated because those correlations inhere in the constructs. Our response to their revelation, then, is something on the order of "no kidding" and "so what?" Or as Alan Wolfe puts it, "Herrnstein and Murray find a strong relationship between race and IQ, but neither race nor IQ are strong phenomena. A strong relationship between weak variables is a weak relationship."

Our response changes, however, when Herrnstein and Murray begin to suggest that "race" and "intelligence" are stronger than they really are, when they suggest that the correlation is inevitable, or natural, or even genetic. It is then that they are speaking nonsense, and we must say as much.

We might add, perhaps as an aside, that their correlations are pretty flimsy. As Stephen Jay Gould notes, even assuming away all the difficulties with their premises, the relationships described by Herrnstein and Murray are very weak. Even on their own terms, they fail to make the case for a genetic correlation between "race" and "intelligence." This is because—conceptual problems aside—the evidence simply does not permit that case to be made.[31]

There have been, to date, essentially four kinds of studies designed to remove the confounding variables of class and culture from an examination of the relationship between race and intelligence. These are

1. *Neurological studies*, which seek to measure cognitive abilities to solve problems that have no cultural foundation;
2. *Physiological studies*, which seek to measure anatomical differences as a way of gauging relative intelligence;
3. *Inheritance studies*, which seek to measure correlations between intelligence and racial ancestry in cross-cultural settings; and
4. *Adoption studies*, which seek to determine whether racial correlations remain constant when the subjects are placed in different environments.

Following is a brief synopsis of the research.

1. Neurological studies. Arthur Jensen's research on "choice reaction time" has defined the field. The results, as we have seen, are equivocal. In one study, Jensen claims that white subjects displayed a superior—faster—choice reaction time. In two subsequent studies, the black subjects displayed a superior choice reaction time. The verdict: a split decision in favor of black intellectual superiority.[32]

2. Physiological studies. This is the domain of the old craniometrists and, today, of J. Phillipe Rushton. Stephen Jay Gould has effectively rebutted the claims of the former, and Zack Z. Cernovsky has tackled the latter. Cernovsky notes, among other things, that Rushton has misrepresented his findings on brain size. Moreover, Cernovsky reports research suggesting that poverty, malnutrition, and climate are correlated with brain size, but that race alone is not. Cernovsky concludes that the use of brain size as an indicator of intelligence is "statistically absurd." The verdict: no evidence of genetic racial difference in intelligence.[33]

3. Inheritance studies. There are a few of these. A study of the German children fathered by American GI's revealed that the children of black fathers had a mean IQ of 96.5 while the children of white fathers had a statistically indistinguishable mean IQ of 97; Flynn reports that the best explanatory model for this data is zero heritability of the black-white IQ gap. A 1934 study determined that extremely high IQ among black children was not correlated with European ancestry. Two different studies from 1973 sought correlations between ancestry and IQ: the correlations varied—+.01 and -.38—but the significant correlation suggested that African blood was associated with higher IQ. A 1977 study of 288 young black Philadelphians sought a correlation between European heritage and IQ: the correlation was .05, "trivial and non-significant." The racial admixture studies, in sum, show near-zero correlation between degree of African or European ancestry and IQ. The verdict: no evidence of genetic racial difference in intelligence.[34]

4. *Adoption studies.* A 1972 study focused on children in a controlled environment (a residential situation): the IQ of the white children was 103, of the black children 108, and the racially mixed children 106. The 1983 Minnesota Transracial Adoption Study is relied upon heavily in *The Bell Curve*, but the researchers' 1994 follow-up study documents the substantial environmental effects on IQ: the performance of black subjects is not constant, but in fact parallels that of their white peers when they are adopted into comparable socioeconomic settings. And a 1986 adoption study revealed the extraordinary impact of the environment (including the "racial" environment): black children adopted into and raised in black middle-class homes attained IQ scores a full standard deviation above the norm for black children; black children adopted into and raised in white middle-class homes attained IQ scores a full standard deviation above that. The verdict: no evidence of genetic racial difference in intelligence.[35]

R. C. Lewontin notes that the claims of inborn racial differences "are made without a shred of evidence and in contradiction to every principle of biology and genetics." Richard Nisbett concludes that the argument that "blacks" are genetically inferior is "not only wrong but irresponsible." Leon J. Kamin writes, "To attribute racial differences to genetic factors, granting the overwhelming cultural-environmental differences between the races, is to compound folly with malice." As Stephen Jay Gould concludes, things might have turned out differently, but in fact our situation is clear: "Human equality is a contingent fact of history."[36]

The myth is wrong, but the myth persists. And *The Bell Curve* is wrong about this too: the myths of merit—and of "race" and "intelligence"—persist *because of*, not in spite of, American politics. Which is to say, in part, that they persist because of, and not in spite of, American law. The final chapter explains how.

7

The Constitution Is Powerless
Myths of Equality under Law

The "natural order" survives because of, rather than in spite of, American law. The law sanctifies the order in theory and secures it as a social fact. Neither the first nor the second Reconstructions has substantially altered this course: indeed, the arguments against both Reconstructions have seemed, in the end, to carry the day. Thus law continues to protect the advantages of some Americans while obscuring the disadvantages of others, all through a carefully crafted set of legal fictions that subvert the constitutional promise of "equality." That promise thus becomes, perversely, a guarantee of privilege for some; and it becomes, tragically, a lifeless abstraction for others. The bell curves of American social life are preserved by law. We cannot be made equal; we are not even permitted to try.

Prologue

> Ask your own soul what it would say if the next census were to report that half of black America was dead and the other half dying.
>
> — W. E. B. Du Bois, *The Souls of White Folks*

Black America, some people said, was dying. And they wondered what they would hear in the souls of white folk when white America heard the news.

Part of the story, perhaps, was told one recent June, by the Supreme Court of all America. The session of the Court had not been convened to determine the fate of black America—not explicitly, at any rate, and not exclusively. Still, it was clearly on the agenda, with no less than three major race-related disputes on the High Court's docket.

What the Court had to say on such matters did tend to matter. As the highest tribunal in the land, it possessed the power to shape the law and, as a consequence, the power to shape the larger society. This last point was the focus of some academic debate—some questioned the societal impact of the Court's decisions—but this much remained fairly certain: the law could be expected to play at least some role in shaping the development of societal conventions, and on matters of law, the words of the Supreme Court tended to be the final ones.

More important, perhaps, the Court helped establish the parameters of cultural discourse. It was a major participant in the national political dialogue, and its voice carried a certain authority not often accorded its elected counterparts. Ironically, perhaps, the paradigms it helped shape were not only legal ones: some were epistemological, some quite political, some downright moral. In reinforcing popular attitudes and beliefs, or in challenging them through new perspectives and dissonant information, it helped establish a national mood. It confirmed or denied the citizenry's sense of what is real and what is right. Over time, it transformed their sense of both the possible and probable, and forever changed the way the people saw one another and saw themselves. Yes, the Court's words mattered.

What the justices of the High Court had to say on this occasion, in the closing weeks of their judicial term, might have mattered more than usual. Their words, after all, were addressed to the most intractable of national problems: the enduring dilemma of racial inequality. For a waiting nation—for judges, lawyers, lawmakers and their constituents, for teachers and students, parents and children, for the American people of every station and every hue—the High Court would do no less than newly define the meaning of racial equality.

It would be a progress report of sorts: how equal was America? But more important, it would set the agenda for the millennium. In this struggle for racial equality, what should be the goals, and how should they be achieved? Whose struggle was it, and when should it end?

Underlying it all was this fundamental question: in the struggle for racial equality, what *could* be done—what equality, and how much, was possible? Only recently, some writers had revived the long-discredited myth of a natural racial order: they had written—or merely hinted, when they knew merely hinting would suffice—that some races were inherently more intelligent than others. The struggle for equality, they concluded, was hopeless in the face of the natural order; worse, the egalitarian effort was unfair to those who were superior, and degrading to the culture the superior race had tried to elevate.

The High Court itself had embraced this view, but over a century ago. Certainly they knew better now; certainly they would teach the nation better now.

There were nine of them—one was black and eight were white—and they would need to explain what *their* souls had to say when they pondered the fate of black America.

They had chosen three specific issues to address: the racial desegregation of America's public schools; the national government's use of preferences or presumptions to benefit racial minorities; and the explicit reliance on "race" in the creation of electoral districts as a device to ensure minority representation in the federal legislature.

The Desegregation Story

It was William H. Rehnquist, the chief justice himself, who began the address to the nation. He selected the desegregation case from the Kansas City, Missouri, School District (the KCMSD) as the basis for his story.[1]

"As this school desegregation litigation enters its 18th year, we are called upon again to review the decisions of the lower courts."

The crowd was still settling into the large chamber. A reporter covering the session noted that the chief justice had barely begun his tale, and already a certain weariness weighed heavily in his voice.

"This case," the chief justice continued, "has been before the same United States District Judge since 1977."

His voice grew heavier.

"After a trial that lasted 7 1/2 months . . ."

Heavier still. The crowd, the reporter thought, sank with it.

"As of 1990, the District Court had ordered $260 million in capital improvements."

And the weariness seemed to give way to frustration.

"Since then, the total cost of capital improvements ordered has soared to over $540 million."

And the frustration yielded to disdain.

"The District Court's desegregation plan has been described as the most ambitious and expensive remedial program in the history of school desegregation. . . . As a result, the desegregation costs have escalated and now are approaching an annual cost of $200 million. These massive expenditures have financed . . ."

It was obvious where this story was going.

The problem, it evolved, was that the district court had done too much to encourage the desegregation of the Kansas City schools. As the chief justice put it, "Proper analysis of the District Court's orders challenged here . . . must rest upon their serving as proper means to the end of restoring the victims of discriminatory conduct to the position they would have occupied in the absence of that conduct."

But the judge in Kansas City had apparently done more than simply "restor[e] the victims" of segregation to their proper place; his remedy for the racial segregation of the Kansas City schools, according to the chief justice, "included an elaborate program of capital improvements, course enrichment, and extracurricular enhancement not simply in the formerly identifiable black schools, but in schools throughout the district."

And still worse, the judge's goal had been to counteract the increasing segregation of the majority black metropolitan schools from the majority white suburban schools. As the chief justice saw it, the judge's plan was "not designed solely to redistribute the students within the KCMSD in order to eliminate racially identifiable schools within the KCMSD. Instead, its purpose is to attract nonminority students from outside the KCMSD schools. But this interdistrict goal is beyond the scope of the intradistrict violation identified by the District Court."

It was axiomatic: "The proper response to an intradistrict violation is an intradistrict remedy."

Associate Justice Sandra Day O'Connor agreed. "Neither the legal responsibility for nor the causal effects of KCMSD's racial segregation transgressed its boundaries, and absent such interdistrict violation or segregative effects, [our decisions] do not permit a regional remedial plan."

But perhaps the effects of the long history of official racial segregation could not be so easily cabined; perhaps disadvantage, oppression, and hostility did not respect "district" lines. Perhaps the KCMSD was largely black, and surrounding districts largely white, precisely because the people of Missouri—indeed, most Americans—had been taught for centuries that racial segregation was both natural and desirable. That, in fact, was the position of the trial court, that the interdistrict segregation it was forced to overcome, the immediate product of the so called white flight from the city district, was ultimately traceable to the segregative policies of the state. Perhaps it was fair to suppose that the state was responsible for the continuing segregation.

No, said the chief justice: "The lower courts' 'findings' as to 'white flight' are both inconsistent internally, and inconsistent with the typical supposition, bolstered here by the record evidence, that 'white flight' may result from desegregation, not *de jure* segregation."

Again, Justice O'Connor agreed. "What the District Court did in this case . . . and how it transgressed the constitutional bounds of its remedial powers, is to make desegregative attractiveness the underlying goal of its remedy for the specific purpose of reversing the trend of white flight. However troubling that trend may be, remedying it is within the District Court's authority only if it is 'directly caused by the constitutional violation.'"

What had "directly caused" the demographic separation of black and white citizens? O'Connor was not certain, but she leaned in favor of the "typical supposition."

"Whether the white exodus that has resulted in a school district that is 68% black was caused by the District Court's remedial orders or by natural, if unfortunate, demographic forces, we have it directly from the District Court that the segregative effects of KCMSD's constitutional violation did not transcend its geographical boundaries."

The segregation, apparently, was caused by the Kansas City judge's own efforts. Or perhaps it was just natural. As O'Connor explained, "In this case, it may be the 'myriad factors of human existence,' that have prompted the white exodus from KCMSD, and the District Court cannot justify its transgression of the above constitutional principles simply by invoking desegregative attractiveness."

"The unfortunate fact of racial imbalance and bias in our society," she continued, "however pervasive or invidious, does not admit of judicial intervention absent a constitutional violation."

The reporter now thought he recognized the genre of the tale: it was tragedy.

The apparent deficits in minority achievement were also insufficient to justify the trial court's plan. "Just as demographic changes independent of *de jure* segregation will affect the racial composition of student assignments," the chief justice continued, "so too will numerous external factors beyond the control of the KCMSD and the State affect minority student achievement. . . . So long as these external factors are not the result of segregation, they do not figure in the remedial calculus."

"External factors"—the reporter briefly wondered what those might be. He waited for the chief justice to elaborate, but there was to be no clarification. Just "external factors"; the details were left to the imagination.

The chief justice continued, "The basic task of the District Court is to decide whether the reduction in achievement by minority students attributable to prior *de jure* segregation has been remedied to the extent practicable."

The Kansas City judge had not done his job. "Although the District Court has determined that '[s]egregation has caused a system wide reduction in achievement in the schools of the KCMSD,' it never has identified the incremental effect that segregation has had on minority student achievement or the specific goals of the quality education programs."

But the reporter knew that identifying the "incremental effect" of centuries of educational inequity would be no easy task. Presumably, the chief justice knew it too.

"Insistence upon academic goals unrelated to the effects of legal segregation unwarrantably postpones the day when the KCMSD will be able to operate on its own." After all, the chief justice noted, "our cases recognize that local autonomy of school districts is a vital national tradition."

But then, racial segregation was a part of that tradition, and so too was resistance to the desegregation effort. So, for that matter, were pervasive educational inequities—racial disparities in funding, in physical resources, in the curriculum itself—inequities that persist to this day, crystallized in the often absurd differences between urban and suburban schools. Would the end of the segregation effort signal a return to these traditions?

The chief justice took a surprising tack. Those awful traditions, he suggested, were already no more; the unfortunate students who labored under them had long since graduated. "Minority students in kindergarten through grade 7 in the KCMSD always have attended AAA-rated schools; minority students in the KCMSD that previously attended schools rated below AAA have since received remedial education programs for a period of up to seven years."

The implications were clear: centuries of racial deprivation caused no lingering racial harms. Depressed academic achievement was due to, well, "external factors." It was not the responsibility of the state; it was not the responsibility of the schools. There was, accordingly, no need for racial redress.

"It may be that in education, just as it may be in economics, a 'rising tide lifts all boats,' but the remedial quality education program should be tailored to remedy the injuries suffered by the victims of prior *de jure* segregation."

It was time for each individual to sink or swim.

Associate Justice Clarence Thomas echoed the chief justice's sentiments: "To ensure that district courts do not embark on such broad initiatives in the future, we should demand that remedial decrees be more precisely designed to benefit only those who have been victims of segregation." The reporter could not help but wonder: how and why would we benefit "only those who have been victims of segregation"?

"The mere fact that a school is black does not mean that it is the product of a constitutional violation."

What, then, did it mean? The justice explained, "The continuing 'racial isolation' of schools after *de jure* segregation has ended may well reflect voluntary housing choices or other private decisions." "The Constitution does not prevent individuals from choosing to live together, to work together, or to send their children to school together, so long as the State does not interfere with their choices on the basis of race."

There was something else on Thomas's mind. "It never ceases to amaze me that the courts are so willing to assume that anything that is predominantly black must be inferior." He spoke, according to some, with special authority: he was, after all, "black."

"'Racial isolation' itself is not a harm; only state-enforced segregation is. After all, if separation itself is a harm, and if integration therefore is the only way that blacks can receive a proper education, then there must be something inferior about blacks. Under this theory, segregation injures blacks because blacks, when left on their own, cannot achieve. To my way of thinking, that conclusion is the result of a jurisprudence based upon a theory of black inferiority."

The crowd stirred. It was, the reporter knew, an extraordinary moment: Thomas was turning a half century of constitutional jurisprudence on its head. Fully five decades ago, in *Brown v. Board of Education*, the Supreme Court had held that racially segregated schools were inherently unequal. In a culture marked by an entrenched racial hierarchy, a hierarchy mutually dependent upon notions of natural racial superiority, the bare fact of state-sponsored separation perpetuated racial supremacy, both as a scientific myth and as a social fact.

Now, remarkably, Thomas was suggesting that it was not segregation but the effort to desegregate that perpetuated the malevolent myths of black inferiority and white superiority. "Two threads in our jurisprudence have produced this unfortunate situation, in which a District Court has taken it upon itself to experiment with the education of the KCMSD's black youth." The reporter winced at the harshness of the metaphor.

"First, the court has read our cases to support the theory that black students suffer an unspecified psychological harm from segregation that retards their mental and educational development. This approach not only relies upon questionable social science research rather than constitutional principle, but it also rests on an assumption of black inferiority."

"Such assumptions," Thomas concluded, "and any social science research upon which they rely certainly cannot form the basis upon which we decide matters of constitutional principle."

Thomas accused the Kansas City judge of "misreading" *Brown* and the early desegregation decisions. Some members of the assembled audience were shaking their heads. Was it disagreement? Dismay? Something worse? Those familiar with the desegregation cases knew that the social science evidence offered to the Court in *Brown*—evidence on which the Court had expressly relied—described a vicious cycle of racism in which racial prejudice generated racial segregation, which in turn generated racial differences in self-concept and achievement, which in turn seemed to legitimate and heighten the prejudice. *Brown* attacked the link in the chain that appeared most vulnerable to law; the segregation it outlawed was, the Court knew, both a cause and an effect of racial inequality.

But Thomas saw it differently. "The lower courts should not be swayed by the easy answers of social science, nor should they accept the findings, and the assumptions, of sociology and psychology at the price of constitutional principle."

"Psychological injury or benefit," Thomas continued, "is irrelevant to the question whether state actors have engaged in intentional discrimination: the critical inquiry for ascertaining violations of the Equal Protection Clause. The judiciary is fully competent to make independent determinations concerning the existence of state action without the unnecessary and misleading assistance of the social sciences."

The reporter was not sure just what Thomas was saying. That there had been no official segregation? That it had caused no harm? That it no longer caused harm? If he was saying the first, then he was clearly mistaken. If he was saying either of the last two, then how did he purport to know?

Ironically, for all of his dismissals of social science, the justice seemed quite willing to draw some social science conclusions of his own. "Given that desegregation has not produced the predicted leaps forward in black educational achievement," he asserted, "there is no reason to think that black students cannot learn as well when surrounded by members of their own race as when they are in an integrated environment." It was both empirical and theoretical, and as the reporter listened to the obligatory citation of authority, he could not help but think that the justice's selective citation belied his every claim.

Compared to the roaring indictment of desegregation's unprincipled failures, *Brown*'s successes—in reducing the gap between black and white achievement, in reducing negative racial attitudes by virtually every conventional measure—became mumbled asides.

"Although the gap between black and white test scores has narrowed over the past two decades,"—Thomas's grudging acknowledgment was barely audible—"it appears that this has resulted more from gains in the socioeconomic status of black families than from desegregation."

Those gains, presumably, were unrelated to the dismantling of segregation.

"It is clear that the District Court misunderstood the meaning of *Brown I*." Thomas was in full voice again.

"Segregation was not unconstitutional because it might have caused psychological feelings of inferiority. Public school systems that separated blacks and provided them with superior educational resources—making blacks 'feel' superior to whites sent to lesser schools—would violate the Fourteenth Amendment, whether or not the white students felt stigmatized, just as do school systems in which the positions of the races are reversed."

The reporter was stunned by this revision of constitutional history. Thomas seemed to be saying that racially separate schools would have been constitutional, provided neither the "black" nor "white" schools were provided "superior" resources. Separate, in other words, was not inherently unequal. But then the justice retreated.

"Regardless of the relative quality of the schools, segregation violated the Constitution because the State classified students based on their race."

But was it correct, the reporter wondered, that the bare fact of classification was unconstitutional? How was classification alone not "equal"? Was it unequal regardless of the purpose? Regardless of the effect? Regardless of the context? Thomas did not explain.

"Of course, segregation additionally harmed black students by relegating them to schools with substandard facilities and resources."

The reporter scribbled furiously; he was losing the story.

"But neutral policies, such as local school assignments, do not offend the Constitution when individual private choices concerning work or residence produce schools with high black populations."

Now, at last, the tale was vaguely familiar. In the aftermath of *Brown*, District Court Judge John Parker had insisted that the Constitution did not require desegregation, but merely an end to segregation—the formal disestablishment, that is, of official segregative policies. In 1968 the so-called Parker doctrine had been unanimously rejected by the Supreme Court.

But not by Thomas. "The point of the Equal Protection Clause is not to enforce strict race-mixing, but to ensure that blacks and whites are treated equally by the State without regard to their skin color."

Yes, that was it: formal equality. "Perfect equality," the opponents of the first Reconstruction had called it; "legal equality," or "no social equality," according to the opponents of the second. In this abstract, legalistic view, real inequalities—the inequities perpetuated by centuries of official oppression—were irrelevant; the responsibility of the state was merely to pretend that race did not exist. Any lingering racial disparities were outside the realm of official power: they were social, private, natural.

Thomas concluded with a critique of the second flaw in desegregation jurisprudence. "Although I do not doubt that all KCMSD students benefit from many of the initiatives ordered by the court below, it is for the democratically accountable state and local officials to decide whether they are to be made available even to those who were never harmed by segregation."

Justice O'Connor concurred. Those "myriad factors" that caused segregation "are not readily corrected by judicial intervention, but are best addressed by the representative branches; time and again, we have recognized the ample authority legislatures possess to combat racial injustice."

There was, then, always the political process. It was ironic, in light of what was soon to come.

The "Affirmative Action" Story

It was Justice O'Connor who took the lead in telling the Court's next tale. This one concerned a federal "affirmative action" law that was designed to increase the participation of economically disadvantaged entrepreneurs in federal contracting; it included a statutory presumption that minority contractors were economically disadvantaged. It was, on the one hand, simply a recognition of an economic reality: statistically, minority contractors were likely to be disadvantaged in a way that white contractors were not. On the other hand, the statute used the "r" word: "race."

The Court had told many stories about "race." Justice O'Connor's story, she said, would be an attempt to reconcile the earlier tales, an attempt to make of them some coherent whole.[2]

"Despite lingering uncertainty in the details," she began, "the Court's cases . . . had established three general propositions with respect to governmental racial classifications." The first of these, she announced, was "skepticism": "'[a]ny preference based on racial or ethnic criteria must necessarily receive a most searching examination.'" It was a relatively uncontroversial start.

With her second proposition, however, the tale took on a sharper edge. "'[T]he standard of review under the Equal Protection Clause is not dependent on the race of those burdened or benefitted by a particular classification.'" "Consistency does recognize that any individual suffers an injury when he or she is disadvantaged by the government because of his or her race, whatever that race may be."

Justice John Paul Stevens, second on the Court in seniority, and Justice Ruth Bader Ginsburg, the second most junior member of the Court, had suggested that the Court's earlier cases told at least two different tales: one when government used "race" to further the oppression of politically vulnerable minorities, the other when government used "race" to assist those minorities in overcoming the disadvantages created by a history of oppression. But for O'Connor, there was just one story.

Thomas agreed with O'Connor, and he took the occasion to express his disagreement with the underlying premise of Stevens's and Ginsburg's positions "that there is a racial paternalism exception to the principle of equal protection." Stevens had questioned whether the different uses of "race" were morally and constitutionally equivalent. "I believe," Thomas responded, "that there is a 'moral [and] constitutional equivalence,' between laws designed to subjugate a race and those that distribute benefits on the basis of race in order to foster some current notion of equality. . . . That these programs may have been motivated, in part, by good intentions cannot provide refuge from the principle that under our Constitution, the government may not make distinctions on the basis of race. As far as the Constitution is concerned, it is irrelevant whether a government's racial classifications are drawn by those who wish to oppress a race or by those who have a sincere desire to help those thought to be disadvantaged."

It was, the reporter thought, an easy argument to comprehend: it offered simplicity, elegance, symmetry. But the Court—Thomas included—was adamant that the only discrimination that mattered was "intentional" discrimination; so why was the character of that "intent" irrelevant? If the constitutional guarantee of equality was implicated only by "purposeful" official action, why should it not matter whether the purposes were benign or malevolent?

Thomas attempted to explain. "There can be no doubt that the paternalism that appears to lie at the heart of this program is at war with the principle of inherent equality that underlies and infuses our Constitution."

The reporter remained perplexed. How did the presumption of economic disadvantage compromise the principle of "inherent equality"? Was it really "paternalistic" to acknowledge the truth of economic inequity and try to offer some redress? Thomas sounded almost, well, Darwinian.

The reporter had barely begun to crystallize this thought when O'Connor abruptly moved on. Her third proposition, she said, was "congruence." It did not matter whether the discrimination was by a federal actor or a state actor, "'[e]qual protection analysis in the Fifth Amendment area is the same as that under the Fourteenth Amendment.'" Stevens, she noted, "claims that we have ignored any difference between federal and state legislatures. . . . It is true that various Members of this Court have taken different views of the authority §5 of the Fourteenth Amendment confers upon Congress to deal with the problem of racial discrimination, and the extent to which courts should defer to Congress' exercise of that authority. We need not, and do not, address these differences today. For now, it is enough to observe that Justice Stevens' suggestion that any Member of this Court has repudiated in this case his or her previously expressed views on the subject, is incorrect."

The reporter smiled. Not that long ago, O'Connor had insisted that the historical truth of national Reconstruction meant that the federal government was entitled to a deference in dealing with "race" that was not applicable to the states. The reporter was glad to hear that she had not repudiated that view. However, precisely what she had done remained something of a mystery.

"Taken together," O'Connor continued, "these three propositions lead to the conclusion that any person, of whatever race, has the right to demand that any governmental actor subject to the Constitution justify any racial classification subjecting that person to unequal treatment under the strictest judicial scrutiny." "The three propositions . . . all derive from the basic principle that the Fifth and Fourteenth Amendments to the Constitution protect persons, not groups."

She had found her unifying theme: only individuals have a right to constitutional protection and governmental redress. Groups, as groups, had no cognizable claims. It was catchy, and Justice Scalia was quick to join in. Individuals, he declared, "who have been wronged by unlawful racial discrimination should be made whole; but under our Constitution there can be no such thing as either a creditor or a debtor race. That concept is alien to the Constitution's focus upon the individual. . . . To pursue the concept of racial entitlement—even for the most admirable and benign of purposes—is to reinforce and preserve for future mischief the way of thinking that produced race slavery, race privilege and race hatred. In the eyes of government, we are just one race here. It is American."

It was stirring language. The reporter surveyed the crowd; he wondered how many were convinced. He himself found the rhetoric oddly unsatisfying. It seemed—he searched for the word—detached. After centuries of discrimination against "individuals" because of their "race," it seemed almost absurd to insist that "individuals" would not receive redress because of their "race." And in a socioeconomic hierarchy rooted deeply in "race," it seemed wholly unrealistic to suggest that the harm could be undone without reference to "race." How else would "individuals" of any oppressed "race" be made truly equal?

"Government cannot make us equal; it can only recognize, respect, and protect us as equal before the law."

It was Thomas again. The reporter shook his head. Precisely how did Thomas imagine we were made unequal in the first place?

"[T]here can be no doubt," he continued, "that racial paternalism and its unintended consequences can be as poisonous and pernicious as any other form of discrimination."

Was it really true, the reporter wondered, that affirmative action was as "poisonous and pernicious" as, for example, compulsory segregation? Thomas explained:

"So-called 'benign' discrimination teaches many that because of chronic and apparently immutable handicaps, minorities cannot compete with them without their patronizing indulgence. Inevitably, such programs engender attitudes of superiority or, alternatively, provoke resentment among those who believe that they have been wronged by the government's use of race. These programs stamp minorities with a badge of inferiority and may cause them to develop dependencies or to adopt an attitude that they are 'entitled' to preferences."

As Thomas concluded his tale, four of his colleagues nodded their approval. Yet none of them, the reporter noted, chose to echo his sentiments.

The reporter, meanwhile, had more questions than answers. Was this "badge of inferiority" the same one that Thomas had so casually dismissed in his desegregation story? Why were "attitudes" so central to this story but so irrelevant in the desegregation tale? Just where, the reporter wondered, was the line between "social science" and "constitutional principle"?

Above all, what possible conception of the relationship between race and ability informed this attitude? It was hard to see how a presumption of economic disadvantage connoted inferiority unless all of the operative variables were assumed to be somehow natural. Was that, the reporter wondered, the premise here? Was Thomas—and the bare majority with whom he concurred—still conceiving "race" as something natural, and "ability" or "merit" or "achievement" as equally natural, such that any effort to bridge the racial gap implied the natural inability of the benefitted group? Did he—did they—not grasp the simple premise of this law: that "races" of people *are* equal, except to the extent that they have been disparately advantaged—made *un*equal? Precisely who, the reporter wondered, was really embracing the myth of inferiority? He wished there was time to ask, but a new story was already starting.

The Redistricting Story

It was Justice Anthony Kennedy who told the final tale of the session. It was to be a short story.[3]

The U.S. Voting Rights Act required states with a history of racial discrimination in elections to obtain federal approval for any changes in their election schemes. The state of Georgia, with a 27 percent black population, had sought approval for a congressional redistricting plan; the federal government refused until Georgia provided that three of its eleven districts would be majority black. One of the majority black districts was the Eleventh District. White voters in the Eleventh sued; perhaps they did not like being in the minority.

The central mandate of the equality guarantee, Kennedy began, "is racial neutrality in governmental decisionmaking." To support his simple assertion, Kennedy reviewed the history of racial segregation. It was not the history of exclusion; it was not the history of oppression; it was instead the history of "race." Segregation and redistricting were, like affirmative action, all part of the same story: the story of "race."

And the reporter knew the end of this story long before Kennedy finished telling it.

"When the State assigns voters on the basis of race," Kennedy said, "it engages in the offensive and demeaning assumption that voters of a particular race, because of their race, 'think alike, share the same political interests, and will prefer the same candidates at the polls.'"

The Eleventh District, he continued, belied this assumption. The district included "the black neighborhoods of metropolitan Atlanta and the poor black populace of coastal Chatham County, though 260 miles apart in distance and worlds apart in culture. In short, the social, political and economic makeup of the Eleventh District tells a tale of disparity, not community."

The reporter failed to see Kennedy's point: why was it that "community" and "disparity" were incompatible? Within any community there were differences; why could that not be true of the "black" community? What was wrong with the simple recognition that among many demographic variables, "race" tended to be prominent, but not exclusive, in defining political communities?

"It is true," Kennedy acknowledged, "that redistricting in most cases will implicate a political calculus in which various interests compete for recognition, but it does not follow from this that individuals of the same race share a single political interest. The view that they do is 'based on the demeaning notion that members of the defined racial groups ascribe to certain "minority views" that must be different from those of other citizens,' the precise use of race as a proxy the Constitution prohibits."

The reporter strained to understand: precisely when did it become demeaning to suggest that racial communities might be united by some political interests? Was that not, after all, substantiated by voting patterns and opinion surveys? Was that not, after all, the precise reason racial minorities were systematically excluded from the polls in the first place? For that matter, was it not the underlying premise of the "white" voters' lawsuit? Why else would they have objected? What else could they point to as their constitutional harm?

The state, Kennedy continued, acts in a presumptively unconstitutional manner whenever the complaining party can prove that "the legislature subordinated traditional race-neutral districting principles, including but not limited to compactness, contiguity, respect for political subdivisions or communities defined by actual shared interests, to racial considerations." The same would be true whenever "race for its own sake, and not other districting principles, was the legislature's dominant and controlling rationale in drawing its district lines."

Race as a proxy? For what? Race for its own sake? As opposed to what? The reporter's head was spinning. He could barely hear Kennedy as he approached the end of his story.

"A State is free to recognize communities that have a particular racial makeup, provided its action is directed toward some common thread of relevant interests."

Just what was Kennedy saying? That there were no communities of race? Or that racial communities had no "common thread" of interests? Or was it that their common interests were not "relevant"?

Kennedy ended with one final observation. "It takes a shortsighted and unauthorized view of the Voting Rights Act to invoke that statute, which has played a decisive role in redressing some of our worst forms of discrimination, to demand the very racial stereotyping the Fourteenth Amendment forbids."

With that, the session ended. The justices left the bench and retired to their offices and, eventually, to their homes. The assembled crowd of media and curious citizenry filed out of the historic chamber and into the hot, humid air of the summer afternoon. A hundred or so schoolchildren raced down the steps of the great building, briefly mingled on the sidewalks below, then scattered into small groups and scrambled onto the buses that carried them on their field trip to the nation's capital. The reporter noted this curious phenomenon: the black students and white students did not ride the same buses.

The reporter managed a smile at the memories of his own field trip to the capital. His schools, he recalled, were racially segregated, but de jure or de facto, he hadn't a clue which. Frankly, his family had moved so much, and he'd been to so many different schools, it was nearly certain that he'd grown up with both kinds of segregation, and maybe a few other types besides.

The reporter watched the schoolchildren as they scrambled to their seats on the buses, laughing and playing, without, it seemed, a care in the world. His mind wandered back again to his own school days, to a day he had nearly forgotten.

He was just six years old, barely beginning the second grade, but already attending his third school. The students were reporting to the rest of the class on their "Most Exciting Day of the Summer," and the reports were filled with gleeful tales of trips to the beach, days at amusement parks, adventurous rides on new bicycles with old friends. When it was his turn, he wasn't sure what to say. "I didn't really do anything," he had said, earnestly hoping that would be the end of the matter. But the teacher was not so easily satisfied, and the ominous silence of the other kids in the class had convinced him that he had better offer something.

So he had spun a magnificent yarn about the day his family went to the farm. Yes, they had driven to a farm in the country, his uncle's farm, where they went every summer. His mother went, and his grandparents, and also his kid sister, who was only three years old and who was afraid of all the animals, especially the pigs. He had been allowed to ride the horses, and feed the pigs and goats, and go swimming with the ducks. And he had become friends with one of the little ducks, a duck named Donald, and when they went to leave at the end of the day, Donald had followed him into the car, and he didn't know what to say or do, with this little duck hiding under his seat, and so Donald had gone home with him, and nobody knew until they got back to his house and Donald waddled up the steps and onto the porch and into the house. And then Donald saw the reporter's kid sister, and started to chase after her to play, because, after all, she walked like a duck, and everybody else started chasing Donald, and feathers were flying everywhere, and they finally caught Donald and took him back to the farm, but he's allowed to come visit now nearly all the time. His voice had grown more and more animated as he told the story, and the laughter of the other kids had grown louder and louder. And when he finished, the kids in the class had clapped, and he, in return, had smiled.

At recess that day, the other kids had all come up to him, wanting to hear more about the farm, the ducks, and even his kid sister. He ended up talking with them about pets, and families, and his one real passion, baseball. And he was feeling really quite good when the teacher found him and said that she wanted to talk to him. He remembered her saying something about "needing to fit in," and something else about "playing by the rules," and when she told him that he was going to get a D on the assignment because he had made the story up, he felt like crying, and maybe he even did. When they got back from recess he had to tell the class another story, a "true story," and he could not think of one, and his grade fell from a D to an F.

That night, the teacher had called his mom, and he had anxiously watched his mother's face as she talked on the phone. When she hung up, she beckoned him to her, smiled, and hugged him. "Well," she had said, "you do have quite an imagination, don't you?" She was not mad at all, she said, but she did hope quite sincerely that he did not plan on bringing any ducks into the house. He promised that he would not, asked if he could have a puppy, and was gently told not to press his luck.

He told a different story to the class the next day, a story about the day he and his friend Huey rode their bikes all day long and into the night and, to their great surprise, did not get punished for missing dinner. It was an okay story, and the kids were attentive, though they did not clap when he finished. The teacher, on the other hand, seemed quite pleased. He got an A this time, which was pretty good, seeing as how he'd never even been on a bike.

A siren wailed in the distance. Police? Ambulance? The reporter had forgotten how to tell them apart.

He was still standing on the hot sidewalk outside the Supreme Court, and the voices of the Justices, still fresh in his ears, began to blend with his distant childhood memories.

He shook his head reflexively, as if to disentangle the past from the present, the memories from the realities, the stories from the truth. But they did not separate. He found himself thinking that it must be the heat.

The White Man's Government

In June 1862, Samuel S. Cox, a Democratic congressman from Ohio, explained his opposition to the receipt of diplomats from Hayti and Liberia; those representatives, Cox explained, would invariably be "negro ministers." Republican William B. Fessenden of Maine interrupted: "What objection," he asked, "can the gentleman have to such a representative?" Cox was incredulous. "Objection? Gracious Heavens! what innocency! Objection to receiving a black man on an equality with the white men of this country? Every objection which instinct, race, prejudice, and institutions make." Cox calmed himself enough to offer his Republican colleague a lesson in civics, one that Democrats would repeat many times in the coming years.

> I have been taught in the history of this country that these Common-wealths and this Union were made for white men; that this Govern-ment is a Government of white men; that the men who made it never intended, by anything they did, to place the black race upon an equality with the white. The reasons for these wise precautions I have not the time to discuss. They are climatic, ethnological, economical, and social. It may be, the gentlemen on the other side intend to carry out their schemes of emancipation to that extent that they will raise the blacks to an equality in every respect with the white men of this country. . . . Do you want to begin by giving national equality to the black republics? After having obtained the equality of black nations with white nations, do you not propose to carry the equality a little further, and so make individual, political and social equality?

The notion that ours is a "white man's government"—of the white man, by and for the white man—provided the cornerstone for opposition to Reconstruction. It was at the heart of nearly every theoretical objection and provided the rhetorical foundation for complaints about each specific measure.

In January 1865, Kentucky congressman Robert Mallory insisted that emancipation must be accompanied by a plan for colonization; opposition to the latter, Mallory insisted, simply reflected Republican desires to employ the freedmen as political pawns. "I have no doubt that that is their leading motive," Mallory insisted. "And in the name of God, is it not a motive for me, and every man who loves the institutions of his country, for every man who wants to see this a great free Government, controlled by the white men during all time, to oppose it?"

A year later, Republican senator William Stewart of Nevada joined the Democratic opposition to black suffrage in the District of Columbia. "I believe the Anglo-Saxon race can govern this country,"

Stewart professed. "I believe it because it has governed it. I believe it because it is the only race that has ever founded such institutions as ours. . . . I believe the white man can govern it without the aid of the negro; and I do not believe that it is necessary for the white man that the negro should vote." "If he ever does vote," Stewart concluded, "it will simply be as a boon to him. I think we can carry on the Government without him." Pennsylvania Democrat John L. Dawson concurred: "We have, then, to insist upon it that this Government was made for the white race. It is our mission to maintain it. Negro suffrage and equality are incompatible with that mission. We must make our own laws and shape our own destiny."

Democratic congressman Andrew J. Rogers of New Jersey was a member of the Joint Committee on Reconstruction, the "Committee of Fifteen." In May 1866, Rogers explained his opposition to the proposed Fourteenth Amendment: "Sir, I want it distinctly understood that the American people believe that this Government was made for white men and white women. They do not believe nor can you make them believe—the edict of God almighty is stamped against it—that there is social equality between the black race and the white." "I have no fault to find with the colored race," Rogers added. "I have not the slightest antipathy to them. I wish them well, and if I were in a State where they exist in large numbers I would vote to give them every right enjoyed by the white people, except the right of a negro man to marry a white woman and the right to vote."

The adoption of the amendment did not end the commitment to a "white man's government." House Democrat James Brooks of New York insisted that "we intend to carry on these reactionary proceedings to the legitimate end." "We don't intend," Brooks conceded,

> to deprive the negro of his liberty or of his civil rights. We do intend to allow them three-fifths representation in Congress in lieu of the three-fifths in the Constitution before it was amended, and we intend to give the negro in the South every right and privilege that the negro has in the North. But we do not intend to let the people of the North be brought into a negro copartnership and be ruled by rotten borough negro communities in the South. We do not intend to sacrifice our white man's government and make it a government of black men, South or North. We intend, in short, to undo all your radical, revolutionary proceedings here, not by force, but by the might and majesty of the people operating through the ballot-box.

In February 1870, Garrett Davis was leading the opposition to the seating of Mississippi senator-elect Hiram Rhoades Revels. Revels was "black"; therefore he was not, Davis insisted, an American citizen. In support of his proposition, Davis cited the Supreme Court's decision in *Dred Scott v. Sandford*, "one of the most learned, argumentative, powerful, and conclusive opinions that was ever written upon that bench." Thus fully two years after the ratification of the Fourteenth Amendment—which, in its opening sentence, explicitly overruled the *Dred Scott* decision—Davis was contending that citizenship of the United States extended only to the "white" race.

The assorted successes of congressional Reconstruction could not all be undone or overtly denied; maintaining the "white man's government" required some limited ingenuity. For the most part, advocates of the old order simply followed the intellectual traditions of the past four score and assorted years—each progressive step toward equality would be tempered by distinctions, disclaimers, and diversions.

The abolition of slavery, for example, was an indisputable fact: the Thirteenth Amendment was explicit on this score. But the end of slavery did not necessarily bring all the concomitants of freedom, or so the opponents of Reconstruction argued. Thus in December 1865, Delaware senator Willard Saulsbury maintained that Congress remained powerless to advance the civil rights of the freedmen. "Slavery is a *status*, a condition," he insisted. "Cannot that *status* or condition be abolished without attempting to confer on all former slaves all the civil or political rights that white people have? Certainly. Your 'appropriate legislation' is confined to the subject matter of your amendment, and extends to nothing else." Republican senator Edgar Cowan of Pennsylvania agreed, and opposed the civil rights bill on that basis. The Thirteenth Amendment, he conceded, "deprived the master of the right" to the proceeds of the slave's labor, "and conferred it upon the negro," but it did no more than that. This led to an interesting distinction: Congress possessed a limited authority to ensure that the freedmen were not returned to slavery, but there "can be no pretense in the world" that Congress had any authority "to legislate in regard to free negroes and mulattoes." Meanwhile, Senator Thomas A. Hendricks of Indiana found another distinction: slavery, he insisted, "is not a relation between the slave and the state; it is not a public relation. . . . It is purely and entirely a domestic relation." The Thirteenth Amendment, Hendricks conceded, "broke asunder this private relation between the master and his slave," but by that amendment no public or civil rights "are conferred upon the freed-man."

The adoption of the Civil Rights Act of 1866, and its subsequent constitutionalization as the Fourteenth Amendment, required some new mental gymnastics, ones that would protect the white man's government from the guarantee of the "equal protection of the law." Reconstruction's opponents were up to the task; they had, after all, some rather obvious precedent. In 1868 Democrat James A. Johnson of California noted that the Declaration of Independence proclaimed that "all men are created equal." But, of course, there was more here—or less—than meets the eye:

> This is the iteration of abstract political principles, applicable alone, governmentally, to those who made it and those who inherit their institutions. That all men are created equal in a general sense is not true, as every one knows. But it is equally as well known that all are equal before the law. Then, by a fair construction, this means that all men subject to the jurisprudence of the State shall receive protection according to his status as fixed by law, and shall receive it according to law. It was not intended to destroy distinctions in society. No change was made or contemplated in the fixed status of the inhabitants of the several States.

That "fixed status," of course, was divided along racial lines: "white men for white men's State governments made the Declaration of Independence," Johnson noted, and so even under that egalitarian charter, "the rights and liberties of the white men of this country are greater than can ever legally be accorded to the inferior races"—thus his objection to those Reconstruction measures that make "citizens not only of the pet negro but of the filthy Chinese."

One task, then, was to insist that the equality ensured by the Fourteenth Amendment was the same as the equality proclaimed by the great Declaration: it was merely an "abstract . . . principle": "legal," not "social"; formal, not real. They consistently referred to it as "perfect equality," and any departure from it was an unwarranted effort to confer "special" privileges on the "negro."

Back in 1864, Senator Waitman T. Willey, Republican from West Virginia, had protested Charles Sumner's efforts to prohibit discrimination in railcars. The effort, Willey insisted, was both unnecessary and unfair:

> The proposition before the committee was to consider whether it was necessary to make special provisions for colored persons in order to secure them equal privileges with other members of the community. The law is as open to a colored person as it is to a white person. So far as that matter is concerned, all members of the community stand, as I conceive it, upon a perfect equality. I do not suppose that it was the object of the honorable Senator from Massachusetts to make a distinction in favor of colored persons over white persons; but any special enactment in regard to their privileges on this road certainly would be a distinction against white passengers, while it would not enlarge under the law, in any respect whatever, the privileges and remedies of colored persons. What, then, is the necessity for any action on this subject on the part of the Senate or on the part of Congress?

Delaware's Saulsbury agreed, and he was certain that it was not "equality" that was at issue: "When these negroes go about sticking their heads into railroad cars, and among white people . . . I think an officer is perfectly right in telling them that they have no business there; because it is evident that the reason they do so is simply to gain notoriety, and to see if they cannot bring themselves into conflict with the officers of the railroad cars."

The "white man's government" was thus more than a historical fact, it was a natural mandate; there could be, then, no equality, unless the white race was to be reduced to the debased level of the black. The three-year debate over Sumner's last civil rights bill—eventually to become the ill-fated Civil Rights Act of 1875—is illustrative. In 1874 the bill was the object of assault by Delaware's Eli Saulsbury, older brother of the former senator; the bill, Eli Saulsbury complained, "proposes the degradation of the white men and white women of the country, and seeks to place them upon an equality socially and in every other respect with a race their inferiors by nature as well as by instinct and civilization."

It was an odd conception of "equality" that they professed, one that could neither disrupt their hypothesized natural order nor intrude into the ever shifting terrain of the "social" order. "Following the great law of association," Missouri's Francis P. Blair proclaimed in opposition to Sumner's bill, "I shall cling to my race in preference to any and all others; and never will submit to have it humiliated and degraded that I may possess the friendship of the negro or any other race, or that I may hold office by his suffrage and at his sufferance. 'Equality before the law' is my motto, but not 'equality before conscience,' nor 'forced social equality.'"

Kentucky congressman Henry D. McHenry championed a similar vision of equality, and opposed Sumner's civil rights bill as a consequence:

> The law can only prevent prejudice from interfering with the legal rights of others; but social prejudice is a social liberty that the law has no right to disturb. Whether it is a prejudice against the negro or a partiality for the whites, it is based upon a manifest and acknowledged superiority of class and race. I certainly have no sort of hostility to the negroes. I want them protected in all their just rights. But I do claim for my race a superiority over them in intelligence, morality, and in all the virtues of true manhood, and I can never consent to have it dragged down to their level; and it is in this view that I speak and protest against the great wrong and outrage this bill attempts against the white people.

They could hardly understand the necessity for the bill, especially the provisions calling for "mixed" schools. Georgia congressman Hiram P. Bell was sure that black Georgians were already well served by the separate schools:

> As to the right to participate in the benefits of our system of public education, they stand upon a footing of perfect equality in every respect with us; they have precisely the kind of schools that we have. . . . This bill does not give them a single right in reference to their education that they do not now possess and enjoy upon terms of perfect equality with us. Except that this bill seeks to coerce an unnatural alliance between the races, unpleasant to them and disgusting to us, in our social relationships; it cannot be disguised that the object of this measure is to enforce social equality between the races.

Even Lyman Trumbull, nearing the end of his eighteen-year career in the Senate, yielded to the formalistic worldview. Civil rights, he insisted, were already secured; the "social equality" bill was unauthorized and unnecessary. Ever the lawyer, Trumbull joined the Democratic opposition in asserting the almost unimaginable: "There is," Trumbull insisted, "perfect equality now."

There was, of course, no refuting such an abstract claim, for it rendered irrelevant even the most grotesque real-world disparities. Separated schools, threatened by the initial versions of the bill, found a similar refuge: in the abstract, they were not demonstrably unequal. "Will it be said the negro child has not the right to go to a white school?" asked North Carolina senator Augustus S. Merrimon. "Then I answer, the white child has no right to go to the negro school." "Like equal legal provisions must be made for each race," Merrimon explained, "and this is the equality of right and protection required by the Constitution."

Such logic permitted Virginia senator John W. Johnston to insist "that in the State of Virginia there is no discrimination at all; that precisely equal privileges are given to the colored people with those given to the white people." Educational inequalities, Johnston commented, are "only apparent, not real."

This logic also permitted the competing vision of equality to be pursued to its absurd conclusion. If "perfect equality" already obtained, then the "negro" would be satisfied only with "perfect social equality." As Kentucky congressman William B. Read explained, Sumner's bill was merely the first step: "the next step will be that they will demand a law allowing them, without restraint, to visit the parlors and drawing rooms of the whites, and have free and unrestrained social intercourse with your unmarried sons and daughters."

One consistent character of this formal conception of equality was its demand for symmetry: any measure that, in motive or effect, targeted the condition of the black race was certain to be condemned as unfair to the white. In 1864 Willard Saulsbury denounced a Sumner bill that prohibited racial discrimination in the District of Columbia's streetcars: "Poor, helpless, and despised inferior race of white men, you have very little interest in this Government; you are not worth consideration in the legislation of the country; but let your superior, Sambo's interests come in question, and you will find the most tender solicitude in his behalf." "What a pity it is," Saulsbury concluded, "that there is not somebody to lampblack white men so that their rights could be secured."

Within a year of Appomattox, former slaves and virtual slaves were already being denounced as the "special favorites" of Republican law.

In early 1866 Democratic congressman John Hogan of Missouri protested against the Freedmen's Bureau: "white soldiers, disabled in the service of the Union, unable to find work, are left to beg upon the streets. What a fault for them to have been born white! Had they been colored, Government would have had an agent to look after them." Garrett Davis made the argument in more personal terms, in opposition to a bill outlawing debt peonage: "I have owed considerable debts and I have worked mighty hard to pay them. All the proceeds of my labor went to the payment of my debts, and I had not the advantage which the peon has; the creditor was not supporting me during the time I was laboring to discharge my debts."

Andrew Johnson sounded the same theme in his message to Congress of March 27, 1866, explaining his veto of the first civil rights bill. The bill establishes, Johnson complained,

> for the security of the colored race, safeguards which go infinitely beyond any that the General Government has ever provided for the white race. In fact, the distinction of race and color is, by the bill, made to operate in favor of the colored and against the white race. . . . The tendency of the bill must be to resuscitate the spirit of rebellion, and to arrest the progress of those influences which are more closely drawing around the States the bonds of union and peace.

Of course, in the zero-sum game that was the struggle for racial dominance, every effort to assist the freedmen was bound to hurt the white man. In 1869 Wisconsin Democrat Charles A. Eldridge explained his opposition to the Fifteenth Amendment as follows:

> It is at the demand of party and in its interest alone that power is sought to be taken from the intelligent and cultivated white man and given to the ignorant, uneducated, and servile negro. It is the inexorable demand of party that is bringing the white and black races in this country in fatal antagonism and conflict, which must end in the utter extermination of the weaker race or in the degradation of the other.

And they were willing to do their part to make certain that the effort to assist the black race did in fact inure to the detriment of the white. Eli Saulsbury was one of many who opposed the desegregation of public or "common" schools, even if it meant an end to public education: "For one, I should regard it as a far less evil to see the common schools in my State abandoned than to see them converted into mixed schools for white and colored children."

Ironically, or perhaps fittingly, "perfect equality" for the white man or white woman occasionally required some obvious inequities. Garrett Davis insisted of black Kentuckians that, "[w]ith a few exceptions, they have all the civil rights that any white man has." Davis explained:

> They are subject to some severer penalties: for instance, rape committed by a white man is punishable by confinement in the penitentiary; when perpetrated by a negro upon a white woman, it is punishable by death, and it will be so punishable until the last trump blows. All the legislation that may be devised by Congress, and all the oppressive and unjust discriminations sought to be introduced against the white man, and to stifle the reserved rights of the States, to overthrow their governments and their independence of legislation—all these measures will never drive the State of Kentucky from a modification of that law.

As this diatribe suggests, the argument on behalf of the white man and the white man's government typically went hand-in-hand with another claim, one on behalf of the sovereignty of the state. At the state level of government, after all, the white man's dominion was generally secure. But federal power, once actively enlisted to support the interests of the slave states, was now decidedly a threat. The expansive conception of federal authority that justified the fugitive slave laws thus underwent a quite magical transformation: grants of federal power were to be strictly construed, strictly limited, and, when literal interpretations were inconvenient, strictly ignored.

Samuel Cox opposed the Thirteenth Amendment because it threatened the integrity of the state governments—the white state governments. "Is your proposition," he asked of Thaddeus Stevens,

> simply to abolish slavery? Or is it a measure to invest the Federal Government with authority to enslave the local white citizen, hold him in vassalage to a central power, and assume the right to dictate to the States what their home policy shall be on home affairs? In fine, is it not an abstract scheme to enfranchise the black, who is really being freed by war, by a total change in the very genius, soul, and body of our Government?

Cox called on Stevens to "[g]ive up his doctrine of negro equality," and "[g]ive up his idea of breaking down State institutions by Federal law." "I ask the gentleman," Cox pleaded, "to give up his idea of the equality of the black and white races before the law." Stevens's reply was brief: "I won't do it."

State sovereignty was invoked in opposition to each act of Reconstruction. Willard Saulsbury insisted that under the original civil rights bill, the states would be "invaded and defrauded of the right of determining who shall hold property"; the bill, he contended, "positively deprives the State of its police power of government." Garrett Davis was convinced the bill would void Kentucky's anti-miscegenation and discriminatory rape laws, an unthinkable result under the federal constitutional scheme. "The result," he maintained, "would be to utterly subvert our Government; it would be wholly incompatible with its principles, with its provisions, or with its spirits. . . . It would produce a perfect and despotic central consolidated Government. All the State governments and State constitutions would be brought in ruins prostrate to the feet of the oligarchy of Congress."

Indiana Democrat Michael C. Kerr derided the "inherent viciousness" of the civil rights bill: "It takes," he claimed, "a long and fearful step toward the complete obliteration of State authority and the reserved and original rights of the States." Andrew Rogers concurred: "it cannot be pretended . . . that there is any authority in the Congress of the United States to enter the domain of a State and interfere with its internal police, statutes, and domestic regulations." The bill, he concluded, is "odious": it will "destroy the foundations of the Government as they were laid and established by our fathers."

Rogers lodged the same complaint against the initial iteration of the Fourteenth Amendment: "This is but another attempt to consolidate the powers of the States in the Federal Government. It is another step to an imperial despotism." His substantive concerns were not unlike Davis's: "under this amendment a negro might be allowed to marry a white woman." Equally disastrous, "Congress would have power to compel the State to provide for white children and black children to attend the same school, upon the principle that all people in the several states shall have equal protection in all the rights of life, liberty, and property, and all the privileges and immunities of citizens in the several states." Davis joined the assault: "the distinguishing feature in our Government is this: the Federal Government has its peculiar and

restrictive duties. It is a Government of limited power and authority."
The proposed amendment, he warned, "is a grant for original
legislation in Congress . . . Congress may arrogate those powers of
legislation which are the peculiar muniments of State organizations."

The proposal was redrafted, but Rogers found the same defect in the
reiteration: the amendment "saps the foundation of the Government;
destroys the elementary principles of the States; it consolidates
everything into one imperial despotism." Democrat Samuel J. Randall
of Pennsylvania concurred: the revised amendment "proposes to make
an equality between the two races, notwithstanding the policy of
discrimination which has heretofore been exclusively exercised by the
States, which in my judgment should remain and continue."

The division of governmental authority was at the root of another
nascent distinction, one eventually to predominate in constitutional
law and theory. The proposed Enforcement Act of 1871 was known
also as the Ku Klux Klan Act, for it largely targeted the oppressive
activities of that organization. But the federal bill, Indiana congressman Michael Kerr complained, criminalized activities that were done
not "under color of state law," but merely by "private" individuals;
thus "jurisdiction is snatched from the State, and the work of
centralization or anarchy goes on." Illinois congressman Jesse H.
Moore was among the Republicans who concurred: "If Congress has
the power thus to prescribe a criminal code for the punishment and
redress of private wrongs in the several States, it does seem to me that
the whole machinery of State government is superseded, that there is
no power reserved to the several States, and that there is an end of the
division of powers between the General and State governments."

Sumner's public accommodations bill, its opponents insisted, went
farther still. It was, Delaware's Thomas F. Bayard claimed, "the
quickest and longest stride toward centralized power which has been
presented to our people." Kentucky congressman Milton J. Durham
insisted that the bill "interferes with State-rights and State sovereignty."
"Social relations," after all, were a matter of "local legislation or of
private contract,"—and, importantly, "local" legislatures knew when
not to interfere:

> when you undertake to legislate as to the civil and social relations of the
> races, then you will have aroused and embittered the feelings of the
> Anglo-Saxon race to such an extent that it will be hard to control them.

The poorest and humblest white person in my district feels and knows that he or she belongs to a superior race morally and intellectually, and nothing is so revolting to them as social equality with this inferior race.

By the end of Reconstruction, another defense of the old order was reemerging. Emancipation had long been challenged as an affront to property; now, so too was antidiscrimination. Sumner's "social equality bill," it evolved, abridged not merely the individual right to choose one's social relations, but also the right to control one's property. Congressman John A. Smith represented the Old Dominion: as he explained, his right to discriminate was a natural property right; even state law—and ipso facto federal—was powerless against it. "[W]here is the boasted right of property," he asked,

> what becomes of its sanctity, if any human power, even that of my own State, can prescribe to me whom I shall admit to my hotel and whom I shall exclude? . . . Sir, I hold that the right of property is so sacred that the Legislature of my State itself cannot dare to say to me, though one of her citizens, that I shall not decide for myself whom I shall admit to and whom I shall exclude from *my* hotel. . . . And so, sir, of my stage-coach, my steamboat, my theater—they are *my* property. (Emphasis in original)

The essence of each complaint, in sum, was that it represented a radical departure from some immutable principle of government. Natural rights in property, the inexorable division of federal and state powers, and an immutable social and natural order all kept intact the white man's government. All were deeply rooted in the national tradition, and all, in spite of Reconstruction, remained permanently enshrined in the constitutional scheme. "I believe," said West Virginia senator Peter G. Van Winkle, "the constitution of society was given to man by the Creator at the time it was instituted, and that whatever conditions were imposed at that time are those to which men should endeavor to live up." New York congressman Robert S. Hale thus complained that the Fourteenth Amendment "is an utter departure from every principle ever dreamed of by the men who framed our Constitution," while Delaware senator Thomas F. Bayard lamented that "the founders of this Government would have shuddered at such propositions as we now see." When John B. Henderson of Missouri proposed the Fifteenth Amendment, Delaware's elder Saulsbury sarcastically raised a point of order: "It is that it is not in order now to attempt to amend the Constitution, that instrument having been blotted out of existence long ago."

Maryland Democratic senator George Vickers explained his party's opposition to the Fifteenth Amendment this way:

> [it] is said that the Democratic party is not a progressive party . . . the Democratic party is not a progressive party because the Constitution is not progressive; the principles of the Constitution are now just as they were when they came from the hands of our fathers; they are plain, explicit, and well defined; and a party which stands upon the Constitution cannot, in relation to constitutional questions, be a progressive party.

Not everyone was interested in preserving the "white man's government." Some, in fact, were certain that there was no such thing. In 1866 Republican senator Daniel Clark of New Hampshire explained his support for black suffrage:

> Mr. President, I am not one of those who believe or assent to the declaration that this is the Government of the white man, and then offer it as an excuse for neglecting or ostracizing the black man; but I hold it to be the government of all men, and for all men and all classes of men. It is its crowning glory that no citizen or person living under it is so high or so powerful that he can refuse or deny its obligation; and none so low that its protection cannot reach him. Its great strength is in its universality of its principles, and its chief danger in attempts to narrow, contract, crib, and confine their application.

In the House, John H. Broomall of Pennsylvania explained that the "white man's government" was a Democratic myth of recent vintage:

> [M]odern Democratic political science discovered and promulgated the dogma that this is the country of the white man, and that no other man has rights here which the white man is bound to respect. When, therefore, this peculiar science culminated in an attempt to overthrow the Government, and was itself overthrown, it is as well that a return to the principles of the founders of the Government should be made manifest to future generations by a declaration upon the statute-books.

Broomall had one final challenge: "Let those who say with the air of such omnipotent authority that this is the country of the white man, explain how it happened that the Ruler of the universe suffered it to be occupied by the red man for countless ages of the past." "No, our country is the country of its inhabitants," Broomall concluded. "Our Government the Government of the governed."

That the Democrats should seek to vindicate their white man's government through continued reliance on the Supreme Court's decision in *Dred Scott*—"that masterpiece of elaborate inhumanity"—left Charles Sumner incredulous: the decision had been wrong when it was first announced, and it had been undone by constitutional Reconstruction. "Is this a white man's Government," Sumner asked, "or is it a Government of 'all men,' as declared by our fathers? Is it a Republic of equal laws, or an oligarchy of the skin?" Sumner was sure that the Fourteenth Amendment offered the conclusive response. Senator Lot M. Morrill of Maine insisted that "this idea of race in the Government of the United States is an absurdity. There is no such thing. Is there any race or color in the Declaration of Independence? Is there any race or color in the Constitution of the United States?" Jacob Benton of New Hampshire demanded, "Away with that dogma—a white man's government; it was born of slavery, let it be entombed with it. As a principle it is narrow, illiberal, anti-republican, unconstitutional, and all unworthy of a liberal and progressive age, in the high noon of the nineteenth century."

And it was, Republicans insisted, a progressive age. If the original construction of the nation had permitted the myth of the white man's government, then a reconstruction was clearly in order. Frederick E. Woodbridge of Vermont supported the Fourteenth Amendment to the Constitution:

> I have the highest opinion of that great charter which was founded by our fathers. But, sir, the age is an age of progress. The conditions of society are different from what the fathers anticipated; and I fully believe that if we meet the obligations which we owe to the country, we must pass an amendment of this or a similar character.

Hiram Price of Iowa also supported the amendment and was growing weary of the appeals to the sacred intent of the "founding fathers." "[G]entlemen rise here and talk about the Constitution of our fathers,"

Price commented, "and I have heard them talk about it here until if I had been a believer in ghosts I would have supposed that our fathers who have been invoked so loudly would have come from the grave to see what was wanted of them." The "fathers," Price observed, may well have thought their charter sufficient to protect the rights of all citizens. "But experience, though it may be a dear school, is one of the best that any man, whether he be foolish or wise, was ever taught in, and the experience of the last quarter of a century ought to have satisfied any gentlemen that the Constitution has not afforded that protection." "I am not one of those," Price concluded, "who believe that we are not to learn anything as we pass through this world."

John Bingham insisted in support of his proposed Fourteenth Amendment that the generation that abolished slavery should not itself be slaves to the past. "I believe," he said, "that the people of the United States have intrusted to the present Congress in some sense the care of the Republic, not only for the present, but for all the hereafter."

If they were willing in some sense to reject the heritage of the founders, it was only because they were certain that they were realizing the nobler aspects of that same heritage. In January 1866 Bingham had insisted that "[t]he spirit, the intent, the purpose of our Constitution is to secure equal and exact justice to all men"; the Fourteenth Amendment merely made this explicit. George F. Miller of Pennsylvania contended of the guarantees contained in the first section of the Fourteenth Amendment that "it is so just, that no State shall deprive life, liberty, or property without due process of law, nor deny the equal protection of the laws, and so clearly within the spirit of the Declaration of Independence of July 4, 1776, that no member of this House can seriously object to it." Luke P. Poland of Vermont insisted that the same guarantees were "essentially declared in the Declaration of Independence and in all the provisions of the Constitution." William Higby of California maintained that the Fourteenth Amendment "will only have the effect of giving vitality and life to portions of the Constitution that probably were intended from the beginning to have life and vitality, but which have received such a construction that they have been entirely ignored and have become as dead matter in that instrument."

As Higby suggested, the framers of Reconstruction were determined to at long last resolve the "constitutional contradiction." Principle this time would not yield to slavery; slavery—and its incidents—would yield to principle. William Windom of Minnesota stood in support of the civil rights bill of 1866. "A true republic," he maintained, "rests upon the absolute equality of rights of the whole people, high and low, rich and poor, white and black. Upon this, the only foundation which can permanently endure, we professed to build our Republic; but at the same time we not only denied to a large portion of the people equality of rights, but we robbed them of every right known to human nature." The civil rights bill, Windom contended, was one of the first efforts "to grasp as a vital reality and embody in the forms of law the great truth that all men are created equal." "Sir, our duty is clear," he concluded; "let no man falter in its performance."

Thaddeus Stevens introduced the Fourteenth Amendment for debate in the House on May 8, 1866. The Joint Committee, he noted, "expected to suggest a plan for rebuilding a shattered nation." It necessitated a genuine reconstruction:

> It cannot be denied that this terrible struggle sprang from the vicious principles incorporated into the institutions of our country. Our fathers had been compelled to postpone the principles of their great Declaration, and wait for their full establishment till a more propitious time. That time ought to be present now. But the public mind has been educated in error for a century. How difficult in a day to unlearn it. In rebuilding, it is necessary to clear away the rotten and defective portions of the old foundations, and to sink deep and found the repaired edifice upon the firm foundation of eternal justice.

They were not dissuaded in their efforts by the too-convenient complaints about federal power. Where were those complaints, they asked, when Congress was passing fugitive slave laws? "States' rights," a "central despotism"—it was all mere verbiage. As Lyman Trumbull responded to Garrett Davis, "The Senator chooses to regard everything to be outside the power of Congress by denouncing it as such."

They insisted as well that the conception of federal power that inhered in the public-private distinction was simply outdated. Opposing Reconstruction's last civil rights bill in 1871, Congressman Kerr of Indiana had denied Congress's power to regulate "private" individuals; that, he had insisted, was the exclusive province of the states. "My honorable friend," Bingham responded, "discussed this question, upon the Constitution as it was and not upon the Constitution as it is." "The powers of the States have been limited by the last three amendments to the Constitution, and the powers of Congress extended by the last three amendments to the Constitution." Among Congress's powers, Bingham insisted, was "a power to protect the rights of citizens against States, and individuals in States, never before granted."

They disputed all the various fictions. It would no longer suffice, they insisted, merely to declare equality, they needed to *realize* it. Initially, this meant a refusal to accept the Democratic proposition that slavery had ended with its formal abolition. Practically, they noted, slavery endured. The "Report on the Condition of the South," submitted to Congress by Major General Carl Schurz on December 19, 1865, documented the persistence of the old order and the need for congressional action. "[W]hile accepting the 'abolition of slavery,'" the report concluded, the old masters "think that some species of serfdom, peonage, or some other form of compulsory labor is not slavery, and may be introduced without a violation of their pledge." "There are a hundred ways of framing apprenticeship, vagrancy, or contract laws, which will serve the purpose," the report continued. "Even the mere reorganization of the militia upon the old footing will go far towards accomplishing the object."

Massachusetts senator Henry Wilson observed that "the law of Mississippi makes every one of these men whom we have made free practically a slave, and he is in a worse condition today than he was when he was a slave, because his master had some interest in protecting and caring for him." Ignatius Donnelly of Minnesota reviewed the "black codes" of Alabama, Mississippi, South Carolina, Tennessee, and Virginia, and concluded that "this means simply the reestablishment of slavery." The Democrats argued that under the Constitution, Congress could do no more than proclaim slavery's demise, merely terminate the "status" of slavery. Lyman Trumbull, Chair of the Judiciary Committee, saw it differently; if the Democratic construction was correct,

> and we have merely taken from the master the power to control the slave and left him at the mercy of the State to be deprived of his civil rights, the trumpet of freedom that we have been blowing throughout the land has given an "uncertain sound," and the promised freedom is a delusion. Such was not the intention of Congress, which proposed the constitutional amendment, nor is such the fair meaning of the

amendment itself. With the destruction of slavery necessarily follows the destruction of the incidents to slavery. When slavery was abolished, slave codes in its support were abolished also.

"Those laws," Trumbull explained, "that prevented the colored man going from home, that did not allow him to buy or sell, or to make contracts; that did not allow him to own property; that did not allow him to enforce rights; that did not allow him to be educated, were all badges of servitude made in the interest of slavery and as a part of slavery." "They never would have been thought of or enacted anywhere but for slavery," he concluded, "and when slavery falls they fall also."

So the Republicans offered the first civil rights bill. Pennsylvania's Martin R. Thayer explained that the bill "is intended only to carry into practical effect the amendment of the Constitution. Its object is to declare not only that slavery shall be abolished upon the pages of our Constitution, but that it shall be abolished in fact and in deed." The bill simply had to be authorized by the amendment ending slavery; "[t]o put any other construction upon this great amendment of the Constitution is to deprive it of its vital force, of its effective value. It is to cheat the world by sounding phrases; and while you pretend to give liberty to those who were in bondage, to leave them in reality in a condition of modified slavery."

The Fourteenth Amendment secured the promise. On January 9, 1866, Bingham had announced,

> I propose, with the help of this Congress and of the American people, that hereafter there shall not be any disregard of that essential guarantee of your Constitution in any State of the Union. And how? By simply adding an amendment to the Constitution to operate on all the States of this Union alike, giving to Congress the power to pass all laws necessary and proper to secure to all persons—which includes every citizen of every State—their equal personal rights.

William P. Fessenden, Senate chair of the Committee of Fifteen, was in ill health on May 23, so it was Jacob M. Howard of Michigan who addressed the Senate. The members of the committee, Howard informed the Senate, "have instituted an inquiry, so far as it was practicable for them to do so, into the political and social condition of the South."   "One result of their investigations" was the proposed Fourteenth Amendment.

As Howard suggested, the amendment was moved by practical concerns, by the very real conditions of "political and social" life that obtained in the South. Its advocates, accordingly, championed a very practical conception of equality, one designed to meet the real needs of the freedmen, one that could not be cabined by the neat rhetorical distinctions offered by Reconstruction's opponents.

It manifestly did not distinguish between "private" and "public" life, if only because the inequalities forced on black Americans did not respect the distinction. Schurz's report observed that "'[a] spirit of bitterness and persecution manifests itself towards the negroes. They are shot and abused outside the immediate protection of our forces *by men who announce their determination to take the law into their own hands, in defiance of our authority*'" (emphasis in original). Planters, the report noted, were enforcing sharecropping contracts that required virtual "peonage"; law, custom, and practice blended to prevent the freedmen from buying or renting property or residing in the community unless employed by a white person; one Louisiana law provided that "it shall be the duty of every *citizen* to act as a police officer for the detection of offenses and the apprehension of offenders" (emphasis in original). The House Committee on Freedmen's Affairs "Report No. 30 on Bureau of Freedmen and Refugees" documented the scope and intensity of white hostility—the threats, violence, and murders. Local sheriffs were routinely among the conspirators; judges and justices of the peace were largely indifferent. It noted ominously the reports "of a secret organization named the 'Ku-klux Klan,' the object of which is believed by the negroes to be their extermination or expulsion."

So much of the "private" oppression of the freedmen was done with the acquiescence or assistance of "public" authority that the distinction was in reality meaningless. It did not matter, the Republicans insisted, whether the state perpetrated the harm on its own or tolerated harm done by others: its duty was to afford "equal protection."   As Massachusetts congressman George F. Hoar observed, "it is an effective denial of the equal protection of the laws when [officers of the state] refuse to extend that protection."

"It is said," observed Kansas congressman David P. Lowe, "that the States are not doing the objectionable acts. This argument is more specious than real. Constitutions and laws are made for practical operation and effect." In practice, Lowe observed, the states had denied equal protection by permitting the harms against the freedmen; such wrongs simply had to be within the meaning of the equal protection guarantee. "What practical security would this provision give if it could do no more than to abrogate and nullify the overt acts and legislations of a State?" After all, as Senator Oliver H. P. T. Morton observed, "[a] criminal law cannot be made against a State. A State cannot be indicted and punished as such. The legislation which Congress is authorized to enact must operate, if at all, upon individuals."

New Jersey senator Frederick T. Frelinghuysen explained that "A state denies equal protection where it fails to give it. Denying includes inaction as well as action. A State denies protection as effectively by not executing as by not making laws." Indiana senator Daniel D. Pratt concurred: "when the equal protection is withheld, when it is not afforded, it is denied." Indiana congressman John Coburn insisted that "The failure to afford protection equally to all is a denial of it." And Henry Wilson insisted that "whether that failure is the result of inaction or inability on the part of one or the other of the coördinate branches of the State government, the remedy lies with Congress."

They also refused to accept the bizarre logic by which the remedy for inequality could somehow be an inequity in its own right. The effort to realize equality, they insisted, meant neither that the black race was to be the "special favorite" nor that the white race was to be degraded. Henry Wilson explained the concept of equality behind the Freedmen's Bureau bill: "the poorest man, be he black or white . . . is as much entitled to the protection of the law as the richest . . . is as much entitled to have [his wife] protected by equal law as is the rich man . . . the poor man's cabin . . . is entitled to the protection of the same law that protects the palace." "[W]e have advocated the rights of the black man," Wilson explained, "because the black man was the oppressed type of the toiling men of this country." But, he continued, "[t]he same influences that go to keep down and crush down the rights of the poor black man bear down and oppress the poor white laboring man." Responding to Edgar Cowan of Pennsylvania, Wilson continued:

The Senator tells us that if all men were equal and all men were learned, we could not get our boots blacked. I believe Henry Clay uttered that folly upon one occasion, and I am not surprised that the Senator should repeat it. It has been the language of the negro drivers in this country for sixty years—of the men who had just as much contempt for the toiling white millions of the country as they had for their own black slaves.

In similar fashion, the Republican Congress rejected Andrew Johnson's veto of the civil rights bill. Trumbull questioned whether it was true, as Johnson had claimed, that the bill "discriminate[s] in favor of the colored person." "Why, sir," he exclaimed,

the very object and effect of the section is to prevent discrimination, and language, it seems to me, could not more plainly express that object and effect. It may be said that it is for the benefit of the black man because he is in some instances discriminated against by State laws; but that is the case with all remedial statutes. They are for the relief of the persons who need the relief, not for the relief of those who have the right already; and when those needing the relief obtain it, they stand upon the precise footing of those who do not need the benefit of the law.

Then there was the inevitable complaint about the inevitably vague "social equality." "The bugbear of 'social equality,'" observed South Carolina congressman Alonzo Ransier, "is used by the enemies of political and civil equality for the colored man in place of argument." Even some Republicans had criticized the public accommodations bill as a "social equality" bill. Charles Sumner responded that "This is no question of society; no question of social life; no question of social equality, if anyone knows what this means. The object is simply Equality before the law."

There was, in truth, a certain hypocrisy to the complaints about "social equality," as there was with its predictable corollaries, "amalgamation" and "miscegenation." Black Americans, after all, had never evidenced any great desire to enter the "drawing rooms" of white Americans; their desperate desire, on the contrary, had always been to keep their white oppressors out. Black legislators helped make this clear. Congressman Richard H. Cain of South Carolina had been among the leading figures at the 1864 National Convention of Colored

Citizens; a decade later, he assumed the House floor to explain to a Democratic colleague why black Americans were perfectly willing to forgo "social equality":

> The gentleman harps upon the idea of social equality. Well, sir, he has not had so much experience of that as I have had, or as my race have had. We have some objections to social equality ourselves, very grave ones. For even now, though freedom has come, it is a hard matter, a very hard matter, to keep safely guarded the precincts of our sacred homes. But I will not dwell upon that. The gentleman knows more about that than I do.

Mississippi congressman John Roy Lynch concurred: "it is not social rights that we desire. We have enough of that already."

Finally, the advocates of Reconstruction refused to be deceived by the beguiling promise of "separate but equal." Nearly eighty years before *Brown v. Board of Education*, Lynch rose in support of Sumner's comprehensive public accommodations bill. The congressman, held in slavery at the time of the great emancipation, explained why "mixed" schools were needed, why separate schools were, in truth, not equal:

> The colored people in asking the passage of this bill just as it passed in the Senate do not thereby admit that their children can be better educated in white schools than in colored schools; nor that white teachers because they are white are better qualified to teach than colored ones. But they recognize the fact that the distinction when made and tolerated by law is an unjust and odious proscription; that you make their color a ground of objection, and consequently a crime. This is what we most earnestly protest against.

Above all, the framers of Reconstruction recognized the dangers that inhered in subservience to ideology or abstraction. As Henry Wilson put it, "In the present condition of the nation we must aim at practical results, not to establish political theories, however beautiful and alluring they may be." Too often, after all, the abstraction was merely a guise; as Pennsylvania congressman Martin R. Thayer noted of New Jersey's Andrew Rogers: "He is for the protection of these men, but he is against every earthly mode that can be devised for protecting them." Equally often, the legalisms obscured the more fundamental truths. Senator Richard Yates of Illinois, himself a lawyer, observed that "the people do not understand that argument which says that Congress may confer upon a man his civil rights and not his political rights. It is the pleading of a lawyer; it is too narrow for statesmanship."

They were after something more, something that transcended ideology, that could not be contained by formalism, that could not be realized through any single canon of construction. William Lawrence of Ohio was also a lawyer: "if we shall give to the Constitution that interpretation which its language requires," he offered, "which is approved of justice, humanity, and God, then we may hope that the men of today and of all time will enjoy its benefits and blessings forever."

They were after something real. Because the end of the old "natural order" promised a better one. "Peace," Henry Wilson said, "can only come in all its power and beauty by the complete triumph of equality and justice."

Legal Fiction

The final Civil Rights Act of the first Reconstruction, Charles Sumner's public accommodations bill, was passed in 1875; eight years later the Supreme Court declared it unconstitutional. The arguments Justice Bradley used to discredit the law were largely those the Democrats had marshaled unsuccessfully against it: the Thirteenth Amendment prohibited slavery, not racial discrimination; the Fourteenth Amendment prohibited state action, not private acts of discrimination; Congress could remedy the wrongful acts of the states, not invade their domain to compensate for their inaction. Black Americans, Bradley insisted, must cease to be "the special favorites of the law." All the claims that the Reconstructors had struggled against—triumphant here in the end.[4]

Sumner was not alive to protest; he had died in the spring of 1874, pleading from his deathbed on behalf of his bill. Henry Wilson was gone too; serving as Grant's vice-president, Wilson had died in the Capitol Building in November 1875. Thaddeus Stevens, perhaps the most radical of Republicans, had died in the summer of 1868; William Fessenden, chair of the Joint Committee on Reconstruction, died in the summer of the following year. Reconstruction, for that matter, was dead too. The Compromise of 1877 killed it; the Supreme Court's decision in the *Civil Rights Cases* was just an epitaph.[5]

The first Redemption was a near total victory for the old order, and it was very nearly a lasting one. Not till halfway through the next century would the nation try again. This time, the Supreme Court helped lead the way. The second Reconstruction desegregated the schools and outlawed racial discrimination not only by governmental actors, but also in public accommodations, housing, and employment. The contrary voices sounded familiar themes: "states' rights," "private rights," "no social equality." Folks didn't much argue on behalf of the "white man's government"; they talked instead of "tradition" and "order." But we knew what they meant.

The second Reconstruction lasted about as long as the first. Within a generation, the contrary voices were carrying the day. Desegregation, it was said, compromised local autonomy: "neighborhood schools" easily triumphed over "forced busing," and desegregation ground to a halt. Racial minorities, it was said, were once again the "special favorites of the law": "color blindness" was an easy winner over "reverse discrimination," and affirmative action fell into disrepute. By the time the second Redemption was complete, writers were proclaiming the "end of racism," and the Supreme Court seemed eager to agree.

There was no denying, of course, that we were still far from equal. Some writers explained that it was only natural: the "bell curve" of intelligence was merely reflected in a "bell curve" of social success. Racial disparities in the latter, alas, reflected principally the racial disparities in the former. Even the corruption of the "white man's government" would not deny the superior race its due: wrongheaded egalitarianism was helpless against the "natural order." Again, the Supreme Court seemed to agree. "Government," one of its members confidently proclaimed, "cannot make us equal."[6]

But he misspoke, just slightly. It is not so much that government *can* not make us equal: almost certainly it can—it made us, after all, *unequal* in the first place. It is rather that government *may* not make us equal—may not, because the law won't let it.

This is the sad truth of American constitutional law in its current iteration: not only does it not require equality, it does not even permit the effort to attain it. The Supreme Court simply won't allow it. It frustrates the effort with a familiar array of distinctions, disclaimers, and diversions—the same legalisms that have sustained the "natural order" through each attempt at Reconstruction. It is law at its worst, divorced from reality, divorced from its moral foundation. Law as rhetorical device: legal fictions. Here, briefly, are just a few.

Federalism and Separated Powers

At some point in nearly every modern "race" case, the Supreme Court is likely to advise that the complaints of racial inequity are either: better addressed to the political branches; matters of state or local concern, or maybe matters of federal concern, but certainly not the business of whichever government has foolishly addressed the racial issue in the immediate case; or best left to the discretion of whichever public official has exercised it in a racially discriminatory matter. Thus the opinions include paeans to local school board authority, to state legislative processes, to prosecutorial discretion, and, when convenient, to congressional expertise—in short, to the unique competence of every public institution in America except the federal courts.[7]

The problem here is not so much conceptual. Of course, the judiciary is not omnipotent: it must accord due deference to the political branches and political processes. It is equally true that the federal government does not have unlimited powers: those not delegated to it by the Constitution remain the reserve of the states. The difficulty is with the utterly arbitrary—and at times simply perverse—deployment of these concepts to frustrate the effort to realize equality.

Consider, first, the role of the courts. It is fairly well settled that in the ordinary course of events, the political branches, state or federal, are entitled to considerable deference when the judiciary reviews the constitutionality of their actions. Typically, this takes the form of a presumption that the acts are constitutional and a modest requirement that the political actor provide a *de minimis* explanation for its actions, that it explains, for example, why an act of discrimination seemed a "reasonable" way to achieve some "legitimate" end. As the Supreme Court's decisions generally suggest, this showing is easily made: almost any logical nexus between the act of discrimination and some plausible purpose will suffice to justify the act.

It is equally well settled that somewhat different rules should obtain when a case implicates the unique functions of the judiciary in a constitutional democracy. The Constitution, after all, explicitly places some rights beyond the reach of the political process: thus a lesser presumption of constitutionality obtains when "fundamental rights" are implicated, and a more compelling justification must be offered when the state attempts to deprive them. Similarly, acts that discriminate against certain minority groups are suspect: groups that historically and in contemporary life are vulnerable to invidious discrimination may often need the special solicitude of the courts to protect them from the majoritarian processes. Accordingly, discrimination against these minority groups also requires a compelling justification.[8]

It rings a little hollow, then, when the Supreme Court responds to complaints from politically vulnerable groups, especially long-suffering racial minorities, that their grievances are best addressed to the political processes. Justice Thurgood Marshall dissented from the Supreme Court's decision to defer to a Texas school financing scheme that disadvantaged the schoolchildren—disproportionately racial and ethnic minorities—in relatively poor districts. The need for reform is apparent, Justice Powell had written for the Court, but "the ultimate solutions must come from the lawmakers and from the democratic pressures of those who elect them." But as Marshall explained, "The disability of the disadvantaged class in this case extends as well into the political processes. . . . [L]egislative reallocation of the State's property wealth must be sought in the face of inevitable opposition from significantly advantaged districts that have a strong vested interest in the preservation of the status quo." "The Court's suggestions of legislative redress and experimentation will doubtless be of great comfort to the schoolchildren of Texas' disadvantaged districts," Marshall concluded. "The possibility of legislative action is, in all events, no answer to this Court's duty under the Constitution to eliminate unjustified discrimination."[9]

The Court's response to "affirmative action" provides an illustrative contrast. No deference at all was granted the Richmond City Council when it acted to benefit minority contractors; and now, after the Court's most recent decision on the matter, no deference is due Congress when it acts to benefit racial minorities. It is fair to ask precisely what vision of constitutional democracy compels the Court to view with heightened suspicion majoritarian actions designed to redress the grievances of minorities. Stated in other words, why do white contractors need or deserve greater judicial protection than, for example, the children of Texas's poor school districts?

The concept of federalism evinced in the Court's decisions—in paeans to "local control," "state authority," and the like—is, if anything, even more incoherent. The original Constitution, of course, did construct a central government of limited powers. But it is important to recall that the Philadelphia convention was called precisely because the initial Confederation had left too much power in the states. Thus Madison warned at the Philadelphia convention that the Constitution must explicate the supreme power of the federal government as a check on the "centrifugal tendency of the States; which, without it, will continually fly out of their proper orbits and destroy the order & harmony of the political system."[10]

Madison, of course, abandoned his "high nationalism" shortly after the convention, but the work was already done. The Supreme Court, under John Marshall's stewardship, rejected the lingering claims of "states' rights" and "state sovereignty": the Constitution, Marshall noted, was ratified by conventions of the people, not by the states. That did not exactly end matters: in 1832, to cite the most famous example, the federal tariff prompted John Calhoun to argue quite unsuccessfully for South Carolina's power of nullification; but ten years later, when Justice Story sustained the constitutionality and supremacy of the federal Fugitive Slave Acts, there were very few complaints from the slave South. "States' rights" arguments arose only when the federal power was a threat to the peculiar institution, and after Lincoln's election, when that threat was great enough, the arguments culminated in secession.[11]

Reunion and Reconstruction should have ended the matter. But "states' rights," of course, remained a significant argument against each act of Reconstruction and, for that matter, of the second Reconstruction in the mid-twentieth century. The historical coincidence of "states' rights" arguments with pro-slavery, pro-discrimination, and pro-segregation politics is enough to make their revival in recent Supreme Court decisions at least a bit, well, unseemly. Context matters when Chief Justice Rehnquist insists that local schools must be saved from the "Draconian remedy" of "indefinite judicial tutelage" in a desegregation case, or when Justice Scalia, in another desegregation case, insists that "[w]e must soon revert to the ordinary principles of

. . . our democratic heritage"—"that public schooling, even in the South, should be controlled by locally elected authorities." Again, the principle is unobjectionable in the abstract: but law is not made in the abstract.[12]

Frankly, it does not have much to do with principle anyway. Again, the affirmative action cases make this clear. In 1980 the Supreme Court upheld a federal set-aside program for minority contractors; under the Fourteenth Amendment, Chief Justice Burger said, Congress was entitled to considerable deference. But in 1989 the Supreme Court invalidated a similar program, this one enacted by the Richmond City Council. In explaining the distinction, Justice O'Connor relied upon a sort of reverse federalism:

> Congress, unlike any State or political subdivision, has a specific constitutional mandate to enforce the dictates of the Fourteenth Amendment. The power to "enforce" may at times also include the power to define situations which Congress determines threaten principles of equality and to adopt prophylactic rules to deal with those situations. The Civil War Amendments themselves worked a dramatic change in the balance between congressional and state power over matters of race.

"We simply note," O'Connor concluded, "what should be apparent to all—§1 of the Fourteenth Amendment stemmed from a distrust of state legislative enactments based on race; §5 is . . .'a positive grant of legislative power' to Congress." Indeed, it was "apparent" also to Justice Scalia: "A sound distinction," he wrote, "between federal and state (or local) action based on race rests not only upon the substance of the Civil War Amendments, but upon social reality and governmental theory."

The following year, Justice Brennan relied upon precisely this distinction to uphold another federal affirmative action plan. O'Connor and Scalia were among the dissenters. But in 1995 they had their majority again, and they overruled the Brennan decision. "Congruence," O'Connor wrote for the Court, requires that affirmative action plans enacted by the federal and state governments receive the same scrutiny. Neither she nor Scalia explained their apparent change of heart. "Ironically," Justice Stevens wrote in dissent, "after all of the time, effort, and paper this Court has expended in differentiating between federal and state affirmative action, the majority today

virtually ignores the issue. It provides not a word of direct explanation for its sudden and enormous departure from the reasoning in past
cases."[13]

The prior opinions became like the Reconstructions themselves: it
was as if they never were.

The Public/Private Dichotomy

There is a world imagined by American constitutional law. It is a
world of free markets, unrestricted by the state; a world of free
individuals, unencumbered by their government. It is a world in
which the law plays no discernable role, a realm of social and
economic life in which the people, freely, make their own way. The
winners and losers in this world are not the "special favorites of the
law"; they are the ones who deserve to win, naturally. Legal rules,
egalitarian or otherwise, are powerless here, in the realm of the
"private."

Such a world, of course, could hardly exist. As a general matter,
there are no purely private choices and no truly free markets. There
never were. The political Progressivism of the late nineteenth and
early twentieth centuries forced perhaps the most coherent defense of
the non-interventionist ideal, and for a while, social Darwinism and
laissez-faire economics had their day. But as John Whiteclay Chambers
notes, the defense of the self-regulating market at the dawn of the
Progressive Era was already somewhat embarrassed by certain political
truths: federal land grants to railroads, protective tariffs, the efforts to
stabilize currency, and, as the labor movement grew, overt antiunion
actions, including the deployment of federal troops to suppress strikes.
Yes, there were "private" rights in free-market America, but they were
created and carefully maintained by public action.[14]

In the specific context of the struggle for equality, however, the
"public-private" dichotomy does have a certain "textual" justification.
The Fourteenth Amendment provides that no "State" shall deny the
equal protection of the laws; the constitutional claim, then, is
necessarily premised on some action or omission by the state that
effectuates a denial of its duty to equally protect. There must be, then,
some public action—or inaction—as a predicate to a constitutional
complaint.

There was plenty of both in the postbellum South: the States enforced, encouraged, and acquiesced in a comprehensive scheme of social and economic oppression of the freedmen. It was neither purely "private" nor always overtly "public," but to the framers of Recon struction, it hardly mattered; if the states weren't actually doing it, they were darned sure not doing enough about it. Either way, the framers deliberately explained, the states were denying the freedmen the "equal protection" of the law.

But Justice Bradley's opinion in the *Civil Rights Cases* rejected this understanding—an understanding he himself seemed to share both before and after the decision—and transformed the "State denial" requirement, by action or inaction, into one of "State action." The rigid public-private dichotomy that resulted had no foundation in the text or history of the Fourteenth Amendment, and it certainly had no experiential foundation; it was, however, a convenient fiction for preserving the principles of the Compromise of 1877. In the process, what was virtually a tautology—there was always some state action or inaction—became a hopeless abstraction and, ultimately, lifeless dogma. As long as "the state" was not guilty of overt formal discrimination, there was no inequality for purposes of the Constitution.

One of the most significant achievements of the second Reconstruction was in realizing the obvious influence of the state on what Justice Bradley—and the anti-Reconstruction Democrats who preceded him—had insisted was purely "private." Thus in 1948 the Supreme Court found "state action" where state courts enforce private discrimination through racially restrictive deed covenants; in 1958, where state officials encourage or cause private racial discrimination; and in 1961, where state agencies are integral participants with private actors in a scheme of racial discrimination, or where they fail to prevent or remedy that discrimination.[15]

Through it all, the Court avoided an outright repudiation of Bradley's public-private dichotomy: it just always found sufficient public action. But reconciling theory and practice is not easy when the theory has no practical integrity; the result was language like this, from a unanimous opinion of the 1983 Court:

The question . . . is whether the reality of private biases and the possible injury they might inflict are permissible considerations for removal of an infant child from the custody of its natural mother. We have little difficulty concluding that they are not. The Constitution cannot control such prejudices but neither can it tolerate them. Private biases may be outside the reach of the law, but the law cannot, directly or indirectly, give them effect. "Public officials sworn to uphold the Constitution may not avoid a constitutional duty by bowing to the hypothetical effects of private racial prejudice that they assume to be both widely and deeply held."[16]

In the past few decades it has become increasingly clear that the public-private dichotomy is very much alive in constitutional decision-making; indeed, the current Court has reasserted it with a vengeance. The recent trilogy of "race" cases is illustrative. Segregation now is not de jure—the product of public action—but de facto—the product of "private decision-making and economics": as such, it is beyond the reach of the federal courts. Economic inequities now are caused not by state actors, but by private decisions, either "societal discrimination" or idiosyncratic "entrepreneurial choices": as a consequence, there is no justification for racial preferences, set-asides, or other remedial legislation. Voting habits now reflect individual decisions, not the logical collective response to a shared experience of official suppression: as such, it is "demeaning" to suggest that there is a "black" political community.

The sub-text to the re-sanctification of the private realm—of private choices, private markets, private decisions—is the vindication of a social and economic order that exists independent of this state action: a natural meritocracy, a natural order. So, in desegregation cases like *Missouri v. Jenkins*, white students attend nearly all-white schools because their parents, after all, can afford to live in suburban (read "better") neighborhoods, and they outperform their minority counterparts in conventional measures of achievement because they are, after all, academically advanced (read "better"). In affirmative action cases like *Adarand Constructors, Inc. v. Pena*, white contractors routinely are awarded contracts because, after all, they submit the lower (read "better") bids. In voting rights cases like *Miller v. Johnson*, white candidates keep winning elections from white electoral majorities because they are, after all, the more popular (read "better") candidates. Socially, academically, economically, and politically, superior efforts and superior talents yield their just rewards.

Of course, there is another perspective, one that recognizes the long-standing role of public forces in shaping the racial hierarchy. It is not a matter of "merit": it is much more a matter of carefully cultivated advantage. Desegregation cases like *Jenkins* suddenly look quite different in this view: residential options, it emerges, have been shaped by generations of official and unofficial segregation, and academic achievement by generations of educational deprivation and cultural hegemony. Affirmative action cases like *Adarand* look different as well: bidding possibilities, it emerges, are limited by the economic realities of bonding requirements, insurance premiums, the economies of scale, and the pervasive network of business connections, realities forged in the long history of economic racial oppression. And new understandings inform voting rights cases like *Miller*: electoral success, it emerges, is fairly traceable not only to the carefully manufactured public obsession with race, but more specifically to well-documented official actions creating minority neighborhoods while simultaneously precluding the possibility of minority electoral districts. There is nothing natural or neutral about any of this: merit, in fact, is not merely contingent, it is racially biased. As the title character of Richard Delgado's *The Rodrigo Chronicles* exclaims, "Merit sounds like white people's affirmative action!"[17]

Delgado's work adds an important experiential element to the critique of "state action": as Delgado writes, "[w]e know, indeed we live, the bogus public-private distinction." Indeed, the sanctification of "private choices" looks particularly bogus from this perspective. Black schoolchildren, after all, do not choose to attend segregated schools; black contractors do not choose an economic scheme that gives their white counterparts seventy-five contracts for their every one; and black voters do not choose to share a common political interest forged by the history and contemporary reality of social and economic oppression. The world too often is not the world subordinated people choose to live in, but is instead the world chosen for them.[18]

Similar criticisms may be leveled against the doctrinal requirement that discrimination be "purposeful." The requirement mirrors the futile search for an individual with the true freedom to act in a truly free market. Quite aside from its failings either as an evidentiary requirement or as a policy tool, the intent requirement depicts a world far removed from the world in which the victims of racial discrimination live. Its focus on the state of mind of the discriminatory actor is, first, quite irrelevant to the experience of discrimination—and, as a consequence, to the fact of inequality—and, second, quite difficult to square with contemporary understandings of human behavior. As Charles Lawrence notes:

> Traditional notions of intent do not reflect the fact that decisions about racial matters are influenced in large part by factors that can be characterized as neither intentional—in the sense that the outcomes are random, fortuitous, and uninfluenced by the decisionmakers' beliefs, desires, and wishes—nor unintentional . . . . We do not recognize the ways in which our cultural experience has influenced our beliefs about race or the occasions on which those beliefs affect our actions. In other words, a large part of the behavior that produces racial discrimination is influenced by unconscious racial motivation.[19]

The cultural context in which these un- and subconscious beliefs and motivations are formed is, of course, significantly the product of official actions. Indeed, law, in all its forms, made "race."

The question begged by all these cases is essentially one of responsibility: when should "the state" be accountable either for the disparate impacts of its own actions (i.e., for discriminatory "effects," whatever the anthropomorphic "intent") or for discrimination not obviously its own (i.e., discrimination that might in part be characterized as "private" or "societal")? The two scenarios tend to collapse in practice: schools are in fact racially segregated, markets are in fact racially skewed, votes are in fact cast along racial lines, and the central question—whether it is conceived in terms of "intent" or "causation"—is whether the state is obliged or permitted to do something about it.

The difficulty with the Supreme Court's approach to these issues is that it has treated the question of "responsibility" as an empirical one: is there evidence of some intentional state action? But state action, even if it is not conceived of in the broad terms envisioned by the Fourteenth Amendment's framers, is everywhere; the question becomes, invariably, one of degree. Attempts to reframe the question in quantitative terms—how much state action is there? how intentional is it? how significant a causal factor is it?—inevitably fail. And they should, because, in the final analysis, the question is not an empirical one at all.

The question is not whether the state intentionally caused discriminatory behavior, or demographic changes, or racial disparities in hiring, firing, or voting: of course it did *not*—entirely—but of course it *did*—in some respects, to some extent. The question is whether, given the nature of the state participation, the severity of the harm, and the necessity and likelihood of redress, it is right and proper to demand or at least permit remedial action by the state. This is not empirical; it is political. It is maybe even moral. And the answers we have been giving are simply embarrassing.

Tradition

In 1896 the Supreme Court upheld Louisiana's "equal but separate" rail accommodations law. Justice Brown explained:

> the case reduces itself to the question whether the statute of Louisiana is a reasonable regulation, and with respect to this there must necessarily be a large discretion on the part of the legislature. In determining the question of reasonableness, it is at liberty to act with reference to the established usages, customs, and traditions of the people, and with a view to the promotion of their comfort, and the preservation of the public peace and good order.

Brown did not explain whose "traditions" he was upholding; it was clear, however, which groups constituted "the people" for purposes of his inquiry.[20]

Fast-forward a century. The Court has ruled that separate is inherently unequal, but its commitment to the desegregation effort appears in doubt. Concurring in a desegregation case, Justice Antonin Scalia writes,

> We must soon revert to the ordinary principles of our law, of our democratic heritage, and of our education tradition: that plaintiffs alleging Equal Protection violations must prove intent and causation and not merely the existence of racial disparity; that public schooling, even in the South, should be controlled by locally elected authorities acting in conjunction with parents; and that it is "desirable" to permit pupils to attend "schools nearest their homes."[21]

Again traditions: legal, political, and social. But whose are they, really? In what sense are they truly "ours"?

There is a danger that lurks behind these invocations of "our" traditions. Not all these traditions will well serve all the people all the time. Traditions nearly always exclude; traditions very often suppress; traditions sometimes subordinate. This is particularly true of our traditions relating to "race," which, perhaps more than most, have neatly divided us into a traditional majority and minority, encouraged each to develop its own traditions, and unfailingly incorporated the majoritarian traditions into meritocratic schemes that deepen the division and rigidify the hierarchy.

"Our" traditions have a color, and that color is usually white.

Even "good traditions" can exclude. When the demand for uniformity precludes the consideration of context and perspective, those traditions that once promised liberation from oppression can become its instruments. Nearly a century ago, the first Justice Harlan dissented from the decision in *Plessy v. Ferguson*; he proposed a countertradition, declaring the Constitution "color-blind." Taken in context, appearing, as it did, in the same paragraph as the otherwise oxymoronic declaration that "the humblest is the peer of the most powerful," Harlan's proclamation was nothing short of an act of existential rebellion: a recognition of the reality of racial subordination and a refusal to accept it. But the meanings of tradition's signs are unstable, and with the shift in cultural valences, "colorblindness" has become the guardian of the status quo. As Patricia Williams writes,

> When segregation was eradicated from the American lexicon, its omission led many to actually believe that racism therefore no longer existed. Race-neutrality in law was the presumed antidote for race bias in real life. With the entrenchment of the notion of race-neutrality came attacks on the concept of affirmative action and the rise of reverse discrimination suits. Blacks, for so many generations deprived of jobs based on the color of our skin, are now told that we ought to find it demeaning to be hired based on the color of our skin. Such is the silliness of simplistic either-or inversions as remedies to complex problems.[22]

The unthinking invocation of tradition excludes too many truths. In its indifference to context, it distorts; in its indifference to perspective, it is biased. In its pretense that the dominant tradition is the one tradition, it oppresses; and in its blindness to its own role in the construction of differences, it enlarges the spaces that separate us.

The claim here is not that "tradition" has no place in constitutional analysis, but only that the term is in need of some critical assessment and more meaningful explication. The caution, in short, is against the nonreflexive reliance on tradition, against the assumption that there is but one "tradition," and that it is unfailingly good. Traditions, after all, may not be universal, or at least not universally beneficial.

Consider the Supreme Court's current favorite tradition, "colorblindness." It finds expression in the contentions that racial classifications are inherently and uniformly suspect, and that, as a consequence, racial quotas, preferences, and gerrymands are presumptively unconstitutional. The tradition has both a normative and a positive dimension.

The former is manifest in an almost obsessive desire to exclude "race" from public discourse, as if, through our willful ignorance, we could make it simply vanish. But this view entails a series of assumptions that should not go unchallenged. One, more or less empirical, is that race will matter less if we consciously refuse to talk about it. But nothing in our history or contemporary reality suggests that the results of the coerced silence approach to public discourse—imposed here quite asymmetrically—will be anything less than perverse. Another is the implicit assumption, made explicit in another of Justice Scalia's concurring opinions, that "race" inherently devolves into questions of better or worse, that we cannot "classify" without "judging." But there is simply no reason that this must be the case, not, at least, if we truly understand "race." Finally, the normative commitment assumes, quite explicitly, that the costs of race-talk outweigh its benefits. Thus the affirmative action decisions, observe T. Alexander Aleinikoff and Samuel Issacharoff, ultimately manifest a program of "equality" "dedicated to the pursuit of social peace rather than social justice." But, perhaps, no justice, no peace.[23]

The positive dimension of the commitment to colorblindness, meanwhile, entails a literal inability or unwillingness to see color and its effects. For example, the Richmond affirmative action decision manifests what Patricia Williams has described as a "lawyerly language game of exclusion and omission," in which the city's evidence of racial discrimination is disaggregated and dismissed. White contractors, Justice O'Connor concedes, were getting over 99 percent of the city's contracts, but that might have been because the black citizens of

Richmond—half the population—didn't really want them: they may have been making different "entrepreneurial choices." Thus, as Williams notes, "the social text, no matter how uniform and exclusive, could not be called exclusionary in the absence of proof that people of color even want to be recipients of municipal contracts." This forced separation of individual choice from social constraint is echoed in the opinion's repetitive invocation of the standard dichotomies: public versus private, state versus federal, past versus present, fact versus opinion. "Societal discrimination" is converted into an amorphous claim by this relentless disaggregation of experience, leaving a fragmented landscape in which "racial power has been mediated out."[24]

What emerges is an almost congenital blindness to the reality of racial hierarchy: "[w]hite folks," writes Richard Delgado, "never see their own racial and class advantage." Buttressed by the metaphysical pretenses of equal opportunity, white justice re-creates a world in which economic disparities reflect not racism, but differences in "special qualifications" and "entrepreneurial choices." In this white-washed tradition, the oppression and privileges of race are consigned to a distant place and time, yielding a myth of innocence and neutrality, "the product of the blissful, self-serving ignorance that comes from never having been on the wrong side of a hiring decision because of race or gender."[25]

The conventional appeals to tradition—to "colorblindness," to "neighborhood schools," to "our democratic heritage"—manifest the desire to ensure that this reimagined past will somehow be the future. But it is a past sanitized by the myopia of colorblindness, cleansed of dissonant voices. What emerges is only a jurisprudence of nostalgia.

But to make a new future, we must come to terms with the past, and not be slaves to it. We must learn how, as Walter Lippman counseled in 1914, "to substitute purpose for tradition."[26]

Formal Equality: Race

It was Justice Brown in *Plessy v. Ferguson* who offered the modern explication of the constitutional guarantee of equality:

> If the two races are to meet upon terms of social equality, it must be the result of natural affinities, a mutual appreciation of each other's

merits, and a voluntary consent of individuals. Legislation is powerless to eradicate racial instincts, or to abolish distinctions based upon physical differences, and the attempt to do so can only result in accentuating the difficulties of the present situation. If the civil and political rights of both races be equal, one cannot be inferior to the other civilly or politically. If one race be inferior to the other socially, the constitution of the United States cannot put them upon the same plane.[27]

To be sure, the specific holding in *Plessy*, that separation does not connote or constitute an inequality, was undone by *Brown v. Board of Education*. And the line of twentieth-century cases that includes *Brown*—*Shelley v. Kraemer* and *Sweatt v. Painter* preceding it; *Cooper v. Aaron*, *Loving v. Virginia*, and *Green v. New Kent County School Board* following it—seemed to reject *Plessy*'s dubious premises and to obliterate its shallow logic.

But no victory in constitutional law is permanent, and so *Plessy* again lives. "Natural affinities" and "racial instincts" are reborn in a hypothesized de facto segregation that represents not centuries of official racism, but "private choices." Affirmative action legislation "is powerless . . . to abolish distinctions based upon physical differences, and the attempt to do so" both demeans the beneficiaries and offends the disadvantaged minority, "accentuating the difficulties of the present situation." Even the formal symmetry of "separate but equal" is revived: "consistency" now requires that a presumption of minority business disadvantage be viewed with the same suspicion as Jim Crow legislation, rendering irrelevant both the context and content of the legislation. Above all, the Constitution secures only a "legal" or "civil" equality: if "one race be inferior to the other socially," the Constitution cannot put them on the same plane, because, well, "Government cannot make us equal."

It is all back: the naturalistic conception of "race" and "racism"; the natural or "social" order against which law is powerless; the empty, arid, isolated guarantee of formal legal equality indifferent to context, blind to all the realities of social life. There was no great outcry in early 1997 when Justice Scalia told a Columbia University audience that, yes, if it had been a case of first impression, he could well imagine voting against the plaintiffs in *Brown v. Board of Education*—no great outcry because, as Reconstruction's framers might have it, his Court has already robbed us of the substance of that decision, and cheated us with the shadow.

Concurring in the Richmond affirmative action decision, Scalia offered this counsel:

> The difficulty of overcoming the effects of past discrimination is as nothing compared with the difficulty of eradicating from our society the source of those effects, which is the tendency—fatal to a Nation such as ours—to classify and judge men and women on the basis of their country of origin or the color of their skin.[28]

It was, of course, a political judgment, and aside from the apparent irony that it emanated from an avowedly *apolitical* justice, it seemed quite unexceptional. But one phrase makes it extraordinary, a coupling of terms that goes quite to the heart of the modern discussion of "race": "to classify and judge." It is indeed true that for centuries, to "classify" was to "judge." But is it invariably the case: must "race"—for all time, in all contexts—carry connotations of superior and inferior?

Scalia and a majority of his Court believe that it must. The story of "race" that they tell remains an essentialist one, a story that understands race as something innate and immutable. Within this story, it is impossible to distinguish between the social, economic, and political forces of racial exclusion, oppression, and disadvantage on the one hand, and the claims of innate inferiority on the other. Within such an understanding of race, the Court is able to suggest that the commitment to desegregation is insulting, that affirmative action is stigmatizing, and that racial bloc voting is oppressive.

It is only within such a story that the recognition of a minority perspective—a "black" voice, for example—is demeaning. But that is the error of essentialism, for there is no need to reduce individuals to "race" or reduce "race" to a single view. Too much, after all, is lost in the process: race is constructed at too many intersections and in too many contexts to permit the suppression of dissonance both within and between racial communities.

Such an untenable conception of "race"—as a natural, inherent, immutable characteristic—obscures the cultural processes of creating "race." It ignores the truth of "race" as a social construct, though perhaps, given the unique role of "race" in the constructions and reconstructions of our official traditions, it is more accurate to speak of "race" as Cornel West does, as a "political and ethical" construct.[29]

But to say that "race" is politically constructed is to assert rather than deny its real salience. It is only when "race" is absurdly divorced from its political meaning that "racism" magically fades from consciousness. Oppression and privilege then become distant memories; equality—formal, symmetrical, elegant, and empty—becomes "perfect." The racial hierarchy left in place by this desiccated vision of equality becomes inevitable, as natural as the "race" that defines it: we simply cannot be made equal. That is the great wrong that inheres in this supposed "color-blindness": that in denying the realities of "race," it simultaneously denies the possibility of a genuine equality.

By focusing on the process of constructing race—on, historically, "racism"—we recover the prospects for a genuinely reconstructed race, for a benign "race"-ism, for differences that are not hierarchical, for a world in which we can indeed "classify" yet not "judge." What, after all, will be left of "race" if the races are—socially, economically, politically, *really*—equal? The tragedy is that we may never find out.

It is simply not plausible that we will be able to reconstruct "race" without the benefit of "race"-conscious measures. Requiring "color-blind" decision making may eliminate the old overt forms of racial discrimination, but it leaves intact—and indeed legitimates—the deeply entrenched biases of American law and life. As Richard Delgado writes, "Facially neutral laws cannot redress most racism, because of the cultural background against which such laws operate. But even if we could somehow control for this, formally neutral rules would still fail to redress racism because of certain structural features of the phenomenon itself." Moreover, the attempt to expose the process is not welcomed: social science evidence is "misleading" and "unnecessary," statistics "inconclusive," context "irrelevant." Nothing matters but the letter of the law; but that law, as Jerome McCristal Culp, Jr., summarizes, "has strained and contorted itself under the constraints imposed by the history of racism."

Some of those who have led the struggle for racial justice are left now to struggle against despair. Derrick Bell now urges a "racial realism": America, he reluctantly concludes, offers no realistic hope of achieving equality through law. The Court's recent decisions are, in this view, not at all anomalous: American law was not designed to ensure real equality. "So law works," Delgado concludes. "But it operates to preserve racial advantage, to maintain the status quo."

It is the worst part of our national heritage. John Hope Franklin writes,

> Racial segregation, discrimination, and degradation are no unanticipated accidents in this nation's history. They stem logically and directly from the legacy that the founding fathers bestowed upon contemporary America. The denial of equality in the year of independence led directly to the denial of equality in the era of the bicentennial of independence. The so-called compromises in the Constitution of 1787 led directly to the arguments in our own time that we can compromise equality with impunity and somehow use the Constitution as an instrument to preserve privilege and to foster inequality. It has thus become easy to invoke the spirit of the founding fathers whenever we seek ideological support for the social, political, and economic inequities that have become a part of the American way.[30]

Formal Equality: Intelligence

"Smartness" provides one of the ways—perhaps now the primary way—that we preserve privilege, and so it should come as no surprise that the conception of "intelligence" in modern American constitutional law substantially mirrors the conception of "race": it too is something innate and immutable. Occasionally, in cases like *Washington v. Davis*, the concepts go hand in hand; in other cases, they are simply different aspects of the natural order. In all cases, essentialism prevails: to be "smart" or not is to be, as with "race," primarily or exclusively *that*, and uniformly that, for all time, and in all contexts.

The Supreme Court's best chance to clarify its conception of the "smart" person came in 1984, when it was called on to determine the status of people with mental retardation in the Court's complex hierarchy of judicial scrutiny. The case involved an effort to establish a group home for mentally retarded adults; a Texas city viewed the group home as a "hospital for the feebleminded" and denied the necessary permit. In the end, the Supreme Court found the city's decision unreasonable.

But it also concluded that mentally retarded people as a class neither needed nor deserved special judicial protection. Unlike discrimination against white contractors, for example, discrimination against people with mental retardation could be justified by the same deferential standard applied in cases of economic distinctions, like the ones between opticians and optometrists, which the Court upheld in one case, or between the manufacturers of filled milk and margarine, which the Court upheld in another. Discrimination against people with mental retardation was no more suspicious than these business distinctions. This was so, Justice White explained, because mentally retarded people "have a reduced ability to cope with and function in the everyday world." "They are thus different," he offered, "immutably so, in relevant respects, and the States' interest in dealing with and providing for them is plainly a legitimate one."

The meaning of "immutably so" was obvious, even if it was also obviously wrong. But what did White mean when he claimed that mentally retarded people were "different . . . *in relevant respects*"? Relevant how, and to what? White elaborated: "we should look to the likelihood that governmental action premised on a particular classification is valid *as a general matter*, not merely to the specifics of the case before us"; and, he concluded, "mental retardation is a characteristic that the government may legitimately take into account *in a wide range* of decisions" (emphasis added).

That the explanation seems on first impression so unobjectionable is a testament to the entrenched nature of the essentialist conception of intelligence generally, and of mental retardation—diminished intelligence—specifically. But Justice Marshall was not fooled. The way he saw it, White's assertion that mental retardation is *generally relevant* violated the most fundamental norm of the equal protection guarantee: it stereotyped. From some perceived difference, it induced a generalized disability, ignoring variations, first, among individuals, and second, among contexts.

Regarding the first, Marshall explained, "that some retarded people have reduced capacities in some areas does not justify using retardation as a proxy for reduced capacity in areas where relevant individual variations in capacity do exist." That someone may have an extremely low IQ may well be "relevant" to, for example, college admissions decisions; but that did not automatically mean that mild or moderate mental retardation was relevant to decisions involving the location of group homes, for example, or the rights to have and raise children.

As for the second:

the suggestion—that the standard of review must be fixed with reference to the number of classifications to which a characteristic would validly be relevant—is similarly flawed. Certainly the assertion is not a logical one; that a characteristic may be relevant under some or even many circumstances does not suggest any reason to presume it relevant under other circumstances where there is reason to suspect it is not.

Marshall offered an example that clearly exposed the dangers of essentialist thought, and the pitfalls of ignoring the significance of context: "A sign that says 'men only' looks very different on a bathroom door than a courthouse door."[31]

But what is so patently clear in the case of gender is too easy to miss in the case of intelligence. It is far too easy to assume, as White did, that diminished intelligence—or, ipso facto, superior intelligence—is somehow "generally" relevant. Performance on an IQ test, however, should not have such an all-pervasive significance. We really should not make it that important.

For two centuries, defenders of the natural order have been certain that they were defending the truth, and equally certain that, in the process, they were defending our culture from the degrading effects of the egalitarian delusion. While they no longer speak overtly of a "white man's government," it is clear that both their truths and their fears have, in substance, remained constant right through this day.

In a recent essay, University of Delaware psychologist Linda S. Gottfredson offers to expose the "egalitarian fiction and collective fraud" that obscures the truth of racial inferiority. "While scientists have not yet determined their source," Gottfredson writes, "the existence of sometimes large group differences in intelligence is as well-established as any fact in the social sciences." In denying or concealing this well-established fact, we perpetuate a most harmful lie:

> enforcement of the lie is gradually distorting and degrading all institutions and processes where intelligence is at least somewhat important. . . . Society is thus being shaped to meet the dictates of a collective fraud. The fiction is aiding and abetting bigots to a far greater degree than any truth could, because its specific side-effects—racial preferences, official mendacity, free-wielding accusations of racism, and falling

standards—are creating deep cynicism and broad resentment against minorities, blacks in particular, among the citizenry.[32]

All the old arguments are here. Egalitarianism is degrading; egalitarianism encourages racial conflict. Egalitarianism, not the history and reality of bias, is distorting our "[s]ociety"; egalitarianism, not the history and reality of racism, is stimulating "broad resentment against minorities, blacks in particular, among the citizenry," a citizenry, evidently, that does not embrace "minorities, blacks in particular." We have nothing to look forward to but continued decline, all because we won't acknowledge one simple truth: white people are smarter than black.

But this truth, on closer examination, is surprisingly equivocal, even as Gottfredson describes it: "While scientists have not yet determined their source, the existence of sometimes large group differences in intelligence is as well-established as any fact in the social sciences." But identifying the "source," it would seem, is a matter of some import; "sometimes large" differences are, presumably, matched by differences that are not so "large"; neither of the operative terms—neither the racial "group" nor the "intelligence" with which it is correlated—is itself "well-established," by Gottfredson or anybody else; and if the "social sciences" are not establishing "facts" any better than this, then "social science fact" is truly an oxymoron.

It is hard not to wonder: if the facts of superiority and inferiority are so well established, then why all the equivocation? And if the equivocation is merely an attempt to manifest good science, then why do all the conditions and qualifiers disappear when the claims shift, as inevitably they do, to the terrain of the political?

Here is a hypothesis: the "truth" of the natural order has to be described in tentative, ambiguous, equivocal terms, because stated directly, it is so obviously a lie. On the other hand, the concomitant political claims must be asserted in strong, clear, and unqualified terms, because only the force of political rhetoric can sustain the "truth" of the natural order: only appeals to the worst parts of our political heritage can obscure the real nature of inequality. The "truth," in short, needs powerful fictions to sustain it.

The net effect of these fictions, political and legal—there is rarely any difference here—is actually twofold: to preserve the concept of a natural order and to preserve in fact the hierarchies of social and economic life, all in spite of, and sometimes even in the name of, the guarantee of the equal protection of the laws. It produces a certain self-perpetuating monotony: it is always the same people and groups of people who are "smart," who are "superior," who are "qualified," who should—and do—end up on top, and who are permitted, as a consequence, to constitute "society" and "the citizenry." The rules that replicate this pattern are "neutral"; the pattern itself—the order—is "natural." Any effort to pierce the veil of legalism is "misleading"; any effort to break the monotony is "distorting and degrading" and creates impermissible "special favorites of the law."

There is no escaping the bell curve, then, because we are not permitted to try. But if the bell curve is the truth, then we should at least abandon the fictions that sustain it.

An Epilogue
The Next Reconstruction

There may be a story within the story here, and it will be the last story of this book. The law is blind, willfully or not, to the steady replication of advantages and biases because, perhaps, it too embraces them, and it is quite oblivious to its own self-perpetuating patterns of disadvantage and exclusion. Law is made by lawyers, and, importantly, lawyers are made by law. There's not a lot of room here for new perspectives.

Consider that law students are admitted into law school based on their aptitude for the study of law, an aptitude measured in substantial part by their performance on a standardized test, the LSAT. Admitted students are then trained to "think like a lawyer," and their success in that task is subsequently measured by examinations that have not much changed in several generations. Performance on those tests, as measured by student grades, are substantially correlated with performance on the LSAT, which, of course, is how the folks who create that standardized test stay in business. At the end of three years' training, graduating students receive one final test of their ability to "think like a lawyer" in the form of a mega-test, the bar examination, performance on which correlates with their law school grades and, hence, the LSAT. Thus students who are admitted into law school based on their measured aptitude for thinking like lawyers are trained to think like lawyers and admitted into the profession based on their success in learning to think like lawyers. When they become professionals, then, we should perhaps not be terribly surprised if, in the course of solving the problems presented to them, they tend to think like—well of course—lawyers.

Folks complain about this all the time. Lawyers, they say, are argumentative; lawyers are coldly deductive; lawyers make big issues

371

out of little words; lawyers talk in circles; lawyers look for loopholes; lawyers always obfuscate; lawyers are savagely competitive; lawyers don't care about people, about their real problems, about the real world. I've done some of this complaining myself, most recently, about fifteen pages' worth.

So here, perhaps, is an idea. It is admittedly quixotic and utopian and optimistic to a fault, but, to borrow a phrase, "you talk about a dream, you try to make it real." And in a few generations, or maybe a few generations more—well, who knows?

So here's the idea: Let's make lawyers out of some people who don't think like lawyers—at least, not in the conventional sense—and maybe out of people who never will. Let's make lawyers out of some people who are smart in different ways, people who are really good at practical problem-solving, and people who are extraordinarily kind and compassionate, and people with a heightened sense of situation and context, and people with a powerful commitment to their community, and people who are especially creative, and deeply spiritual, and moral and ethical and maybe even just. Some of them won't have done so great on the LSAT; some of them will have done just plain lousy. And they'll be the ones we recruit most heavily.

We will have, of course, certain assessment problems. Identifying people who are real kind or spiritual or committed to their community may not be an easy matter: there are, to date, no standardized tests of these qualities. But if we can create tests to determine somebody's aptitude for conventional legal analysis—if we can create, for that matter, tests for something as broad and organic as "general intelligence"—then I am quite certain that we could create tests for these other qualities, if we merely put our minds to it and our hearts into it. Maybe, for that matter, we would not be constrained by standardized tests at all: maybe we could gauge kindness, spirituality, or community commitment in more practical or experiential terms, by considering, for example, how our applicants actually live their lives.

It may take a while to work out the particulars, and it may take a while longer for us to transcend our long-held biases. Eventually, though, we'll get all kinds of different folks into our schools, with all kinds of different aptitudes. We'd get folks with some different perspectives too. Would that mean, for example, that we'd get more black Americans, do they have a unique, and uniquely valuable, perspective? Of course they do, and so do other minorities of "race," and so do poor folks, and so do folks with disabilities, and so do all the uniquely gifted people we'd be recruiting, and if we can get enough of them into law school, they just might be willing to share their perspective, and share their gifts, and help us rebuild the profession in ways that reflect their various strengths, instead of excluding folks because of their supposed weaknesses.

Some people won't much like this plan. They'd fuss and fume about merit, and inferiority, and qualifications and all that old tired nonsense they've been trotting out to exclude people for centuries. Ironically, many of the people who would throw a tantrum if we really tried to democratize the legal profession are the same ones who are always carping about the lawyers. Well, now we'd see where they really stand.

And when we were done, when we'd really democratized "lawyers," I'll bet you we then democratize the laws. Not just in letter, not just in theory, but in practice, in the way law is experienced. Our new lawyers would not tolerate empty formalisms, and neither would our reconstructed laws.

Some of the old hierarchies would be swept away quickly. "Race" would surely be one; it never had anything going for it anyway, except the inequities fashioned by law. Take away those inequities—really take them away—and there won't be much left to be "race"-ist about.

Some other hierarchies might take longer. Some parts of the order are so hard to escape; some changes would really require some faith. But maybe, at some point, perhaps several more generations down the line, we'd take a really bold chance. Some day, at some law school, we'd admit somebody who had a lousy LSAT and a low IQ to boot. He'd need some help: we'd have to modify our curriculum some, and the way we taught, and also our examinations. And when he became a lawyer, he'd still need our help: some things he couldn't do alone. But maybe that would be the beauty of it, maybe that's when we'd really learn about the law.

What insights would he offer? What clarifications would he demand? What would be his vision of the law as it is practiced, as it is lived? How would the law change, when it included—I mean really included—him? It's hard even to imagine; but then, we knew we had a long way to go.

Some things, we might suspect, would never make sense to him. The fuss over affirmative action might be one. It might not be easy to explain why we got into this business of labeling people, or why we could not use those labels to get us out of the mess we created. It may be especially hard to convince him that laws designed to help people had to be treated the same as the laws that were designed to hurt them in the first place. He'd probably see things more like a fellow named Ed Murphy, a guy who knows something about labels, seeing as how he's lived with one of the toughest labels all his life:

> It is very hard to go through life with a label. You have to fight constantly. Retarded is just a word. We have to separate individuals from the word. We use words like "retarded" because of habit—just like going shopping every week and getting up in the morning. The word "retarded" must be there if you are going to give people help, but what the hell is the sense of calling someone retarded and not giving them anything?

So our best efforts to explain might fail; it might never make sense to him. And then maybe it would stop making sense to the rest us.

Some people would be skeptical, some scornful, some would mock us for what we were trying to do. "A mentally retarded lawyer," they'd scoff, "there's certain proof that you've gone off the deep end." We could tell them it was only a label, but they know that, and they don't care. So we'd say instead that "it's only law—it's not like it's nuclear physics." "And besides," we'd say, "we've seen what the 'smart' people have done with law, and frankly, we're not all that impressed."

Or maybe we wouldn't say that at all. Maybe the response would be different, different because it came from a voice that, until only recently, had not much been heard. Maybe it would sound like Ed Murphy: "I don't know. Maybe I used to be retarded. That's what they said anyhow. I wish they could see me now. I wonder what they'd say if they could see me holding down a regular job and doing all kinds of things. I bet they wouldn't believe it."[1]

Notes

Except where otherwise indicated, quotations from congressional debates are from the CONGRESSIONAL GLOBE or CONGRESSIONAL RECORD, and biographical information on the participants is from the BIOGRAPHICAL DIRECTORY OF THE AMERICAN CONGRESS, 1774-1971 (1971).

CHAPTER 1: INTRODUCTION

1. *Buck v. Bell,* 274 U.S. 200 (1927), upholding *Buck v. Bell,* 130 S.E. 516 (1925). On the story behind the opinion, see Paul A. Lombardo, *Three Generations, No Imbeciles: New Light on* Buck v. Bell, 60 NEW YORK UNIVERSITY LAW REVIEW 30 (1985).

2. See Robert L. Hayman, Jr., *Presumptions of Justice: Law, Politics, and the Mentally Retarded Parent,* 103 HARVARD LAW REVIEW 1201 (1990), and sources cited therein.

3. *Davis v. Washington,* 348 F. Supp. 15 (D.D.C. 1972); *reversed,* 512 F.2d 956 (D.C.Cir. 1975); *reversed, Washington v. Davis,* 426 U.S. 229 (1976). Test 21 is reprinted in full as an appendix to the Court of Appeals opinion.

4. See Robert L. Hayman, Jr., & Nancy Levit, *The Constitutional Ghetto,* 1993 WISCONSIN LAW REVIEW 627, and sources cited therein.

CHAPTER 2: THE FIRST OBJECT OF GOVERNMENT

1. Thurgood Marshall, *Reflections on the Bicentennial of the United States Constitution,* 101 HARVARD LAW REVIEW 1 (1987).

2. Eugene D. Genovese, THE SOUTHERN TRADITION: THE ACHIEVEMENTS AND LIMITATIONS OF AN AMERICAN CONSERVATISM 22-24 (1994); Winton U. Solberg, *The Genesis of American Constitutionalism,* in Winton U. Solberg, ed., THE CONSTITUTIONAL CONVENTION AND THE FORMATION OF

THE UNION xliv (2d ed. 1990); *The Federal Convention: Madison's Notes of Debates*, in *id.* at 67, 166, 176, 178; THE FEDERALIST NO. 10 (Madison).

3. Jean-Jacques Rousseau, THE SOCIAL CONTRACT, chap. 11; THE FEDERALIST NO. 10 (Madison); I. Bernard Cohen, SCIENCE AND THE FOUNDING FATHERS: SCIENCE IN THE POLITICAL THOUGHT OF JEFFERSON, FRANKLIN, ADAMS, AND MADISON 211, 222 (1995); Solberg, *supra*, note 2, at xxxviii.

4. *James Wilson's Speech at a Public Meeting*, in Bernard Bailyn, ed., THE DEBATE ON THE CONSTITUTION: FEDERALIST AND ANTI-FEDERALIST SPEECHES, ARTICLES, AND LETTERS DURING THE STRUGGLE OVER RATIFICATION 63, 68 (1993); Noah Webster, *Reply to the Pennsylvania Minority*, in *id.* at 553, 554; *James Madison to Thomas Jefferson*, in. *id.* at 192, 200; Oscar Handlin & Lilian Handlin, LIBERTY IN AMERICA, 1600 TO THE PRESENT, VOLUME 2: LIBERTY IN EXPANSION, 1760-1850, at 378-89 (1989).

5. Fabius [John Dickinson], *Observations on the Constitution Proposed by the Federal Convention*, in Bailyn, *supra* note 4, at 408, 424; *A Citizen of America*, in *id.* at 129, 158.

6. Edmund S. Morgan, AMERICAN SLAVERY, AMERICAN FREEDOM 4 (1975).

7. Solberg, *American Constitutionalism*, *supra*, note 2, at 181, 252; Morgan, *supra*, note 6, at 376; *id.* at 24.

8. Peter J. Parish, SLAVERY: HISTORY AND HISTORIANS 1-23 (1989); Thomas D. Morris, SOUTHERN SLAVERY AND THE LAW, 1619-1860, at 101 (1996); Robert William Fogel, WITHOUT CONSENT OR CONTRACT: THE RISE AND FALL OF AMERICAN SLAVERY 10 (1989); Solberg, *American Constitutionalism*, *supra*, note 2, at 216, 246.

9. Morgan, *supra*, note 6, at 380.

10. *Id.* at 3, 385.

11. William Lee Miller, ARGUING ABOUT SLAVERY: THE GREAT BATTLE IN THE UNITED STATES CONGRESS 132, 439 (1996); *id.* at 162; Handlin & Handlin, *supra*, note 4, at 303; Solberg, *supra*, note 2, at 209, 279, 280, 281, 283; *id.* at 279-81.

12. A. Leon Higginbotham, Jr., IN THE MATTER OF COLOR: RACE AND THE AMERICAN LEGAL PROCESS: THE COLONIAL PERIOD 92-95 (1978); Handlin & Handlin, *supra*, note 4, at 304-12; Morris, *supra*, note 8, at 164, 181.

13. GEORGE WASHINGTON: WRITINGS 900, 1002 (John Rhodehamel, ed. 1997). Eric Foner, FREE LABOR, FREE SOIL, FREE MEN: THE IDEOLOGY OF THE REPUBLICAN PARTY BEFORE THE CIVIL WAR xxx (1995); Handlin & Handlin, *supra*, note 4, at 312-14.

14. Miller, *supra*, note 11, at 354; Foner, *supra*, note 13, at 85; *id.* at 74-76; William S. McFeely, FREDERICK DOUGLASS 172-73 (1991).

15. Christine Leigh Heyrman, SOUTHERN CROSS: THE BEGINNINGS OF THE BIBLE BELT 50-52, 67-69 (1997); Donald G. Mathews, *Religion and Slavery: The Case of the American South*, in Christine Bolt & Seymour Drescher, eds., ANTI-SLAVERY, RELIGION, AND REFORM: ESSAYS IN MEMORY OF ROGER ANSTEY 207,

211-16 (1980); Louis S. Gerteis, MORALITY AND UTILITY IN AMERICAN ANTISLAVERY REFORM 118 (1987)

16. Eric Foner, *Abolitionism and the Labor Movement in Antebellum America*, in Bolt & Drescher, *supra*, note 15, at 254, 259; George M. Fredrickson, BLACK LIBERATION: A COMPARATIVE HISTORY OF BLACK IDEOLOGIES IN THE UNITED STATES AND SOUTH AFRICA 25 (1995); Handlin & Handlin, *supra*, note 4, at 312.

17. *Scott v. Sandford*, 60 U.S. 393 (1856); Foner, *supra*, note 13, at 87.

18. Thomas Jefferson, *Notes on the State of Virginia*, in THOMAS JEFFERSON: WRITINGS 123, 264-70 (Merrill D. Peterson, ed. 1984); Cohen, *supra*, note 3, at 297-300; *id.* at 191.

19. Ira Berlin et al., eds., FREE AT LAST: A DOCUMENTARY HISTORY OF SLAVERY, FREEDOM, AND THE CIVIL WAR 447-49 (1992).

20. James M. McPherson, THE ABOLITIONIST LEGACY: FROM RECON-STRUCTION TO THE NAACP 13 (1975); C. Vann Woodward, THE STRANGE CAREER OF JIM CROW (3d rev. ed. 1974); C. Vann Woodward, *STRANGE CAREER Critics: Long May They Persevere*, in THE FUTURE OF THE PAST 295 (1989); Eric Foner, RECONSTRUCTION: AMERICA'S UNFINISHED REVOLUTION 469-72 (1988).

21. See generally Woodward, STRANGE CAREER OF JIM CROW, *supra*, note 20; Foner, *supra*, note 20; Leon Litwack, BEEN IN THE STORM SO LONG: THE AFTERMATH OF SLAVERY (1979); Emily Field Van Tassel, *"Only the Law Would Rule between Us": Antimiscegenation, the Moral Economy of Dependency, and the Debate over Rights after the Civil War*, 70 CHICAGO-KENT LAW REVIEW 873 (1995).

22. McPherson, *supra*, note 20, at 19-20; C. Vann Woodward, REUNION AND REACTION: THE COMPROMISE OF 1877 AND THE END OF RECONSTRUCTION 150-62 (1951); John Hope Franklin, *The Enforcement of the Civil Rights Act of 1875*, in RACE AND HISTORY: SELECTED ESSAYS, 1938-1988, at 116-31 (1989); John A. Scott, *Justice Bradley's Evolving Concept of the Fourteenth Amendment from the Slaughterhouse Cases to the* Civil Rights Cases, 25 RUTGERS LAW REVIEW 552, 568 (1971).

23. *Civil Rights Cases*, 109 U.S. 1 (1883); *Blyew v. United States* (1871) (Bradley, J., dissenting); 1871 Letter from Joseph P. Bradley to Hon. William B. Woods, quoted in *Bell v. Maryland* 378 U.S. 226 (1964) (Goldberg, J., concurring); Joseph P. Bradley, MISCELLANEOUS WRITINGS 240-45 (Charles Bradley, ed. 1901).

24. Woodward, STRANGE CAREER OF JIM CROW, *supra*, note 20, at 81; *Plessy v. Ferguson*, 163 U.S. 537 (1896).

25. See, for example, David Garrow, BEARING THE CROSS: MARTIN LUTHER KING, JR. AND THE SOUTHERN CHRISTIAN LEADERSHIP CONFERENCE (1986); Henry Hampton & Steve Fayer, VOICES OF FREEDOM: AN ORAL HISTORY OF THE CIVIL RIGHTS MOVEMENT FROM THE 1950S THROUGH THE 1980S (1990); Richard Kluger, SIMPLE JUSTICE: THE HISTORY OF BROWN V. BOARD OF EDUCATION AND BLACK AMERICA'S STRUGGLE FOR EQUALITY (1975).

26. *Shelley v. Kraemer*, 334 U.S. 1 (1948).

27. *Sweatt v. Painter*, 339 U.S. 629 (1950).

28. *Brown v. Board of Education of Topeka* (Brown I), 347 U.S. 483 (1954).

29. *Brown v. Board of Education of Topeka* (Brown II), 349 U.S. 294 (1955); Derrick A. Bell, Jr., AND WE ARE NOT SAVED: THE ELUSIVE QUEST FOR RACIAL JUSTICE (1987); Garrow, *supra*, note 25, at 119

30. Hampton & Fayer, *supra*, note 25, at 35-52; Melba Patillo Beals, WARRIORS DON'T CRY 92-145 (1994); *Cooper v. Aaron*, 358 U.S. 1 (1958).

31. James T. Patterson, GRAND EXPECTATIONS: THE UNITED STATES, 1945-74, at 24 (1996); *Loving v. Commonwealth of Virginia*, 388 U.S. 1 (1967).

32. *Green v. New Kent County School Board*, 391 U.S. 430 (1968).

33. Marshall, *supra*, note 1; see also John Hope Franklin & Genna Rae McNeil, AFRICAN AMERICANS AND THE LIVING CONSTITUTION (1995); *San Antonio School District v. Rodriguez*, 411 U.S. 1 (1973); *Keyes v. School District No. 1*, 413 U.S. 189 (1973) (Rehnquist, J., dissenting); *Milliken v. Bradley* (Milliken I), 418 U.S. 717 (1974).

34. *Board of Education v. Dowell*, 498 U.S. 237 (1991) (Marshall, J., dissenting); *Missouri v. Jenkins*, 115 S. Ct. 2038 (1995) (Thomas, J., concurring); *Adarand Constructors v. Pena*, 115 S. Ct. 2097 (1995) (Thomas, J., concurring).

CHAPTER 3: IN THE NATURE OF THINGS

1. W. E. B. Du Bois, *The Souls of White Folk*, in W. E. B. DU BOIS: WRITINGS 923 (Nathan Huggins, ed. 1986); Bernard Crick, *Foreword*, in Ivan Hannaford, RACE: THE HISTORY OF AN IDEA IN THE WEST xiii (1996); Frank M. Snowden, Jr., BEFORE COLOR PREJUDICE: THE ANCIENT VIEW OF BLACKS 63 (1983); Jan Nederveen Pieterse, WHITE ON BLACK: IMAGES OF AFRICA AND BLACKS IN WESTERN POPULAR CULTURE 23 (1992).

2. Ronald Segal, THE BLACK DIASPORA 3 (1995); Snowden, *supra*, note 1, at 106; George M. Fredrickson, BLACK LIBERATION: A COMPARATIVE HISTORY OF BLACK IDEOLOGIES IN THE UNITED STATES AND SOUTH AFRICA 62 (1995); Pieterse, *supra*, note 1, at 24-26, 34-36, 45-49; Hannaford, *supra*, note 1, at 187-88.

3. Michael L. Blakey, *Passing the Buck: Naturalism and Individualism as Anthropological Expressions of Euro-American Denial*, in Steven Gregory & Roger Sanjek, eds., RACE 270, 272 (1994); Albert H. Yee, Halford H. Fairchild, Frederic Weizmann, & Gail E. Wyatt, *Addressing Psychology's Problems with Race*, 48 AMERICAN PSYCHOLOGIST 1132 (November 1993); Hannaford, *supra*, note 1, at 371-72.

4. See Robert L. Hayman, Jr., *Presumptions of Justice: Law, Politics, and the Mentally Retarded Parent*, 103 HARVARD LAW REVIEW 1201 (1990), and sources cited therein.

5. Martha Minow, MAKING ALL THE DIFFERENCE: INCLUSION, EXCLUSION, AND AMERICAN LAW 80 (1990); Christine A. Littleton, *Reconstructing Sexual Equality*, 75 CALIFORNIA LAW REVIEW 1279 (1987); see generally Robert L.

Hayman, Jr., & Nancy Levit, JURISPRUDENCE: CONTEMPORARY READINGS, PROBLEMS, AND NARRATIVES 325-82 (1995).

6. I. Bernard Cohen, SCIENCE AND THE FOUNDING FATHERS: SCIENCE IN THE POLITICAL THOUGHT OF JEFFERSON, FRANKLIN, ADAMS, AND MADISON 191 (1995); Fredrickson, *supra*, note 2, at 67; Hannaford, *supra*, note 1, at 207-8; James M. McPherson, THE ABOLITIONIST LEGACY: FROM RECONSTRUCTION TO THE NAACP 352 (1975).

7. Franz Boas, ANTHROPOLOGY AND MODERN LIFE 19, 22, 37, 63, 71, 226 (1928).

8. Michael Omi & Howard Winant, RACIAL FORMATION IN THE UNITED STATES 10 (1994); Hannaford, *supra*, note 1, at 374, 391; Pieterse, *supra*, note 1, at 50.

9. F. James Davis, WHO IS BLACK? ONE NATION'S DEFINITION 21 (1991); R. C. Lewontin, Steven Rose, and Leon J. Kamin, NOT IN OUR GENES: BIOLOGY, IDEOLOGY, AND HUMAN NATURE 121-27 (1984); Stephen Jay Gould, THE FLAMINGO'S SMILE: REFLECTIONS IN NATURAL HISTORY 193-95 (1985); see also Christopher Wills, *The Skin We're In*, in Richard Delgado & Jean Stefancic, eds., CRITICAL WHITE STUDIES: LOOKING BEHIND THE MIRROR 12 (1997). Writer Charles Johnson says, "I believe in my bones that the things that separate us make up one percent of who we are, that ninety-nine percent of our lives are similar. . . . We have given so much over the years to that one percent, complexion, it's a travesty. I think it's one of the great tragedies of our species." Studs Terkel, RACE: HOW BLACKS & WHITES THINK & FEEL ABOUT THE AMERICAN OBSESSION 218 (1993).

10. Yee et al., *supra*, note 3.

11. James G. Leyburn, *The Scotch-Irish in America*, in John A. Garraty, ed., HISTORICAL VIEWPOINTS: NOTABLE ARTICLES FROM AMERICAN HERITAGE 118 (5th ed. 1987); Eric Foner, FREE LABOR, FREE SOIL, FREE MEN: THE IDEOLOGY OF THE REPUBLICAN PARTY BEFORE THE CIVIL WAR xi-xxvi (1995).

12. Pieterse, *supra*, note 1, at 213-15; Robert William Fogel, WITHOUT CONSENT OR CONTRACT: THE RISE AND FALL OF AMERICAN SLAVERY 372 (1989); John Whiteclay Chambers II, THE TYRANNY OF CHANGE: AMERICA IN THE PROGRESSIVE ERA, 1900-1917, at 67-75 (1980); Thomas E. Watson, *The Negro Question in the South*, in Paul F. Boller, Jr., & Ronald Story, A MORE PERFECT UNION: DOCUMENTS IN U.S. HISTORY, VOLUME 2: SINCE 1865, at 99 (2d ed. 1988).

13. Chambers, *supra*, note 12, at 10-12, 37, 67, 81.

14. *Id.* at 75-77; Karen Brodkin Sacks, *How Did Jews Become White Folks?*, in Gregory & Sanjek, *supra*, note 3, at 78, 80, 87-97; Roger Sanjek, *The Enduring Inequalities of Race*, in *id.* at 1, 9; see also the materials collected in Delgado & Stefancic, *supra*, note 9, at 337-421.

15. See, for example, Edward Countryman, AMERICANS: A COLLISION OF HISTORIES (1996); Ronald Takaki, A DIFFERENT MIRROR: A HISTORY OF MULTICULTURAL AMERICA (1993).

16. M. Annette Jaimes, *American Racism: The Impact on American-Indian Identity and Survival*, in Gregory & Sanjek, *supra*, note 3, at 41; Alden T. Vaughn, ROOTS OF AMERICAN RACISM: ESSAYS ON THE COLONIAL EXPERIENCE 136-74 (1995). Although both the historiography and the synthesis offered here differ in some respects from Vaughn's, I think that the essential similarities are within the consensus I describe. See also James Campbell & James Oakes, *The Invention of Race: Rereading* White over Black, 21 REVIEWS IN AMERICAN HISTORY 172 (March 1993).

17. A. Leon Higginbotham, Jr., IN THE MATTER OF COLOR: RACE AND THE AMERICAN LEGAL PROCESS: THE COLONIAL PERIOD 62 (1978); Edmund S. Morgan, AMERICAN SLAVERY, AMERICAN FREEDOM 115, 154, 325 (1975).

18. Vaughn, *supra*, note 16, at 160; Thomas D. Morris, SOUTHERN SLAVERY AND THE LAW, 1619-1860 20 (1996).

19. Vaughn, *supra*, note 16, at 161; Higginbotham, *supra*, note 17, at 103.

20. Higginbotham, *supra*, note 17, at 148, 308, 313; *John Pendleton Kennedy: A Southern View of Slavery*, in Robert D. Marcus and David Burner, eds., AMERICA FIRSTHAND, VOLUME 1: FROM SETTLEMENT TO RECONSTRUCTION 222 (1989); Ira Berlin, SLAVES WITHOUT MASTERS: THE FREE NEGRO IN THE ANTEBELLUM SOUTH 86 (1974).

21. Hannaford, *supra*, note 1, at 210; Vaughn, *supra*, note 16, at 160-74; Peter Kolchin, UNFREE LABOR: AMERICAN SLAVERY AND RUSSIAN SERFDOM 184 (1987); Morgan, *supra*, note 17, at 154-55.

22. Higginbotham, *supra*, note 17, at 38; Morris, *supra*, note 18, at 22-27; Luther Wright, Jr., *Who's Black, Who's White, and Who Cares*, 48 VANDERBILT LAW REVIEW 513 (1995); Morgan, *supra*, note 17, at 327-31; Berlin, *supra*, note 20, at 8.

23. Vaughn, *supra*, note 16, at 167-73; Fields cited in *id.*; Berlin, *supra*, note 20, at 190-93; Peter M. Bergman & Jean McCarroll, THE NEGRO IN THE CONGRESSIONAL RECORD, VOLUME 8: 1821-1824 (1970).

24. Jaimes, *supra*, note 16, at 43; Stephen Jay Gould, THE MISMEASURE OF MAN 50, *passim* (1981).

25. Morgan, *supra*, note 17, at 154-55; Kolchin, *supra*, note 21, at 184; Berlin, *supra*, note 20, at 261-68.

26. Segal, *supra*, note 2, at 4; Higginbotham, *supra*, note 17, at 216; Peter J. Parish, SLAVERY: HISTORY AND HISTORIANS 19, 128 (1989); Peter Kolchin, AMERICAN SLAVERY, 1619-1877, at 242 (1993).

27. Leon Litwack, BEEN IN THE STORM SO LONG: THE AFTERMATH OF SLAVERY xi, 22, 57 (1979); Parish, *supra*, note 26, at 7, 130; *Henry Bibb: Letters from an Abolitionist to His Former Master*, in Marcus and Burner, *supra*, note 20, at 247.

28. Berlin, *supra*, note 20, at 15, 39, 74-76, 135-38, 156-60, 318, 343, 371-79; C. Vann Woodward, *The Antislavery Myth*, in THE FUTURE OF THE PAST, 265, 268-71 (1989).

29. Pieterse, *supra*, note 1, at 60; Litwack, *supra*, note 27, at 147-53, 156, 179; Felix Haywood et al., *Black Reactions to Reconstruction*, in Marcus and Burner, *supra*, note 20, at 288, 292-93; Litwack, *supra*, note 27, at 223; Davis, *supra*, note 9, at 43; Eric Foner, RECONSTRUCTION AMERICA'S UNFINISHED REVOLUTION (1988).

30. John Egerton, SPEAK NOW AGAINST THE DAY: THE GENERATION BEFORE THE CIVIL RIGHTS MOVEMENT IN THE SOUTH 35 (1994); McPherson, *supra*, note 6, at 70, 249-55; *Berea College v. Commonwealth of Kentucky*, 211 U.S. 45 (1908).

31. Fredrickson, *supra*, note 2, at 99; McPherson, *supra*, note 6, at 203, 222; Booker T. Washington, *Atlanta Exposition Address*, in Boller & Story, *supra*, note 12, at 61; W. E. B. Du Bois, *Niagara Movement Address*, in *id.* at 71; Fredrickson, *supra*, note 2, at 109; W. E. B. Du Bois, *Dusk of Dawn*, in Huggins, *supra*, note 1, at 549, 629.

32. Fredrickson, *supra*, note 2, at 103; McPherson, *supra*, note 6, at 371; Vanessa Siddle Walker, THEIR HIGHEST POTENTIAL: AN AFRICAN AMERICAN SCHOOL COMMUNITY IN THE SEGREGATED SOUTH 2, 200-201 (1996).

33. Fredrickson, *supra*, note 2, at 232-35; Egerton, *supra*, note 30, at 273, 503; Gunnar Myrdal, AN AMERICAN DILEMMA: THE NEGRO PROBLEM AND MODERN DEMOCRACY 583-86 (1944); John Hope Franklin, FROM SLAVERY TO FREEDOM: A HISTORY OF NEGRO AMERICANS xvi, 412 (1947); Egerton, *supra*, note 30, at 415, 431, 509.

34. Martin Carnoy, FADED DREAMS: THE POLITICS AND ECONOMICS OF RACE IN AMERICA 60-67 (1994).

35. *Id.* at 62-63; Amy Wallace, *Minority College Enrollment Still Lags Education*, L.A. TIMES D27 (July 21, 1996).

36. Segal, *supra*, note 2, at 260.

37. Carnoy, *supra*, note 34, at 75, 147; Marc Breslow, *Last In, First Out: Black Men Take the Heat*, DOLLARS & SENSE 24 (January 11, 1997).

38. House Committee on Education and Labor, 101st Cong., 2d sess., *A Report on Shortchanging Children: The Impact of Fiscal Inequity on the Education of Students at Risk* 19-24, 44 (Comm. Print 1990) (prepared by William L. Taylor & Diane M. Piche); Jonathan Kozol, SAVAGE INEQUALITIES: CHILDREN IN AMERICA'S SCHOOLS (1991); Carnoy, *supra*, note 34, at 133-39, 118; Blakey, *supra*, note 3, at 277; Carnoy, *supra*, note 34, at 162; Sharon M. Collins, *Black Mobility in White Corporations: Up the Corporate Ladder but Out on a Limb*, 44 SOCIAL PROBLEMS 55 (February 1997).

39. *Correspondence: Excess Mortality in Harlem*, 322 NEW ENGLAND JOURNAL OF MEDICINE 1606 (1990); *Correspondence: Mortality among Black Men*, 322 NEW ENGLAND JOURNAL OF MEDICINE 205, 205-6 (1990); Segal, *supra*, note 2, at 353; Fredrickson, *supra*, note 2, at 320.

40. Du Bois, *Dusk of Dawn*, *supra*, note 31, at 549, 650.

41. *Plessy v. Ferguson*, 163 U.S. 537 (1896); Egerton, *supra*, note 30, at 37.

42. Boas, *supra*, note 7, at 64-65, 71, 78-79.

43. Fredrickson, *supra*, note 2, at 32-35; Hannaford, *supra*, note 1, at 341; Myrdal, *supra*, note 33, at 669.

44. John F. Dovidio & Samuel L. Gaertner, *Changes in the Expression and Assessment of Racial Prejudice*, in Harry J. Knopke et al. eds., OPENING DOORS: PERSPECTIVE ON RACE RELATIONS IN CONTEMPORARY AMERICA 119-43 (1991); Paul M. Sniderman & Michael G. Hagen, RACE AND INEQUALITY: A STUDY IN AMERICAN VALUES 112 (1985); Howard Schuman et al., RACIAL ATTITUDES IN AMERICA: TRENDS AND INTERPRETATIONS 193-95 (1985); Howard Schuman & Lawrence Bobo, *An Experimental Approach to Surveys of Racial Attitudes*, in Hubert J. O'Gorman ed., SURVEYING SOCIAL LIFE: PAPERS IN HONOR OF HERBERT HYMAN 60, 67-68 (1988); Gerald G. Pine & Asa G. Hilliard III, *Rx for Racism: Imperatives for America's Schools*, 1990 PHI DELTA KAPPAN 593, 593-95; Thomas F. Pettigrew, *The Nature of Modern Racism in the United States*, 2 REVUE INTERNATIONALE DE PSYCHOLOGIE SOCIALE 291 (1989); Donald R. Kinder, *The Continuing American Dilemma: White Resistance to Racial Change 40 Years after Myrdal*, 42 JOURNAL OF SOCIAL ISSUES 151, 154 (1986); Fredrickson, *supra*, note 2, at 320.

45. Dovidio & Gaertner, *supra*, note 44, at 127-28; Marc Howard Ross, *The Role of Evolution in Ethnocentric Conflict and Its Management*, 47 JOURNAL OF SOCIAL ISSUES 167, 182 (1991); Gary M. Ingersoll, *Race and Ethnic Relations among High School Youth: Perspectives from Psychology*, 18 INTERNATIONAL JOURNAL OF GROUP TENSIONS 20, 21-22 (1988); Patricia G. Ramsey & Leslie C. Myers, *Salience of Race in Young Children's Cognitive, Affective, and Behavioral Responses to Social Environments*, 11 JOURNAL OF APPLIED DEVELOPMENTAL PSYCHOLOGY 49 (1990); Patricia G. Ramsey, *The Salience of Race in Young Children Growing Up in an All-White Community*, 83 JOURNAL OF EDUCATIONAL PSYCHOLOGY 83 (1991); Janet Ward Schofield, BLACK AND WHITE IN SCHOOL 220 (1989); Judith H. Skillings & James E. Dobbins, *Racism as a Disease: Etiology and Treatment Implications*, 70 JOURNAL OF COUNSELING & DEVELOPMENT 206 (1991); Donald R. Kinder & David O. Sears, *Prejudice and Politics: Symbolic Racism versus Racial Threats to the Good Life*, 40 JOURNAL OF PERSONALITY & SOCIAL PSYCHOLOGY 414 (1981); Paul M. Sniderman et al., *The New Racism*, 35 AMERICAN JOURNAL OF POLITICAL SCIENCE 423 (1991); Irwin Katz & R. Glen Hass, *Racial Ambivalence and American Value Conflict: Correlational and Priming Studies of Dual Cognitive Structures*, 55 JOURNAL OF PERSONALITY & SOCIAL PSYCHOLOGY 893 (1988); Marguerite Ross Barnette, *Educational Policy Trends in a Neoconservative Era*, in Willy DeMarcell Smith & Eva Wells Chunn, eds., BLACK EDUCATION: A QUEST FOR EQUITY AND EXCELLENCE 36, 44 (1991); Omi & Winant, *supra*, note 8, at 159; Blakey, *supra*, note 3, at 278; Fletcher A. Blanchard et al., *Reducing the Expression of Racial Prejudice*, 2 PSYCHOLOGICAL SCIENCE 101 (1991).

46. Anthony Appiah, *The Uncompleted Argument: Du Bois and the Illusion of Race*, in Henry Louis Gates, Jr., ed., "RACE," WRITING, AND DIFFERENCE 35 (1985); Cameron McCarthy & Warren Crichlow, eds., RACE, IDENTITY, AND

REPRESENTATION IN EDUCATION xix (1993); Douglass quoted in Howard Zinn, A PEOPLE'S HISTORY OF THE UNITED STATES 176 (1990).

CHAPTER 4: A NEUTRAL QUALIFICATION

1. Leon Litwack, BEEN IN THE STORM SO LONG: THE AFTERMATH OF SLAVERY 505-22 (1979); Eric Foner, FREE LABOR, FREE SOIL, FREE MEN: THE IDEOLOGY OF THE REPUBLICAN PARTY BEFORE THE CIVIL WAR xxxvi (1995); Litwack, *supra*, at 257.

2. *Washington v. Davis*, 426 U.S. 229 (1976).

3. *Arlington Heights v. Metropolitan Housing Corporation*, 429 U.S. 252 (1977).

4. *Personnel Administrator of Massachusetts v. Feeney*, 442 U.S. 256 (1979).

5. *McCleskey v. Kemp*, 481 U.S. 279-367 (1987); David C. Baldus, George Woodworth, & Charles A. Pulaski, Jr., EQUAL JUSTICE AND THE DEATH PENALTY: A LEGAL AND EMPIRICAL ANALYSIS 378 (1990); *Warren McCleskey's Long Road to the Death Chamber*, AMNESTY ACTION, (November-December 1991); John C. Jeffries, Jr., JUSTICE LEWIS F. POWELL, JR. 451 (1994).

6. *My Cousin Vinny* (Twentieth Century Fox 1992).

7. Bronwen Hriska, *The "Eraser" Effect*, PHILADELPHIA INQUIRER E-1, 10 (June 19, 1996).

8. *The Verdict Is In*, DELAWARE TODAY 42, 138 (October 1996); Joshua W. Martin et al., *Minorities in the Delaware Bar*, in Helen L. Winslow, ed., THE DELAWARE BAR IN THE TWENTIETH CENTURY 658, 659-63 (1994).

9. *City of Richmond v. J. A. Croson Co.*, 488 U.S. 469 (1989).

10. Studs Terkel offers additional examples:
Hank de Zutter feels he understands it. He teaches at a black urban college. "There may be a literacy problem in terms of the written word. But there is no literacy problem when it comes to reading people. . . . Why aren't my students, who have this unique ability to read people, working where this quality is so important? They're experts and could be marvelous at managing people."
Studs Terkel, RACE: HOW BLACKS & WHITES THINK & FEEL ABOUT THE AMERICAN OBSESSION 16-17 (1993). See also Stephanie M. Wildman, with Margalynne Armstrong, Adrienne D. Davis, & Trina Grillo, PRIVILEGE REVEALED: HOW INVISIBLE PREFERENCE UNDERMINES AMERICA (1997).

CHAPTER 5: CREATING THE SMART CULTURE

1. Stephen Jay Gould, THE FLAMINGO'S SMILE: REFLECTIONS IN NATURAL HISTORY 282 (1985); Thomas Jefferson, *Notes on the State of Virginia*, in THOMAS JEFFERSON: WRITINGS 123, 264-70 (Merrill D. Peterson, ed. 1984).

2. William Lee Miller, ARGUING ABOUT SLAVERY: THE GREAT BATTLE IN THE UNITED STATES CONGRESS 139, 365 (1996); Leon Litwack, BEEN IN THE STORM SO LONG: THE AFTERMATH OF SLAVERY 16, 189 (1979).

3. Steven Fraser, ed., THE BELL CURVE WARS: RACE, INTELLIGENCE AND THE FUTURE OF AMERICA 1 (1995).

4. James M. McPherson, THE ABOLITIONIST LEGACY: FROM RECONSTRUCTION TO THE NAACP 333, 339 (1975); Arthur S. Link, WOODROW WILSON AND THE PROGRESSIVE ERA, 1910-1917, at 63-66 (1963); John Hope Franklin, The Birth of a Nation: *Propaganda as History*, in RACE AND HISTORY: SELECTED ESSAYS, 1938-1988, at 10, 16 (1989); Eric Foner, RECONSTRUCTION: AMERICA'S UNFINISHED REVOLUTION xix-xxi (1988); Stephen Jay Gould, THE MISMEASURE OF MAN (1981); *The Ku Klux Klan: In Its Own Words*, in Robert D. Marcus and David Burner, eds., AMERICA FIRSTHAND, VOLUME 2: FROM RECONSTRUCTION TO THE PRESENT 235 (1989).

5. Carl Degler, IN SEARCH OF HUMAN BEHAVIOR 17-19 (1991); Gould, *supra*, note 4, at 35, 80, 120, 190; McPherson, *supra*, note 4, at 341; R. C. Lewontin, Steven Rose, & Leon J. Kamin, NOT IN OUR GENES: BIOLOGY, IDEOLOGY, AND HUMAN NATURE 86 (1984).

6. James MacGregor Burns, ROOSEVELT: THE LION AND THE FOX, VOLUME 1: 1882-1940, at 20, 198 (1956); Doris Kearns Goodwin, NO ORDINARY TIME: FRANKLIN AND ELEANOR ROOSEVELT: THE HOME FRONT IN WORLD WAR II, at 521-23 (1994); Robert William Fogel, WITHOUT CONSENT OR CONTRACT: THE RISE AND FALL OF AMERICAN SLAVERY 155 (1989); Peter J. Parish, SLAVERY: HISTORY AND HISTORIANS 6-7 (1989); Foner, *supra*, note 4, at xxi; Miller, *supra*, note 2, at 55; McPherson, *supra*, note 4, at 346.

7. Degler, *supra*, note 5, at 61-76, 89-92; Gould, *supra*, note 4, at 191.

8. Miller, *supra*, note 2, at 317-21.

9. Degler, *supra*, note 5, at 26-28, 109-15.

10. *Muller v. Oregon*, 208 U.S. 412 (1908).

11. Degler, *supra*, note 5, at 132-37.

12. Gould, *supra*, note 4, at 159-68; Leon J. Kamin, THE SCIENCE AND POLITICS OF I.Q. 8 (1974).

13. Kamin, *supra*, note 12, at 10; Gould, *supra*, note 1, at 308; Degler, *supra*, note 5, at 128.

14. Degler, *supra*, note 5, at 139-50.

15. Gould, *supra*, note 4, at 171-74; Gould, *supra*, note 1, at 313.

16. *Id*. at 80-123.

17. Gould, *supra*, note 4, at 146-49; Lewontin, Rose, & Kamin, *supra*, note 5, at 89.

18. Gould, *supra*, note 4, at 154-57, 194-214; Walter Lippman, *The Mental Age of Americans*, in Russell Jacoby & Naomi Glauberman, eds., THE BELL CURVE DEBATE: HISTORY, DOCUMENTS, OPINIONS 561, 562, 565 (1995).

19. Gould, *supra*, note 4, at 80-123; Kamin, *supra*, note 12, at 20.

20. Gould, *supra*, note 4, at 231, 271-74.

21. McPherson, *supra*, note 4, at 348; Degler, *supra*, note 5, at 173-81.

CHAPTER 6: THE SMART CULTURE

1. R. C. Lewontin, Steven Rose, & Leon J. Kamin, NOT IN OUR GENES: BIOLOGY, IDEOLOGY, AND HUMAN NATURE 89 (1984); Monica Rosen, *Gender Differences in Structure, Means and Variances of Hierarchically Ordered Ability Dimensions*, 5 LEARNING AND INSTRUCTION 37 (1995).

2. Alan S. Kaufman, James E. McLean, & Cecil R. Reynolds, *Sex, Race, Residence, Region, and Education Differences on the 11 WAIS-R Subtests*, 44 JOURNAL OF CHILD PSYCHOLOGY 231 (March 1988); Michael Lind, *Brand New Right*, in Steven Fraser, ed., THE BELL CURVE WARS: RACE, INTELLIGENCE, AND THE FUTURE OF AMERICA 172, 177 (1995); Andrew Hacker, *Caste, Crime, and Precocity*, in *id.* at 97, 104.

3. Vicki Ritts, Miles L. Patterson, & Marke E. Tubbs, *Expectations, Impressions, and Judgments of Physically Attractive Students: A Review*, 62 REVIEW OF EDUCATIONAL RESEARCH 413 (1992); Lewontin, Rose, & Kamin, *supra*, note 1, at 89; Orlando Patterson, *For Whom the Bell Curves*, in Fraser, *supra*, note 2, at 187, 203.

4. Stephen Jay Gould, THE MISMEASURE OF MAN 151 (1981).

5. Carl Degler, IN SEARCH OF HUMAN BEHAVIOR 39 (1991); Howard Gardner, *Scholarly Brinkmanship*, in Russell Jacoby & Naomi Glauberman, eds., THE BELL CURVE DEBATE: HISTORY, DOCUMENTS, OPINIONS 61, 62 (1995).

6. Maynard Goff & Phillip L. Ackerman, *Personality-Intelligence Relations: Assessment of Typical Intellectual Engagement*, 84 JOURNAL OF EDUCATIONAL PSYCHOLOGY 537 (1992); Robert J. Sternberg, SUCCESSFUL INTELLIGENCE: HOW PRACTICAL AND CREATIVE INTELLIGENCE DETERMINE SUCCESS IN LIFE 47 (1996).

7. Patterson, *supra*, note 3, at 196.

8. Dona J. Matthews & Daniel P. Keating, *Domain Specificity and Habits of Mind: An Investigation of Patterns of High-Level Development*, 15 JOURNAL OF EARLY ADOLESCENCE 319 (1995).

9. Kaufman, McLean, & Reynolds, *supra*, note 2.

10. Gould, *supra*, note 4, at 234-316; F. Allan Hanson, *Testing, the Bell Curve, and the Social Construction of Intelligence*, TIKKUN 22 (January 1995).

11. Lewontin, Rose, & Kamin, *supra*, note 1, at 73.

12. Gould, *supra*, note 4, at 153.

13. *Id.* at 154, 179; Irwin D. Waldman, Richard A. Weinberg, & Sandra Scarr, *Racial-Group Differences in IQ in the Minnesota Transracial Adoption Study: A Reply to Levin and Lynn*, 19 INTELLIGENCE 29 (1994).

14. Lewontin, Rose, & Kamin, *supra*, note 1, at 71; Bernie Devlin, Michael Daniels, & Kathryn Roeder, *The Heritability of IQ*, NATURE 468 (July 31, 1997); Anthony J. McMichael et al., *Port Pirie Cohort Study: Environmental Exposure to*

Lead and Children's Abilities at the Age of Four Years, 319 NEW ENGLAND JOURNAL OF MEDICINE 468 (1988); Herbert L. Needleman et al., *The Long-Term Effects of Exposure to Low Doses of Lead in Childhood: An 11-Year Follow-up Report*, 322 NEW ENGLAND JOURNAL OF MEDICINE 83, 86 (1990).

15. Ned Block, *How Heritability Misleads about Race*, 56 COGNITION 99 (1995).

16. *Id.*; Jonathan Crane, *Exploding the Myth of Scientific Support for the Theory of Black Intellectual Inferiority*, 20 JOURNAL OF BLACK PSYCHOLOGY 189 (1994); Stephen Jay Gould, *Mismeasure by Any Measure*, in Jacoby & Glauberman, *supra*, note 5, at 3, 4.

17. R. C. Lewontin, BIOLOGY AS IDEOLOGY: THE DOCTRINE OF DNA 29 (1992); Richard Nisbett, *Race, IQ, and Scientism*, in Fraser, *supra*, note 2, at 36, 36-50; Richard Nisbett, *Dangerous, but Important*, in Jacoby & Glauberman, *supra*, note 5, at 110, 112-13; Christiane Capron & Michel Duyme, *Assessment of Effects of Socio-Economic Status on IQ in a Full Cross-Fostering Study*, 17 NATURE 552 (1989); Waldman, Weinberg, & Scarr, *supra*, note 13; K. C. Cole, *Innumeracy*, in Jacoby & Glauberman, *supra*, note 5, at 73, 78.

18. J. Phillipe Rushton, *The Equalitarian Dogma Revisited*, 19 INTELLIGENCE 263 (1994); Balabam quoted in Gregg Easterbrook, *Blacktop Basketball and* The Bell Curve, in Jacoby & Glauberman, *supra*, note 5, at 30, 37.

19. Binet quoted in Gould, *supra*, note 4, at 151; Lewontin, Rose, & Kamin, *supra*, note 1, at 27; Edward Lurie, LOUIS AGASSIZ: A LIFE IN SCIENCE 257 (1988); Gould, *supra*, note 4, at 69, 199-219.

20. Leon J. Kamin, THE SCIENCE AND POLITICS OF I.Q. 20 (1974); Gould, *supra*, note 4, at 218-20; Degler, *supra*, note 5, at 179.

21. Rushton, *supra*, note 18; Zack Z. Cernovsky, *On the Similarities of American Blacks and Whites*, 25 JOURNAL OF BLACK STUDIES 672 (1995); Zack Z. Cernovsky, *J. P. Rushton's Aggregational Errors in Racial Psychology*, 19 JOURNAL OF BLACK PSYCHOLOGY 282 (1993); Leon J. Kamin, *Lies, Damned Lies, and Statistics*, in Jacoby & Glauberman, *supra*, note 5, at 81, 82-88; Adam Miller, *Professors of Hate*, in *id.* at 162, 165.

22. Gardner, *supra*, note 5; Gould, *supra*, note 16; John Carey, *Clever Arguments, Atrocious Science*, in Jacoby & Glauberman, *supra*, note 5, at 53, 55; Nisbett, *Race, IQ, and Scientism*, *supra*, note 17; Kamin, *supra*, note 21; Allan Ryan, *Apocalypse Now?* in Jacoby & Glauberman, *supra*, note 5, at 14, 22; Jeffrey Rosen & Charles Lane, *The Sources of* The Bell Curve, in Fraser, *supra*, note 2, at 58; Jacqueline Jones, *Back to the Future with* The Bell Curve: *Jim Crow, Slavery, and G*, in *id.* at 80, 93; see also Joe L. Kincheloe, Shirley R. Steinberg, & Aaron D. Gresson III, eds., MEASURED LIES: THE BELL CURVE EXAMINED (1996).

23. Nancy Levit, *Listening to Tribal Legends: An Essay on Law and the Scientific Method*, 58 FORDHAM LAW REVIEW 263 (1989); Lewontin, Rose, & Kamin, *supra*, note 1, at 31-33.

24. Lewontin, *supra*, note 17, at 31.

25. Gould, *supra*, note 4, at 231; Henry Louis Gates, Jr., *Why Now?* in Fraser, *supra*, note 2, at 94, 96; House Committee on Education and Labor, 101st Cong.,

2d sess., *A Report on Shortchanging Children: The Impact of Fiscal Inequity on the Education of Students at Risk* 19-24, 44 (Comm. Print 1990) (prepared by William L. Taylor & Diane M. Piche); Robert L. Hayman, Jr., & Nancy Levit, *The Constitutional Ghetto*, 1993 WISCONSIN LAW REVIEW 627, 697-709; Hanson, *supra*, note 10.

26. Crane, *supra*, note 16; Hayman & Levit, *supra*, note 25; Nisbett, *supra*, note 17, at 53.

27. Nisbett, *Dangerous, but Important*, *supra*, note 17, at 43; John U. Ogbu, *Overcoming Racial Barriers to Equal Access*, in John I. Goodlad & Pamela Keating eds., ACCESS TO KNOWLEDGE: AN AGENDA FOR OUR NATION'S SCHOOLS 59, 61-64 (1990); John I. Goodlad, *Common Schools for the Common Weal: Reconciling Self-Interest with the Common Good*, in *id.* at 1, 9; Hayman & Levit, *supra*, note 26; Robert J. Vallerand & Robert Bissonnette, *Intrinsic, Extrinsic, and Amotivational Styles as Predictors of Behavior: A Prospective Study*, JOURNAL OF PERSONALITY 60:3 (September 1992).

28. Rushton, *supra*, note 18; Elsie G. J. Moore, *Ethnic Social Milieu and Black Children's Intelligence Test Achievement*, 56 JOURNAL OF NEGRO EDUCATION 44 (1987); Kaufman, McLean, & Reynolds, *supra*, note 2; Thomas Sowell, *Ethnicity and IQ*, in Fraser, *supra*, note 2, at 70; Paglia quoted in Joe Chidley, *The Heart of the Matter*, in Jacoby & Glauberman, *supra*, note 5, at 119, 122. For a critique of the linearity that constrains THE BELL CURVE and like works, see Patrick Slattery, *Chaos and Complexity: A Quantum Analysis of* The Bell Curve, in Kincheloe, Steinberg, & Gresson, *supra*, note 22, at 291.

29. Gardner, *supra*, note 5, at 68; Ritts, Patterson, & Tubbs, *supra*, note 3.

30. K. Anthony Appiah, *Straightening Out* The Bell Curve, in Jacoby & Glauberman, *supra*, note 5, at 305, 309; Rogers Elliot, *Tests, Abilities, Race, and Conflict*, 12 INTELLIGENCE 333 (1988).

31. Block, *supra*, note 15; Alan Wolfe, *Has There Been a Cognitive Revolution in America? The Flawed Sociology of* The Bell Curve, in Fraser, *supra*, note 2, at 109, 122; Gould, *supra*, note 16.

32. Nisbett, *Race, IQ, and Scientism*, *supra*, note 17.

33. Cernovsky, *Similarities of American Blacks and Whites*, *supra*, note 21.

34. Nisbett, *Race, IQ, and Scientism*, *supra*, note 17.

35. *Id.* at 38; Waldman, Weinberg, & Scarr, *supra*, note 15; William E. Cross, Jr., The Bell Curve *and Transracial Adoption Studies*, in Kincheloe, Steinberg, & Gresson, *supra*, note 22, at 331.

36. Lewontin, *supra*, note 24, at 26; Kamin, *supra*, note 20, at 177; Stephen Jay Gould, THE FLAMINGO'S SMILE: REFLECTIONS IN NATURAL HISTORY 195 (1985).

CHAPTER 7: THE CONSTITUTION IS POWERLESS

1. *Missouri v. Jenkins*, 115 S. Ct. 2038 (1995).
2. *Adarand Constructors v. Pena*, 115 S. Ct. 2097 (1995).

3. *Miller v. Johnson*, 115 S. Ct. 2475 (1995).

4. *In re Civil Rights Cases*, 109 U.S. 3 (1883).

5. C. Vann Woodward, REUNION AND REACTION: THE COMPROMISE OF 1877 AND THE END OF RECONSTRUCTION (1951).

6. *Adarand Constructors v. Pena*, 115 S. Ct. 2097 (1995) (Thomas, J., concurring).

7. See *Freeman v. Pitts*, 112 S. Ct. 1430, 1445 (1992); *Board of Education v. Dowell*, 498 U.S. 237, 248 (1991); *Employment Division v. Smith*, 494 U.S. 872, 890 (1990); *McCleskey v. Kemp*, 481 U.S. 279, 319 (1987); *City of Richmond v. J. A. Croson Co.*, 488 U.S. 469, 490-91 (1989) (distinguishing *Fullilove v. Klutznick*, 448 U.S. 448 (1980)).

8. See generally *United States v. Carolene Products Co.*, 304 U.S. 144 (1938); compare *Skinner v. State of Oklahoma*, 316 U.S. 535 (1942) ("fundamental right"), *Korematsu v. United States*, 323 U.S. 214 (1944) ("race").

9. *San Antonio School District v. Rodriguez*, 411 U.S. 1 (1973).

10. *City of Richmond v. J. A. Croson Co.*, 488 U.S. 469 (1989); *The Federal Convention: Madison's Notes of Debates*, in Winton U. Solberg, ed., THE CONSTITUTIONAL CONVENTION AND THE FORMATION OF THE UNION 117 (2d Ed. 1990).

11. Solberg, *supra*, note 10, at 68; *Prigg v. Pennsylvania*, 41 U.S. 539 (1842).

12. *Board of Education v. Dowell*, 498 U.S. 237 (1991); *Freeman v. Pitts*, 112 S. Ct. 1430 (1992).

13. *City of Richmond v. J. A. Croson Co.*, 488 U.S. 469 (1989); *Metro Broadcasting v. F.C.C.*, 497 U.S. 547 (1990); *Adarand Constructors v. Pena*, 115 S. Ct. 2097 (1995).

14. John Whiteclay Chambers II, THE TYRANNY OF CHANGE: AMERICA IN THE PROGRESSIVE ERA, 1900-1917, at 4-6 (1980).

15. *Shelley v. Kraemer*, 334 U.S. 1-23 (1948); *Cooper v. Aaron*, 358 U.S. 1 (1958); *Burton v. Wilmington Parking Authority*, 365 U.S. 715 (1961).

16. *Palmore v. Sidoti*, 466 U.S. 429 (1984).

17. Richard Delgado, THE RODRIGO CHRONICLES: CONVERSATIONS ABOUT AMERICA AND RACE 6 (1995).

18. Richard Delgado, *The Ethereal Scholar: Does Critical Legal Studies Have What Minorities Want?* 22 HARVARD CIVIL RIGHTS—CIVIL LIBERTIES LAW REVIEW 301, 311 (1987).

19. Charles R. Lawrence III, *The Id, The Ego, and Equal Protection: Reckoning with Unconscious Racism*, 39 STANFORD LAW REVIEW 317 (1987).

20. *Plessy v. Ferguson*, 163 U.S. 537 (1896).

21. *Freeman v. Pitts*, 112 S. Ct. 1430 (1992) (Scalia, J., concurring).

22. J. M. Balkin, *Tradition, Betrayal, and the Politics of Deconstruction*, 11 CARDOZO LAW REVIEW 1613 (1990); Patricia Williams, *The Obliging Shell: An Informal Essay on Formal Equality*, 87 MICHIGAN LAW REVIEW 2128 (1989).

23. T. Alexander Aleinikoff & Samuel Issacharoff, *Race and Redistricting: Drawing Constitutional Lines after Shaw v. Reno*, 92 MICHIGAN LAW REVIEW 588, 639 (1993).

24. Williams, *supra*, note 22, at 2139.

25. Richard Delgado, *Rodrigo's Eighth Chronicle: Black Crime, White Fears—On the Social Construction of Threat*, 80 VIRGINIA LAW REVIEW 503 (1994); Derrick Bell & Linda Singer, *Making a Record*, 26 CONNECTICUT LAW REVIEW 265, 274 (1993).

26. Robert L. Hayman, Jr., *The Color of Tradition: Critical Race Theory and Postmodern Constitutional Traditionalism*, 30 HARVARD CIVIL RIGHTS—CIVIL LIBERTIES LAW REVIEW 57 (1995). Chambers, *supra*, note 14, at 231.

27. *Plessy v. Ferguson*, 163 U.S. 537 (1896).

28. *City of Richmond v. J. A. Croson Co.*, 488 U.S. 469 (1989) (Scalia, J., concurring).

29. Cornel West, RACE MATTERS 26 (1993).

30. Derrick Bell, *Racial Realism*, 24 CONNECTICUT LAW REVIEW 363 (1992); Delgado, *supra*, note 17, at 80-81; Jerome McCristal Culp, Jr., *Toward a Black Legal Scholarship: Race and Original Understandings*, 1991 DUKE LAW JOURNAL 39; John Hope Franklin, *The Moral Legacy of the Founding Fathers*, in RACE AND HISTORY: SELECTED ESSAYS, 1938-1988, at 153, 161 (1989).

31. *City of Cleburne v. Cleburne Living Center*, 473 U.S. 432 (1985).

32. Linda S. Gottfredson, *Egalitarian Fiction and Collective Fraud*, SOCIETY 53 (March-April 1994).

EPILOGUE

1. Murphy quoted in R. Bogdan & S. Taylor, INSIDE OUT: THE SOCIAL MEANING OF MENTAL RETARDATION 92 (1982).

Index